BIBLE AND LITERATURE
SERIES

Editor
David M. Gunn

KINGSHIP of GOD in CRISIS

A Close Reading of 1 Samuel 1-12

LYLE M. ESLINGER

ALMOND • 1985

BIBLE AND LITERATURE SERIES, 10

Library of Congress Cataloging in Publication Data:

Eslinger, Lyle M., 1953-
  Kingship of God in crisis.

  (Bible and literature series, ISSN 0260-4493; 10)
  Bibliography: p.
  Includes indexes.
    1. Bible. O.T. Samuel, 1st I-XII - Criticism,
interpretation, etc. I. Title. II. Series
BS1325.2.E85 1985   222'.4307   85-18685
ISBN 0-907459-40-4
ISBN 0-907459-41-2 (pbk.)

ALMOND is an imprint of
JSOT PRESS
Department of Biblical Studies
The University of Sheffield
Sheffield, S10 2TN, England

Origination & Editorial:
THE ALMOND PRESS
Columbia Theological Seminary
P.O. Box 520
Decatur, GA 30031, U.S.A.

Printed in Great Britain by
Dotesios (Printers) Ltd.
Bradford-on-Avon, Wiltshire

CONTENTS

Chapter Four
1 SAMUEL 1-12:
A CLOSE READING OF THE NARRATIVE   *63*

ACKNOWLEDGEMENTS

I would like to thank the following institutions for financial support for this work:

The Memorial Fund for Jewish Culture
The Social Sciences and Humanities Research Council
    of Canada
The Calgary Institute for the Humanities
The University of Calgary

Thanks, also, to A. Eugene Combs, Alan M. Cooper, and T. Ray Hobbs for numerous comments and improvements.

Special thanks to Jan P. Fokkelman for his copious trans-oceanic comments and encouragements.

Last, but first, thank you Gloria.

Lyle Eslinger
The University of Calgary
1984

KINGSHIP OF GOD IN CRISIS

LYLE M. ESLINGER

The man is like a wise fisherman who cast his net into the sea and drew it up from the sea full of small fish. Among them he found a large and good fish; that wise fisherman, he threw all the small fish back into the sea and he chose the large fish without difficulty.

Gospel of Thomas
Saying 8

CHAPTER ONE

THE LITERARY ANALYSIS
OF 1 SAMUEL 8-12

1. Review of Scholarship

The modern interpretation of 1 Sam 8-12, a narrative
description of the rise of the Israelite monarchy, has
usually been done using the methodology of historical
criticism. The goal of such criticism is to answer the
questions 'What actually happened?' and 'Why?' about
events reported in the Bible (Krentz 1975:37). In view
of this goal the historical critic must be circumspect
about his or her sources, the biblical books, which
also have a history that must be investigated.

> The writer's position as an observer, his internal
> consistency, his bias or prejudices, and his
> abilities as a writer all affect the accuracy of
> what he knows and the competence of the report.
> Where more than one report exists, they must be
> compared. If they disagree, this does not automat-
> ically mean that one is wrong. Differences may
> arise from the writers' position for observation
> (Krentz 1975:44).

Before one can approach 'what happened and why it
happened,' one must penetrate through the socio-
historical context of the narrator who has filtered
'what happened and why' in constructing his own
narrative account.

The history of historical-critical reckoning with 1
Sam 8-12 shows a continual focus on two features of

the narrative that block the path to 'what happened and why.' First, there seem to be three conflicting accounts of Saul's inauguration as king: 1. Chapters 9.1-10.6, Saul is anointed to be *nagîd,* 'designate'; 2. Chapter 10.17-27, Saul is chosen by lot to be king; 3. Chapter 11.1-15, Saul is made king in Gilgal after proving himself in battle (Weiser 1961:159f). The seeming redundancy and inconsistency among these three accounts has led to the explanation that separate traditions or redactors have contributed to the narrative in the course of its transmission (e.g. J. G. Eichhorn, cited by Stoebe 1973:35).

Secondly, these separate accounts or traditions in 1 Sam 8-12 seem to display markedly different attitudes towards the monarchy as an institution and towards King Saul himself. For example, in 8.7-8 the people's request for a king is characterized as rejection of God and equated with idolatry. This negative perception of the monarchy is also evident in 10.17-19 and 12.1-25. On the other hand, in 9.1-10.16 God himself sends a man to Samuel to be anointed 'designate' (*nagîd*). The task of the designate is strikingly reminiscent of Moses' task in Exod 3.7-10. He is to save Israel from the hand of the Philistines (9.16). Saul himself is praised in 9.2 and 10.23-24 but disparaged in 10.27.

Historical criticism has accounted for this multiplicity of opposing viewpoints on 'what actually happened' with a hypothesis of multiple authorship in various periods of Israelite literary history. So Julius Wellhausen, who discerned only two separate literary sources in 1 Sam 8-12, suggested that 'In the great difference which separated these two narratives we recognize the mental interval between two different ages' (1973:253).

The history of modern critical examination of 1 Sam 8-12 before Wellhausen exhibits several variations on the hypothesis of multiple successive authorship /1/. Wellhausen wove the separate strands of his predecessors' hypotheses into one unified account of the narrative's development. He was able to correlate the two basic problems in 1 Sam 8-12 - the three varying accounts of the inauguration of a monarchy and the two conflicting views of that institution - by dividing the narrative into what he saw as two separate versions (1899:240). One, anti-monarchic in viewpoint, appears in chs. 8, 10.17-27, and 12. The other, pro-monarchic, is seen in chs. 9.1-10.16 and 11.

It is obvious from the number of Wellhausen's literary strands - two - that he has subsumed the problem of three varying accounts to the criterion of pro- or anti-monarchism. He accomplishes this conjunction of two of the accounts, 9.1-10.16 and ch. 11, by noting that 9.16 is inconclusive and requires the events of ch. 11 for a satisfactory resolution of events initiated in 9.1-10.16 (1973:251). What seemed, therefore, to be two accounts of Saul's rise to power is in fact one; in 9.1-10.16 Saul is only king *de jure*, he becomes king *de facto* when he proves himself in ch. 11 (1973:250).

Having resolved the literary problems of the narrative, Wellhausen explains the relationship between the two versions. He sets each within the context of Israelite history and the history of Israelite literature. The pro-monarchic version is earlier and expresses ancient Israel's gratitude to the men and institutions that ended the anarchy and oppression characteristic of the period of the judges (1973:254). The anti-monarchic version presented in chs. 8, 10.17-19, and 12 is the product of the exilic or post-exilic religious community. Those people knew nothing of government or statehood and so retrojected their theocratic concerns back to the early history of the monarchy (1973:255f). The anti-monarchic version is much later than the pro-monarchic and is dependent on the latter; the anti-monarchic is unhistorical, the pro-monarchic is the genuine tradition (1973:255).

For Wellhausen, the establishment of an historical setting for each strand of the narrative takes the

place of specific textual interpretation. Any statement
or view in either version is understood in the context
of the historical milieu of its author rather than in
its existing literary context. The two versions are
compared and contrasted but the explanation of their
differences is always traced to their separate historical contexts /2/. Wellhausen's analysis of 1 Sam 8-12
was the classic formulation of scholarship in his day,
but it is even more important for the paradigmatic role
it has played in subsequent scholarship. Although there
have been two broad shifts in hypotheses about the
mechanisms of literary growth and accretion in the
narrative - from Wellhausen's two separate versions
to three separate and possibly contemporary traditions
(e.g., Weiser 1962; Wallis 1968; Hauer 1967), to
complexes of one, two or even three redactions or
earlier traditions (e.g., Noth 1967; Boecker 1969;
Birch 1976; Veijola 1977; Langlamet 1978; McCarter
1980) - few examinations have stepped outside Wellhausen's paradigm.

Wellhausen's Paradigm:

1. The separated components that together make up 1
Sam 8-12 must be isolated. This first step presupposes
that the two problems of conflicts and redundancy in
the narrative are the result of composite authorship
over an extended period of time. The theoretical framework of historical criticism is so heavily dependent on
the literary dissection of narratives exhibiting conflicts or redundancies that it is almost impossible for
any alternative explanation of these literary phenomena
to occur. That these conflicts and redundancies might
be functional exemplifications of narrative conventions
is ruled out *a priori* /3/.
2. Each component is analyzed to determine its auth-
or's intention and point of view.
3. A particular group or stratum of Israelite society is tentatively assigned authorship. In addition, a

date and purpose for the composition is suggested.

The whole of the narrative can now be said to have been interpreted. All aspects of the text, especially the problems of conflicting viewpoint and redundancies, have been explained as the product of a particular school or view in a particular period of Israelite history. According to Otto Eissfeldt it is only after determining the extent and nature, date, place, and purpose of the narrative components that the structure and composition of a biblical book become intelligible (1965:130). The extrinsic nature of the historical approach is apparent. The narrative is explained and accounted for by tracing its origins /4/.

The historical-critical approach has endured, albeit with modifications. Instead of literary sources, one speaks of 'traditions' and 'redactions.' More importance is now given to the redactor's control over the content and shape of traditions that he uses. Nevertheless, interpretation is decidedly historical; the meaning of the sources (or traditions, or redactions) is discovered in the particular time and place in Israelite history in which they were supposedly composed.

In the following review of works on 1 Sam 8-12, the dominance of the historical-critical paradigm will be illustrated by schematization of each treatment according to the three steps described above. Representative examples of the three major varieties of historical criticism are reviewed under the headings source, tradition and redaction criticism /5/.

A. Source Criticism

Karl Budde

i) Budde divides the narrative into two parallel independent sources (1902:xii, xviii, xix). His primary criterion for this division is the pro- or anti-monarchic viewpoint of the narrative components (1902:

xii). Budde finds the pro-monarchic source in 9.1-
10.16; 11.1-11, 15; 14.1-46, and the anti-monarchic in
7.2ff; 8; 10.17-24a; 12; 15 (1902:xii). These two
sources were combined by a deuteronomistic redactor,
whose hand is apparent in 1 Sam 7.13-17; 14.47-51; 2
Sam 8 (1902:x). Although Budde agreed that his two
sources were aggregates of pre-exilic traditions, he
saw no visible evidence that would allow for a division of these sources into their respective components.
'There are no signs of redactional activity, no vocabulary differences, no factual disparities between the
two source documents, and no independent traditions
at [our] disposal' (1902:xvii).

ii) Budde's analysis of the content of each source
and their respective vocabularies brings him to recognize them as the Hexateuchal sources J and E (1902:
xviii-xix). The contents and tendencies of each source,
J being the pro-monarchic and E the anti-monarchic,
are explained with reference to the hypothetical characteristics of J and E in the Hexateuch (1902:xviii-xix).

iii) The identification of the two sources as J and
E supplies a previously established place and date for
them. Budde's identification of the anti-monarchic
source with E caused him to date it much earlier than
Wellhausen's post-exilic dating (Wellhausen 1973:254).
The tone of the anti-monarchic E is prophetic in viewpoint with particular dependence on Hosea (1902:xix).
The pro-monarchic source reveals its identity in its
exact correspondence with preceding J narratives in
Joshua and Judges, and in its extensive agreement with
the viewpoint and vocabulary of J (1902:xix).

Budde's examination follows Wellhausen's division of
the narrative into two sources. His main contribution
is to demonstrate the feasibility of other socio-
historical settings, besides Wellhausen's post-exilic
Judaism, to explain the anti-monarchic stance of what
he called E.

Otto Eissfeldt

i) Eissfeldt is the most recent and probably the last proponent of a purely source-critical explanation of the narrative. Eissfeldt agrees with Budde that the narrative sources J and E make up most of 1 Sam 8-12, but makes further subdivision in J, the pro-monarchic source. To J, he ascribes 9.1-10.15; 11.6a; 13.3-15, and to his L, ch. 11 (excluding v. 6a); 13.1-2, 16-23; 14 (1965:275). The two parallel strands J and L stand against E, and relate to one another like J and L in the Pentateuch (1965:208-09). L presents older, cruder, more historically credible narratives (1965:275).

ii) Eissfeldt's comments on the contents of the narrative are almost exclusively devoted to showing how the narrative components assigned to each source exhibit the typical characteristics of their respective sources. For Eissfeldt, these observations confirm the validity of the divisions made in the narratives and the ascription of the resultant components to the pentateuchal sources. An order of dependence is established: from available pre-formed materials to L, to J (with subsidiary reliance on 'living popular tradition'), to E, who undertakes a religiously biased reshaping of L and J, again, with access to 'popular tradition' (1965:279-80). Points of view and intentions of the narrative components are, of course, identical with those previously established for L, J, and E.

iii) For Eissfeldt, as for Budde, the task of determining a date and social setting for each source is solved by pointing to the prior determination of this information in the analysis of the Pentateuch. The division of 1 Sam 8-12 into the sources L, J, and E (in order of dependence) reveals the structural evolution of the narrative. For Eissfeldt the latter result is equally as important as the analysis of single narrative components, in which it is presumed that 1 Samuel can be understood as a simple collocation of numerous individual narrative components (1965:270). There is no question, however, in Eissfeldt's view, of any narrative unity in 1 Sam 8-12.

B. *Tradition History*

A change in approach to the books of Samuel took place after Hermann Gunkel inaugurated his methods of tradition history and form criticism (Stoebe 1973: 47). Gunkel tried to come to terms with the long and varied history of the traditional elements that had been combined to form a narrative, or for that matter, any of the supposed sources.

It was Gunkel's goal to compile a historical catalogue of the literary types represented in the Old Testament. 'We must take the writings of the Old Testament, and, as many of these are collections of writings, we must take their constituent parts out of the order in which they happen to appear in our Canon and in which "Old Testament Introduction" usually studies them, and then rearrange them according to the type to which they belong' (1928:59). Such literary history, 'will only merit the title it claims when it can show how the literature emerged from the national history and was the expression of its spiritual life' (1928:67) /6/. The text as it now exists is, therefore, comprehensible only when the long history of traditions - the separate narrative components - has been traced and comprehended as a product of changing historical and social contexts. Speaking of the Genesis sagas Gunkel says, ' . . . the sagas have already had a history in oral tradition before literary fixation; and this prehistory, ultimately of sole importance, is not to be reached through literary criticism' (quote from Knight 1975:79).

Hugo Gressmann

Gressmann developed Gunkel's view that it was important to examine the prehistory of narrative components

in order to understand both the features of the resulting conglomerate narratives and the historical information purportedly contained therein.

i) Gressmann suggests that the conflicts and redundancies in the books of Samuel are not the result of a
combination of sources such as is the case in the
Hexateuch. He sees the isolated conflicts and mutually exclusive redundancies as the product of variant
manuscript readings that have been combined in the
present MT (1921:xviii). As the recension represented
by LXX shows, these manuscript variants represent
variant traditions which are more or less valuable.

> The Hebrew manuscripts were compared at some
> point and the variants were placed one after anoth-
> er within the body of the text - unlike the modern
> edition which places variants in the margin. The
> variants are thus the product of pedantic exacti-
> tude (1921:xviii) /7/.

The MT has been further complicated by a long
history of glossing, the effects of which must be
eliminated by excluding these later additions to the
traditional material (1921:xviii).

1 Samuel 8-12 is divided into two groupings of
traditions according to their attitudes to the monarchy
and Samuel. 7.2-8.22, 10.17-27, and 12.1-25 are anti-
monarchic and in them Samuel is a judge and central
administrator (1921:46). 9.1-10.16 and 11.1-15 are pro-
monarchic and Samuel plays only a minor role (11.1-15)
or is simply a seer (9.1-10.16).

Although in the present text ch. 11 is required as
a resolution and conclusion of 9.1-10.16, they were
originally separate; 9.1-10.16 is a saga while ch. 11
is a historical narrative, which gives us the only
reliable information on the rise of the Israelite
monarchy (1921:43).

ii) Gressmann understands the intent and point of
view of a narrative component according to its generic

traits. Once each tradition is generically categorized, it is dated and place within the general framework of the Israelite literary periods established by Gunkel /8/. It is primarily the place of a tradition (narrative component) in Israelite literary history that allows modern readers to understand its nature and intent.

Gressmann finds three genres in the narrative: 1. historical narrative represented by ch.11; 2. saga represented by 9.1-10.16; 3. legend in 7.2-8.22, 10.17-27, and 12.1-25.

1. Historical narrative presents contemporary material or material from the immediate past. It deals, by Gressmann's definition, with leading political figures and events (1921:xiv). Only ch. 11 fits this definition while also fulfilling the requirement of agreement with the facts of Israelite history as known from the general history of the Ancient Near East /9/.

2. Saga (German: *Sage*) primarily portrays events from the past. The focus is on individuals, personal relationships, and only incidentally on political events (1921:xiv). While historical narrative portrays what really happened, saga only simulates such relation to reality, 'lacking, as it does, any sense of reality' (1921:xiv). Chapters 9.1-10.16 fit this category admirably 'governed, as it is, by the conventions of the miraculous' (1921:34).

3. Legend is Gressmann's third generic category. It is distinguished from saga by its tendentious edifying purpose (1921:xvi). The legend cycle of Samuel (7.2-8.22; 10.17-27; 12.1-25) fits easily here, 'with the portrayal of Samuel bearing the obvious signs of an edifying purpose' (1921:26).

Having categorized each narrative component, Gressmann continues his exegesis by noting how genre and contents manifest the particular style and viewpoint of a certain period in Israelite literary history. The great detail and leisurely pace of 9.1-10.16 are, for example, the result of a poet's immersion in his heroic subject, of a folk perception of folk heroes. The numerous similarities of this section to fairytales are characteristic of *Sage*, which includes miracles amongst its literary conventions (1921:34).

iii) Chapter 11 is a sober, factually based account of the rise of the monarchy (1921:44). It stands close in time to the events described and little critical sifting is required to determine what actually happened. Since by definition ch. 11 represents the earliest of the three genres present in 1 Sam 8-12 and since it is pro-monarchic, the anti-monarchic viewpoint of the legends must be later and unhistorical (1921:46).

Second in reliability and age is the saga in 9.1-10.16. Many details in this narrative are embroidery of a basic historical kernel, the result of a process of oral transmission in which beliefs became imperceptibly mixed with fact (1921:xii-xiv). Nevertheless, it is the oldest of the sagas and legends in 1 Sam 8-12 and stands relatively close to the events.

Finally, the legends in 7.2-8.22, 10.17-27 and 12 are late deuteronomistic reflections on the narrative (1921:xvi-xvii). Hosea was the first prophet to voice similar anti-monarchic sentiments (1921:28). Gressmann's opinion of these legends is reflected in his comment on 10.17-27. 'A pious nature requires that the king be designated by lot, but history determines in other ways' (1921:41).

All important in Gressmann's exegesis is the narrative component's historical content, the value of the component varying proportionally with its historicity. His analysis of the literary history of the narrative is in fact a byproduct of his attempt to obtain what he considers to be true historical knowledge about the rise of the monarchy from the traditions found in the text. Given that even the literary history of 1 Sam 8-12 is secondary to the goal of historical knowledge, it is obvious that the meaning of the narrative in its existing shape is totally irrelevant to Gressmann.

In *Mose und sein Zeit*, Gressmann summarizes his approach to texts that are 'unreadable and imcompre-

hensible' in their final form because they are simply
a chaotic conglomeration of recensions, variations and
glosses. They become readable and understandable only
when taken out of their present literary context and
reset in a historical context. The claim that these
separated traditions should then be replaced in their
literary context and interpreted there is to be strongly rejected. That is like asking an archaeologist to
take the rubble and finds from his excavations and
replace them in their unexcavated positions and interpret them there. 'Science has nothing to do with such
tasks' (1913:23).

Martin Noth

Gressmann's work set the stage for alternatives to
the source-critical approach to the narrative, but it
was not until the publication of Noth's *Überlieferungs-
geschichtliche Studien* (1943; 2nd edn 1957, reprinted
1967; English trans. 1981) that a traditio-historical
approach to this narrative found wider acceptance.
According to B. C. Birch, Gressmann's analysis was
found unacceptable because it lacked an adequate explanation of how the independent narrative components
came together (1976:2). In Noth's case, it appears that
at least part of his success was due to his emphasis on
the conglomerative process and on the redactional meaning thereby imposed on the traditions. One could view
the scholarly rejection of Gressmann in favour of Noth
as an indication that interpretation of narrative is
more satisfactory when it includes the final form in
its purview.
    1) Noth agrees with Wellhausen's literary-critical
divisions in the narrative, and so his analysis conforms to the paradigmatic explanation of conflicts and
redundancies as indications of multiple authorship. On
the basis of characteristic vocabulary and perspective,
7.2-8.22, 10.17-27a and 12.1-25 are identified as
deuteronomistic (1967:54-55). In these sections, the

deuteronomistic redactor (dtr) has attempted to modify the older traditions in 9.1-10.16 and 11.1-15.

ii) Again Noth follows Wellhausen's reading of the viewpoints expressed in the narrative. Dtr is anti-monarchic. The request for a king in 8.5 is portrayed as an expression of the people's sinful desire not to be dependent on God and his missionary judge for protection against enemies (1967:57). On the other hand, the older traditions (9.1-10.16, 11.1-15) '. . . of the election of Saul to the throne obviously refer to the event with unfeigned satisfaction; they see in it a work of the God of Israel and they show an obvious delight in the personality and the first actions of the new king' (1960:172).

iii) Noth accepts the relative dating of the pro- and anti-monarchic traditions established by Wellhausen. Nowhere does he explicitly say why the pro-monarchic traditions are to be regarded as older. Noth does say, of dtr's anti-monarchic viewpoint, that '. . . it is likely that in this an attitude to the monarchy as such was being expressed which was certainly later confirmed time and again by the experiences which the people had of the institution, but which had, however, existed from the very beginning and had made itself felt even before the rise of the monarchy' (1960: 172-73). By implication, the only time in Israelite history when a pro-monarchic view would have been possible was its birth /10/. As Noth observes, 'For the time being, however, the emergency was so great that there was hardly time for detailed discussion, and the hope placed in the new king, who had proved his worth so brilliantly in the battle against the Ammonites, was so great that all doubts about him faded into the background' (1960:173).

Noth's most basic interpretation of the pro-monarchic elements of 1 Sam 8-12 is, therefore, historical. The views expressed in 1 Sam 9.1-10.16 and 11.1-15 are the product of specific situations in Israelite history. We understand them by understanding the events that they describe.

The anti-monarchic stance of dtr's redactional sections in the narrative is congruent with the remainder of the dtr history, the purpose of which according to Noth is to collect Israel's historical traditions and compile them in such a way as to illumine the course of Israelite history in light of its conclusion. To explain Israel's catastrophic end from his exilic vantage, the dtr portrays the nation's history as a continual sequence of Israelite defections from the covenant with God. The terms of the covenant and the justice of God both require the punishment of Israel for the continual apostasy, and so Israel was destroyed and its people sent into exile.

Noth's interpretation of the anti-monarchic sections of the narrative is historical; the text is the product of an individual (dtr) trying to comprehend his own time by composing a historical etiology. All of Noth's literary observations and interpretations of the text are directed toward one end: the history of Israel (cf. Knight 1975:166f).

Artur Weiser

Weiser's views on 1 Sam 8-12 represent a reaction to both Wellhausen's source criticism and Noth's redaction-critical adaptation of Wellhausen. Weiser labels these views of the apparent conflicts of viewpoint a 'typical case of literary criticism' (1962:28). He proposes instead, a traditio-historical study in which he would seek to discover the particular time, place, and group in Israelite history that might have produced the various traditions that we see. Only then will the historical questions get a proper answer (1962:1).

It is evident that Weiser rejects only the hypothetical division of the narrative into pro- and anti-monarchic strands, whether the latter are conceived as literary sources (Wellhausen *et al.*) or as traditions and redaction (Noth). His exegetical goal is still to establish an historical context in which the text can be set and from which it is comprehensible.

i) Weiser begins from the same observations as his predecessors. The narratives of Samuel 'are not all of a piece' (1961:159). The 'books of Samuel must be regarded as a compilation of heterogenous literary compilations' (1961:159). The narrative complex is not explicable, as in the Pentateuch, as a compilation of continuous parallel strands running throughout the complex. Rather, the narrative complexes such as 1 Sam 8-12 are composed of groups of narratives '. . . which are not so much intermingled with each other as strung after each other, partly on a very loose thread' (1961: 162).

Weiser, like Gressmann, uses a generic criterion to divide 1 Sam 8-12 into its component traditions: 1. 9.1-10.16, a popular saga; 2. 11.1-15, a historical narrative; and 3. chs. 7, 8, 10.17ff, 12, cultic and prophetic formulations and reshapings of earier traditions (1961:162f, 169f).

ii) Weiser finds one central concern in each narrative component: in ch. 7, to honour Samuel as an authoritative and powerful prophetic figure and to outline his role in the religious and political crisis posed by the Philistine threat (1962:23, 28); in ch. 8, to describe the proceedings leading to the establishment of a specifically Israelite monarchy (1962:43f); in 9.1-10.16, to narrate the anointing of Saul (1962: 49); in 11.1-15, to portray the connection between Saul's heroic deeds in the Ammonite war and his subsequent elevation to kingship (1962:72); in 10.17-26, to point out that Saul was elected by lots (1962:65); and in 12.1-25, to show how Samuel managed the transition from theocracy to monarchy (1962:81).

Throughout his investigation, Weiser attempts to demonstrate that neither the so-called anti-monarchic nor the pro-monarchic source exhibits the unitary characteristics and point of view that it should if

it really were a separate literary source /11/. For example, the starting point and primary criterion for spec-
ifying 7-8.22, 10,17-27a, and 12 as one literary source
is the so-called anti-monarchic viewpoint common to
these narrative components. Yet in Weiser's reading,
ch. 7 reveals no anti-monarchic tendencies (1962:27).
Chapter 8 rejects only the non-Israelite monarchic model proposed by the people (8.5, 20) and not kingship
per se (1962:27). Chapter 10.17-27a portrays the choice
of Saul as the will of God and differs from ch. 8 in
the representation of the historical motivation for the
people's request for a king (1962:62). Chapter 12 differs from both chs. 8 and 10.17-27 in its recollection
of the setting and reason for the request (1962:80). In
Weiser's view, the disagreements outweigh any commonality of viewpoint these traditions are said to
share.

Although he is able to discern the efforts of a
redactor to impress a single chronological and factual
context on the disparate traditions, Weiser is more
concerned with the specific and idiosyncratic details
of each separate tradition (1962:25). The differing
details of each tradition are the product of the different social and religious contexts from which the
tradition arose. The narrative, therefore, as well as
the individual traditions and the apparent conflicts
between them is best understood from the combined
historical, sociological, and anthropological perspective that Weiser calls 'tradition history' (1962:48).

iii) Weiser's explanation for the development of
such markedly different recollections of the same
basic historical events is historical. During the period before the construction of the central sanctuary at
Jerusalem, various cultic centres existed in Israel. It
was at these cultic centres that the business of tradition transmission was carried on. Each centre nurtured
and promoted its own distinctive version of what had
happened in the past. Obviously, when these various traditions were compiled by a pious redactor, who dared

not alter sacred tradition, contradictions and confusions would result (1962:79).

Chapter 7, with its cultic interests, points to a setting in a Yahwistic cult at Mizpah (7.5) (1962:13, 22). Chapter 8 stems from the circles of Samuel's like-minded friends in Ramah (1962:44).

Chapter 9 is the combined result of Benjaminite tribal conceptions of the rise of Saul, and sacral elements from the circle of Samuel's successors (1962:57). Chapter 10.1-16 contains several different traditions on the question of the *Königscharisma* (1962:59). Chapter 10.17-27 is the product of an Israelite assembly at Mizpah and is shaped in accordance with the sacred covenant traditions (1962:67). Chapter 11 is a cult tradition of Gilgal (1962:78). And Ch. 12 is also a product of the Gilgal cult; like 10.17-27, it is closely linked with Israel's covenant ideology (1962: 88, 91). In each case, Weiser's understanding of each tradition's significance is contingent upon the correct determination of its time and place of origin.

C. Redaction Criticism

Bruce C. Birch

i) Birch rejects the customary divisions of 1 Sam 8-12 because, for the most part, they are based on content and not critical analysis (1976:132). Instead, he divides the narrative into fragmentary old traditions /12/, a pre-deuteronomistic edition of the old traditions that unified them in a coherent theological perspective (1976:141), and finally the deuteronomistic redaction supplementing the prior redaction (1976:135).

ii) The old traditional narrative fragments are functionally categorized by Birch as aetiological (7.7-12; 10.10-12), folkloristic (9.1-14, 18-19, 22-24; 10.2-4, 9, 14-16a), archival (14.47-51), historical (13.19-22), and military encounters (11.1-11) (1976:132). Generally the old traditions are favourable to the monarchy although they also give evidence of some opposition (1976:134). Samuel plays a less prominent role in the old traditions, either as a judge (magistrate) (7.15-17; 8), or seer/man of God (chs. 9 and 10) (1976:134f).

The first edition of the old traditions gives indications of prophetic interest lying behind the edition. Certain characteristic prophetic genres such as the call narrative and judgement speech are found in the narrative (1976:142). The prophetic editor used the old traditions to illustrate his theological viewpoint. The king as the anointed of God bears special responsibility to fulfill God's law (1976:148).

The deuteronomistic redaction allows that God has granted Israel a king, but is not enthusiastic about this fact (1976:137). 'His main concern, however, is to fit the kingship into the larger framework of covenant obedience . . . The kingship is not in itself a sin, but it contains a potential for sin' (1976:137). The deuteronomist is, therefore, not an anti-monarchist viewing kingship as inherently evil (1976:138).

iii) Birch is cautious when it comes to dating each contribution to the narrative. In general it may be said that the traditio-historical approach as a whole, of which Birch's study is one example, is more concerned to establish a sociological context for any given tradition or narrative component, than to establish an exact historical context. This caution is a product of both the great uncertainties in Israelite history and literary history, and an increasingly sophisticated awareness of the complexity and diversity of Israelite society. Even having established a date for a tradition, the latter cannot be correctly understood until it has been placed in particular social context.

Of the old traditions, Birch says that little more can be said than that there is no reason to date them at any great distance from the time of Saul (1976:133). The prophetic edition exhibits forms dating to the second half of the 8th century B.C. The picture of the king accords better with the northern kings and so would be composed not much later than 721 when the northern kingdom fell (1976:152). The prophetic edit-ion's concern to demonstrate Saul's failure to live up to his charismatic designation is possibly an attempt at theological interpretation of the fall of Samaria (1976:153). Saul, a northern king, failed in obedience and was rejected. David, a southern king, received the boon of an eternal royal dynasty (1976:153).

Birch notes that the deuteronomist is dated anywhere from Josiah in the late seventh century to 550 B.C, He maintains that the 'wait and see' attitude towards the monarchy excludes the view that the anti-monarchic views in 1 Sam 8 and 12 support an exilic date (1976: 140). Beyond this suggestion, Birch does not attempt to interpret the deuteronomistic sections of the narrative by dating them.

Tryggve Mettinger

i) Mettinger follows divisions of the text customary since Wellhausen: the framework, consisting of 7.2-8.22 and ch. 12, is an important part of the dtr composi-tion, separable by vocabulary and ideology from 9.1-10.16, 10.17-27, and 11.1-15 (1976:64-98).

ii) According to Mettinger the dtr framework exhib-its a negative attitude to Saul's kingship. The place-ment of ch. 7 before the request for a king in ch. 8 makes the request seem unwarranted; Israel has Yahweh and Samuel to deliver it from its enemies (1976:80). Chapter 8.11ff criticizes certain aspects of the mon-archy and denigrates Saul and his kingship (1976:81). Chapter 12 demonstrates Yahweh's continued preserva-tion of his people and consequently the willfulness of their request for a king.

Chapters 9.1-10.16 are a composite narrative con-sisting of an old tale about Saul's search for his father's asses reworked to include an anointing by Samuel. The original tale testifies to the conception of the divine election of the king. Its exhortations to the new king to perform a deed of valour (10.7) reveals a martial ideal of kingship (1976:79). The reworking of the old tale adds further emphasis to the concept of a divinely elected king by adding the official designation of Saul as *nagîd* (1976:79).

Chapter 10.17-27 presents Samuel as the last of the pre-monarchic saviours and supplies a link between those figures and the monarchy of Saul. 'The presentation of Samuel as having personally arranged to lot-casting at Mizpah serves to create something of an "apostolic succession": Saul is brought into line with the great pre-monarchic leaders' (1976:90f).

Chapter 11.1-15 presents a very ancient conception of the divine election of a king in which the divine choice is revealed in the course of events that occurred in the rescue of Jabesh (1976:87). Saul is seen to be the same type of man as the earlier saviours (1976: 96). Chapter 11:1-5 is the oldest and historically most reliable tradition of the beginning of Saul's kingship.

iii) Mettinger is among those scholars who suppose multiple deuteronomistic redactions (1976:20). Although he remains non-committal on the exact dating of these redactions he does say that the dtr redactions are the last elements in the process of development of traditions that resulted in 1 Sam 8-12 (1976:96).

The original tale of 9.1-10.16 is dated from the reign of Saul. 'When Saul had proved to be a good warrior and had established his reputation as a hero of Israel his youth became an interesting topic for tradition' (1976:75). Mettinger explains the text as a product of historical events. The interpretive strand of 9.1-10.16 indicates a date near Solomon's death and a social setting in northern prophetic circles (1976: 79).

Chapter 10.17-27 was shaped 'not by the actual historical circumstances in connection with the beginning of Saul's kingship but by the needs of a later time characterized by a tension between different ideals of kingship' (1976:87). Mettinger suggests that many of

the features of 10.17-27 are explicable if the tradition is dated in the reign of Solomon and interpreted
as a northern polemic against Solomon's kingship
(1976:92-95).

Chapter 11.1-15 is the oldest and most historically
reliable tradition. It is to be read as an account of
actual events (1976:86-88).

Timo Veijola

Veijola's redactional analysis of the narrative
(1977) signals a return to an interpretation of the
individual narrative components along the lines established by Wellhausen. Rather than explaining the pro-
and anti-monarchic tensions and the redundancies in
the narrative as the result of the confluence of various
traditions from different times, places, and social
situations, Veijola sees the tensions and redundancies
in the narrative as the product of two dtr redactors,
one pro-monarchic and the other anti-monarchic.

i) Veijola, basing his hypothesis upon the prior
studies of Smend (1971) and Dietrich (1972), suggests
that it is possible to discern two different layers in
the dtr history by paying careful attention to the
vocabulary of the redactor (1977:12f). Veijola makes
the following divisions in 1 Sam 8-12: 1. DtrG - Judg
17-21; 1 Sam 7.5-15, 17, 8.1-5, 22b; 9.1-10.16 (a pre-
dtr composition used by DtrG); 10.17-18a*a*, 19b-27a;
10.27b[LXX]-11.15 (pre-dtr), 2. DtrN - 1 Sam 7.2-4; 8.6-
22a; 10.18a*bc*b-19a; 12.1-25 (1977:115f, 119).

ii) After dividing the narrative between the two dtr
redactors and claiming that division to be based upon
discernible differences in vocabulary (1977:13),
Veijola proceeds to suggest that the tensions and redundancies in 1 Sam 8-12 are the result of two *consecutive* redactions of the narrative.

The first dtr redactor made use of old pro-monarchic
traditions to compose a narrative with the intention of
portraying the monarchy as the answer to the anarchy

and official corruption prevailing in pre-monarchic
Israel (1977:68). Veijola calls this redactor 'the true
historiographer, DtrG' (1977:115). For DtrG, King Saul
is an important figure in salvation history, DtrG gives
Saul a central role as a great deliverer, freeing
Israel from the hand of all its enemies round about
(following 1 Sam 10.1b [LXX]) (1977:118).

The second dtr redaction is a supplementary modification of DtrG's work. Veijola calls the second
redactor DtrN (Nomistic) due to the characteristic way
this redactor evaluates all characters and events from
the perspective of deuteronomic law (1977:119-22). For
DtrN, the 'later student' of DtrG, the monarchy had
become highly suspect (1977:115). The anti-monarchic
DtrN has almost totally obscured the pro-monarchic tone
of DtrG through his extensive revision of DtrG's work
(1977:119).

Armed with this explanation of the chronological
development of the narrative, the exegetical difficulties posed by the narrative are quickly overcome. Read
separately the two redactions are coherent, if contradictory, presentations of the place of the monarchy in
Israel. All that remains to be done in order for us to
understand these two presentations is to determine, if
possible, who made them and when.

iii) Veijola does not offer specific datings for DtrG
and DtrN. He does place DtrN after DtrG based upon
his analysis of dependency between the redactions. The
lack of specific datings for DtrG and DtrN is not an
indication that these are unimportant to Veijola's
approach, but rather that he has taken them for granted
as established by his previous work (1975:137-42).
Veijola's concern in his 1977 book is to supply further
confirmation of the validity of the multiple deuteronomist hypothesis developed to explain the Davidic
traditions.

Frank Crüsemann

Crüsemann's primary interest in 1 Sam 8-12 lies in the anti-monarchic expressions. The purpose of his book is to interpret anti-monarchic texts throughout the O.T. as the product of a particular group or social class in a particular period of Israelite history. Speaking of the anti-monarchic texts, Crüsemann says, 'To do them justice means in the first instance one must reconstruct the situation out of which they arose and the polemical context in which they stood' (1978: 16). Crüsemann outlines four steps leading to an understanding of the anti-monarchic texts: 1. The literary analysis of individual texts; 2. The development of a hypothesis about the possibility and locality of an anti-monarchic movement in Israelite history; 3. An analysis of the pro-monarchic texts and comparison with the anti-monarchic texts. (As polemical political writings they may only be objectively interpreted in comparison with each other.); 4. The construction of a sociological model in which the sociological, political, and theological aspects of the text may be correlated (1978:16f).

i) Crüsemann divides 1 Sam 1-12 between two redactors, each of whom has made use of pre-exisitng materials. The first redaction is found in chs. 9-11. Three separate traditions, 9.1-10.16, 10.21b*b*-27, and ch. 11, have been roughly incorporated, joined by redactional links (9.2b; 10.13b-16, 26b, 27a; 11.12-13) (1978:58). Subsequently a dtr redactor has inserted material in 10.17-21b*a*, 24a*a*, and 25, which alters the meaning of this first redaction and links it with the dtr redaction of chs. 8 and 12 (1978:55). The dtr redaction of chs. 8 and 12 presupposes the prior redaction of chs. 9-11 and includes within itself older traditions in 8.1-3, 7, 11-17; 12.3-5, 12 (1978:61f, 75). The remainder of chs. 8 and 12 exhibit the vocabulary and ideology that characterizes the dtr history.

ii) The intention of the pre-dtr redaction in chs. 9-11 is to defend the legitimacy of the Saulide dynasty (1978:59). The anti-monarchism of the dtr redactor is especially visible in chs. 8 and 12 (1978:60). Even some of the the traditional material used in the dtr redaction is anti-monarchic. Chapter 8.11-17 can only be understood as a strong polemic against the monarchy (1978:65) like 8.7 and 12.12 (1978:84).

iii) Crüsemann's interpretation of the traditions and redactions that comprise the narrative are particularly conditioned by the effort to define the historical and social settings of the individual units.

The theological problem is indivisible from the sociological. When did which group in Israel say no to this institution; when did which say yes? How, therefore, are the various theologies for and against the monarchy connected to a sociologically tangible opposition in Israel?' (1978:15)

Crüsemann says that the question, against whom did the redactor of chs. 9-11 direct his polemical legitimation of Saul, is at the same time the question of the date of this redaction (1978:59). He dates the redaction to the period of the Davidic-Solomonic regime and suggests that it was an appeal to anti-monarchists to join forces with partisans of the Saulides, the legitimate and deserving claimants to the throne (1978:59-60). Crüsemann does not offer a specific dating for the dtr redaction but seems to concur with Boecker's post-monarchic dating (1978:12, cf. Boecker 1969:98).

The pre-dtr unit of 8.11-17 is an early attempt to arouse opposition to the monarchy among the landed gentry (1978:73).

According to vv. 11-17, this group of well-established Israelites can only lose from a monarchy; the economic consequences of the monarchy for the landed gentry are used as an exhortation to anti-monarchic

agitation (1978:73). Crüsemann states, therefore,
that the piece is only comprehensible in the historical context of the early monarchy (1978:72). Verses
8.7 and 12.12, which express the unique view that
divine kingship and human kingship are mutually exclusive options for Israel, require explanation of
how such a conflict had arisen. Such an explanation
requires in turn an approximate date (1978:76). Crüsemann, however, thinks it impossible to be more specific
than the Solomonic period as a *terminus a quo* and the
fall of the northern kingdom as a *terminus ad quem*
(1978:83).

2. Summary and Critique

The historical critical interpretations of 1 Sam 8-12
see the narrative as composite and incomprehensible
in its present form. This judgement is based upon the
interpreters' presuppositions about the genre and conventions of the text. The historical critic approaches
the text in search of the historical realities which
are also supposed to be the object of biblical narrative. Historical truth becomes the standard by which
biblical narrative is evaluated. Whether one is a
conservative historical critic, expecting revelation
in scripture to be truthful and accurate, or simply a
historian desirous of understanding the events described, the principle of historical analogy requires
that biblical narrative give a clear, logical, sequential representation of what happened /13/.

When a narrative does not seem to meet this criterion and, like 1 Sam 8-12, contains conflicting evaluative statements and supposed repetitions such as could
not conceivably have taken place, the historical critic
temporarily switches attention from the subject matter
of the narrative to the level of the narrative itself.
The narrative, as a source for historical knowledge,
has shown itself to be in need of preliminary examination and evaluation.

This evaluation takes the form of a shift from historical analysis of the narrative to literary analysis of the separated narrative components. The perceived lack of narrative logic is replaced with a historical logic by explaining the separate narrative components as products of separate socio-historical contexts. Once each component is reset in its new non-narrative context it may be evaluated for its suitability as a historical source (cf. Mettinger 1976: 16f).

In the course of historical critical studies of 1 Sam 8-12 the literary disunity of these chapters has become axiomatic. Differences of opinion arise, but only on where to divide the narrative, and on what hypothetical socio-historical context best explains any given narrative component. Buber's reading of 1 Sam 7-12 as a unity (with some accretion) has not been seen as a serious enough threat to warrant serious refutation /14/.

Despite the fact that dissenting voices have been almost non-existent there is a relatively unexplored alternative to the historical-critical reading. It is possible that the historical-critical impression of literary disunity is not the result of any inherent quality of the narrative, but of the evaluative literary standards by which historical critics have judged the narrative. It is even conceivable that the methodological predisposition to fragmentary reading of biblical narratives has barred the way to any reasonable attempts to read the narrative as a unit. A reading of scholarly works on 1 Sam 8-12 reveals that the theoretical and empirical basis for the literary fragmentation of the narrative has been based at best on suggested differences in vocabulary, and on ideological and geographical horizons in the material, and at worst on impressionistic evaluations of what constitutes a unitary narrative /15/.

Speaking of the tensions in 1 Sam 8-12, H. P. Smith stated, 'So great a discrepancy, not in details of the narrative only, but also in the whole view of the same period, is not conceivable in one author. It can be accounted for only on the hypothesis that various works have been combined in one' (1899:xvi). Smith's view, characteristic of the majority of critical readings of the narrative, fails to examine the possibility that the differing viewpoints within 1 Sam 8-12 may be subordinate to a single encompassing authorial point of view that is expressed and can only be heard in the narrative as a whole.

Within the study of literature, literary critics have perceived ideological tensions differently. T. E. Hulme, for instance, suggests, 'A powerful imaginative mind seizes and combines at the same instant all the important ideas of its poem or picture, and while it works with one of them, it is at the same instant working with and modifying all in their relation to it and never losing sight of their bearings on each other - as the motion of a snake's belly goes through all parts at once and its volition acts at the same instant in coils which go contrary ways' (cited from Preminger 1974:846). Before passing judgement on the literary continuity of 1 Sam 8-12, the applicability of Hulme's approach should be tested.

J. R. Vannoy (1978) has, in fact, recently suggested that the apparently diverging pro- and anti-monarchic tendencies are reconciled in a final covenant renewal ceremony in ch. 12. In ch. 12, the relations and respective roles of theocracy, monarchy, and people are defined and any ideological conflicts between pro- and anti-monarchic factions are resolved. The aim of such a narrative might be to explore all sides of the theological-political problems of government in the special case of Israel, people of Yahweh. Such an aim is far from the tendentious purposes that have been suggested for the separated narrative components.

F. Crüsemann notes the existence of many other biblical texts that are uniformly either pro- or anti-monarchic (1978:19-53, 85-193). The polemics of such

texts are manifest and straightforward, as is expected
from literature designed to persuade its audience to
accept a particular perspective on the topic of discussion. When, on the other hand, we are faced with a
text that holds the two contrary views in a state of
narrative tension, and we read unencumbered by the
theoretical predisposition to regard such tension as
prima facie evidence of a composite text, the possibility that a neutral perspective - a study of a debated problem - is being voiced cannot be overlooked.
In fact, the tables can be turned. The existence of a
text containing contradictory views should be assumed
to present an examination of a controversy. Only if
such an assumption proves unfruitful should genetic
explanations be considered as a last resort.

A small number of scholars have recently suggested that the interweaving of pro- and anti-monarchic
voices is intentional and meaningful (e.g. Childs 1979:
278; McCarthy 1973; Tsevat 1980). David Gunn (1980)
has treated 1 Sam 8-12 as a literary unity, part of a
larger 'final form' reading of 1 Sam 8 - 2 Sam 1,
the 'story of Saul.' What is lacking in all existing
treatments of the unity of 1 Sam 8-12, however, is a
detailed and comprehensive descriptive reading of
the narrative to support the various positions taken,
which otherwise are too easily ignored by supporters
of the traditional historical-critical position. A
detailed demonstration of coherent plot and a formal
narrative design in 1 Sam 8-12 should obviate the
resort to hypothetical sources, traditions, or subsequent redactions on the principle of parsimony /16/.
A comprehensive attempt at reading the narrative as a
unity, that is, at interpretation of the existing
narrative, is therefore necessary and desirable.

The approach to any biblical text as a narrative
unit does not exclude the possibility that there are
redactional additions or modifications in the text.
But it must be stressed that the act of labelling any
part of the narrative as secondary and contextually

incoherent is a last resort and may be a failure in interpretation rather than in the narrative itself (cf. Fokkelman 1975:2). Gunn suggests that even if a narrative has a complex redactional history, the perceivable unity of the text is a product of mutual interacting influence between existing narrative elements (plot, character, insights, and values) and those who have worked with the narrative. Subtlety in the story, says Gunn, is not necessarily the intentional contrivance of one author: 'rather it may be a subtlety created unconsciously in the dialectical process by which the story is created, a subtlety which is the logical resolution of the variously nuanced contributions and not a property of the contributions themselves' (1980:15) /17/. Gunn's view is helpful in directing the focus of interpretation away from tangential diachronic hypothesis, which is inherently non-verifiable, back to the interpretation of the existing text.

Another weakness of historical-critical literary analysis, as B. S. Childs has suggested, is that the practice of isolating individual components of the narrative may lead to an unbalancing and overemphasis of certain aspects contained in those sections:

> The final form of the text performs a crucial hermeneutical function in establishing the peculiar profile of a passage. Its shaping provides an order in highlighting certain elements and subordinating others, in drawing features to the foreground and pushing others into the background (1979:77).

The practice of dividing a narrative such as 1 Sam 8-12 into separate redactional sections followed by an interpretation of the individual sections as separate expressions of different socio-historical situations may mistakenly attribute independent status and even socio-historical existence to themes, viewpoints, and concepts that owe their existence and

particular nuances solely to their actual setting in
the context of the whole narrative, the final form
of the text /18/. The only pro- and anti-monarchists
that we become acquainted with in 1 Sam 8-12 are
those voices that find complementary expression in
their intertwined appearance in the narrative. It is
the whole text that supplies the formal and semantic
context that is necessary for interpretation.

3. A New Approach to 1 Samuel 8-12

The purpose of this reexamination of 1 Sam 8-12 is
to try to interpret the narrative by reading it as a
unity, without ruling out the possibility that there
may be some aspects that may not, or cannot be comprehended. The method employed can be described as
close reading of the text, a reading strategy akin
to that used by 'new criticism.'

The label 'new criticism' has been applied to a
practical and theoretical approach to English literature that was concerned with close readings of the
individual work rather than with its socio-historical
milieu. New criticism explored the structure of a work
rather than attempting to divine the mind and personality of the author or audience; it attempted to deal
with the literary object rather than its origins and
effects (Preminger 1974:568). Each text is treated as
a structural whole made up of many contributing and
participatory parts. A close reading of a text seeks
to uncover and describe the intricate reticular connections that unite the narrative (or poem), making it into
a singular entity, however complex or devious its plot
may be.

Though 'new criticism' is now seen as a phase in
literary study that has rightly been superseded as an
overreaction to a previous overconcentration on historical criticism (Lentricchia 1980), its methods and
theoretical emphases are still of great value to biblical studies, where scholarship is just beginning to

explore avenues outside historical criticism.

Descriptions of structure in narrative are often divided into two categories. Seymour Chatman, for example, first describes the 'what' of narrative, which he calls its 'story.' 'Story' is composed of events and existents, character and setting (1978:9). Chatman's second analytical category is the 'way' or 'discourse' of narrative. Narrative discourse is the means by which a story is transmitted. Similarly, Charles Conroy divides narrative analysis into two categories, the text as narrative ('what') and as language system ('how') (1978:viii-ix). Under 'text as narrative,' Conroy describes macro- and micro-contextual narrative patterns, plot of action and character, meaning and theme, narrator and reader (primarily point of view) /19/. Under 'text as language system' he places sound stratum (phonology), vocabulary, uses of direct speech (grammar and syntax), and techniques of organization (rhetorical structure).

Although this twofold division is well-suited to Chatman's purpose, which is to generate a general theory of narrative, it is not as useful when the goal is a comprehensive understanding of the meaning of a single work /20/. As P. M. Wetherill notes with regard to his own typology of the textual features that contribute to a text's meaning, 'these categories should not be interpreted narrowly, nor should they be seen as watertight compartments: [they] represent different angles from which a text may be approached. They are therefore independent' (1974:xvi). The meaning of a narrative arises from the union of content (Chatman's story or 'what') and form (discourse or 'way'). The line between form and content is indefinite; the events of a narrative are part of its content and, arranged in a plot, they constitute its form (Wellek & Warren 1975:140). Since it is the goal of this study to understand the meaning of 1 Sam 8-12, the form/content division, though taken into consideration in all analysis, cannot be studied sequentially as first 'form' and then

'content,' or vice versa. To arrive at meaning of a
scene, sermon, or sentence we must view form and content together. As Ellis says, 'the attempted distinction between 'what is said' and 'how it is said' when
analyzed turns out to be no more than a distinction
between 'gross surface meaning' and 'more differenti-
ated investigated meaning" (1974:183).

An interpretation produced by close reading will
follow the order of presentation given in the text,
noting along the way the various contributions of
linguistic and literary devices to the developing
meaning of the text /21/. At the same time, the close
reading of any biblical text, and especially of 1 Sam
8-12, must be carried out in the light of the previous
historical-critical readings of the text. We have been
cued to the tensions, doublets and varying points of
view and their location in the narrative by historical
criticism. A close reading will have to describe the
contextual role of such phenomena if the hypothesis
that the narrative can be read as a unity is to be
maintained /22/.

CHAPTER TWO

DEFINING THE LITERARY UNIT

A major difficulty that the reader of biblical narrative faces is to determine the appropriate contextual boundaries within which to interpret the story that the reader wishes to read. A basic convention of communication is to build interpretation on a completed communication. The meaning of a sentence can only be apprehended by taking all the words together. The same holds true for a paragraph, a chapter or an entire book. Any interpretation that disregards this rule is usually unacceptable to other members of the communicating community. The traditional division of the Bible into books, chapters, and even verses has posed problems with respect to this convention, by separating material that often seems should be read together, or uniting material that should be separate /1/.

A response to the problem that has received some acceptance is what David Robertson calls, 'a literary approach' to context. The contextual decision is determined by the question that the interpreter puts to the text, which is in turn conditioned by the potential of the text to respond (Bar-Efrat 1980:185). Robertson gives the example of an interpretation of Job as a Greek tragedy. Such an interpretation may be judged valid if there are certain conventions in Job that function as the conventions of Greek tragedy do (1977: 10).

The reversal in the role of the interpreter - from a passive recipient of a completed communication to an active questioner who sets contexts - is only apparent. No matter what the communicative situation, context is always produced by objective determinants (completed communications and the possibilities of texts) and the audience's subjective input (a decision as to what context, generic or thematic, is appropriate to an utterance).

Central to the reading of every literary work is the interaction between its structure and its recipient. This is why the phenomenological theory of art has emphatically drawn attention to the fact that the study of a literary work should concern not only the actual text but also, and in equal measure, the actions involved in responding to that text. The text itself simply offers 'schematized aspects' through which the subject matter of the work can be produced, while the actual production takes place through an act of concretization [by the reader] (Iser 1978:20f).

With regard to the interpretation of a text, the would-be interpreter must first pose a question such as, 'What happened when Israel's government changed from theocracy to monarchy?,' before the answer of 'schematized aspects' in the text can be heard. The definition of the literary unit, then, is part of the question and part of the answer. The interpreter has a specific question in mind when seeking to determine what part of the text answers the question posed and the text simultaneously begins its answer by presenting structural and semantic features that influence the interpreter's contextual determinations. The definition of the literary unit is the beginning of the interpretational dialectic and there is no set point of entrance into this hermeneutical circle (cf. Gunn 1980:13).

As Shimon Bar-Efrat notes, biblical narrative is particularly intractable when it comes to establishing the boundaries of a literary unit. Narratives, complete in themselves, are linked with others to compose large literary units such as the patriarchal cycles; the larger units comprise books which in turn make up the Bible. Bar-Efrat responds by suggesting that structure may be legitimately discerned and analysed in both small sections and comprehensive units (1980:156). We may find an idea completely presented in a sentence, a verse, a chapter, or a book.

Similarly, Rolf Knierim suggests that the text contains different possible units depending on the way a question is put to it and on the structural characteristics of the text. The number of contextual delimitations of any text is only limited by the number of the various themes and concepts in the text (1968:25). This suggestion may also be put in different terms. A text may be viewed from the analytical perspective of story and scenes that comprise story. An interpreter of story must read all scenes in proper order to understand story. It is, nevertheless, a valid enterprise to analyse a single scene by itself as long as the reader bears in mind that the scene and its interpretation should ultimately be reintegrated with the story. In fact, as a reader progresses through a story composed of several scenes, he or she takes the course just described interpreting each new scene as it comes and integrating it into the reading of subsequent scenes.

To illustrate: there are now several 'final form' studies of various overlapping sections within the books of Samuel. This study suggests 1 Sam 1-12 can be studied as an integral unit treating the causes and consequnces of initiating a monarchy in theocratic Israel. Within the unit a character, Saul, is introduced and the narrative subsequently tuins to focus on his career as Israel's first king. Thus David Gunn suggests that 1 Sam 9-31 can be studied as a unit treating 'King Saul' (1980:12-18; cf. W. L. Humphreys 1978; 1980; 1982). Gunn, nevertheless, recognizes the importance of the issues about theocracy and monarchy in ch. 8 for understanding 'King Saul' so he adds ch. 8 to his text of concern; the addition is a reflection of the way 'one thing leads to another' in the ongoing

story of God and Israel. Similarly in the middle of
the story of King Saul another character, David, is
introduced (1 Sam 16). Though studies of 'King David'
usually take 2 Sam 9 as the beginning of his story
(cf., however, Gunn 1978:65-84) it is entirely legitimate to study 1 Sam 16 - 1 Kgs 2 as a unit with a
focus on David. Again, the story of Saul leads directly into that of David. There is no abrupt disjuncture
between the two because the events of Saul's demise
are precisely the events of David's rise. The process
continues from David to Solomon, though thereafter the
junctures between successive reigns become more obvious and abrupt. The point, of course, is that like the
body there are identifiable parts which nevertheless
make up an inseparable whole. Specialized study of
the parts is equally as legitimate and profitable as
general study of the whole. The analogy of general
practitioners and specialists in medicine is illum-
inating in this respect.

A practical limitation also imposes itself on all
biblical interpreters in their attempts to determine
the correct literary context for interpretation. The
time and the writing space needed to write a good close
reading of a text do impose real limitations on the
amount of biblical text that can be encompassed in any
single examination. Faced by such limitations one must
be resigned to some measure of inexhaustiveness (cf.
Conroy 1978:7).

The accepted boundaries of the narrative treating
the rise of Israel's monarchy are chs. (7)8 and 12 of 1
Samuel /2/. These chapters have been seen as a history
of the inauguration of the Israelite monarchy /3/. The
primary criterion for this textual delimitation has
been thematic unity, the assumption being that thematic
unity is basic to any narrative. This thematic concern
has also been used to distinguish chs. 8-12 from their
immediate context. Alfons Schulz, for example, suggested the following thematic division of 1 Sam 1-15:

   1. Samuel's youth, chs. 1-3;

2. The Ark, 4.1-7.1;
3. Samuel and the monarchy, 7.2-12.15; and
4. Saul, the victorious king, and his rejection,
   chs. 13-15 (1919:vii).

Whether or not chs. 7, and 13-15 are included in the narrative on the rise of the monarchy or the rise of Saul's monarchy, as the case may be, there is virtual unanimity that at least chs. 1-6 must be treated separately. Although stylistic observations and arguments are advanced to support this division /4/, the principle evidence is the seeming lack of thematic continuity between accounts of Samuel's birth and youth, the 'ark narrative' (1 Sam 4-6), and 1 Sam 8-12. So, for example, Hertzberg states that chs. 1-3 show how Samuel replaces the Elides, chs. 4-6 are a history of the ark, and chs. 7-15 are the history of the beginnings of Israelite monarchy (1964:43, 62, 130).

Hertzberg's separation of chs. 1-3 and chs. 4-6 within chs. 1-6 exemplifies a scholarly consensus that has only recently been criticized as too fragmentary. In a series of articles (1971, 1972, 1979), Willis has suggested that chs. 1-7 must be viewed as a meaningful whole that is thematically and stylistically unified; the theological concern expressed in chs. 1-7 is presented in a well-attested biblical literary pattern:

1. Yahweh prepares a man to lead Israel through some crisis (1.1-4.1a);
2. The crisis is described (4.16-7.1);
3. The successful guidance of Israel out of the crisis is accomplished by the chosen man (7.1-17)(1971:298).

The character of Samuel is obviously an important unifying element in Willis's reading, and yet it is partly because of Samuel's absence in 4.1b-7.1 that scholars have separated all or part of chs. 1-3 from chs. 4-6. Willis suggests that Samuel's absence from chs. 4-6 emphasizes that without him Israel's situation was rapidly deteriorating under the Elides. The failure of the Elides in chs. 4-6 is contrasted with the deliverance accomplished by Samuel in ch. 7 (1971:299).

Whether Willis's analysis is judged right or wrong, the ability of his interpretation to include ch. 4-6, where the main character does not appear, is based on a more sophisticated understanding of narrative technique and character. The most important justification of his reading of chs. 1-7 as a whole is that he can suggest a theme that unites the narrative, utilising in support the numerous rhetorical connections between those parts of the narrative separated in the conventional historical-critical reading (1979:208 n.29).

If Willis's reading of chs. 1-7 is more satisfactory than one in which the chapters represent a series of disconnected events and conglomerate historical descriptions, it is because his interpretation reveals meaning and order in the sequential combination of chapters. This reading does not differ in the logic of the reading process from historical-critical readings. Just as Hertzberg argued from thematic unity to justify his claim that chs. 1-3 were a unit, Willis argues for the unity of chs. 1-7. His reading does differ, however, quantitatively: it unites seven chapters; Hertzberg's unites only three.

M. Perry describes the reading process as the construction of a system of hypotheses or frames to create the greatest amount of correlation between the various data of a text. These frames or hypotheses explain the 'co-presence' of data in the text in reference to models derived from 'reality,' or from literary or cultural conventions (1979:43). Willis's 'frame' for chs. 1-7, for example, is a literary convention (1971:298-99).

Perry describes the logic of frame construction in the reading process as a hierarchy of three considerations:

1. The reader prefers a frame that links the highest number of textual data;
2. The frame that connects the data most closely allowing them the least degree of 'freedom' takes precedence;

3. The simpler, more conventional and more typical a frame is, the more acceptable it is. 'The validity of a hypothesis will increase in a direct ratio to the variety of the items it organizes and to the heterogeneity of the textual dimensions where they originate' (1979:45).

Perry's three considerations are in the nature of self-evident descriptions of what we find acceptable in interpretation rather than being hypotheses about the reading process. It is unlikely that anyone would dispute the claim that the goal of interpretation in any field of human inquiry is an explanation (frame) that is comprehensive, provides a single explanatory structure for all or most of the data, and last, but not least, that is elegant. Yet these three qualities of a superior interpretation are simply adjectival paraphrases of Perry's three considerations. Willis's reading of 1 Sam 1-7 is more valid in Perry's terms because it has greater organizing powers, granted that the text does exhibit the features of Willis's 'OT hero narrative' /5/.

Valid as Willis's reading of chs. 1-7 may be, it is possible to construct an interpretational frame that is preferable to Willis's reading in all three of Perry's considerations. The hypothesis to be tested in this study is that *neither chs. 1-7 nor 8-12 can be properly understood in isolation from each other.* The narrative extending through chs. 1-12 should be interpreted as a coherent theological-political exploration of human and divine leadership in Israel. This exploration is presented in the form of a literary representation of the events leading to the establishment of a monarchy in Israel /6/.

In the the context of the so-called deuteronomistic history this important narrative is thematically distinguished from the preceding events, the period of the judges, and from the following events, the period of the monarchies. Chapters 1-12 belong wholly to neither of these periods, and focus, instead, on the moment of transition lying between the two eras. Although there are obvious connections between chs. 1-12 and the stories of subsequent monarchs - especially Saul - in the deuteronomistic history, it is legitimate to study this narrative as a self-contained unit focused on one particularly important moment within the history.

The description of Israel's transition from theocracy to a theocratically subordinate monarchy is an *episode*, which differs from preceding *scenes* in that it is a *digression* in the story of Israel's theological-political relationship with God /7/. As an episode, the description of the movement away from theocracy towards monarchy is separable from the on-going story of covenant and theocracy, yet it arises naturally from that story. And, subsequently (1 Sam 13ff) the book of Samuel returns to the theocratic story. Ultimately, of course, my interpretation of chs. 1-12 will have to be incorporated, and thereby certainly modified, into an interpretation of the whole of the deuteronomistic history (cf. the similar position taken by Gunn 1980: 14f). Such a task, however, is far beyond the scope of a single study, especially in view of the novelty of this approach /8/.

Several stylistic features distinguish the episode from its context. The unit occupies the important position of the opening of a book. Perry cites a number of psychological experiments studying the 'primacy effect' - the effect on the reader of situating information at the beginning of a message - that have shown that the beginning of a message receives more attention than its continuation (1979: 50-58; cf. Sternberg 1978, index under 'Primacy effect'). The literary text can exploit the 'primacy effect' for rhetorical purposes by placing first information that will guide the reader's construction of hypotheses about the story so that subsequent material is always read in light of these interpretations.

As Budde observed, 1 Sam 1.1 differs from the opening verses of the two preceding books of the deuteronomistic history, Judges and Joshua: 'The book does not connect explicitly to the book of Judges, as the latter does to Joshua and Joshua to the Pentateuch (cf. Judg 1.1; Josh 1.1)' (1890:167). The opening verse thereby sets the following episode, which it introduces, apart from the previous series of scenes in Israel's theocratic history. The small stylistic difference between 1 Sam 1.1 and the introductory verses of Joshua and Judges is a subtle hint about the special significance of the *episode* that follows. Another obvious guideline for the establishment of the proper opening contextual boundary is the simple fact that the book begins at 1.1. As Lewis Carroll says, 'Begin at the beginning' (1963:158).

The episode ends in ch. 12 with Samuel's great oration in which he surveys Israel's history of defection and lays down the law for the future. As Noth suggests, ch. 12 is one in a series of speeches made by the Israelite leaders in the deuteronomistic history (1967:5). These speeches punctuate the narrative; they are placed at the close of important epochs in Israel's theocratic history. In the view of Noth, and most scholars since, 1 Sam 12 constitutes a summary and conclusion to the period of the judges, which in the biblical narrative, stretches from Judg 1.1 to 1 Sam 12.25.

One function of the formula in 13.1 is that it is the narrator's customary way of introducing the beginning of a king's reign by stating the king's age at accession and the length of his reign (cf. Driver 1913:96f; McCarter 1980:222f). The placement of this introductory formula immediately after Samuel's speech indicates that the period of the judges is, indeed, finished and that the age of the kings has begun. Chapter 12 also functions more specifically as the conclusion of the narrative begun in 1.1. Samuel, the last of the judges (7.8, 12.11) is introduced in ch. 1, and in ch. 12 he makes his concluding speech as *sole* political representative. In the speech, he specifically mentions the length of his service, which

reaches back to events narrated in 2.11. Another link
to the narrative prior to ch. 8, the accepted introductory limit for the interpretation of chs. 8-12, is
found in 12.10f, which refers, among other things, to
the events of ch. 7.

The renewal of the covenant relationship in ch. 12
at least partially resolves the covenantal tensions
that begin in 2.12ff with the Elide abuses of the
priestly office. At that time, Yahweh was provoked
to annul his promise of a priestly dynasty to Eli's
forefathers (2.30f). The covenantal issue continues
through chs. 4-7, in which Yahweh's apparent abandonment (4.3) and open rejection of Israel (6.20) lead
Israel to a reluctant worship of other gods (7.2f). A
reconciliation is achieved in ch. 7. Israel is repentant (7.3-9) and Yahweh acts again to save Israel from
its enemy (7.9-12). Immediately thereafter, however,
the covenant is again in jeopardy (8.7f); this time,
though, in contrast to chs. 4-6 where Yahweh abandoned Israel (4.3; cf. Exod 23.22f), it is Israel that expresses a wish to have a king like the nations and to
be like the nations (8.5, 20). Yahweh and Samuel
correctly interpret the request as an attempt to break
free from the theocratic covenant (8.7f; 10.19; 12.12).
Yahweh takes the initiative in chs. 9-10 and makes an
effort to avoid a covenantal breech by granting the
people's request for a human king. It is important to
note, however, that Yahweh gives them a king and a
monarchy that remain within the covenantal framework. Saul is not a king 'like all the nations': on the
contrary, he is described in the same words as Moses,
the paradigmatic theocratic representative (cf. Exod
3.7, 9), as a deliverer given to Israel by its all-
seeing, protective God (1 Sam 9.16). Saul's victory in
11.11 is described as deliverance wrought by Yahweh
in 11.13 /9/. Finally, the covenantal inconstancies are
disposed of in ch. 12 which redefines (vv. 13-15) and
reestablishes the covenant (vv. 6-15) in terms that
emphasize Yahweh's initiative in the original covenant

(v. 22; cf. Deut 7.6; 14.2). It was Yahweh who decided to elect Israel and to covenant with them; it is also Yahweh, therefore, who will say whether the covenant ends or continues, and not Israel.

This brief survey of the causal linkage provided by the theme of covenant relationship reveals that the section comprised by chs. 1-12 is also distinguished as an integral unit by internal considerations. A problem is introduced in ch. 2 and a resolution is not reached until ch. 12. And ch. 1, as Willis has demonstrated (1979), cannot be separated from the rest. Taken together, the internal causal concatenations and the external stylistic boundary markers permit the exploration of the hypothesis that chs. 1-12 may be read as an episode in Israel's theocratic history.

CHAPTER THREE

1 SAMUEL 1-12:
SUMMARY OF THE NARRATIVE

The literary method of painstaking, close reading requires description of the text within a narrowly circumscribed field of view. If analytic description increases reader appreciation of the importance of detail in narrative study, it is always at risk of losing sight of the larger narrative context. To avoid this problem - losing sight of the forest for the trees - it seems advisable to provide the reader with a summary of the narrative, a literary map to lead him or her through the mass of detail to follow (cf. Conroy 1978:10). The summary is the product of several readings of 1 Sam 1-12. The reader who has not had a chance to read chs. 1-12 through several times can use the summary as an introduction and as a contextual guide for checking his or her understanding at any point in the study.

Of special importance are several parallels and points of contact between chs. 1-7 and chs. 8-12. A quick read through chs. 1-12 probably would not lead the reader to see that chs. 1-7 are important to the subject, presented in chs. 8-12, of Israel's monarchy. Numerous existing studies of chs. 1-7 and chs. 8-12 as separate, and within themselves fragmented, narratives reveal that close reading is necessary before a reader can appreciate the connections. Like an illuminated manuscript, biblical literature needs careful attention to be understood and appreciated.

The summary is also of practical utility; my analytical description follows the order of the narrative's

own expositional patterns. Since the relevance of chs.
1-7 for chs. 8-12 does not surface until the crucial
ch. 8, the significance of the detailed study of chs.
1-7 for an understanding of Israel's monarchy also
remains hidden until ch. 8. The summary should help
the reader to traverse the first seven chapters, whose
intrinsic merit and interest are unquestionable, but
whose importance to the development of Israel's monarchy is initially unapparent. The omission of any
introductory statement by the narrator in 1 Sam 1 -
'Here follows a description of the causes, conditions,
and consequences leading to the establishment of our
king' - places this narrative closer to literature
than to historiography. The order of presentation and
narratorial exposition is designed more to entertain
and educate the reader than to inform and accurately
portray events for the reader.

Most studies of 1 Samuel 1-12 see a definite break
between ch. 7 and ch. 8, though some have suggested
that ch. 7 complements the so-called anti-monarchic
bias of ch. 8 (e.g. McCarter 1980:150f). The widespread agreement on this division suggests that some
feature of the narrative promotes such a reading. In
my view, ch. 7 does indeed describe a momentary resolution of tensions developed in chs. 1-6. With ch. 8
the very same tensions are reintroduced and the narrator describes a related but different series of events
leading to a second resolution in ch. 12.

1 Sam 1-6 traces the development of a crisis in
covenantal relations between Yahweh and Israel. The
priestly leaders have become corrupt (2.12, 23-25, 29;
3.13f) and debilitated (2.22, 25; 3.2, 13). Yahweh
decides to punish his priests by destroying them and
denying his promise to them of a perpetual priestly
dynasty (2.28-30; 3.12-14). He inflicts the punishment
(2.31-34; 4.11, 18) but in doing so also makes innocent
Israelites suffer (4.2f, 10).

Divine responsibility for the indiscriminate slaughter of innocent Israelites along with the guilty priests

is underlined by chs. 5-6. Israel was defeated by Yahweh at Ebenezer, not by the Philistine god Dagon. Yahweh is more than equal to Dagon (5.1-5; cf. Miller & Roberts 1977:46). To make things worse, Yahweh caps his victorious return to his own people by striking them for looking 'at' or 'in' - the Hebrew is ambiguous - the ark.

Israel seems worse off for the return of the victorious Yahweh than it was without him. The question put by Israel in 6.20, 'And to whom shall he go up from upon us?,' parallels the Philistine reaction to the presence of Yahweh's palladium (5.8, 10, 11; 6.2). Yahweh's behavior forces Israel to respond as if they were Philistines. What has become of the covenant relationship that was supposed to distinguish and privilege Israel as Yahweh's own 'peculiar people' (Exod 19.5; Deut 14.2)?

In fact Yahweh, in his efforts to punish his sinful priests, had neglected his promise to make Israel's enemies his own enemies (e.g. Exod 23.22). He even treats Israel as if he were bringing the covenant curse on it, as a comparison with Deuteronomy's curses shows:

1 Sam 4.2,10: *wayyinnagep* yisra'el *lipnê pelištîm*
. . . *wayyanusû*
Deut 28.25: yittenka yhwh *niggap lipnê 'oyebeyka*
. . . *tanûs* lepanayw
Sam: And Israel was defeated before the Philistines
. . . and they fled
Deut: Yahweh will cause you to be defeated before
your enemies . . . you shall flee before them.

The men of Bethshemesh respond to Yahweh's action by raising the question whether it is possible to continue in a covenantal relationship with such a God (6.20). The expression 'to stand before Yahweh' frequently occurs in covenantal usages /1/. Israel seems to find it difficult to maintain a covenant relationship with this holy, incomprehensible God, who punishes where no apparent wrong has been done (cf. 4.3). Like the Philistines before them (5.7ff), the men of Beth-shemesh decide that the best course is to unload the burden of the ark on someone else /2/.

The covenant relationship reaches a new low in 7.1f. The ark (and its God) is put into 'cold storage' (Hertzberg 1964:61), and Israel mourns Yahweh as though he were dead (Buber 1956:118; cf. Ezek 32.18; Mic 2.4; and the noun form in Jer 9.9, 17-19; Amos 5.16). From Samuel's subsequent exhortation, we see that Israel truly believed that the relationship was ended and that Yahweh was no longer a viable national god. Accordingly, the nation turned to the worship of other gods (7.3).

Samuel proposes a scheme for renewal of relations between Israel and Yahweh (7.3), which they both accept (7.4, 9). At the conclusion of ch. 7 covenantal relations are back to normal. Yahweh is again on Israel's side (7.13) and lost territories are regained (7.14). There is even peace with the Amorites (7.14). Order and regularity prevail. Samuel serves Israel as circuit-judge, making his rounds 'year by year' (7.16). All is well in Israel.

Previous readers have been right, therefore, to suggest that ch. 7 resolves the conflicts and tensions of chs. 2-6. They also rightly observe that, surprisingly, ch. 8 opens with the description of another disturbance in the relationship. The new crisis is strikingly dissonant with the conclusion of ch. 7. Historical-critical reader reaction to the dissonance has generally been to see in chs. 7 and 8 the end and the beginning of two separate and unrelated literary complexes (e.g. Stoebe 1973:175).

As others have observed, however, the pastoral conclusion to ch. 7 provides an interesting setting for the radical request of ch. 8 (e.g. McCarter 1980:151; Birch 1976:11). Why would Israel request a king, a replacement for both Samuel and God (8.6-8), when things were going as smoothly as they were in ch. 7?

If ch. 7 is read by itself as the context for ch. 8
then McCarter is right to say that it sets the request
for a king in a very bad light (1980:151). But ch. 7
itself cannot be divorced from its own context and that
includes chs. 1-6. Could there be some rationale for
the request for a king in the events described in chs.
2-6? The possibility deserves examination.

Intervening between the request for a king (8.5) and
the conclusion to ch. 7 are four verses of narration.
In vv. 1-3 the decaying state of affairs in Samuel's
family is described. In v.4 the narrator describes the
elders convening and then going to Samuel. The convention is obviously a response to the family affairs of
Samuel (cf. 8.5). Remarkably, the deterioration in the
house of Samuel, Israel's judge and covenantal mediator, is virtually identical to the state of affairs
that had existed in the priestly Elide house. And, it
was that very state of affairs that had brought on the
catastrophe in ch. 4 - an old theocratic representative
(8.1, 5; cf. 2.22; 3.2; 4.18) has two sons who inherit
the office but depart from the requisite morality (8.2,
3, 5; cf. 2.11, 16) /3/. In both situations the leadership of Israel, whether responsible for cultic or civil
affairs, - both being governed by the theocratic constitution - has failed in the transition to a new generation /4/.

Is this paralleling done intentionally by the narrator? Is Israel aware of the parallel and requesting
a king to avert a repetition of the disaster at Ebenezer (ch. 4)? If the request is made in view of events
described in chs. 2-6, why ask for a king such as all
the nations have (8.5)?

The covenant had made Israel 'a people dwelling
alone, not reckoning itself among the nations' (Num
28.9). Israel became Yahweh's own possession, unique
and separate from all the other peoples and nations on
the earth (Exod 19.4-6; 33.16; Deut 7.6; 14.2; 26.18f;
32.8f). The request for a king 'like all the nations'
could be a bid to escape from this special status. When

Samuel tries to dissuade Israel, the response reveals even more clearly Israel's desire to step outside the relationship. 'No; we want a king over us, and we, yes we, will be like all the nations' (8.19-20, my translation). If the request is a response to the recurrence of a potentially dangerous disorder in the house of the theocratic mediator, could the anti-covenantal content of the request be a reaction to Yahweh's hostilities towards Israel in ch. 4 and in 6.19?

Yahweh's decision to accede to the elders' request, even though he understands their anti-covenantal intentions (8.7, 8, 22), seems even stranger than the request itself first did. Why does he give in so easily? He does, after all, regard the request as one in a series of Israel's rebellions against him (8.8). Is the reader supposed to understand Yahweh's accession to the request as an admission that he had gone too far in his zealous allotment of punishment for the Elide sin? When the provocative situation reappears in the mediator's house and Yahweh agrees to the request for a king, is he himself realizing that this wish to be 'like the nations' is justified in view of his behavior towards Israel? He did, after all, treat them very much like he treated the Philistines (6.19).

If Yahweh does give his consent to the request, and he seems to give that impression (8.9, 22; 9.15-16; 10.18-19), he certainly has a strange way of showing it to Israel. The request is indeed granted, but only in a vitiated form (Buber 1956:121). At Yahweh's command Saul is anointed as 'designate' (*nagîd*) and not as king. Saul's mission as 'designate' is set out by Yahweh in much the same words that he used to describe Moses' mission to Israel in Egypt (9.15f; cf. Exod 3.7-10). The requested king, leader of a new, profane Israel, is a far cry from the granted 'designate,' the 'new Moses' sent by Yahweh to save(!) Yahweh's people /5/. But how does Yahweh, the actual cause of Israel's 'outcry' (4.13f), expect to pass off his 'designate' as an answer to the 'cry of his people' (9.16), which by

implication is the request for a profane king? Surely
Israel will not stand for such an obvious perversion of
its seemingly just request. Does Yahweh have something
up his sleeve, or will he simply impose his will as God
over humankind?

As it happens, Yahweh resorts to both means of getting Israel to accept his 'designate' as their king. In
10.17-27 Samuel reconvenes Israel at Mizpah, with the
object of presenting Yahweh's proposal for the people's
approval. Samuel's rhetoric in his introductory speech
conveys the impression that Yahweh is reluctantly granting the request (10.18-19). Unaware that Saul is not
exactly what they asked for, the people unanimously
and officially acclaim him (10.24). Their acclamation,
'Long live the king!,' is a binding recognition of the
new royal authority (de Boer 1955:231). Having obtained this binding response, Samuel proclaims the
actual basis and constitution (*mišpaṭ hammelukâ*)
of the new monarchy (10.25).

Response to this case of entrapment is mixed. Some,
with a little help from God, - he touches their hearts
(10.26) - accept Saul and go with him /6/. Others, untouched 'renegades' (*benê belîyaʿal*), reject Saul
as unsuitable for their purposes (10.27). Such doubts
about Saul's suitability continue through into 11.1-5,
where the nation is in desperate need of a leader, yet
refuses to even consider Saul let alone follow him as
king (cf. 8.20).

Saul, stirred into action by an injection of divine
spirit (11.6), forcibly conscripts his unwilling subjects and leads them to a sound victory over the Ammonites (11.11). The victory convinces all the people
to unite in support of Saul, and they ceremoniously
reaffirm their allegiance to him and to Yahweh (11.15).
The description of the location for the renewal, 'before Yahweh,' uses the verbal cue *lipnê yhwh* to recall 10.25, where the new monarchic constitution was
installed, also 'before Yahweh' (*lipnê yhwh*). The
renewal at Gilgal constitutes a conscious acceptance

by all the people of the theocratic monarchy proposed by Yahweh.

In ch. 12 Yahweh, through Samuel, ensures that the people accept his designate on his terms by using his other option, the coercive power of man's justifiable fear of God. The conditions and stipulations that are established for the new theorcratically subordinate monarchy are no different than those of the pre-monarchic, theocratic covenant. Ch. 12 exhibits the same literary form and the same requirements as the Sinaitic (Exod 19) and Shechemite (Josh 24) covenants (Muilenburg 1959:361-65).

Nothing has changed (12.14; cf. Exod 19.5). Israel's capitulation is obtained by a show of divine force (12.17f) and the people respond as we would expect. They turn to Samuel - not Saul - and request his intercession on their behalf (12.19). Samuel reassures the people of his prayers for them (12.23) and of Yahweh's good intentions towards them (12.22). No evil will come upon Israel so long as it is faithful to Yahweh (12.22-25).

With ch. 12, then, the story arrives at a second resolution. Both the problems of chs. 4 and 8 - renegade behavior on the part of one of the covenantal partners - are laid to rest. Whether the narrative encourages the reader to regard the resolutions as satisfactory or not is another question. For the moment what matters is that the reader be able to follow the story line throughout chs. 1-12, however roughly sketched here, and so have some sense of the direction that the following close reading will take.

1 SAMUEL 1-12:
A CLOSE READING
OF THE NARRATIVE

Rather than analytically separating the different aspects of narrative composition that create its meaning, as Conroy (1978) has done in his innovative study of 2 Sam 13-20, I shall follow the order of the text and discuss any feature of the narrative as the occasion arises. Separate treatment of the various literary phenomena, though suitable for attempts to compose a biblical narratology, detract from the comprehensive understanding of a narrative when the goal is interpretation. The focus of this study is not biblical narrative in general, but the specific narrative in 1 Sam 1-12 for which Buber's label, the 'Biblical Politeia,' is an appropriate title (1964:734).

1 SAMUEL 1-2:
A CLOSE READING
OF THE NARRATIVE

CHAPTER FOUR:
PART ONE

1 SAMUEL 1

Verse 1

The narrative begins with an introductory phrase also
found in the stories of the judges (Judg 13.2; 17.1; 19.1).
'There once was a man' (*wayehî 'îš 'eḥad*), is a common
formula indicating that the following narrative is a
new story (cf. Stoebe 1973:92). McCarter's suggestion
to follow the opening in LXXB (*anthropos en*) instead
of MT, which has supposedly been influenced by Judg
13.2, bypasses the significance of this parallel in MT.
McCarter offers a genetic explanation for the form of
the introductory formula in MT and uses this explanation as an argument in favour of the reading of LXX
(1980:51). Such explanations are common enough in textual criticism. but their adequacy is questionable /1/.
   The fact that the opening of MT uses the sequence
wayehî 'îš, which regularly introduces new stories
in a series, arouses certain expectations in the reader about the nature of the material that follows, and
about how he is to approach it. Buber's observations
about repeated 'keywords' (*Leitwörter*) are pertinent;
'They function to open up or clarify a significance of
the text otherwise not seen, or to make a perceptible
meaning even more obvious' (1964: 1131). The same is
true of the influence of Samson's birth narrative on v.
1 and elsewhere in ch. 1.
   Already with the first three words of Samuel's birth
story, construction of a framework is begun, and it is
within this framework that the reader understands the

narrative. If the narrative begins like the Samson birth narrative, do we gain more knowledge about it by speculating about the 'superiority' of versional alternatives that do away with the parallel, or by noting the effects of the similarity on the reading process? Given the other similarities between Samuel's and Samson's birth stories (cf. McCarter 1980:64-66), and the fact that one of the four roles (priest, judge, prophet, and seer) that Samuel plays is that of a judge (ch. 7, esp. vv. 6, 15-17; 8.1-5 [by implication]; 12.11), the connection between 1.1 and the stories of the judges seems to be in accord with the conventions of the scene as a whole. The story about to be told should, therefore, be read in the light of the prior stories of the judges (cf. Schulz 1919:2).

The place of Elkanah's origin has sparked many vexed topographical discussions. According to Driver, Ramathaimzophim is grammatically indefensible. He suggests that the final 'm' of *sôpîm* is a dittographic repetition of the initial 'm' of the following words (1913:1). Driver's reading is coincidentally supported by LXX and provides a balanced appositional sentence, roughly translated:

'There once was a man from *haramatayim*,
a Zuphite from Har *'eprayim.'*

His suggestion receives further support from the name and tribal affiliation of Elkanah's great-great-grandfather. He is *sûp*, an *'epratî*. Driver's reading suitably identifies Elkanah as a *sûpî mehar 'eprayim*.

The dual ending on *haramatayim* creates a rhyme with the word *'eprayim*, which supports the parallelism of the two lines /2/. Both geographical names serve to locate Elkanah and concretize the story from the very beginning.

Paradoxically, the names in Elkanah's genealogy are important because of their unimportance. They are all names of insignificant obscure people /3/. This type of genealogy, labelled a 'linear' genealogy by Robert Wilson, traces a single line of descent from a given ancestor (1977:9). Linear genealogies are normally used to link a descendant with an earlier ancestor for social, political, or religious legitimation (Wilson 1977: 40-45, 155, 164). The Elkanah genealogy is so employed in 1 Chr 6.11-13. There the genealogy places the family amongst the Levites, thereby making Samuel a Levite. As it appears in 1 Sam 1.1, however, the genealogy accomplishes anything but legitimation. Samuel's natural lineage grants him no claim to any important rank. If he has or attains any status at all it is not because of his family tree.

This reading of the genealogy is reinforced by the fact that Samuel, the son of a barren woman, only comes into being as a miraculous grant of God. He may be well-connected, but his connections are definitely not drawn from any Israelite social structures /4/.

Besides introducing the reader to Elkanah, v. 1 also establishes the 'narrative situation' from which the narrator will relate the story. By framing his introduction to Elkanah in the preterite (*wayehî 'îš*), the narrator reveals that he views the events at some temporal remove from their occurrence. At this point the length of the intervening period of time between the events and the situation of the narrator, that is the narrative distance, is left undetermined.

A second, very important implication of the temporal distance between the events of the narrative and the event of narration is that the narrator thereby indicates his position beyond the world that he describes. Franz Stanzel observes that this exterior position of the 'authorial' narrative situation - a situation in which author and narrator are usually indistinguishable - 'enables the authorial narrator to assume a position of superiority over his figures' (1971:38f). The reader, who perceives and comes to understand the narrated events only as they are presented by the narrator is thereby also placed in a position of conscious superiority to the characters and exteriority to the story.

This definition of the relationship between the

narrator and reader, on the one hand, is an important function of the preterite introduction. The importance of this definition for the proper understanding of the narrative cannot be overemphasized. All subsequent features of the narrative, such as the presence of conflicting evaluations and viewpoints within the narrative, are subject to this basic framework.

Verse 2

Verse 2 continues to sketch the background for the events of the birth story. A similar pattern of gradually increasing specificity lies behind both v. 1 and v. 2. The characters are gradually brought into focus by beginning with general specifications followed by ascending list of particularizations:

	VERSE 1	VERSE 2
1. gender & no.	wayehî 'îš 'eḥad	welô šetê našîm
2. place	min haramatayim	Women assume the situation of their husband.
3. name	ûšemô 'elqanâ	šem 'aḥat ḥannâ wešem haššenît peninnâ
4. progenitors/ progeny	genealogy	Peninnah has children, Hannah does not.

The specifications in v.1 end with Elkanah's genealogy, which is not illustrous. In v. 2, the final concern is again with the family lines. In this case, however, it is with respect to their potentialities as preservers of Elkanah's line that Hannah and Peninnah are characterized. With respect to Samuel, v. 1 suggests his unimportance in Israel's social hierarchy, and now v. 2 suggests that it is unlikely that he should even become an insignificant character. At this point he *is* the son of a barren woman.

In conjunction with the introduction of characters, v. 2 also introduces the biblical motif of two wives, one barren and one fruitful /5/. This motif serves as the impetus for the main events of the chapter. Hannah

is explicitly called the 'first' wife while Peninnah is
the 'second' (McCarter 1980:58). Elkanah's love for
Hannah is stated explicitly; the contrasting lack of
such a statement about his feelings for Peninnah is
conspicuous in absence. It seems that she is 'second'
and unloved. As in the Jacob cycle, the barrenness of
the favorite wife is attributed to Yahweh's direct
intervention (v. 5; cf. Gen 29.31).

Hannah may be the first wife, but the chiastic
patterning of names in v. 2 places her last with her
barrenness. Peninnah comes first with her children.

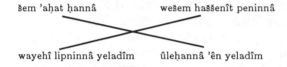

šem 'aḥat ḥannâ   wešem haššenît peninnâ

wayehî lipninnâ yeladîm   ûleḥannâ 'ên yeladîm

The combination of contrasting fortunes in one
woman is also a recurring element in this motif.

Any reader who is familiar with the motif will
immediately become suspect that the reversal of fortunes elegantly represented by the chiastic syntax
of v. 2 is a result of divine intervention (cf. Gen
29.30f; Matt 19.30). The reader who detects the conventional usage of the motif does not receive explicit
confirmation of his suspicions until v. 5. The narrator withholds confirmation to pique reader interest
with an element of suspense. Even the suspicion of
divine intervention in the lives of these characters
is enough to begin to stir the reader's interest and
speculation about the larger significance of the rather
simple tale.

Verse 3

Elkanah's character receives further specification.
The waw-consecutive perfect verb, *we'alâ*, has a frequen-
tative force (Driver 1913:5; GKC para.112dd), which
along with the expression *miyyamîm yamîmâ*, 'from days

to days' (cf. below on v. 21), depicts Elkanah first and foremost as a pious observer of sacrificial duties.

Two important new characters, Hophni and Phinehas, are unobtrusively introduced as the priests at Shiloh, where Elkanah regularly went to worship. Eli is also introduced here as the father of the two priests (cf. Willis 1979:206). J. Bourke sees this introduction of the Elides in conjunction with the description of Elkanah's piety as the first instance in a series of contrasts drawn between Samuel (and Israel) and the Elides throughout chs. 1-3 (1954:82).

At least, the reader is prepared for future contrasts by the paralleling of Elkanah 'at Shiloh' (*bešiloh*) and the Elides 'there' (*wešam*). The topographical parallelism is made prominent by placing *wešam* first in its own sentence, immediately following *bešiloh*, which is last in its sentence. Elkanah actively sacrifices and worships at Shiloh in contrast to the Elide priests, who are just there. The contrast is reinforced by using an active verb taking two infinitive constructs to describe Elkanah's action. The Elide priests, on the other hand, do not even get a single verb to describe their functioning as priests; in their case the verb 'to be' is simply assumed.

Elkanah's sacrificial activity is further highlighted by the numerous alliterations in the description of his activity:

1. *ha'îš hahû'*;
2. *miyyamîm yamîmâ*;
3. *lehiš . . . weliz . . . lay. . .*

The Elides' inactivity receives similar treatment:

1. wešam *šenê benê - 'elî*;
2. *hopnî ûpinḥas*.

The inclusion of the name of God, *yhwh ṣeba'ôt,* in v. 3a introduces the reader to the warrior god who will play such an important role in connection with the ark in chs. 4-6 (cf. Budde 1902:4). Verse 3 concludes the reader's introduction to the major characters appearing in chs. 1-3.

Verses 4-5

The portrait of Elkanah's piety is even more definite in v. 4. Here, again, he is sacrificing. The introductory temporal clause specifies the action to follow
as an example of one of the days when Elkanah would
sacrifice (GKC #126s; Schulz 1919:10).

The narrator continues to develop the theme of
tension between the wives. Elkanah gives portions of
the sacrifice first to Peninnah and to all her sons
and daughters. To Hannah he gives only one portion,
'for though he loved Hannah, Yahweh had sealed her
womb' /6/. Elkanah is fair in his dealings with his
wives even though he loves Hannah more.

Verses 4-5 continue to stress the difference between
Hannah and Peninnah. Peninnah is described as Elkanah's wife; she and all her sons and daughters receive
portions first /7/. Only then does Hannah, who unable
to fulfill her childbearing role as a wife and who is
not called his wife, get her single portion. Prominent
here is the ignominy of Hannah's position. Although
she is the number one wife, *'ahat* (v. 2), she receives
only a single portion, *manâ 'ahat.*

The final sentence of v. 5 provides the anticipated
confirmation that Yahweh is indeed responsible for
the recurrence of this typical familial situation in
biblical narrative. Hannah's sterility is explicitly
attributed to the fact that Yahweh sealed her womb.
The statement is an unusual way to describe sterility.
The usual term for sterility is *'aqar,* 'barren,' e.g.
Gen. 11.30; 25.21; 29.31; Exod 23.26; Deut 7.14; Judg
13.2f; 1 Sam 2.5, etc. The narrator, who now reveals
his 'omniscience' for the first time, tells us that
Yahweh has intervened to close Hannah's womb. This
expositional comment is addressed to the reader alone,
and encourages him to continue to speculate about the
larger significance of these events. The reader can
now be certain, as he could not be on the basis of the
convention alone, that Yahweh is working behind the

scenes and probably directing events toward some goal, as is his wont.

Why has Yahweh closed Hannah's womb? What is the goal towards which divine guidance is leading? The answers to these and similar questions are obviously available to the omniscient narrator, but he temporarily withholds them from the reader. The simple technique of withholding information, which is by implication available to himself, is the narrator's principal means of achieving 'one of the primary aims of fiction - the creation and manipulation of narrative interest' (Sternberg 1978:45). At this point in the narrative, interest is increasingly directed onto the question of the meaning of Hannah's sterility. Where mystery goes, the reader's curiosity will follow.

Verse 6

Hannah's vexation is made complete in v. 6. The tension between the two women is brought to the surface. Peninnah is Hannah's rival who sorely vexes Hannah until the latter vociferates. It is the fact that Yahweh has sealed Hannah's womb that provides Peninnah with the ammunition to vex Hannah to the point of vocal thunderings. The *kî* of v. 6b is, therefore, causal (GKC #158a b; R. J. Williams 1976 #444).

The emphatic repetition of the final sentence in both vv. 5 and 6 links the two verses, both of which focus on Hannah's infertility /8/. Elkanah, though he loves her, can only give her one portion because Yahweh has sealed her womb /9/. Peninnah is able to vex Hannah both with her inabilities as a wife and with her resultant single portion, because Yahweh has sealed her womb. Even the verb *harre'imâh*, 'vociferate,' by its phonetic similarity to *raḥmâh*, Hannah's 'womb,' points to her sterility as the cause of her distress (cf. Dhorme 1910:19).

Bourke has also suggested that Hannah and Peninnah

are stylized characters conforming to conventional
themes in Hebrew literature. A barren woman is oppressed by a cruel rival blandishing her own fecundity.
Hannah belongs to the *'anawîm*, the humble, afflicted, poor, and righteous whom Yahweh loves. She is
described in *'anawîm* terms such as bitterness of
soul (v. 10), afflicted (v. 11), pouring out her soul
(v. 16), and having an abundance of complaint (v. 16).
(Bourke 1954:84 supplies comparative examples.) By
drawing these lines between the heroine of ch. 1 and
her opponent, the narrative begins the process of
associating Samuel with the side of right and just
causes, here through his oppressed mother. Although
the oppression of Hannah by the vindictive Peninnah
is not central to the narrative - Peninnah and the conflict leave the narrative after v. 7 - it introduces an
important thematic contrast between the two characters.
Such contrasts will come to occupy a central position
in chs. 2-3.

The final sentence of v. 6 is introduced by a conjunctive *kî*; 'Because (*kî*) Yahweh had sealed up
her womb.' The ostensible function of this sentence is
to explain the behaviour of the two wives in v. 6.
Peninnah is successful at taunting Hannah because
Hannah is sterile.

The sentence also achieves less obvious ends. As
a repetition of the last sentence in v. 5 it is foregrounded and the reader's attention is firmly directed
towards its content. Events on the place of the human
characters in the story are being manipulated by God,
who operates from the divine plane.

The repeated sentence is almost identical to the
last sentence of v. 5 except for the addition of the
preposition *be'ad,* which functions idiomatically with
the verb *sgr* (cf. BDB p. 126 , col. 1 para.1b). The
addition of the preposition seems to stress the totality of Hannah's barrenness; whereas v. 5b might be
translated 'Yahweh sealed her womb,' v. 6b would be
'Yahweh sealed *up* her womb.' As in v. 5, the narrator

does not reveal the reason for Yahweh's intervention in the regular course of biological events; his repeated address to the reader simply stresses that events on the human plane of the narrative are the product of an initiative from the divine plane.

The effect on the reader of this repeated expositional address by the narrator is to divert a large amount of attention away from the plane of events on the human plane towards the divine, and onto the as yet unrevealed goal that is the presumable object of the divine initiative. The narrator's exposition creates distance between the reader's and the human characters' perceptions so that the reader begins to perceive the larger meaning in these events. As Wayne Booth says, 'distance is never an end in itself; distance along one axis is sought for the sake of increasing the reader's involvement on some other axis' (1961: 123).

Booth's observation is also applicable to the effect of the expositional comment on the reader's relationship with the narrator. When the narrator addresses the reader with a piece of exposition such as this, he temporarily elevates the reader to his own level of omniscience. The information conveyed - that Yahweh *had* closed Hannah's womb - is privileged as both omniscient and after the fact. Possession of such information distances the reader from both human and divine characters, and even from involvement in the effort to decipher the divine manipulation of the human characters. In return, the reader's involvement and identification with the level and perspective of the omniscient narrator - the level of discourse - is greatly increased. Here, after all, the reader recognizes the answer to all puzzles and riddles not answerable from a reading that views from the plane of human characters or even from the level of the divine character. The expositional comment in v. 6b functions as one of the explicit invitations for the reader to perceive from the broadest perspective available in this narrative world, that of the omniscient narrator, the author and finisher of our reading.

Verse 7

The verse provides a summary of the events of vv. 4-6, and notes that such was the regular sequence whenever the Elkanahs went to Yahweh's house. The parallel (with a difference) between the two phases of action is made prominent by the twofold repetition of *ken,* and captured by Keil and Delitzsch. 'So did he from year to year as often as she went up to the house of the Lord. So did she (Peninnah) provoke her (Hannah), so that she wept and did not eat' (1880:22f). Hannah's sorrow is such that she cannot even eat the single portion that she gets.

Verse 8

Elkanah is dissociated from Peninnah's mistreatment of Hannah. Hannah may not be able to fullfill her role as childbearer, but Elkanah is still her husband and cares for her.

The narrator emphasizes the special relationship between Hannah and Elkanah by attaching the seemingly redundant description 'her husband' to the proper name Elkanah in v. 8. In contrast, Elkanah is never described as Peninnah's 'husband.' The alliterative complex of names at the beginning of the verse also emphasizes the bond between them:

(wayyo'mer) lâh 'elqanâ 'îšâh hannâ.

Elkanah's threefold repetition of *lameh,* 'why,' stresses that in terms of their marriage she has nothing to worry about. 'Am I not better to you than ten sons' expresses his reassurance. No matter how many sons Peninnah may have, Elkanah's love for Hannah should be worth more to her than ten sons without his love. Peninnah's vindictiveness supports Elkanah's claim.

Verse 9

Hannah appears to humour Elkanah by eating for we next see her getting up 'after she had eaten' (*'aḥarê 'akelâ;* cf. GKC para.91e, against Stoebe's repointing to *'akelâh,'* 1973:91) /10/. As v. 10 shows, however, her eating does not signify any change of heart over her childlessness.

Verse 9b is contemporaneous with v. 9a (Driver 1913:12; cf. GKC #116d; R. J. Williams 1976 #237). The verse structure recalls v. 3:

3. The man goes up from his city to worship and sacrifice to Yahweh at Shiloh.
9. Hannah gets up after eating and drinking at Shiloh.
3. There Eli's two sons are priests to Yahweh.
9. Eli the priest is sitting on his throne beside the doorpost of Yahweh's temple.

The statement that Hannah was at Shiloh when she got up after eating is not 'oddly repetitious' (McCarter 1980:53), but meaningfully so. As in v. 3 the Elide priests are specifically associated with Shiloh. In both cases, we see the beginnings of the contrast schema that governs chs. 2-3 (cf. Bourke 1954:82ff.; Willis 1971:289). Elkanah actively goes up to worship and sacrifice at Shiloh; Eli's sons, the priests, are simply there. Hannah rises after eating and drinking at Shiloh; Eli is sitting at the doorpost. The contrast is not yet developed into an opposition of right and wrong, or good and evil, but is simply one of active and passive roles at the temple.

The narrator introduces these vestigial contrasts between the Elide priests and the family of Elkanah as foreshadowings of the coming contrasts between the Elides and Samuel, Hannah's son. The narrator leaves the full significance of this foreshadowing implicit, thus increasing narrative interest in the attentive reader.

Verses 10-11

In desperation, Hannah turns to Yahweh. As the reader reads about her bitterness of soul and about her cries and prayers to Yahweh he is being allowed to share the narrator's knowledge that, ironically, Hannah is seeking help from exactly the right source. Though Hannah does not know it, Yahweh is the one who sealed her womb (vv. 5, 6) and he is therefore the logical choice to open it.

Hannah's dedicatory vow of any forthcoming offspring to Yahweh has attracted attention because of the Nazirite element in it. McCarter suggests that the additional note, 'wine or strong drink he will not drink,' of LXX*B* is supported by space considerations in 4QSam*a* (1980:53f). Whether the variant is included or not, the allusion to the Nazirite status of any offspring is present /11/. If Yahweh will give to his maidservant the seed of men, she will give to Yahweh one upon whose head a razor has not gone /12/. The act of dedication will turn an ordinary 'seed of men' into a Nazirite, set apart from the rank and file, if Yahweh agrees /13/.

The emphasis on the uniqueness and distinction of the requested child is made even stronger by the way Hannah phrases her vow in terms drawn from Exod 3:7. Samuel will be the answer to Hannah's affliction as Moses was the answer to the Israelites' affliction in Egypt:

v. 11: 'im ra'oh tir'eh ba'onî 'amateka
Exod 3.7: ra'oh ra'êtî 'et-'onî 'ammî.

This allusion to the Exodus material and the Mosaic role of Hannah's future son begins a process of legitimating Samuel as a worthy replacement for the Elides. Not only is he to be born of a barren woman, but he will even be a new Moses. The verbal reminiscence brings the exodus event to the mind of the reader, who will be reminded of the paradigmatic significance of the exodus throughout the narrative.

Verses 12-13

The two verses are connected as one single event by a syntactic chiasmus of verb forms:
Hannah, active verb ⟍ Eli, participle
Hannah, participle ⟋ Eli, active verb.

Hannah fervently multiplies her prayers while Eli is watching her mouth. Hannah's prayer is silent, only her lips move and Eli takes her for a drunk. Eli's mistaken identification provides Hannah with the opportunity to proclaim her abstinence from alcoholic beverages, a basic requirement for a woman who would bear a Nazirite (cf. Judg 13:4; Stoebe 1973:97).

Willis suggests that Eli's misjudgement of Hannah's mental state is the beginning of the contrast between Hannah/Samuel/Israel and the Elides (1971:289). Perhaps it is better to regard this mistake as the first instance where the reader is led to favour Hannah over against Eli. The contrast between Elkanah and Hannah and the Elides has already appeared twice (vv. 3, 9) although with less explicit differentiation. The reader knows from vv. 11-12 that Hannah's outward appearance is the expression of deep inner distress and piety. When Eli takes Hannah for a drunk the reader sees him as a man grown old and imperceptive. The narrator leads the reader to favour Hannah by allowing him a privileged insight into Hannah's thoughts but only an external view of Eli (cf. Booth 1961:245-49).

Verses 14-15

Hannah's polite response to Eli's mistaken rebuke

strengthens the reader's favourable impression of her /14/. The forwardness of Eli's rebuke is foregrounded by the assonance in the second two words of v. 14 and is contrasted to Hannah's submissiveness, similarly highlighted by assonance:

v. 14: wayyo'mer 'eleyha 'elî
v. 15: watta'an ḥannâ watto'mer

Eli is completely mistaken. As Hannah points out, her actions are not the manifestation of drinking (šatîtî) spirits, but of pouring out ('ešpok) her spirit; not of pouring into herself, but of out-pouring herself.

Thenius's widely accepted suggestion to read Hannah's self-description as qešat yôm, 'one in misfortune,' instead of qešat rûaḥ, 'hard-spirited,' is unnecessary (1864:6). The entire episode between Hannah and Eli is a result of her fervent multiple prayers (v. 12), which are in turn the result of an embittered soul (marat napeš, v. 10). Hannah explains her behaviour by the fact that she is a 'determined' woman ('iššâ qešat rûaḥ) pouring out her soul (Ahlström 1979:254). Eli's question 'ad-matay, 'how long,' also implies that it was the incessancy of her prayer that provoked him (v. 14).

Verse 16

The continuation of Hannah's answer confirms this reading of qešat rûaḥ. She continued speaking for so long ('ad hennâ) because of the greatness of her complaint (cf. v. 12) and vexation (cf. v. 10).

The introduction of the term bat belîya'al here prepares for the subsequent occurrence of the expression in 2:12 (cf. Willis 1979:207). Hannah interprets Eli's rebuke as making her out to be a renegade woman (bat belîya'al).

Verse 17

Eli accepts Hannah's explanation, though without apology for his error in judgement. He sends Hannah off with his approval, 'May the God of Israel grant you your request.' Although neither he nor the reader know it, Eli has approved a request for his successor. Eli's endorsement of his own replacement is suitably a result of his lack of awareness of what is really going on in the worship at the temple. He demonstrates the need for a successor at the same time that he gives his blessing on the request for one.

Verse 18

Schulz suggests that Hannah's reply, 'implies nothing more than the request that Eli maintain the friendly attitude towards her that he had already demonstrated' (1919:17). Hannah's actions agree with Schulz's reading. She goes 'her way,' meaning that she takes up her regular activities again (cf. Koch 1978: 276). Her renewed eating is a sign, as before (v. 9), that she has accepted consolation. Most commentators read the word *paneyha* in the final sentence as 'sad' or 'troubled countenance.' The parallel in Job 9:27 supports this reading (Thenius 1864:6; Nowack 1902:6; Driver 1913:15-16; Schulz 1919:18).

The adverb *'ôd* positioned last in v. 18 is another temporal hint that Hannah's troubles will be resolved sometime in the future. Hannah's firm resolve to have a child has been sufficiently described so far for the reader to surmise that if she was not sad any more (*'ôd*) it was because her wish eventually comes true.

Verse 19

Verse 19 concludes the events begun in v. 3, where the man (Elkanah) had left his city (*we'alâ me'îrô*) to worship (*lehištahawot*) and sacrifice (*welizboah*) to Yahweh at Shiloh. In v. 19, they worship (*wayyiš-tahawû*) before Yahweh and return home to Ramah (*wayyašubû wayyabo'û 'el-bêtam haramatâ*). The inclusio between vv. 3 and 19 shows that Elkanah has accomplished all that he set out to do. The events may be schematically outlined in correlation with Hannah's troubles as follows:

v.2		Introduction to Hannah's problem.
v.3	we'ala ha'îš hahû'	That man alone, signifying division in
	me'îrô lehištahawot	the family.
	welizboah	
v.4	wayyizbah	Intensification of Hannah's difficulties.
v.18b		Indication of a future resolution to
		Hannah's problem ('ôd).
v.19a	wayyištahawû	They worship together
	wayyašubû wayyabo'u	and return home.
	'el bêtam haramatâ	Division disappears.
v.19b		Hannah's problem is resolved.

As the outline shows, v. 19 describes both Elkanah's accomplishment of his purposes and the unification of the family in worship and in their return home. The statement that they return specifically to their home contrasts with Elkanah's departure in v. 3, which is simply from his city. The contrast emphasizes that previous alienation amongst family members has received some measure of resolution.

The narrator immediately goes on to relate the consummation of the resolution to Hannah's problem, a resolution he has so far only hinted at. No sooner has he traced the family's return journey home, than the narrator describes Elkanah in action, 'And Elkanah knew Hannah, his wife.' Elkanah's role, while essential, is not a sufficient cause to end Hannah's barrenness. Without further ado, the narrator adds the vital piece of information for the reader and the efficient cause to end Hannah's sterility; Yahweh remembers (*zkr*) Hannah, just as she had asked (cf. *zkr* in v.

11). The latter statement is the actual climax of the story, and the description in v. 20a simply works out the details of the birth process.

Verse 20

In due time Hannah becomes pregnant and bears a son /15/. The key element, which makes the birth possible, is Yahweh's remembrance of Hannah. Elkanah may 'know' her, but Yahweh 'remembers' her. Hannah recognizes this fact and commemorates it by naming her son 'Samuel.' She explains the name in a recollection of her request for Samuel from Yahweh. The explanation of the name also expresses Hannah's understanding that her son is evidence that Yahweh has agreed to the terms of the vow in v. 11. Hannah has not forgotten that Samuel is the rightful property of Yahweh.

The name Samuel and Hannah's explanation have pro-voked many lengthy examinations of the connection between them (cf. Driver 1913:16-19; Van Zyl 1969: 125). Several studies have proposed the traditio-historical hypothesis that the birth story originally applied to Saul, whose name seems to fit the explanation better than Samuel (Hylander 1932:11-13; McCarter 1980:62, 65-66; cf. Zakovitch 1980:41 n.45). Given the focus of the present study on the existing narrative, however, discussion of the traditio-historical hypothesis about the text's prehistory is unnecessarily speculative /16/. In addition, Zakovitch notes that all of the details concerning the family of Elkanah are applicable to the story of Samuel but not to that of Saul (1980:41). Even historical critics sympathetic to the endeavour have either regarded the supposed underlying Saul story with suspicion or rejected it (Hertzberg 1964:26; Noth 1963:395 ['so unwahrscheinlich wie möglich']; Stoebe 1973:97f). As Driver notes, the relationship between the name and the explanation is alliterative; the name

šemû'el 'recalls' the word ša'al (1913:16). Kimḥi's
reasoning supplies semantic explanation of the connection that Driver regards as assonantal: 'For among the
letters of Samuel (šmw'l) there is Saul (š'wl), and
among these letters there is also "of the Lord" (m'l),
as if she had said š'l m'l ("lent of the Lord")' (cited
from Zakovitch 1980:42). Hannah's explanation emphasizes that Samuel is from Yahweh by placing myhwh
before še'iltîw. Here, at last, is Samuel's real genealogy; he is from Yahweh.

In biblical etymologies Zakovitch suggests that
we can discern a trend from an earlier derivatory
explanation that did not aim at exact resemblance between a name and its derivation, to a later form in
which attempt was made to embed all the sounds and
elements of the name in the explanatory derivation
(1980:31); Hannah's explanation of Samuel's name falls
into the earlier, less precise class; however accurate
or inaccurate from a linguistic perspective, it gives an
accurate assessment of the miraculous element in the
birth of her son. She calls her son Samuel, which may
be explained as 'his name is God' (VanZyl 1969:125-
26), or more simply 'the name of God' (Weingreen 1976:
64). Samuel's name forever marks him as one standing
close to God. Hannah's explanation is very simple;
Samuel gets a name that celebrates and identifies the
divinity because he is the answer to her request from
Yahweh.

Samuel exists and his name celebrates his existence
as a unique and special boon from Yahweh who is God.
The traditional motif of the barren woman who is
granted a son by God is used here, as elsewhere (Judg
13; and especially Luke 1), to characterize and legitimate the son who results. Elkanah's genealogy, non-
descript in the first place, fades into the background
in the presence of Samuel's true genealogy. The name
Hannah gives to Samuel thus focuses the entire chapter
on two things, the amazing divine capacities of Yahweh
and the special character of her son Samuel.

Verse 21

A new stage in the history of Elkanah's sacrificial pilgrimages, v. 21 parallels v. 3 but also exhibits some differences:
1. Elkanah is mentioned by name; instead of *ha'îš hahû'* we read *ha'îš 'elqanâ*. In the preceding description of v. 3, I suggested that the narrator described Elkanah as simply 'that man' and sent him off alone to sacrifice as a means of supporting the general impression of strife and division in the family. Between v. 3 and v. 21, however, Samuel is born and the source of conflict in the family thereby disappears. Domestic disputes being settled, the narrator evokes the opposite associations of familiarity and intimacy by using the proper name, Elkanah, in place of the pronominal description, 'that man.'
2. Verse 21 explicitly states that Elkanah's whole family goes with him. Again the contrast with v. 3 creates the impression of a unified family. The entire household now acts in unison.
3. The family goes only to sacrifice and not to worship, as Elkanah did in v. 3. By leaving out one part of the hendiadys *lehištaḥawot welizboah* the narrator separates this particular occasion from the previous practise, which occurred 'from days to days.' The sacrifice in v. 21 is more specific than that of v. 3.
4. Instead of having Elkanah go up to sacrifice 'from days to days,' the narrator says he went to sacrifice 'the sacrifice of the days' /17/. The expression *zebah hayyamîm* is much more specific than *miyyamîm yamîmâ'* of v. 3. The only previous mention of *yamîm* with the definite article comes in v. 20, where it refers to the completion of days associated with Hannah's pregnancy and delivery.

As noted by Wellhausen (1871:40) and Driver (1913:16), these two occurrences of *hayyamîm* are related, as one would expect given their close proximity (cf. Stoebe 1973:99). I view of the em-

phasis in v. 21 on the united household (*kol-bêtô*)
going up with Elkanah to offer a special sacrifice,
it seems likely and especially appropriate that the
sacrifice be a celebration of the 'completion of the
days.' Hannah's successfully completed pregnancy resolves the tensions between the two wives. Therefore,
they all go, *kol-bêtô*, to celebrate the sacrifice of
'the days.' The *zebaḥ hayyamîm* celebrates both the
birth of Samuel and the family reunion. 5. Elkanah
also 'sacrifices' a vow in v. 21 in contrast to v. 3,
which makes no mention of vows. There is no previous
mention of any vow made by Elkanah. Noting that
neder is not the object of *zabaḥ* elsewhere, McCarter
suggests that LXXL gives a clue to the meaning of
'his vow' (1980:55). He restores 'and to redeem his vow
and all the tithes of his land,' supposedly lost by haplography. The LXXL reading does not, however, solve
the difficulty of what vow Elkanah is redeeming. The
reference to land tithes has no obvious contextual ref-
erent and seems designed to ease the oddity of a vow
that Elkanah did not make.

Hertzberg suggests that perhaps the narrator assumes that Elkanah has taken on Hannah's vow in accordance with the regulations for vows in Num 30:1ff
(esp. v. 14). A husband could confirm or invalidate
any vow made by his wife. 'Elkanah even went beyond
a confirmation of this nature by his personal participation in the vow' (1964:28). Aside from the difficulty
of what 'participation in the vow' might mean and how
that would relate to the text's 'to sacrifice . . . his
vow,' Hertzberg's explanation does not take serious
account of Hannah's vow. She vowed to give back
Samuel. It is hard to see how Elkanah's sacrifice of'
(MT), or 'participation in' (Hertzberg) his vow has anything to do with Hannah's vow. Yahweh 'remembered'
Hannah because she vowed to return Samuel, not to
sacrifice for him or to elicit Elkanah's 'participation'
in the vow.

Verse 22

In the case of a nonsensical text, the way lies open for a judicious use of emendation. Supposing a dittography of a *waw*, a contextually suitable reading may be obtained: *we'et(!)-neder(w) weḥannâ lo' 'alâ*; 'But *with* a vow, Hannah did not go up.' The narrator reverses the usual word order to emphasize the important fact that Hannah is not quick to fulfill her vow (cf. R. J. Williams 1976:96 #573). 'And the man Elkanah and all his household went up to offer the sacrifice of the days [in celebration of Samuel's birth], but with a vow Hannah did not go up.' The chiastic juxtaposition of the actions of the household and the non-action of Hannah captures the reader's attention:

wayya'al ha'îš 'elqanâ wekol-bêtô lizboaḥ lyhwh 'et-zebaḥ hayyamîm

we'et(!)-neder weḥannâ lo' 'alatâ

Hannah's procrastination contradicts the reader's expectations of her. All along she has been the protagonist and Peninnah the antagonist. In v. 21, however, Peninnah is included among the 'entire household' going up to celebrate Samuel's birth while Hannah stays back with the vow. Will Hannah shirk the responsibility and so defeat the mysterious purpose of Yahweh? He was after all the real cause of her sterility in the first place. The resolution of Hannah's personal difficulty has unexpectedly jeopardized Yahweh's purpose. Ironically it is the very maternal instinct that drove Hannah to make her vow that now appears as a potential source of frustration for the divine purpose.

By reading 'But with a vow' as the first part of v. 22 instead of with v. 21 the syntax and meaning of v. 22 become less problematic than they have appeared in previous studies (e.g. Cross 1953:18; McCarter 1980: 55f). The verse may be translated, 'But with a vow

Hannah did not go up for she told her husband (wait) until the boy is weaned. (Then) I will bring him and he will appear before Yahweh and remain there forever' (cf. GKC #112a, d).

Hannah seems to be stalling for time. Although her action is understandable and captures the reader's sympathies (Hertzberg 1964:28), she is obligated, as she recognizes, to present Samuel as she vowed.

Verse 23

Hannah is allowed a period of grace but, as the three-fold repetition of the words *'ad gamal* in vv. 22-23 emphasizes, only until Samuel is weaned. Elkanah respects his wife's wishes, trusting her judgement to do as she sees fit (*hattôb be'ênayik*).

Elkanah's reminder to Hannah about her vow and petition, to which the birth of Samuel corresponds as the divine answer, also serves to remind the reader that the entire series of events evolves as the manifestation of a divine plan, initiated by God himself, as we know already in v.5. When Elkanah says, 'Only may Yahweh establish his word,' he expresses his understanding that the birth of Samuel after the vow indicates that the vow is in accord with Yahweh's purpose. The vow irrevocably establishes the future actions of Hannah and especially of Samuel. Yahweh's assent to Hannah's request signals that the vow is his plan for the future; it becomes 'his word.' Hannah would not have given up her son had she not been made sterile by Yahweh. We have proof of this in her actions after the birth, when she hesitates to fulfill the vow. Hence from the beginning to end, the narrative reveals that Samuel is 'from Yahweh' (v.20), 'for Yahweh' (v.11).

Gerhard von Rad has suggested that the so-called deuteronomistic concept of Yahweh's word in historical manifestation behind Elkanah's words in v. 23. Samuel's future life of sanctified devotion to Yahweh has become Yahweh's word. Thereby the birth and future life of

Samuel are incorporated into a historical perspective
in which the word of Yahweh is 'the real motive force
and creator of Israel's history' (1965 :II/94 n.23, 95).

Elkanah's words reinforce the narrator's presentation of preceding events - Hannah's sterility her vow,
and Samuel's birth - which affords the reader a few
glimpses of the divine hand working behind the scenes.
The sketchiness of these few insights into the larger
significance of the birth story serves to increase narrative interest. The reader wants to know why God has
arranged to have this boy dedicated to his service.

So far the narrator has given the reader no real
clues as to any historical cause or situation that
might have prompted Yahweh to this course of action.
Instead of explaining these historical antecedents with
a piece of preliminary exposition, the narrator plunges
the reader directly into the outworkings of the divine
plan in progress. The reader can only speculate on the
wider context that brings about this miraculous birth,
and must patiently wait for further developments and
narratorial exposition in order to understand completely the birth of Samuel.

The final sentence of v. 23 summarizes the brief
period of Hannah's time with the child. The poignancy
of the scene is sharpened by the choice of words. Hannah nurses the child, now specifically 'her son' (*benâh*),
until he is weaned. The physical bond, about to be broken, between mother and child is in the forefront.

Verse 24

Hannah makes good her promise; the first sentence
of v. 24 stands in clear contrast to vv. 21/22:

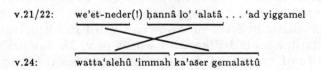

v.21/22:   we'et-neder(!) hannâ lo' 'alatâ . . . 'ad yiggamel

v.24:   watta'alehû 'immah ka'ašer gemalattû

Hannah's forthright action lays to rest any doubts created by her hesitation in vv. 21/22.

Both Cross (1953:18) and McCarter (1980:56) see *ka'ašer gemalattû* as redundant and syntactically awkward here and insert it in v. 22 following LXXB and a reconstructed 4QSam*a*. Given the doubts in vv. 22-23 about Hannah's intention to fulfill the vow, however, the phrase is an appropriate and emphatic depiction of Hannah's faithfulness /18/.

Hannah takes a 'three year old bull' /19/, an ephah of flour, and a skin of wine. The final two sentences of v. 24 with v. 25 are radically different in MT and LXXB (cf. McCarter 1980:57). Before attempting to determine the 'original' or 'correct' reading, we must first determine if MT has meaning as it stands. Recalling that the first sentence in v. 24 corresponds to vv. 21/22, a similar response can be seen in the last sentence of v. 24:

v.22: wahabi'otîw wenir'â 'et-penê yhwh weyašab šam 'ad-'ôlam
v.24: wattebi'ehû bêt-yhwh šilô wehanna'ar na'ar.

The narrative reemphasizes Hannah's faithfulness by describing the enactment of her promise, which she carries out quite literally.

The parallel may also afford an understanding of the obscure concluding sentence, *wehanna'ar na'ar*. Tsevat has proposed that 'The boy takes up his service as servant' (quote from Stoebe 1973:99 n.24d). Samuel takes up his role as *na'ar* to the priests once he gets to Shiloh, just as his mother had said he would in v.22.

Verse 25

The subjects of the verbs are unspecified. Perhaps it was this unspecificity that provoked the longer LXX reading in v. 25, though this cannot be proven. The ambiguity of the text allows the reader to entertain several possibilities /20/:

1. The subjects could be Elkanah, his household, and Hannah, since Elkanah has not returned home from his journey in v. 21;
2. They could be Hophni and Phinehas, who are the priests at Shiloh;
3. They could be Hophni, Phinehas and Hannah.

The ambiguity invites speculation from the reader but also forces the holding of all possibilities in abeyance until further information is received. Whoever the subjects are, the most important point is that the proper sacrifice is performed and that Samuel is brought to Eli, fulfilling the vow.

Verse 26

Hannah, at least, must be included amongst the subjects of v. 25. Here in v. 26 her address to Eli is introduced by the narrator using the waw-consecutive (*watto'mer*), which implies temporal sequence (cf.R. J. Williams 1976:33 #178).

Hannah identifies herself to Eli as the woman who stood near him and prayed to Yahweh for Samuel. Again she is supremely humble before Eli, recalling her previous bearing in vv. 15f, 18. This time Samuel is physically associated with his mother when she exhibits such behaviour in Eli's presence. The association is an important prelude to the stark contrast to be made between Samuel and the Elides in chs. 2-3.

Verse 27

The first three words in v. 27 pick up and develop the last three words of v. 26. In v. 26, Hannah describes her prayer to Yahweh. Immediately following the words 'to pray to Yahweh' (v. 26) she says, 'for this child' (v. 27). Taken together, the six words exhibit a chiastic symmetry that reinforces the semantic emphases of the words:

lehitpallel 'el-yhwh

'el-hanna'ar hazzeh hitpallaltî.

The repetition of the verb *hitpallel*, 'to pray,' uni-
fies the two lines and accents the fact that the only resort of a barren woman is prayer directly to Yahweh
/21/. The paralleling of the indirect object 'Yahweh,'
with the direct object, 'this lad,' both modified by
the preposition *'el*, suggests a connection between
Yahweh and the lad. The demonstrative adjective *zeh*
modifying *hanna'ar* calls attention to the fact that
the prayer was answered - 'this (*hazzeh*) lad' is the
result. The small chiastic structure sets up an important parallel that emphasizes one thing. Hannah
prayed to Yahweh and Samuel is the result. The importance laid upon this state of affairs may be gauged
by its three fold repetition, once in v. 20 and twice
in v. 27.

Using different language, Hannah repeats again her
explanation of Samuel's miraculous birth to Eli. Almost
word for word, she repeats what Eli said to her when
she left the temple after her prayer in v. 17. Yahweh
has granted her her request in the form of Samuel.
Yahweh, we are told, is the answer to Hannah's problems.

Verse 28

Hannah attempts to show how her own response to
Yahweh's gift parallels the granting of her request:

v.27: wayyitten yhwh lî 'et-še'elatî
v.28: wegam 'anokî hiš'iltihû lyhwh.

The correlative *wegam* (R. J. Williams 1976:64 #381),
and the long form of the first person pronoun in the
emphatic syntactic position before the verb highlight
Hanna's response: 'And I, for my part, grant him to

Yahweh.' The doubts raised in v. 22 about Hannah's
ability to overcome her maternal instincts and to fulfill the vow by handing over her child are laid to
rest. She willingly repays the vow.

As she promised, 'All the days for which he shall
be, he is granted to Yahweh' (Driver's translation,
1913:22). The special grant of Yahweh to Hannah is
specially dedicated to Yahweh. He will be Yahweh's
man.

Hannah's remarks about the background to Samuel's
birth and about his life-long career of dedication to
Yahweh supply the reader with a conclusive definition
of Samuel's role. Hannah recalls the almost miraculous
birth and ties Samuel's career to his special birth;
his pre-natal dedication, his birth, his name, and his
public dedication all show that he is inseparably
linked to Yahweh. The only thing that is not yet revealed about Samuel is the part he will play in Yahweh's plans. That Yahweh does have some purpose for
this Samuel has been evident ever since the narrator
told us that Yahweh sealed Hannah's womb (v. 5).
Though we do not know what Samuel is going to do,
we do know that Samuel, whose name means 'the name
of God,' will act in the interest of his namesake,
'God.'

Few scholars since Hylander have failed to note
the connection between the repeated emphasis on the
verb ša'al in connection with Samuel, and the name
of Israel's first king, Saul /22/. Most recently, Mc-
Carter has also adopted Hylander's position, suggesting that an account of Saul's birth and Nazirite dedication lie behind the narrative in ch. 1, which has
been adapted for Samuel (1980:65f).

McCarter provides two reasons for his suggestion:
first, the word-play on ša'al, and secondly, the points
of contact between ch. 1 and Judg 13. The word-play
fits Saul's name better than Samuel's, and the birth
story in ch. 1 involves Nazirite elements that parallel
the Samson birth story in Judg 13. Yet Samson and

Samuel are not alike. Samson was a great military figure more comparable to Saul than Samuel.

To suggest that the Nazirite elements of ch. 1 must
originally have described a military man assumes, on
the basis of the Samson story, that all Nazirites were
military men. Yet the case of Samson is more the exception than the rule for Nazirite status and function.
W. R. Smith, citing Wellhausen, observes that the
Arabic *nadhara* and the Hebrew *nzr* both mean primarily 'to consecrate' (1969:482). The law of Nazirite
dedication in Num 6 also focuses on sanctification
rather than any explicit tasks or actions such as military duties. In fact, military function is not even mentioned in Num 6. Nor as Exum notes, is the Nazirite
vow mentioned in Judg 14-15 which describe Samson's
military endeavours. 'Samson's fidelity to the Nazirite
vow is not central to the theological message of the
saga as it now stands' (1981:25 n.1).

Without further proof the assumption that Samson
was a typical Nazirite is unwarranted. The Nazirite
elements of 1 Sam 1 are perfectly suited to the character of Samuel as outlined so far. The primary focus
in the Nazirite life is that it is to be a life dedicated to Yahweh (Rylaarsdam 1962:526). Samuel, requested from Yahweh (v. 20), given by Yahweh (v. 27),
and given to Yahweh (v. 28), is an eminent Nazirite
candidate.

Without the support of the suggested Nazirite connection between Samson and Saul, who incidentally does
not appear anywhere in the course of 1 Sam 9-11 as a
Nazirite, the connection between the verb *ša'al* and
Saul's name lends but weak support to speculation about
the pre-history of ch. 1. The 'whole narrative concerning the birth of Samuel cannot be declared a Saul birth
story merely on account of this pun. Except for the
verb *ša'al*, there is nothing in the present Samuel
narratives that exhibits any connection with a possible
Saul birth narrative (Van Zyl 1969:124).

The genetic explanations of the word-play on *ša'al*

with reference to Samuel have been unpalatable even to historical critics (e.g. Noth 1963:395; Stoebe 1973: 97f). The observation that the word-play, especially in v. 28, applies more naturally to Saul than Samuel is, however, valid and requires explanation. Hertzberg suggests that the application to Samuel may contain a criticism of Saul. 'The real deliverer is not the first king, but the last judge' (1964:26; cf. Stoebe 1973: 98). Alternatively the connection may not be so much a criticism of Saul as a conditioning of the reader. When one reads the events of ch. 9 and realizes that Saul is going to be Israel's king, one recalls a previous person - Samuel - described as *ša'ûl*. Samuel was *ša'ûl,* 'granted' to Yahweh to serve him all the days of his life. Saul's very name in ch. 9 thereby cues the reader to the possibility that Saul, too, may be or become one dedicated to Yahweh.

Whether or not this is, in fact, the correct explanation of the narrative function of the connection between *ša'al* in ch. 1 and Saul in chs. 9-11, it is, I believe, a correct approach to an explanation. The reader of 1 Sam 1-12 encounters ch. 1 before ch. 9 and so the reader reads and interprets Saul's name in terms of the previous associations he has encountered in ch. 1. *Ša'ûl* in 1:28 foreshadows the name Saul in 9:2, which, in turn, may contain a subtle hint about the type of monarchy to be given to Israel.

If the connection between the verb *ša'al* in ch. 1 and the name Saul in ch. 9 is exploited by the narrative, it is the prior occurrence that will determine the frame within which subsequent occurrences will be read (cf. Perry 1979:40; Sternberg 1978:35-55). The traditio-historical explanation reverses the conventional sequential order of reading, and interprets the prior occurrence in terms of the sequent. The basis for this reversal is the hypothetical historical priority of the latter. The dynamic structure built into the narrative in its ordering of information is thereby disregarded and distroyed. Instead, the meaning of the text is sought in its compositional history.

The root š'l is, nevertheless, of great importance for ch. 1 and the reader's view of Samuel. If there is one thing that ch. 1 is about, one single thing or person that frames the episode, it is Samuel. Yahweh closes Hannah's womb so that she promises to give her child to Yahweh if he will only let her have one. Yahweh opens her womb and she gives him Samuel, one requested from Yahweh and returned back to him to serve him. Samuel is the miraculous gift of Yahweh to a barren woman. He is a part of a mysterious divine plan of which the reader is allowed only glimpses at this point. The repetition of the root š'l in vv. 27-28 recapitulates these various emphases of the chapter.

Chapter 1 ends, therefore, with a reminder of exactly who and what Samuel is; the various nuances given to the root š'l are various nuances given to the character of Samuel. Repeatedly the final verses of ch. 1 emphasize Samuel's uniqueness and divine origination. He is the answer to prayer, the granted request. He has come into the world in response to Hannah's human need. Subsequently, he is granted to Yahweh, devoted to him all his days. In short, Samuel is a God-given man of God.

The subject of the final sentence in v. 28 is not defined. Most commentators have followed Wellhausen, who himself followed LXX (1871:42). Instead of 'He worshipped there to Yahweh,' LXX reads, 'And she left him there before Yahweh and returned to Ramathah' /23/. The LXX reading is unambiguous and logical, so an attractive alternative to the obstacle posed by MT's ambiguity. And, as Wellhausen notes with respect to Elkanah's absence in LXX 2:11, 'If, in contrast to LXX, it is in fact Hannah's departure that is reported that [reading] would more likely be original, since there would be no point in reducing here Elkanah's part in the action, which was so extensively granted him in v. 24' (1871:42).

It is possible, on the other hand, that the ambiguity of this sentence is intentional rather than an inadvertent textual corruption. Previously in v. 25 the subjects of the verbs were also left undetermined and there too LXX made them specific. In MT, Elkanah does not explicitly return from his journey of v. 21 until 2.11. The text allows the reader to include him in v. 25 and perhaps also as the subject of the last sentence in v. 28. The reader recalls that Elkanah went up to sacrifice and to worship in v. 3. In v. 21, he goes up to sacrifice. Perhaps he completes his religious observances in v. 28, and then goes home as in 2.11 /24/.

Another possible subject for *wayyištaḥû* in v. 28 is Samuel (cf. H. P. Smith 1899:13). He is the subject in Hannah's preceding participial clause and could be the subject of the final sentence, which is a description from the narrator.

When Hannah finishes speaking about Samuel, it is possible that the narrator might not identify the subject of his descriptive conclusion. Since the topic of Hannah's utterance is Samuel, the narrator adds a sentence with an unspecified subject and assumes that the reader will understand that the topic of discussion - Samuel - has not changed. Viewed from the alternative perspective, the sentence would be strange and difficult to follow if the narrator intended to change the topic of discussion from Samuel in Hannah's utterance to someone else in his own, but did not tell his audience who he was talking about.

If Samuel is to be understood as the subject of the last sentence - though it is far from certain that he or anyone else can be conclusively chosen - the sentence would show Samuel demonstrating his willingness to take up the role prescribed for him by worshipping his new employer.

A third possibility suggested by de Boer is that the verb be read as 'hitpal. 3rd pers. plur.' with Hannah and Samuel as subject (1938:82; cf. Thenius 1864:9). Eli, while possible, is an unlikely candidate.

Neither in the preceding context nor in the following is he or either of his sons cast in a clearly positive light. Contrast Elkanah, Hannah and Samuel. Worshipping Yahweh is not amongst the characteristics of the Elides. Eli even mistakes prayer for drunkenness (v.14).

The positive function of the ambiguity of this sentence in v. 28 might be to cause the careful reader to do exactly what has been done above, namely to run through the possibilities noting who could and could not be subject. The process of recollection groups Elkanah, Hannah and Samuel as characters that could be expected to worship Yahweh and contrasts them with Eli. Such ambiguity, 'plurisignation,' is a valuable addition of richness and complexity to the structure of meaning in the narrative (Wimsatt & Brooks 1957: 2/ 639f; Perry 1979:46-49). The unambiguous LXX reading does not contain the opportunity for reader participation created by MT. The attempt to understand the ambiguity forces the reader to struggle with the text, thereby testing and modifying or confirming his understanding of it. Premature decisions to read MT here and LXX there dodge the obstacles in the text instead of confronting them and seeking to determine their significance.

Though summaries are doomed to misrepresent literary texts (cf. Brooks 1947:192-214), it may be useful to present such a 'misrepresentation' at this point in order to reorient readers. Chapter 1 centres on Samuel, aiming at a definition of his pre-determined role. Subsidiary accomplishments include the veiled revelations of divine purpose, and the introduction of a series of contrasts drawn between the Elide priests and ordinary Israelites such as Elkanah and Hannah. These three aspects of ch. 1 are all on the level of story, the subject matter of the narrative.

On the level of discourse, the level of literary technique and narrative structure, the narrator introduces himself to the reader in ch. 1. The narrator shows that he reports to us from an undetermined time subsequent to the events of the narrative. He is a so-called 'omniscient' narrator with access to God's hidden actions (e.g. v. 5), though he does not commit himself to telling all to his reader. On the contrary, he is interested in narration, and the creation of narrative interest, as his many ambiguities and denials of necessary expositional material show. From ch. 1, we are given to understand that the voice describing everything belongs to a narrator telling a *story*, and not to a historian providing *information*.

Chapter 1, therefore, introduces the reader to two important persons, Samuel and the narrator.

CHAPTER FOUR:
PART TWO

1 SAMUEL 2

Excursus on the 'Song of Hannah'

The majority of critical studies on the song of Hannah have concluded that it is secondary in its present context (Thenius 1864:9; Wellhausen 1871:42; H. P. Smith 1899:14; Budde 1902:13f; Nowack 1902:9; Dhorme 1910:29; Hertzberg 1964:29; Brockington 1962:319; Mauchline 1971:50; Stoebe 1973:106f; McCarter 1980: 75f). Two positions have been taken on the question of the redactional logic for the insertion of the song.

Exemplifying the first position, Thenius suggests that a redactor who inserted the song saw a connection between vv. 1 and 5 of the song and the preceding situation of Hannah's infertility (1864:9; cf. H. P. Smith 1899:14). Because the connection is slim, almost spurious, the redaction critic is able to label the song redactional. He can then go on to suggest an original setting in which the song may be correctly understood (e.g., Budde 1902:13f.).

The presumption that an author of a work would not introduce a poem only minimally linked with its context has received neither demonstration nor analysis. Gutbrod, for example, simply asserts, 'It requires no special insight to see that this hymn of praise has little, or to be exact, no connection with the personal story of Hannah and her son' (1956:19). We are to assume, therefore, that the psalm pre-existed its present context and has been inserted. 'We should take this in the same way as the addition of a suitable hymn to a Bible reading' (Hertzberg 1964:29). But if it is 'suitable,' why call it redactional? Lacking are objective criteria for determining whether or not the song is redactional or integral to its context.

Scholars of the second position build on the redactional label attached to the song in the first position. They differ, however, in their perception of a broader thematic connection between the song and its context. McCarter is able to say that 'the song is not wholly unsuited to its secondary context . . . the little hymn is fitting enough on Hannah's lips' (1980: 76; cf. Hertzberg 1964:31). As for the subsequent context, 'the song of Hannah sounds a clear keynote' (McCarter 1980:76). Similarly, Gutbrod says that although we cannot answer the question of whether or not the song was sung by Hannah, it does introduce the central concerns of the subsequent narratives. With the poem we see a transition from the family affairs of Elkanah and Hannah to the leading themes of the book. Samuel is part of a divine plan and is introduced at the beginning of an important moment in the history of the theocracy. 'Thus the text invites an open-mindedness towards this theme' (Gutbrod 1956:22).

The historical critic's recognition of such important thematic continuity undermines his reason for calling the song redactional. The redactional label is left supported only by the fact that 2.1-10 is written as poetry while its context is written as prose. By itself this difference allows no conclusions about the text's compositional history, unless one were to go as far as to suggest that poetry and prose cannot coexist in the same literary unit.

The redactional label, originally applied because 2.1-10 was regarded as contextually isolated, becomes a vestigial appendage inherited from a historical-critical mode of reading when vv. 1-10 are recognized as thematically appropriate. As Stoebe suggests, if there is a lack of specific reference in ch.1 it is because even ch. 1 is not so much concerned with the details as with the larger implications of those developments. 'The characters of Hannah and Samuel are of no interest in themselves, but rather for the significance that Samuel has for the rise of the monarchy' (1973:106).

Both chs. 1 and 2.1-10 relate to Israelite politics, the basic subject matter of the books of Samuel. The song of Hannah according to Stoebe is a thematic introduction, by which 'The entire subsequent story is presented as the outflow and manifestation of God's wisdom (vv. 2-3)' (1973:106). Despite his correct observations, Stoebe still feels compelled to doff his historical-critical hat to his predecessors. 'Should this conclusion seem to go too far, one could nevertheless maintain that the song was at least an interpolation with the same viewpoint as the whole story' (1973:107).

Scholars of the 'second position' have rejected the view that the song of Hannah is contextually isolated, yet at the same time they have been unable or unwilling to give up the now questionable redactional label. Stoebe's statement that the song was at least interpolated in view of the entire narrative says nothing about the narrative and everything about the historical-critical predisposition to interpret the text in terms of literary history.

McCarter suggests that since the lyrics presuppose the monarchy (v. 10), the song cannot have been contemporary with the events with which it is related. He suggests, therefore, that it is a redactional insertion made, perhaps, quite late in the literary history of the book (1980:75). It seems that he assumes that the prose context of 2.1-10 was composed at the same time as the events it describes. Yet such historical information is neither explicit in the text nor does McCarter supply a method for dating Hebrew prose. It is just as difficult to date the narrative context of Hannah's song as it is to date the song itself /1/. The narrative context offers no certain historical evidence about itself or its relative dating with respect to the song.

The only existing context for an interpretation of the song is to be found in its present narrative context. If the song does offer 'an interpretive key' to the narrative (Childs 1979:273), then one can only discover how it unlocks subsequent events by a careful scrutiny of the contours of the key we see.

The hermeneutic options for reading the song of Hannah are at least two. We can read the song in a hypothetical historical context, interpreting it as the literary record of a specific socio-historical setting. Or, we can read it in its given narrative context. The problem facing the historical-critical reading is the hypothetical nature of the undertaking. 'Though criticism is of one opinion in recognizing the song of Hannah as a late insertion, there is little agreement about the interpretation of the song or its date of composition' (Dhorme 1910:32).

Even granting a correct determination of the socio-historical context, the historical critic is still faced with a problem analogous to that single problem facing a literary interpretation. Both approaches must show how the features of the poem engage the context, whether it be socio-historical or narrative. The most satisfying interpretation will be the one that is able to show the greatest degree of engagement between the poem and its context.

Robert Polzin has even suggested that literary contextual analysis should have operational priority over socio-historical analysis. Citing K. Pomorska, he says, 'if we move in the opposite direction, basing synchronic analysis on historical studies 'we always run a risk of applying ready-made theories to something not suited to them" (1980:6; cf. Ellis 1974:118-21, 133-54). Further socio-historical discussion of Hannah's song should at least consider the contextual engagement of the poem within the narrative before removing it to a separate place and distant time (e.g. McCarter 1980:75f).

Verse 1

Hannah expresses a prayer of thanksgiving and praise, apparently in celebration of her fulfillment of her vow (cf. 1.11). The repetition of the verb *wattitpallel,* forms an inclusio with the prior occurrences in 1.26-27:

```
┌ 1.26f    Hannah prayed to Yahweh, praying for Samuel (this lad).
│  1.27    Yahweh gives Samuel to Hannah.
│
│  1.28    Hannah dedicates Samuel to Yahweh.
└ 2.1      Hannah prays (to Yahweh, thanking and praising him).
```

The inclusio, with the intervening chiastic summary of the main events of ch. 1, specifically indicates that the following prayer of thanksgiving is Hannah's response to the result of the previous petitionary prayer /2/. She is able to pray this prayer, which celebrates divine strength, because Yahweh answered the first. Since this prayer in 2.1-10 is structurally linked to the prayer for Samuel in 1.26-27, we are also led to expect some correlation between Samuel and the message of the poem. In fact, Samuel becomes more and more the sole representative of the theological and political point of view expressed in Hannah's prayer.

Verse 1 exhibits a chiastic structure of the A B : B' A' type. A and A' are semantically parallel. Both describe Hannah's exultation in Yahweh and his deliverance. The two verbs *'alaṣ* and *šamah* also appear elsewhere in parallel construction (Pss 5.12; 9.3; 68.4). In all cases, the verbs describe the joyful response of humble worshippers of Yahweh, who exult in the strength of their God. Also associated with all occurrences are statements about the futility and wickedness of man's pride and efforts at self-help, whether done in defiance or ignorance of the deity.

B and B' are also connected semantically: 'my horn becomes high in/by Yahweh, my mouth stretches wide ov-

er my enemies.' They also share a connotation of power
possessed by Hannah; in B she exults in the strength
that Yahweh gives her and in B', in the consequent
power over her enemies (I owe this observation to a
letter from Jan Fokkelman). The connection is reinforced by the alliterative parallelism between the
verbs. Both begin with 'r' and describe metaphorical
physical enlargements resulting from Yahweh's sponsor-
ship /3/.

In addition to the chiastic structure of the verse,
which sets off the exultation (A, A') against the cause
of exultation (B, B'), there is a logical progression
in the verse indicated by the grammatical construction
of each line:

My heart exults in Yahweh
My horn is exalted in Yahweh
My mouth extends over my enemies
So I rejoice in your deliverance.

The *kî* introducing A' should not be omitted to
agree with LXX (against McCarter 1980:68). It highlights the uniqueness of A', which is the only line of
the verse in which Hannah is subject. The switch from
third person description in A, B, and B' to first person in A', an exclamation addressing Yahweh directly
in the second person, structurally conveys the mounting
pressure of Hannah's exuberance. She finally bursts out
in direct address to Yahweh because her descriptive
praise is not expressive enough. The single *kî*, the
change in person of the verb, and the change from description to address to Yahweh in the 2nd person all
combine to give prominence to A'. As James Muilenburg says, *kî* 'is characteristically associated with emphatic words or clauses . . . [it] frequently appears
in a strategic position in the poem or narrative, . . .
[and] often confirms or underlines what has been said,
or, at times, undergirds the whole of the utterance
and gives point to it' (1961:150). A third pattern

(pointed out by Fokkelman in a letter) in v. 1 is related to the pattern of logical progression. The first two lines are paralleled in A*1*A*2* pattern, as are the second two lines, B*1*B*2*. The first two lines are linked semantically and by the perfect rhyme of *yhwh*. The B*1*B*2* pair end in contrasting terms 'my enemies,' and 'your deliverance.'

There are, therefore, at least three structural patterns exhibited by v. 1. Rather than trying to decide which pattern is predominant it seems better to regard all three as equally important, The reader of such intricately constructed and integrated plural structure must study each verse with care to discover the wealth of meaning contained therein. The time necessarily spent on such a reading ensures that the reader cannot leave the poem without a thorough understanding and appreciation of the message presented by the poem.

In the particular case of Hannah's poem the utility of such poetic technique is readily apparent, since the message of the poem is one pole in the subsequent examination of the question of human need in relation to divine aid. The reader who has read Hannah's poem as it should be read cannot fail to carry its message with him as he reads on. The three structures in v. 1 are, therefore, rhetorically complementary.

McCarter notes that the idiom, 'raise, exalt the horn' denotes visible success and can refer specifically to progeny acquired (e.g. 1 Chr 25.5; 1980:71). Hannah's praise refers directly back to the birth of Samuel who is figuratively representative of her raised horn. As a result of his birth her mouth stretches (*raḥab*) over her enemy.

Just as Moses and the people of Israel sang a song of praise to Yahweh for his deliverance (Exod 15.2) from their enemies (vv. 6, 7, 9) so Hannah rejoices. Both poems celebrate Yahweh's deliverance (*yešû'â*) of his people, who praise him for it. Again in both cases the immediate context provides a contrast in the representation of the fate of those whose strength is in their own hand (1 Sam 2.4-10a; Exod 15.4-10; cf. Isa 10.12-15). Hannah regards Yahweh's deliverance in the same terms as the Israelites looked upon their deliverance from Egypt.

Hence the rhetorical emphasis on the final *kî* clause is seen to agree with the semantic emphasis of the poem, which celebrates Yahweh's deliverance of the weak and helpless. As the *kî* clause is distinguished as the climactic conclusion of v. 1, so it also introduces the leitmotif of the poem - salvation is from Yahweh. The only action to be taken by the one delivered is to rejoice. This notion is especially important in the light of Israel's subsequent decision to take matters into its own hands by ousting Yahweh as their king and replacing him with a human king (1 Sam 8). Though the reader does not read Hannah's song in light of 1 Sam 8, he will relate the two passages in the course of his reflections on ch. 8.

It is important to note at this point that the narrator does not himself espouse the notion of total reliance on Yahweh. Instead, he allows Hannah to do the talking. In her mouth, such an idea is motivated and supported by her personal experience. Given the location of the motivation for the expression of this notion *within the story itself*, the reader is not at liberty to think that the narrator shares Hannah's point of view. The narrator presents the notion through Hannah so that the reader will consider it together with preceding and subsequent narrative situations and events. The reader must, however, wait for further evidence of the narrator's own point of view before making any firm decisions on his or her relation to the ideas expressed in *Hannah's* song. Given that the narrator has already supplied the reader with the story of Samuel's miraculous birth, a story that supports Hannah's position in 2.1-10, it seems that he at least understands such views and knows how they arise.

Verse 2

Practically all commentators regard this verse as conflate. Usually the second line is taken to be the intruder, although McCarter suggests that MT contains three separate variants (1980:68f; cf. Talmon 1975: 231ff.). It is, nevertheless, possible to include all three variants in a reading of the verse even though the first and third lines are syntactically parallel, while the second deviates from the structure. It may be that the obtrusive appearance of the second line is designed to draw attention to it. If so, we would expect the foregrounded element to have a semantic role commensurate with its unusual form.

All three variants say more or less the same thing: Yahweh is unique and incomparable. The second line sums up the first and third, and includes all other comparisons that might be made. The unified voice of all three lines is that Yahweh is a sure source of refuge without rival. Parallel occurrences all stress the same idea (Deut 32.4, 15, 18, 37; Pss 18.3, 32, 47; 28.1; 31.1, etc.) /4/.

Hannah's assertion of this widespread notion is important in light of the people's request for a human king to replace Yahweh in ch. 8. She presents the standard theological view, which is supported by the events of ch. 1.

By allowing Hannah to speak directly, the narrator begins to equip his reader for the exploration of the theological-political problem that is presented in his narrative. Hannah gives voice to the standard view of the proper relation between Israelite need and divine response to need. It is important to note, however, that the standard view is supported here by the deliverance of a pious *individual.* The events of ch. 1 prove the truthfulness of the standard view but the application is limited to the individual's case.

Because the reader reads the exaltation of Yahweh as deliverer of those in need in light of a supportive example (ch. 1), he is compelled to admit to the validity of the idea, at least within the framework of this narrative. The order of presentation, example followed by theological statement, is designed to convince. Since it is the author/omniscient narrator who has arranged this order of presentation, it would seem that he wants his reader to see the validity of the ideas presented by Hannah. Through an awareness of the rhetorical function of the narrative's order of presentation, we can watch how the narrator carefully guides the reader's reflections and perceptions of the events and their significance.

Again one must be careful to maintain a distinction between views the narrator wants his reader to understand and views that he, the narrator, holds. The reader, therefore, is prudent to avoid attributing perspectives voiced within the narrative to the narrator until the whole narrative has been studied. It is primarily in the structural whole, which includes all aspects of his narrative, that a narrator presents his views.

Verse 3

Verses 1-2 constitute a positive celebration of both Yahweh's deliverance of Hannah from her enemies and his preeminence as a haven for his people. That is, the positive implications of Yahweh's power and incomparability for humanity are presented. Verse 3 presents the reverse side of the coin. It advises against arrogant boasts because Yahweh is a knowledgeable God who weighs such practises.

The two key words *gebohâ* and *'ataq* converge on the self-sufficient attitude of the person who makes such utterances. According to Donald Gowan, the basic meaning of these words is haughtiness. They are the biblical Hebrew equivalent to the Greek word *hybris* (1975:20f). Self-sufficiency is contrary to the proper attitude of dependence on Yahweh. He is the sole deter-

minant of human fortunes. Arrogance and boastful
speech are characterized as *'alilôt,* 'evil practises' /5/.
The evil deeds are, however, balanced by Yahweh /6/.
As in Zeph 3.11ff, the evil deeds of the proud are pun-
ished, while the humble are given divine protection.

A series of seven contrasts follow v. 3 and illustrate the 'balancing' or weighing of deeds by Yahweh
(Brownlee 1977:43). The reversals of fortune exhibit
the standard Israelite belief that Yahweh downgrades
human self-sufficiency and rewards the helpless, who
have no basis for pride or self-sufficiency /7/.

Verses 4-10

The warrior's broken bow is, as in Jer 51.56, symbolic of the insignificance of human strength. The
reversal makes the strong weak and the weak strong.
One cannot rely on apprearances, which mean nothing
when it comes to Yahweh (cf. 1 Sam 16.7). The obvious
conclusion is that one should rely solely on Yahweh.
He is the only 'rock,' the God who girds the weak with
strength (Ps 18.32f; cf. 2 Sam 22) /8/.

The reversals of fortune receive further illustra-
tion, thereby driving the point home by repetition /9/.
Human fate is totally in Yahweh's hands (v. 6; cf. Deut
32.39). Ehrlich describes the intent of the references
to the physical creation in v. 8: 'Because Yahweh is
the creator and preserver of the world he can do as
he pleases in it' (1910:170). Verse 9 openly states the
basis of all the unexpected reversals. A man does not
become mighty by his own strength, but must resort to
Yahweh for preservation (cf. Ps 33.16f).

Verse 10

Yahweh shatters (*yehattû*) his opponents just
as he shattered the bows of the mighty (v. 4). By
implication one could say that his opponent is human
self-sufficiency as symbolized by the warrior's bow

/10/. The situation of Yahweh in heaven, thundering and judging the inhabitants of earth, stresses man's helplessness before this God (cf. Ps 33.13-15) /11/. Obviously any posture other than humble submission is absurd.

Hannah's song also bears some implications for the character of Samuel. He is born to the woman who believes in the necessity of pious submission and utter dependence on Yahweh. Samuel, the fruit of such faith, will continue to bear that torch throughout the following events. He is the living proof and will become the adamant exponent of the viewpoint expounded in Hannah's song.

The last two lines of v. 10 openly anticipate the coming conflict of political ideologies. In keeping with the entire poem we are told that it is Yahweh who gives strength to his king and raises the horn of his anointed. That is to say, if a king has any power at all, it is delegated to him by Yahweh. By attaching the third person masculine singular pronominal suffix to each noun describing the monarch the verse stresses the fact that the king is Yahweh's king (cf. 2.35, on which see below). He derives his power from him and owes obedience and allegiance to him.

The references to a king in v. 10 are usually taken as a clue that the song is from the later monarchic period. They are thought to be the clearest evidence that the poem is a redactional insertion. (Willis (1973:148 n.43) gives a list of early modern proponents to which add all recent commentators.) This genetic explanation fails to perceive the unity of the poem, and its thematic linkage to its prose context.

As Willis has observed, the poem begins with Hannah's description of her horn, raised by Yahweh, and concludes with a note that Yahweh raises the horn of his anointed (1973:148). An equivalence between Hannah and the anointed is thereby established. Hannah's horn-raising was accomplished through her prayerful, but submissive request for divine activity on her behalf.

The structural inclusio suggests that the anointed's horn, raised by Yahweh, requires a similar stance of the king. If the reader has followed the logic of the poem, he cannot deny this implication, 'For it is not by strength that a man becomes mighty' (v. 9).

To reiterate, the song of Hannah begins to prepare the reader for the future controversy over who shall rule in Israel - God or man. The poem directs us to the simple fact that Yahweh is the great leveller, the controller of human destiny. From this perspective the notion that a human king could rule and successfully guide Israel independent of Yahweh is nonsense. The point is not, however, made polemically, which is to say that redaction critics should not jump to label the poem anti-monarchic. Rather Hannah sets forth this view upon the basis of her own experience, the examples of vv. 4-10, Yahweh's obvious superiority (vv. 2, 3, 4, 6, 8, 10), and the common tradition about the fate of the proud.

The poem is a theological reflection on the principles underlying the events of ch. 1. At the same time, Hannah's song sounds a key note for the subsequent story of Israel's political evolution. The poem suggests that an Israelite monarchy can only exist in a subordinate role determined by Yahweh. Verse 10 anticipates the turn of events in chs. 9-12 but its weight is balanced by the intervening chapters (2.11-ch. 8) which support Israel's request for a secular king, just as ch. 1 supports Hannah's exultation in the standard view about the necessity of total dependence on Yahweh.

The narrative in chs. 1-12 exhibits a dialectical structure. In ch. 1 and especially in 2.1-10 Yahweh's supreme sovereignty over humanity is affirmed. In the concatenation of narrative events following Hannah's poem, however, the desirability of Yahweh's sovereignty over Israel is called into doubt and even rejected by Israel (8.5, 20) /12/. Finally, chs. 9-12 reaffirm both Yahweh's status as Israel's real king and the covenant between Israel and Yahweh. The reaffirmation is especially visible in the terms laid down by Samuel in ch. 12.

Hannah's song also serves as an appropriate introduction to the events of chs. 2-3, which set up a contrast between the Elides and Samuel. Samuel is of the same humble sort as his mother, with whom he is directly associated (2.18-21). Samuel is portrayed as a servant of God and his priests (2.11, 18; 3.1, 4-10). He calls himself 'your servant' (*'abdeka*, 3.9) when addressing Yahweh just as his mother called herself 'your maidservant' (*'amateka*, 2.11) in her prayer to Yahweh. Samuel is as humbly submissive to Eli's brusque cross-examination after Yahweh's visit (3.17-18) as Hannah was when Eli accused her of drunkenness when she was praying to Yahweh (1.15-16).

The Elides, on the other hand, are far from submissive types. Eli's sons put themselves before Yahweh in the sacrifices (2.15-17), thereby despising (2.30) and blaspheming Yahweh (3.13). They sin against Yahweh (2.25). They are anti-types of Samuel and Hannah and can be grouped with those whose fate takes a turn for the worse in Hannah's song. It is Yahweh's will to slay them (2.25) just as he cuts off the wicked in Hannah's song (2.6, 9; cf. below on vv. 25-26).

Verse 11

The narrative thread is picked up from 1.28. Once again the text leaves the reader wondering about the place and action of a character, this time Hannah. Elkanah goes home and Samuel ministers to Yahweh, but where is Hannah and what is she doing?

R. Ingarden has called such narrative lacunae 'places of indeterminacy.' 'Each object, person, event, etc., portrayed in the literary work of art contains a number of places of indeterminacy, especially the descriptions of what happens to people and things' (1973a:50; cf. Iser 1974:280; Chatman 1978: 28-30).

The reader's response to indeterminacies is to supply elements that agree with the context to concretize the indeterminacy. Ingarden focuses on the aesthetic effects of different concretizations. One way of filling out may flatten the work while another gives it greater depth, introducing new, aesthetically valuable qualities (1973a:54).

The text-critical concretization of Hannah's indeterminacy is to follow LXX in v. 11: 'after Hannah had returned to Ramah.' This decision removes the gap between 1.28 and 2.11, but in doing so it also neglects the aesthetic possibilities of MT. Furthermore, there is no reason, other than the indeterminacy itself, for rejecting MT. McCarter's explanation for MT's supposed corruption rests on two weak supports: supposed scribal incompetence and redactional hypothesis. He suggests that the redactional intrusion of 2.1-10 obscured the connection between 1.28 and 2.11 (1980:78). But why would an obscured connection be even more obscured by filling in Elkanah instead of leaving Hannah as subject in v. 11? Wouldn't the scribe who was confused by the insertion of Hannah's prayer try to eliminate his confusion by reading the same subject in 1.28 and 2.11? As Ingarden suggested - and the examples of LXX and numerous text critics who have followed it support him on this - the usual response to an indeterminacy or obscurity is to clarify and not to obscure. There is in fact no basis for suggesting that either MT or LXX is superior or inferior.

An alternative is to take MT seriously and to seek a concretization that is both aesthetically and contextually acceptable. We can recall that when Elkanah went up to offer the sacrifice of the days in 1.21 Hannah stayed behind so as to extend her time with Samuel (1.22). The poignancy of her situation was emphasized by the repetition of the phrase 'until he is weaned' in 1.22-24, and the final sentence of v. 23, which pointedly emphasized the mother and child union.

Perhaps in 2.11 Elkanah finally goes home for the first time since 1.21, leaving Samuel at the temple. Hannah's absence at this point can be explained by the conflict she experiences between her vow to leave Samuel at the temple and her obviously strong maternal attachment. She does not go home with Elkanah because of her attachment to Samuel, and she does not stay with Samuel because of her promise to leave him 'before Yahweh' when he is weaned. Hannah, as the text's indeterminacy suggests, is left nowhere, caught between her vow and her maternal instincts.

Of course there are virtually limitless alternative concretizations of Hannah's indeterminacy. Each reader fills in gaps in his or her own way (Iser 1974:280). All that is claimed is that this concretization is contextually and aesthetically defensible.

Verse 11 immediately introduces Samuel in what will be his almost singular role in chs. 2-3. 'And the lad was ministering to Yahweh before Eli the priest.' Samuel is obviously a 'flat' character according to E. M. Forster's division of characters into 'flat' and 'round.' Forster's statement that the 'really flat character can be expressed in one sentence' might have been written about Samuel in ch. 2 rather than Mrs Micawber (1976:73).

Forster suggests that flat characters have two advantages: they are easily recognized and easily remembered. 'They remain in his [the reader's] mind as unalterable for the reason that they were not changed by circumstances' (1976:74). Samuel is the faithful servant in ch. 2, whose only development is to grow 'in stature and favor with Yahweh and men' (v. 26). As a flat character, we easily recognize him as the unpretentious protagonist, continuing in his mother's footsteps. He represents the same religious type as Hannah and will continue to express and exemplify the views she expresses in 2.1-10. His flatness makes him the unbending standard of right action by which other characters will be measured.

According to Driver, Samuel's action in v. 11 is simultaneous with the deeds about to be dealt with in v. 12 (1913:28). The synchronicity of Samuel's action with Eli's sons' misdeeds introduces the explicit contrast between them /13/. While Samuel is ministering *'et-yhwh* the sons of Eli do not know *'et-yhwh* (v. 12). As in other occurrences of the expression, 'to know Yahweh' describes a conscious interaction of the knower with Yahweh in a covenantal relationship. To know Yahweh is to acknowledge his divinity (Exod 5.2 by implication) and claim on Israel (Judg 2.10), to enter into covenant with him (Isa 19.21), to obey the ethical requirements of relationship with Yahweh (Jer 9.2, 5, 15, 23), and to participate in a covenant with him (Jer 31.34; Hos 2.22; 5.4; 6.3; 8.2). While it is not stated here that Samuel knows Yahweh, the contrast between the lad who serves Yahweh and the priests who are supposed to maintain the covenant but do not even participate in 'covenantal knowledge,' is clear and strongly in favour of Samuel.

Samuel has not yet been introduced to the knowledge of Yahweh, and will not attain such knowledge until Yahweh comes and personally introduces himself to Samuel (3.7-21). By implication, the existing priests, supposed mediators of the knowledge of Yahweh, are incapable of introducing Samuel to it, Even though he lacks this important knowledge, however, Samuel remains a faithful servant of God, in contrast to the priests, who should have the knowledge, but do not/14/.

Verse 12

The focus shifts completely from Elkanah and Samuel to the sons of Eli. By means of paronomastic assonance and consonance the *benê 'elî* are characteristically redefined as *benê belîya'al*. According to Benedikt Otzen, who reviews the various attempts at etymological explanation, there is no convincing solution to the derivation of *belîya'al* (1977:133).

Within the context of 1 Sam 1-12, however, the three occurrences of the term all describe characters offensive to Yahweh: the drunken woman in the temple (1.16), those who do not know Yahweh (2.12), and those who reject Yahweh's compromise kingship (10.27).

In each instance, the children of *beliyaʻal* trespass against the covenant, or a covenantal institution: the supposedly drunken woman violates the sanctity of the temple (1.16), the sinful priest neglects the convenantal knowledge of Yahweh (2.12), and the rebellious dissenters refuse to honour the king that Yahweh has granted (10.27).

The prior use of the term to describe the sanctum transgressing woman in the temple supports the narrator's use of the term in v. 12. The narrator's interruption of the narrative sequence to give us his judgement of Eli's sons is a measure of the importance that he attaches to the reader's acceptance of this description of the Elides. He relies on his proven authority to ensure that the reader accepts the categorization of the Elides as covenant transgressors without question. Functionally like the omniscient narrator's assertion of the innocence of Job (Job 1. 1), this characterization of the sons of Eli must be accepted as true if the reader is going to follow the logic of the story. Since it is the sins of Eli's sons that catalyze the subsequent Israelite defeat (2.26, 31-34; ch. 4, esp. v. 11) the narrator takes pains, in the form of explicit exposition, to assure that the reader follows the logic at the course of events /15/.

Verses 13-14

These verses describe the customary practise of the priests when any person made a sacrifice (Buber 1964: 737) /16/. The introduction to v. 13 indicates that it should be read as a separate syntactic unit from v. 12, which tells us about the Elides' actions with respect to Yahweh; v. 13, on the other hand, describes their actions with respect to the people.

v.12 lo' yade'û 'et-yhwh
v.13 ûmišpaṭ hakkohanîm 'et-ha'am /17/

Verses 13-14 are laid out in a symmetrical chiasmus:

A   The priests' custom with respect to ['et] the people when anyone sacrificed.

B   The priest's servant comes with his trident [hammazleg šeloš-haššinnayim] when the flesh boiled.

B'   (The priest's servant) thrusts his fork [hammazleg] into the pots and the priest gets whatever is on it.

A'   So they (the priests) do to any Israelite coming to Shiloh.

The chiastic structure, with its parallel between 'et-ha'am in A and lekol-yiśra'el in A', also shows that A in MT should be read separate from v. 12 with the verbal idea implied by ûmišpaṭ /18/.

The two verses themselves contain neither explicit nor implicit condemnation of the priests or the priests' servant's actions. H. P. Smith's view that this method of obtaining the priestly portion 'could scarcely be more offensive' (1899:18) has little basis in the text. Instead the two verses seem designed to establish the regular practise in order to highlight the irregularities of v. 15 /19/.

Verse 15

The sin of the sons of Eli is foregrounded by placing the words *gam beṭerem* first in the verse. Emphasis thereby falls on the fact that the priests demand their portion *even before* the god gets his in the form of smoke from burnt fat. It is exactly this prematurity that provokes Yahweh to anger /20/; in 2.29 he accuses Eli and his sons of fattening themselves on the *first* parts (*mere'šît*) of every Israelite offering (cf. McCarter 1980:90). Even the common

Israelite saw the priestly indiscretion in the prematurity of their request for raw flesh. 'Let the fat be burnt first (*kayyôm*)' (v. 16; cf. Driver 1913:31). The words *gam beṭerem* might, therefore, be translated as 'But even before . . .'

The reason for the priest's impatience is that he wants roasted meat rather than boiled. The gastronomical motivation for putting himself before Yahweh makes the priest out to be nothing more than a piggish lout (cf. Schulz 1919:37). As Yahweh points out the motivation for Eli's sons' priestly crassness is to get fat on the first parts of all Israel's sacrifices (v. 29). The Elides are far from being the prometheans of Israel's sacrificial system.

Verse 16

As most commentators have recognized, v. 16 portrays an upside-down situation in Israel's cult. The layman tells the official how the sacrifice should be done (Hertzberg 1964:35). The offer to take whatever he desired after the fat had been burned is refused by the priest's servant. What is at stake is not the question of raw or boiled meat; that is a foregone conclusion ('take whatever you want'). The point is that the priests will not wait for Yahweh.

The reply of the priest's servant puts the issue succinctly. 'Give it *now*!' (*kî 'attâ titten*). According to Driver the apodosis containing the 'bare perfect' is uncommon and emphatic. 'And if not I take it by force' (1913:32). Not only do the priests disregard the regular sacrificial custom (vv. 13-14), but they threaten violence to any who would obstruct them. Sacrifice in their eyes is only a means to their own ends, which are pursued with total disregard for sacrificer or Yahweh.

Verse 17

The verse assumes that the servants' actions are sinful, and declares only that the magnitude of their sin was very great in Yahweh's view (*'et-penê yhwh*). The gravity of the sin is explained by the fact that 'the men' treated the offering of Yahweh with contempt. 'The men' who are subject of the verb do not appear in LXX and are omitted by some commentators (e.g. McCarter 1980:80). If retained, however, the shift in the verse from *hanne'arîm* to *ha'anašîm* lays emphasis on the hybris of the act. It is an act of contempt by man (or men) against God /21/. We expect, on the basis of Hannah's song, that such sinful hybris will not go unrequited by Yahweh.

Again in v. 17 the narrator employs his omniscience to inform his reader about the relationship between the divine and human planes in the narrative. In ch. 1, he described a situation where a divine initiative changed the course of events on the human plane (1.5). Now, however, he shows a reverse causality, in which human actions have an effect on the divine character. Just as the reader was led to expect some future result of the divine intervention in ch. 1, he is now led to expect some future result, or reaction on the divine plane. A difference between the two situations is that while the human characters can only respond blindly, and so, from the reader's perspective often ironically to divine action, God responds directly and consciously to human actions that impinge on him. The expositional note in v. 17 assumes this difference and uses it to create narrative interest by leading the reader to anticipate a divine reaction.

Verse 18

As Willis observes (1979:208), v. 18 contrasts Samuel, ministering before Yahweh (*'et-penê yhwh*), with Hophni and Phinehas (or more correctly, the servants of the latter) whose sin is exceedingly great *'et penê yhwh* (v. 17; cf. Hertzberg 1964:35; Peter-Contesse 1976:313).

Samuel is introduced by name for the first time in an active role. It is possible that he is mentioned by name to avoid any misunderstanding that would identify him - the priest's servant (*na'ar*, v. 11) - with the priest's servant of vv. 13-17.

The description of Samuel's garb also seems designed to contrast him with the Elides. Roland de Vaux suggests that the linen ephod, worn here by Samuel, was a loin-cloth worn by priests performing their offices (1965:350). While the Elides are misbehaving as priests, Samuel behaves as one both in appearance and conduct.

Verses 19-21

These verses recall the series of events leading to Samuel's birth, reminding the reader of his special character.

The reminder, coming as it does just after an explicit contrast between the Elides and Samuel, and just after the expositional comment in v. 17, is an example of the narrator's subtle use of structural associations created by the order of presentation to make veiled suggestions to the reader. Here he is reminded that Samuel was brought into the world for some divine purpose, just after the narrator has told the reader about the impingement of the Elides' actions on God. The association of these two transactions across the divine/human border seems to be aimed at arousing reader speculation about a possible relation between the two.

Hannah brings a little robe for Samuel every year when her husband brings her up to commemorate the birth of Samuel by sacrificing 'the sacrifice of the days' /22/. Eli joins in the commemorative celebrations, blessing Elkanah and Hannah.

The scene parallels that in 1.17-18. The results
are also similar. Eli blesses and Hannah/Elkanah or
Hannah leave. Subsequently, God 'remembers' or visits
Hannah and she conceives and bears a child/children.
The parallel indicates that Yahweh repays Hannah's
faithfulness to her vow (v. 20) by giving her five
children for the one child, who came out of the previous visit and whom she gave back to Yahweh (cf. 2.5).

The final sentence in v. 21 describes Samuel's
physical maturation and his deepening relationship
with Yahweh. Coming just after the notice of Hannah's
continuing fecundity and her expanding family, this
final sentence makes Yahweh the sole family for Samuel. Samuel's period of growth takes place with Yahweh, while Hannah is kept busy with his replacements.

We will hear no more from Hannah or Elkanah. They
have fulfilled their task of introducing Samuel and
now they retire. Samuel and his relationship with Yahweh take up where Hannah leaves off. Verse 21 accomplishes this shift in focus by a 'fade-out' scene of
Hannah with her five new offspring followed by a
'fade-in' on the lad Samuel, who is growing with Yahweh (v. 21). Hannah is bountifully repaid for her part
in Yahweh's plan, and Yahweh has the person dedicated to his service.

It was in order to get Samuel that the whole process
of events involving Hannah was initiated. The reader
has been informed about Samuel's special identity by
the special circumstances of his birth and his subsequent temple career. The reader has also been made
aware of a problem amongst the priests serving at the
temple.

The associations of vv. 17-21 have intimated that
here may be some causal relationship between the two
instances of actions from one side of the divine/human
border with an influence or effect on the other side.
The principal characters have been introduced and the
stage is set. The plot begins to take shape.

Verse 22

While Samuel is growing with Yahweh, Eli has become very old. The intended contrast is clear:

	subject	predicate	modifier
v. 21	the lad Samuel	grew	with Yahweh
v. 22	Eli	(was) old	very

The mention of Eli's old age here is important for
subsequent events (Miller & Roberts 1977:62). Eli's
age will play an important part in his death in 4.15-
18. It is the 'old man' (*zaqen*) of the Elide household who is promised death in 2.31f.

More important, however, is the paradigm established by the conjunctive description of old Eli and his
wicked sons in v. 22. When the paradigm is repeated
later in the narrative, all of the meanings, associations, and consequences that are connected to the
Elide instance are brought to bear on the recurrence.
The paradigmatic Elide affair provides commentary
on all subsequent reappearances of a similar state of
affairs.

By providing the reader with this specific description of the Elides, the only leaders visible in the
story, the narrator directs attention to a problem in
the political structure of Israel, namely the problem
of bad representation.

The theocratic system is utterly dependent on the
proper functioning of the role of the mediator. In the
specific instance of the priesthood it is clear that
bad priests and abuses of the sacrificial system destroy the utility of the institution as a mechanism for
maintaining normal covenantal relations between Yahweh and his people.

Eli hears of his sons' sacrificial misdeeds and how
they 'laid' (*yiškebûn 'et*) the women serving at the
entrance to the tent of meeting. Willis is inclined to
see a case of sacral prostitution here (1972:56). Given

that the narrator is listing the abuses of Eli's sons
and the fact that the women are described neutrally as
tent servants, it seems more likely that it is simply
another example of the Elides' 'heart's desire' taking
precedence over cultic propriety. Just as they contemned the sacrifices of Yahweh so Eli's sons now abuse
Yahweh's servants.

The women abused by Eli's sons are those 'serving'
(*haṣṣobe'ôt*) at the door of the tent of meeting.
This description alludes to one of the divine titles,
yhwh ṣeba'ôt, introduced to us by another woman,
Hannah, when she prayed for a son (1.11) in the same
locale, the cultic sanctuary. Eli's sons are violating
the 'hostesses' of 'Yahweh, God of hosts' (noted by
Fokkelman in a letter to me). The allusion repeats the
suggestion that the sinful acts of Eli's sons transmit
an effect across the divine/human border.

Verses 23-25

Eli's attempt to warn his sons away from their dan-
gerously sinful ways distinguishes him from his sons.
He is neither a party to their misdeeds nor does he con-
done them. The fact that he rebukes his sons because
of the bad reports he has heard from the people (v.
23) has been taken by Willis to suggest an irrespon-
sibility on Eli's part (1971:292). Presumably Willis
thinks that Eli should have been aware of the problem
on his own. Why present Eli rebuking his sons at all,
though, if the goal is to criticize Eli at this point
in the narrative?

The fact that Eli hears the bad report from the
people is not so much a criticism of Eli as a reflection of Eli's agedness. He is old and out of touch
with the affairs of the priesthood. His knowledge of
his sons' misdeeds is not second-hand because he is
willfully ignorant and out of touch with reality.
Rather, it is his age, over which he has no control,
that renders him out of touch and unable to control

his sons. Since the narrator supplies this mitigating explanation of Eli's ignorance about his sons' activities, it is a mistake to suggest that the narrator is accusing Eli of willful wrong-doing in vv. 22f.

Willis' understanding of v. 23 is, in fact, the result of reading it in light of Yahweh's subsequent rebuke and condemnation of Eli (2.29; 3.13; 1971:292). In doing so he makes two mistakes, First, by reading any element in a narrative in the light of a subsequent element, the reader subverts the order of presentation created by the narrator. Since the order of presentation - the structure of a narrative - is an extremely important device for the narrator's creation of meaning, we actually destroy the existing meaning structure and create a new one by rearranging the order of presentation (cf. Perry 1979; Sternberg 1978).

Secondly, Willis' reading of the narrator's comments in vv. 22f together with Yahweh's condemnation of Eli in 2.29 and 3.13 disregards the voice structure of the narrative. An elementary convention in narratives told by omniscient narrators sometime after the narrative events is that the voices of all characters, even God, are subordinate to the voice of their creator, the omniscient narrator. One cannot simply combine the voice of the narrator with the voice of a character, even if it is God, and expect to have gotten it right. If a reader suspects that the narrator and a character share a common perspective, the suspicion must be supported by proof from the narrative before it is incorporated into an interpretation.

Whatever the relationship between the narrator's voice and Yahweh's voice may turn out to be, Yahweh's comments should not be removed from their subsequent position to modify the narrator's existing evaluation of Eli in 2.22f. Eli really does warn his sons of the danger of their acts. The reader is given no indication in these or any preceding verses that Eli is culpably lax in his warning. The narrator presents Eli as trying, within the limits imposed by age, to turn his sons

from their sin. If a negative evaluation of Eli's efforts is later voiced by Yahweh, the reader will have
to understand it in connection with the narrator's
voice, and in subordination to it.

Eli mentions twice that the people are spreading
the report of his sons' evil deeds. This repetition is
an indication of the importance attached to absolving
the people from any complicity in their priestly
officials' sin (vv. 23f). The emphasis lies on the
people's universal judgement of their priests; Eli
hears the reports 'from *all* this people' (v. 23); the
rumor is *circulating* amongst the people of Yahweh
(v. 24). This emphasis on *all* the Israelites denounc-
ing their priests (*lô'-ṭôbâ haššemu'â*, v. 24) is another vital part of the theological-political problem
that is being developed in these events. The people
are innocent and are expressly called 'Yahweh's
people' (v. 24).

Though Eli's unintentional absolution does not
itself have the authority of the narrator's explicit
evaluations (e.g. the evaluation of Eli's sons in v.
12, which is complementary to Eli's absolution of the
people here), it receives the necessary support from
the narrator's descriptions of the people's propriety
in vv. 13-16. In addition, there is no mention of any
sin on the part of the people anywhere in the preceding (or subsequent) context.

Eli points out the extreme danger of his sons' actions. Their abuses of cultic procedures and personnel
are sins against Yahweh to whom all cultic activities
are directed. Eli's professional opinion about the
effects of his sons' action supports the narrator's
observation about its effect on the divine plane (v.
17). There is no one to offer intercessory prayer for
one who sins against Yahweh. Intercession by God,
available in the case of a man sinning against another,
is impossible when Yahweh is the injured party (v. 25).
Eli's words are ominous portents.

If he is correct, and the reader is given no reason

to doubt him, then we must expect disaster to be approaching. Here Eli himself is allowed to create narrative interest by making suggestions about impending doom.

Driver observes that the position of *lyhwh* in the apodosis of v. 25 is emphatic (1913:35). This emphasis supplements that of the nouns in the protasis. God (*'elohîm*) can mediate when a man (*'îš*) sins against a man (*'îš*) /23/. But when it is against Yahweh, Israel's sovereign, that a man sins mediation is out of the question. Even the possibility of an efficacious prayer is doubtful; 'Who will pray for him?' (v. 25).

Eli's rhetorical question places grave doubts on the future of his sons. They have sinned against Yahweh (v. 17) and even Eli, their own father, castigates them rather than praying for them.

The final sentence in v. 25 explicitly prepares for the ensuing, but as yet unspecified, death of Eli's sons. Yahweh is the one character in the story whose ability to enact any wish or plan is unquestionable. The death of Eli's sons is a foregone conclusion; it is only how and when that are unspecified, again creating narrative interest. When they do die the reader will be absolutely certain that their death and the conditions surrounding the event are the fruit of Yahweh's desire.

Few would debate the assertion that the repentance of the sinner is a predominant theme in the O.T., or that it is favoured by man and especially God /24/. In Ezek 33.11 (cf. 18.32) Yahweh says, 'I have no pleasure (*ḥpṣ*) in the death of the wicked, but that the wicked turn back from his way and live.' Here in 1 Sam 2.25, however, the failure of Eli's sons to listen to him, that is, to repent, is directly attributed to Yahweh's pleasure (*ḥpṣ*) in killing them /25/. Eli's efforts to turn his sons from their path to destruction is a predetermined failure. Try as he might his words fall on ears closed by Yahweh himself.

As in ch. 1, the narrator affords his audience a

clear view of the divine marionetteer working behind
the scene. As he sealed Hannah's womb to get Samuel so
now Yahweh prevents Eli's sons from listening to their
father.

The fact that this revelation is preceded by only
one other such insight into the direct divine intervention into human affairs provides an important and
obvious linkage of the two distinct actions. The birth
of Samuel and the ensuing deaths of Eli's sons are
henceforth inseparable. The rudimentary pattern of
birth (1.5) followed by death (2.25) suggests that the
birth was engineered in anticipation of the death. The
pattern at least makes room for such a hypothesis,
which can be confirmed or rejected as it conforms or
departs from the pattern of subsequent events.

Just as the divine initiative served as the efficient cause of events on the human plane leading up to
Samuel's birth and dedication, Yahweh's desire to kill
Eli's sons takes over in v. 25 as the efficient cause
of subsequent events. Had he not intervened, Eli's sons
might have repented and so changed the shape of subsequent events. Whatever happens, therefore can and
must be understood as the result of Yahweh's intention.
The sins of Eli's sons are hereafter causally subsidiary to Yahweh's desire.

It is worthwhile noting that v. 25 contains another
point to which the narrator has lent his own omniscient
authority. As with the description of Eli's sons in 2:12,
it is thereby mandatory for the reader to accept the
point. There can be no doubt about Yahweh's responsibility for the deaths of Eli's sons, as well as for
any circumstances directly attendant on their deaths.
Yahweh's 'desire' is the fourth such key to be given to
the reader for a proper understanding of the subsequent
course of events /26/.

Verse 26

Samuel is contrasted with the wicked Elides, as

many have noted (Smith 1899:20; Bourke 1954:82, 89; Hertzberg 1964:37; Willis 1971:289, 291; Péter-Contesse 1976:313f; McCarter 1980:85). The implication of Eli's warning in v. 25 was that his sons had sinned, perhaps against man, perhaps against Yahweh. Samuel, on the other hand, 'continued growing greater and better' (Driver 1913:36), with Yahweh and with men. The contrast is foregrounded by a chiasmus of objects, and the syntactic foregrounding is supplemented by the similar sounding prepositions that modify the objects:

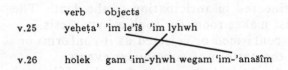

	verb	objects
v.25	yeḥeṭa'	'im le'îš 'im lyhwh
v.26	holek	gam 'im-yhwh wegam 'im-'anašîm

The effect of the contrast is a striking confirmation of the hypothesis that Yahweh has brought Samuel into the world as a replacement for Eli's sons, who are well on their way out. Eli's sons are sinning against man and God, who plans to kill them because of their sin. Samuel, on the other hand, is prospering with respect to the very persons - God and man - with whom the Elides are failing.

Hannah offers this prophetic comment on the fates of Eli's sons and her own son Samuel, 'The Lord killeth, and maketh alive: he bringeth down to the grave, and bringeth up' (1 Sam 2.6).

Verse 26 also serves to confirm the predominant traits of each of the three main characters. Explicitly it portrays Samuel, the good. By way of contrast it confirms Eli's sons as the bad. Finally, and also by way of the juxtaposition of Samuel and the Elides, vv. 25f presents, in an ugly mood, Yahweh, manipulator. He has arranged for a Samuel to replace the sons of Eli, whom he desires to kill.

Excursus on Verses 27-36

The man of God and his word of Yahweh have often been regarded as late-coming intruders imported by a deuteronomist (e.g. Smith 1899:21; Nowack 1902:xxxf [citing Kittel, Wellhausen, Budde, Smith, and Löhr in agreement]; Bourke 1954:73; Hertzberg 1964: 37; de Ward 1976:117; McCarter 1980:92f). Others have suggested that vv. 27-34 have only been elaborated by deuteronomistic additions, especially in vv. 35f (Press 1938: 187f; Buber 1964:819f; Tsevat 1961:195; J. Mauchline 1971:54; Stoebe 1973:118; Miller & Roberts 1977:21, 30f).

There are, nevertheless, several explicit literary connections between this episode and its preceding and subsequent contexts (Willis 1971:292f; 1972:38; 1979:208; Stoebe 1973:86, 117; Miller & Roberts 1977: 30). More important is the fact that this section of the narrative can be read, 'deuteronomistic additions' and all, as an important integral development in the narrative. As in the case of textual criticism, when the text itself presents us with a cohesive intelligible sequence there is no call, other than the siren song of genetic explanation, for supposing multiple composers and compositional periods. Even if the passage is 'replete with the devices and cliches of the Josianic historian' (McCarter 1980:92) and the latter could be convincingly dated, there are no comparable linguistic criteria by which the hypotheses of earlier literary versions could be substantiated. What we are faced with, instead, is an integral narrative punctuated with so-called deuteronomistic ideology.

Verse 27

That a man of God comes to Eli to make known to him the word of God is an ironic comment on the state of the Elide priesthood. The very first thing mentioned in the message is that God revealed himself to Eli's forebears while they were yet in Egypt and belonged to Pharaoh /27/. Now, in Israel, to the priests of his temple, Yahweh speaks only through a man of God.

The interrogative particle prefixed to *nigloh* expresses the belief that the subsequent information is well known and unconditionally admitted by the hearer (GKC #150e; cf. Gen 3.11; 27.36; 29.15; Deut 11.30; Judg 4.6, etc.). Yahweh states the grounds for his displeasure at the Elide priesthood. Their 'house' became priests because Yahweh graciously revealed himself to them and so they owe their privileged position to him.

According to H.-J. Zobel the niphal of *glh* is a specific technical term for revelation (1977:484). The revelation of Yahweh establishes a communicative channel between God and man (cf. Gen 35.7). The subsequent statement (v. 28) that Yahweh chose Eli's forebear shows that the revelation of Yahweh is the first step in the call to be a priestly intermediary (1977:484).

Verse 28

Yahweh privileged Eli's predecessors with a divine revelation, and established a permanent (*'ad-'ôlam*, v. 30) office wherein they could act as intermediaries between the God revealed to them and the men amongst whom they lived. The verse stresses the unique status of the priesthood bestowed upon the Elide predecessors. They are chosen *mikkol-šibṭê yiśra'el*. Horst Seebass' observations on *bḥr* neatly descibe the situation of Eli's predecessors, 'Everywhere that *bḥr* occurs in relationship to persons, it denotes choice out of a group (generally out of the totality of the people), so that the chosen one discharges a function in relationship to the group' (1977:82f).

The freedom bestowed by the revelation, releasing Eli's father from 'being [subject] to the house of Pharoah' (*biheyôtam lebêt par'oh*, v. 27) is not unlimited. His new allegiance is to Yahweh; he is now 'to Yahweh' (*ûbaḥor 'otô lî*, v. 28). In return for his liberating revelation Eli's father was given the duties of a priest. Remuneration for his services is given in the form of all the *'iššê* of the Israel- ites /28/.

An obvious parallel to the choice of the priests is alluded to in the mention of Egypt and Pharoah in v. 27. Israel too was freed from Egypt (Exod 19.4; Deut 7.8). It was chosen (*bḥr*, Deut 7.6) and given stipulated covenantal duties (Exod 19.5; Deut 7.11f). On the basis of these parallels it seems that what Yahweh rehearses in vv. 27f is the covenant he estab- lished with Eli's predecessors. Although the 'six common elements of the treaty form' are not given, Yahweh does rehearse those points vital to his case against the Elides /29/. They are indebted to Yahweh because he revealed himself to them in Egypt. They were commissioned to be his priests and were given specific benefits in payment for their services.

Verse 29

The Elide abuse of their covenantal election to the priesthood is described as *b'ṭ*, 'to kick.' The only parallel is found in a similar context in Deut 32.15. Jeshurun waxes fat (*wayyišman*) and kicks (*way- yib'aṭ*). He forsakes and scoffs at the God who saved him. The context reveals that Jeshurun has broken his covenant obligations to Yahweh. Similarly the Elides kick at Yahweh's sacrifices and offerings which he had commanded on 'account of sin' /30/. As in Deut 32.15, this 'kicking' is associated with the fact that the kickers have grown fat.

The 'kicking' is particularly heinous in the Elides' case. Not only do they desecrate Yahweh's provision for expiation of sin, but they get fat by taking the first part (*mere'šît*, cf. McCarter 1980:86) of the sac- rifice (cf. 2.15f). Obviously Yahweh sees this as an example of adding insult to injury.

Yahweh's accusation that Eli has honoured his sons before Yahweh must be weighed against the narrator's description of Eli's rebuke of his sons in vv. 23-25 and against the narrator's comment that Yahweh desired the death of Eli's sons /31/.

Verse 30

The obligatory covenantal requirements are laid out in vv. 27f, the infraction in v. 29, and now comes the punishment. The formal idiom of an oracle of doom is used as an ominous introduction (Hertzberg 1964:38; McCarter 1980:90). The use of the infinitive absolute *'amôr* before the verb *'amartî* recalls the previous use of this emphatic construction in v. 27. Yahweh reemphasizes his graciousness to the Elide line and the prosperous future that had awaited them.

The promise of a perpetual priesthood is revoked /32/. Yahweh only honours (*kbd*) those who honour (*kbd*) him, not those who honour (*kbd*) their sons more than God (v. 29). Those who treat him with contempt (*ûbozay*), as Eli's sons have (2.17), are cursed.

The requital Yahweh offers to the Elides reflects the language of covenantal retribution used in passages such as Exod 34.7; Num 14.18; and Deut 7.9f. According to J. A. Thompson these expressions have the appearance of liturgical formulae or confessional phrases (1974:131). Yahweh recites the confessional view of covenantal retribution in v. 30, and follows this recitation with the particulars to be meted out to the Elides /33/. He obviously sees himself as within his rights, as such are defined by the covenant.

Verse 31

In punishment Eli is to have his 'arm' and the 'arm' of his father's house cut off. The Elide dynasty is to be broken by cutting off its strength (*zeroa'*, Driver 1913:38). The statement that there will not be an old man (*zaqen*) in his house is pointed directly at Eli, who we know is *zaqen me'od* (v. 22).

The reference to a future implementation of the punishment (*yamîm ba'îm*) sets the reader in expectation of a specific fulfillment of Yahweh's words in the future. Any subsequent events that can be taken as fulfillment of the oracle will be so taken /34/.

Verse 32

As in v. 29, Seebass repoints *ma'ôn*, which is incomprehensible, to *me'awon* (1966:80). The verse would then read (ignoring Seebass' further emendations), 'And you will see affliction, on account of [your] sin, in everything that should/will be good for Israel. There will not be an old man in your house anymore.' The occurrence of the two words *me'awon* in v. 29 describes the reason for the sacrificial system. The priests and the system were chosen and commanded by Yahweh to provide a means of atoning for sin. Ironically in v. 32 it is because of sin, by implication the priests', that affliction will be seen in what should have been good for Israel. The repetition of *me'awon* draws attention to this reversal of the priestly effect on the people. Instead of averting the consequences of the people's sin by obtaining sacrificial atonement for it, the priests bring the evil consequences of their own sin down on everything that should have been good for Israel.

The ambiguity of the verb form *yêṭîb* does, however, allow for two readings /35/. Either Yahweh is hinting at the fact that the priests' sin will bring affliction to all Israel instead of the 'good' that they expect to gain from the priestly offices, or he is saying that future benefits to Israel will appear as afflictions to Eli.

Two factors militate against the second alternative.

First, Yahweh says that Eli, 'the old man,' will see this affliction. Since he dies in 4.18, the event referred to must occur prior to that verse. Secondly, the second sentence states that there will not be an old man in Eli's house in the future. That is, there will be no Eli (cf. v. 22) in the future to see all the good that is supposed to be done for Israel. In view of these two considerations the first possibility, that v. 32a refers to the affliction that Eli will see over-taking Israel because of the sin of its priests, is attractive /36/. In v. 32b, Eli is told that having seen the affliction, he, himself an old man, will cease to exist.

In this reading of what Smith appropriately called 'so desperate a passage,' v. 32 contributes to an anticipation of impending disaster already developed in v. 31. A specific chronological pattern has been given, and it coincides with the events of ch. 4. First, Eli sees the expected Israelite victory (*kol 'ašer-yêṭib 'et-yiśra'el*) turned into a terrible defeat (4.1-11) /37/. Then he himself is killed (4.18). The exact nature of the affliction and the potential good to Israel is left for the reader to discover in ch. 4.

Verse 32 introduces a central issue in chs. 1-12. In the theocratic system the people are very much affected by their leaders. Yahweh had established the priests as covenant mediators in charge of the cult. The latter, as Yahweh notes in vv. 28f, is an essential feature of the covenant, allowing as it does for the expiation of sin. When the officials of this vital institution are themselves sinful and contemptuous of Yahweh their sin cannot be expiated or palliated by prayer (2.25f; 3.14). The priests must die. The theocratic political system, that is the covenant in which Yahweh is sovereign and Israel subject, requires upright human leaders for its smooth operation.

But this problem carries with it an even worse consequence which is mentioned here in v. 32. The sin of the priests, and they are the only ones who have sinned

so far, brings affliction to Israel. That Yahweh is
able to tell Eli, before the fact, that Israel will be
adversely affected by the sin of its priests, indicates
that the defeat and slaughter of innocent Israelites is
not spontaneous. Israel's fate is closely tied to that
of its priestly leaders in the covenantally constituted
theocracy.

On this point, A. F. Campbell has suggested that the
punishment of the Elides is incommensurate with the
national catastrophe of ch. 4 (1975:175). 'The loss of
the ark, two defeats and the death of 34,000 men is a
steep price to pay for the punishment of two or three
errant priests. Can this be justified by the central
role of these priests in the nation?' (1979:35). He
concludes that the concerns of ch. 4 are largely unrelated to those of ch. 2.

Campbell, however, has unknowingly put his finger
on a key issue in chs. 1-4, and indeed in chs. 1-12.
The defeat at Aphek is the fulfillment of the prophesied punishment and the question posed by Campbell
is the question posed by the narrative. Is the theocracy with its covenant, its intermediaries, its
stipulations, and especially its unpredictable God a
desirable system? Are there imbalances in the system
that create political havoc for all on the basis of
the sacral misdeeds of a few who happen to be leaders?

Verses 33-36

Verses 33, 35-36 have occasionally been interpreted
as the *vaticinia ex eventu* insertions of a deuteronomist /38/. R. Press, for example, suggests 'thus v.
33 heralds the catastrophe at Nob' (1938:191). The
debate over the historical identification of the events
and characters referred to in vv. 33, 35f has a long
history. (Keil & Delitzsch, 1880:44-48, give early
examples.)

Keil and Delitzsch offer the suggestion that we

should allow the possibility of multiple fulfillments
of the prophecy within a typological framework (1880:
46f). Certainly that option is able to accommodate all
possible identifications, thereby conforming interpretation to the ambiguity inherent in the prophecy itself.
Depending on the context in which a reader has chosen
to read the prophecy, different possibilities arise
/39/.

The typological approach to the identity of the
referents in the text comes close to certain modern
theories of reader-oriented and structuralist critics.
The following statement of Jonathan Culler exhibits
important similarities to the typological approach.
'To read a text as literature is not to make one's mind
a *tabula rasa* and approach it without preconceptions;
. . . the semiological approach suggests, rather, that the
poem be thought of as an utterance that has meaning
only with respect to a system of conventions which the
reader has assimilated. If other conventions were oper-
ative its range of potential meanings would be different' (quote from Tompkins 1980:xviif) /40/. 'The Rabbins' could never agree with Keil and Delitzsch or
Gutbrod about the identity of the faithful priest in v.
35 because they operate from different conventional
bases of interpretation.

Since the present reading is made from the context
of 1 Sam 1-12, the present concern is to determine
what, if any, subsequent characters and events are
referred to by vv. 33, 35f. The decision to read within this context is no more or less arbitrary than the
decision to read in terms of the so-called deuteronomistic history (McCarter), the Hebrew Bible ('the
Rabbins'), or the Old and New Testaments (Gutbrod).

An indication of the validity of a reading of the
prophecy made upon the basis of its immediate context
is found in the favourable comments on this option by
those who have chosen different contexts. McCarter,
for example, says, 'Indeed we are bound to say that on
the basis of our reading of the childhood narrative of

Samuel up to this point and of the sequel to this passage in 3.1-4:1a, Samuel emerges incontestably as the successor to the prerogatives of the house of Eli' (1980:92). He then rejects this 'incontestable' reading in favour of one made in the context of the deuteronomistic history. Tsevat too sees the possibility of a connection between 2.27-36 and chs. 3-4, but rejects it (1961:207).

Verse 33

The man left to Eli at Yahweh's altar after the death of Eli (v. 32) and his sons (vv. 31, 33, 34) could be either Ichabod (4.20, 21) or Samuel, who can be said to be 'to Eli' (*leka*) as a servant and apprentice. Samuel and Eli are close enough, in fact, for Eli to call him 'my son' (3.6, 16). Against Ichabod is the conclusion of v. 33, which says that all the increase of Eli's house will die as men. Ichabod is presumably included here and so will be at Yahweh's altar (*'im mizbeḥî*) neither as a cultic functionary nor even as a man. Furthermore it is difficult to see how the continued existence of Ichabod can be construed as a punishment that would waste Eli's eyes and make his soul pine away /41/.

Samuel, on the other hand, would be a suitable candidate for this role. The fact that a temple servant will outlast Eli and his house would be sufficient cause for grief to Eli. The identification of Samuel as the *'îš* of v. 33 also fits the immediate context of complete doom for the Elides. Finally, it should be noted that Samuel builds an altar to Yahweh in 7.17 and survives through the remainder of the narrative as the only active priest (7.9f; 9.12-14; 10.8; 12.23). He does, in fact, replace Eli at Yahweh's altar.

Verse 34

The sign given to Eli is that his sons will both die

on the same day. It is given because Eli will not be around to see the installation of his successor; it is to be taken by Eli as an indication that the various events prophesied are about to take place (cf. Keil & Delitzsch 1880:45; Smith 1899:23). The fulfillment of this prophecy in 4.11 is an incontestable link between chs. 1-3 and ch. 4.

Campbell, however, reasons that if ch. 4 was intended as the accomplishment of the prophecies in chs. 1-3 one would justifiably expect an indication, such as that in 1 Kgs 2.26-37, that the prophetic word had come to pass (1975:175). The answer to Campbell's difficulty may be found in 2.34. Yahweh says that the death of Eli's sons is an *'ôt*, a sign. As Gunkel notes, a sign 'is an object, an occurrence, an event through which a person is to recognize, learn, remember, or perceive the credibility of something' (quote from Helfmeyer 1977:170). 'The significant thing about a sign is not the sign itself, but its function . . . it calls attention to, confirms, or corroborates something beyond itself . . .' (p. 183).

The fact of the simultaneous death of Eli's sons in 4.11 is all that is needed, at that point, for both Eli and the reader to know that they are witnessing prophecy fulfilled in ch. 4. The functional nature of the sign along with the several other links between 2.27-36 and ch. 4 justify reading them as prophecy and fulfillment.

Verse 35

The substitute for the Elide priests is characterized. According to Buber the faithful priest of 2.35 is, in fact, the reliable prophet of 3.20, namely Samuel. The prophet shall take over from the priest, whose office is destroyed along with the temple (1964: 820).

Buber supplements this observation with the links between 2.27, 3.7; and 3.21: the repetition of the verb

glh in the Niphal signifies, he argues, that the old
priestly revelation, now become unworthy, is replaced
by a new prophetic revelation.

Buber is correct in his observation that Samuel is
not simply a cultic priest. Instead he combines several
occupations in one career /42/. Included among his activities is his priestly role, prepared for in chs. 1-3 and
implemented in chs. 7-12. The case for Samuel grows
stronger when Samuel's origin and priestly apprentice-
ship are considered. One recalls that his birth to a barren woman bears the mark of divine intervention and
purpose. He is Yahweh's all the days of his life (1.11,
28) and grows up as an apprentice to Eli (2.11, 18, 26;
3.1, 3). He wears the priestly clothing (2.18). Finally, the juxtaposition of the 'outgoing' priests and the
growing favour of Samuel in 2.25f foreshadows the succession.

Consequently, when Yahweh says he will raise a
faithful priest for himself the reader is encouraged by
preceding events to conclude that Yahweh is simply
making explicit the developments he had planned ever
since he closed and then opened Hannah's womb. This
conclusion will be subsequently confirmed both in the
literary links noted by Buber and in the simple facts
of Samuel's subsequent actions as Israel's new covenant
mediator.

Hertzberg sees a problem arising for this reading
in the statement that Yahweh will build a faithful
house for Samuel. As we know from 8.3-5, Samuel's sons
also go astray. Samuel's house does not, therefore,
seem to continue from generation to generation as the
prophecy implies (1964:38). It should be noted, however, that unlike Eli's sons, who are killed for their
sins, Samuel's sons are still around in 12.2. From
the context it appears that they still operate in an
official capacity. Subsequently we hear no more of
Samuel's sons due to the shifting focus of the narrative. We cannot conclude, however, that Samuel's
house was not 'faithful.' Alternatively, one might

note that Yahweh's promises of unending tenure to his chosen officials (e.g. 2:30) are conditional upon good behavior, Samuel's house included.

The final statement in v. 35 can be read as an anticipation of the monarchy established in chs. 9-12. The reader is prepared for subsequent events, albeit more with perplexity than anticipation or foreknowledge. Throughout the prophecy, Yahweh demonstrates his own awareness of future events and reveals his plans for those events. In fact, one of Yahweh's most constant traits throughout the whole of chs. 1-12 is fore-knowledge of future situations in his covenantal relationship with Israel.

Yahweh's prediction also contains a subtle indication of the type of monarchy to be introduced. The fact that the king is referred to as *mešîḥî* suggests that some future monarch will be established by Yahweh and be held responsible to him. Anointment makes the king a theocratic vassal of Yahweh (Szikszai 1962:139). Without a prior awareness of the issues raised in ch. 8 the reader is unlikely, however, to comprehend Yahweh's surreptitious anticipation of chs. 9-12. It is a private irony enjoyed by Yahweh alone.

Verse 36

It is especially in v. 35 that the identification of the faithful priest encounters difficulty. Nowhere can this prediction be seen in Samuel's career. Scholars have, therefore, turned to Zadok as the priest and suggest that v. 36 refers to the Levites, who in consequence of the Josianic reform (2 Kgs. 23.9) were forced to come begging at the Temple (Mauchline 1971: 56; Tsevat 1961:192f; McCarter 1980:93).

Noth agreed, at first, with this judgement and labelled the prophecy a *vaticinium ex eventu* product of the deuteronomist (1967:61). He later repudiated this view of the prophecy, correctly observing 'Verse 36 is not a deuteronomistic formulation and cannot be

reconciled, on the basis of context, with the details
of 2 Kgs 23.8f' (1963:394). Noth's solution to the
referential problem posed by v. 36 is to suggest that
we have no certain grounds for dating it and even less
certain grounds to specify a situation in which it was
fulfilled: 'An inspired word of a 'man of God' against
the earlier Shilonite priesthood and its thorough de-
generation and for the royal priesthood of Jerusalem
is in itself quite conceivable' (1963:394).

In view of their radically different presuppositions
it is remarkable that Keil and Delitzsch arrive at a
similar result. Just as they see the prophecy of the
faithful priest fulfilled in both Samuel and Zadok so
'the threat announces deep degradation and even destruction to all the priests of the house of Aaron who
should walk in the footsteps of the sons of Eli . . .'
(1880:46).

The readings suggested by Noth and especially by
Keil and Delitzsch are most compatible with the vagueness of the prophecy. The only specific information
given is the sign. The death of Hophni and Phinehas
is supposed to show both Eli and the reader that the
fulfillment of the prophecy is beginning. The reader
is thereby provoked to identify the other events prophesied, and is given opportunity to do so for all
except v. 36 in the course of reading chs. 3-12.

For v. 36, the reader is required to continue
through the books of Samuel and Kings in search of a
suitable referential candidate. The apparent lack of
correspondence between the prophesied situation of v.
36 and that of the 'Levites' in 2 Kgs 23.9 suggests
that most readers will come to identifications some-
where between Keil and Delitzsch's multiple typology
and the identification of Levites as in 2 Kgs 23.9.

The prophecy of the man of God in vv. 27-36 exhibits the characteristics of the literary phenomenon that
Iser calls 'blanks":

The blank, however, designates a vacancy in the over-

all system of the text, the filling of which brings
about an interaction of textual patterns . . . It is
only when the schemata of the text are related to
one another that the imaginary object can begin to
be formed, and it is the blanks that get this con-
necting operation under way. They indicate that the
different segments of the text are to be connected,
even though the text itself does not say so. They
are the unseen joints of the text, and as they mark
off schemata and textual perspectives from one another they simultaneously trigger acts of ideation
on the reader's part. Consequently, when the schemata and perspectives have been linked together,
the blanks 'disappear' (1978:182f)

The prophetic sign says 'begin here,' but it is up to
each reader to decide what fulfills what (Iser's 'acts
of ideation on the reader's part'). It is important to
note, however, that 4.11 presents an explicit textual
directive forcing the reader to scrutinize the immediately subsequent context. This explicit connection
stacks the odds in favour of reading the subsequent
events and characters, insofar as possible, as those
referred to by the prophecy.

Perry's notion of a reader's frame construction is
also relevant here. The reader who has read the prophecy will not fail to construct a 'frame' that incorporates the events of chs. 3-7 as the fulfillment of
the prophecy in 2.27-36. 'The reader does not wait until the end before beginning to understand it, before
embarking upon its semantic integration' (Perry 1979:
46). If subsequent information is given that contradicts the constructed frame the reader will then modify or reject it.

Within chs. 1-12, however, such contradiction does
not occur. If the final verse of the prophecy cannot be
recognized as fulfilled before ch. 12 the reader will
wait and watch for its subsequent fulfillment, whatever
that may be.

PART THREE

1 SAMUEL 3

Excursus on the Context of Chapter 3

In ch. 3, the narrator describes the concluding events
in the transfer of human authority from the priestly
Elides to Samuel, who begins the chapter as a priestly
servant (v. 1) and ends as a prophet (vv. 20f). It is
to this end that the miraculous birth story (ch. 1),
the contrasts between the families of Samuel and Eli
(chs. 1-2), and the prophetic rejection of the Elide
priests (2.27-36) have been moving. Events in ch. 1-
2.26 proceed in mysterious concatenation towards the
climactic message from Yahweh in 2.27-36. Though the
narrator gives several hints at the connections between
the fates of the Elides and Samuel, he never provides
an explicit and detailed prediction of the end towards
which their intertwining paths are surely proceeding.
The veiled structural hints about that end, as well as
the revelations that there is a divine purpose behind
the events of chs. 1-2, are only specific enough to
allow the reader to create hypotheses about the significance of the events. The result is the creation
of a great deal of narrative interest, which prods the
reader on in hopes of discovering the connection or of
having it openly revealed to him.

In the prophetic message of 2.27-36, God reveals his
reading of preceding events and lays out a rather ambiguous prophetic plan for the future. Though some of
the possible contextual readings of the prophecy were
explored in anticipatory fashion in the preceding dis-

cussion of 2.27-36, these were not intended to suggest
that the reader would entertain all or any such hypotheses. While trying, of course, to interpret the prophecy on first reading it (and even, perhaps, arriving at
hypotheses such as those suggested above), the reader
will remain absolutely dependent on the narrator to
conform or reject these suspicions. Chapter 3, following hard on the heels of the divine revelation, does
exactly that, as the narrator describes the events in
which the Elide priestly presence is obviated.

In accord with the general narrational principles
described by Ruhl's algorithm /1/, the narrator has
placed Samuel's call immediately after the prophecy,
leading the reader to see events in ch. 3 as the fulfillment of ch. 2. The narrator takes obvious care
to ensure that his reader follows the logic of his
plot. The reader must be aware that the prophecy
is being enacted and that Yahweh is guiding these
events.

Chapter 3 describes the state of Israelite leadership in terms of the revelation of Yahweh, both aural
and visual; it contains six references to visual revelation or sight, and sixteen to aural revelation. Good
leadership allows for open communications from Yahweh (vv. 19-21), bad leadership restricts it (vv. 1f).

A link with the prophecy in 2.27-36 is also forged
with the vocabulary of revelation. The Elide line had
been elected to the priesthood when Yahweh revealed
himself (*hanigloh niglêtî*) to them in Egypt
(2.27). The Elide corruption is cause for annulment
of their election (2.30) and contact with Yahweh via
vision or word thereafter becomes very rare (v. 1; cf.
Willis 1971:292f).

As compensation for the loss of divine revelation
through the medium of the priestly Elides, Yahweh
grants Samuel a vision (v. 15), and speaks directly to
him (vv. 4-14). As a result of the fulfillment of the
message he then transmits, Samuel becomes established as the reliable prophet of Yahweh (3.20). Yahweh

reappears at Shiloh *because of* (*kî*) his self-revelation (*niglâ yhwh*) to Samuel (3.21). Samuel replaces the Elides as the human receptor and agent of the divine revelation. His installation in this important mediating office allows for renewed communication from Yahweh (cf. Newman 1962:89f; Buber 1964:819).

Verse 1

The introductory description of the lad Samuel resumes the characterization of him begun in ch. 1 (Noth 1963:392). He is Yahweh's servant. The portrait of Samuel has an even closer link with 2.11, with which it is almost identical. There are several significant variants (underlined below), however, which can be viewed as the product of intervening events:

3.1 wehanna'ar šemû'el mešaret 'et-yhwh lipnê 'elî
2.11 wehanna'ar hayâ mešaret 'et-yhwh 'et-penê 'elî hakkohen

As always when the name 'Samuel' is used, the narrator reminds the reader of the special meaning of Samuel's existence and of the purpose which brought him into being. Immediately after the prophecy of the Elide rejection the reader is led to recall that Samuel is Yahweh's missionary. The contrast between Elides and Samuel is, again, obvious. We know from the prophecy that Yahweh plans to replace Eli and his sons. Samuel's appearance, serving Yahweh, immediately after the promise of a new priest is conspicious and invites the reader to entertain the thought that Samuel is that priest.

In 2.11, the lad serves Yahweh and 'the face' of Eli, both of which are modified by the accusative particle *'et*. In 3.11, however, Samuel serves only Yahweh, doing so 'before' or 'in the presence of' (*lipnê*) Eli. The reason for this change is revealed by the final variant: Eli is no longer called 'the

priest' in 3.11; he is simply called Eli. Samuel no
longer serves Eli 'with' Yahweh because Eli has lost
the rank and title of priest. Already Eli takes a back
seat to Samuel in the priestly service (against
Mauchline 1971:57).

The second two sentences in v. 1 describe the state
of divine communications in the period after the Elide
rejection. It is the only description of the conditions
of that time, and serves as an important indicator of
the effects of the upheaval in covenanted relations
between Yahweh and his priests. The preciousness of
Yahweh's word and the sparsity of vision could indicate either that Yahweh has nothing to say to Israel,
or that the official receptors of the vision, the
Elides (cf. 2.27), were unfit to mediate any revelations. Given that Eli is no longer called 'priest,'
it is most likely that there is no suitable recipient
for the revelations of Yahweh. In fact, this is exactly
the point, for when Samuel has come to know Yahweh
through the revelation of his word, Yahweh reappears
at Shiloh (v. 21).

The narrator momentarily shifts the reader's attention away from the characters to the state of affairs
in covenantal communication with this brief note
about the lack of such communication. He thereby
exhibits his concern that the reader bear in mind the
effect that the sin of the priests and the counter
measures of Yahweh are having in the larger arena
of the theocracy as a whole. Obviously it is a dangerous situation for the union when the political
leader refuses to communicate with the citizens.

Verse 2

Commentators have expressed doubts about how to
read the initial temporal clause in v. 2 and about its
bearing on the events at hand (e.g. Wellhausen 1871:
51; Smith 1899:25). According to GKC (#126s), the
phrase simply means 'one day.' McCarter translates 'at

that time' and states that the phrase introduces a syntactical sequence of ordinary past narration (1980: 97). What follows the phrase would, according to McCarter's translation, take place at the same time as what immediately preceded.

More significant is the link that the phrase provides with v. 1. In v. 1, we read that 'In those days (*bayyamîm hahem*) the word of Yahweh was precious, and the vision sparse.' In v. 2, we read that 'At that time (*bayyôm hahû'*) Eli was lying in his place, his eyes were failing and he could not see.' The repeated temporal phrase reinforces the semantic parallel between the two verses. The scarcity of word or vision from Yahweh is a parallel, and perhaps even the logical result, on the physical plane of the blindness of Israel's priestly leader.

The attention drawn to this parallel by the temporal phrases reinforces the point made in v. 1. Together, vv. 1-2 suggest that a capable, functioning priest is necessary for the regular communication of messages from God, which are necessary for the maintenance of the theocracy. As in the Mosaic model, the institutional mediator receives the message from God and transmits it to the people (Exod 20:18-26). When the mediator is nonfunctioning, the quantity of divine communication is reduced.

The communications that are sent when the institutional mediator is out of commission, such as that delivered by the man of God in 2.27-36, are exceptional and few in number. The purpose of such special revelations is not simply to continue the regular communications through a different channel. Rather, as the example of 2.27-36 shows, they often are directed against the institutional means of communication, and aim only at tearing down the existing figures. The task of building up is left to God's own subsequent action.

The description of Eli, lying in his place, contrasts unfavourably with that of Samuel in both vv. 1 and 3. While Samuel actively serves Yahweh in v. 1,

Eli lies dormant in v. 2. Whereas Eli lies in *his* place, Samuel lies in Yahweh's temple (v. 3) /2/. Samuel attends to Yahweh's needs while Eli attends to his own. These contrasts support the succession of Samuel to Eli's position in the mediating office.

Though the narrator has not agreed with Yahweh's criticisms of Eli (cf. above on 2.22-25 and 29), he has suggested that Eli's great age is having a detrimental effect on his ability to carry out his important duties as the head priest. In the contrast between Eli and Samuel in 3.1-3 it is also Eli's feebleness in old age that serves as the basis for the narrator's contrast. The young Samuel remains in the temple, ready, able and willing to carry out any duty immediately. Eli, on the other hand, lies in his own place; the reader recognizes the familiar image of a tired, old man who relies on the comfort and security of his own place. In the narrator's contrast Eli is not sinful, just old. The contrast does show, however, that a transition from Eli to Samuel is desirable.

Verse 3

In contrast to the atmosphere of darkness and unknowing in vv. 1f, symbolized by Eli's blindness and the scarcity of vision, v. 3 presents the hope of the future. The technique of foreshadowing a resolution to a present problem used in v. 3 has already been seen in 1.18. Here in v. 3, the insertion of the word *terem* in the sentence 'The lamp of God has not yet (*terem*) gone out,' indicates that, though the situation described in vv. 1f is gloomy, there is still hope. The flame is not yet completely extinguished.

The lamp of God, still burning, is a symbol that God has not totally cut off relations with Israel on account of the Elides. In Exod 27.2 (cf. Lev 24.2), Yahweh commands that a lamp be kept ever lit in the tabernacle. As with the other furnishings and the tabernacle itself, the lamp represents the presence of

Yahweh, in accord with his covenanted pledge to be with Israel (Lev 26.12-13; cf. Childs 1974:540). Helmer Ringgren suggests that the lamp provided a vivid image of the divine presence (1966:91) /3/.

Associated with the lamp of God, symbol of God's presence and communication with Israel, is Samuel who lies in the temple. Through this associative parallelism the narrative identifies Samuel as a glimmer of light in the general darkness of that time (cf. Bourke 1954:85). The narrative has drawn the comparison between Samuel and Eli in terms of clear-cut opposites:

Samuel	Eli
lies in the temple	lies in his place
the light still burns	blindness, lack of vision or word from God

Commentators have generally missed the symbolic contrast between Samuel and Eli. The significance of God's burning lamp is seen to lie in its temporal definition (it was not yet dawn) (Thenius 1864:16; Keil & Delitzsch 1880:49; Smith 1899:26; McCarter 1980: 98). Although the temporal dimension of the lamp does function as part of the general setting for the events of ch. 3 it has much greater significance as a symbol. As Stoebe noted with respect to ch. 1 the importance of details in this narrative lies in their significance for the theological-political issues raised by the narrative. Hence the reading that sees the mention of the still burning lamp as a temporal detail should be expanded to include the symbolism. As the still-burning lamp shows that dawn was near, so Samuel lying in the temple is a sign that a new dawn in Israelite leadership is also near.

Similarly, Buber observes that the mention of the ark, at first glance a mere scenic elaboration, is in fact of special significance in view of subsequent events. The introduction of the ark here links it with Yahweh's message of doom. Samuel receives the message

in the presence of the cultic object that will play a
major role in the subsequent destruction of the Elides
(1964:825; cf. Stoebe 1973:124) /4/.

In addition, it should be noted that like the still-
burning lamp, the ark appears in immediate association
with Samuel in the temple. The reader finds Samuel
sandwiched between these two symbols of God's presence and covenantal relationship with Israel. The narrator seems to be trying to rub some of this symbolism
onto the figure of Samuel by literally surrounding him
with it (cf. below on 4.4).

Verses 4-10

That Yahweh has to try three times before he can
talk to Samuel is an indication of both Samuel's
ignorance about Yahweh and Eli's lack of perceptive-
ness. Samuel's ignorance is youthfully innocent, for
Yahweh has not yet revealed his word to him (v. 7).
Eli's unperceptiveness, on the other hand, is probably
again a result of his failing powers in old age. In
addition, Yahweh's persistence indicates that he has
something important to say and that it is intended
specifically for Samuel's ears.

The reader, who is by now well aware of the general
direction that events are taking, remembers Yahweh's
last revelation through the man of God which contained a reference to a replacement for Eli. Samuel's continual failure to receive his divine visitor is a
source of increasing tension to the reader, who begins
to doubt Samuel's intelligence. Will Yahweh abandon
the attempt to communicate with the duteous but ob-
tuse Samuel?

Samuel's speedy response to Yahweh's call is to
run to Eli, in the belief that Eli had called. Three
times Yahweh calls and three times Samuel presents
himself to Eli. Samuel appears as the young man with
great things in store for him, who still runs to Eli
in boyish respect when he thinks he is being called

(Stoebe 1973: 125). The insight into Samuel's character afforded by this incident, nevertheless, evokes a positive response from the reader. Though naive, Samuel is willing and responsive. Even his ignorance makes Samuel shine in the reader's eyes.

Press, discussing the rhetorical function of the threefold call, suggests that the tension produced by Samuel and Eli's continuing misunderstanding creates 'an intensification of interest and a prominencing of the expected oracle' (1938:184). Yet as in the description of the lamp in 3.2, a future resolution to a problem, in this case Samuel's ignorance of Yahweh, is hinted at by a temporal modifier attached to the description of the problem. Samuel does not yet (*terem*) know Yahweh, the word of Yahweh is not yet (*terem*) revealed to him (3.7). The reader is given to understand, even before Yahweh successfully communicates to Samuel, that Yahweh will eventually get a message through, Samuel will know Yahweh, and the latter's word will be revealed to him (cf. *terem*, as it functions in 3.3).

Verse 11

When Samuel finally responds correctly to Yahweh's call, with the knowledge of who is calling, Yahweh is able to speak.

It is Eli who is responsible for the success of Yahweh's third attempt to communicate with Samuel. Eli finally discerns (*wayyaben*, v. 8) that Yahweh is calling the boy, and so tells Samuel how to respond. The narrator could have arranged his narrative so that Eli had no part in the success, but he did not. It is ironic that Eli should contribute to his successor's rise, but it is not a condemnation. If anything, Eli comes out of ch. 3 as a tragic figure.

Yahweh's mention of the location, 'in Israel,' of the thing he is going to do, and the statement that it will make all its auditors' ears buzz, seem to indicate

an event of national significance /5/. Gutbrod understands the national import of the punishment in terms
of the loss of the covenantal mediation of the priesthood (1956:34). While he is correct, it is also possible that Yahweh is hinting at the even more horri-
fying repercussions of the priests' punishment seen
in the Israelite defeat in ch. 4. Whether or not this
allusion is contained in v. 11, the effects of Yahweh's
action are such as to affect *all* Israel. The reader
familiar with the conventional implication of an 'ear-
buzzing' event is at least certain that the impending
disaster will not be limited to an effect on the Elide
priesthood alone.

Verses 12-14

As often noted, v. 12 refers directly back to 2.27-
36 (e.g. McCarter 1980:98). Samuel is alerted to the
fact that all is not right between Yahweh and Eli.
Yahweh claims that Eli knew of his sons' sin yet did
not 'rebuke' them (v. 13) /6/.

Again (cf. 2.29), the reader must evaluate Yahweh's
claim in the light of the authoritative information
provided by the narrator that Eli *did* warn his sons
and that they did not listen because Yahweh desired
to kill them (2.25). Yahweh is not telling the whole
story to Samuel. As the reader watches the innocent
young man being indoctrinated with an explanation of
the ensuing disaster that is only partially true, he is
once again filled with foreboding about the future of
the people whose fate lies in the hands of this God.

Yahweh's half-truth also compromises Samuel's
innocence by indoctrinating him with an understanding
of what has happened and will happen that will make
him an unquestioning ally and representative of Yahweh's position. Samuel was born to serve Yahweh. but
the reader did not know until now just what such
membership in the theocratic service might mean.

Yahweh's revelations to Samuel confirm the reader

in the view that was forced upon him by the narrator's differences with Yahweh in ch. 2. Yahweh has engineered the unnecessary destruction of the Elides and now he is grooming his own pawn to take their place. If he had not desired to kill Eli's sons, perhaps they would have listened to their father, and if he told Samuel the truth about Eli's efforts to reform his sons perhaps Samuel would not be quite so dogmatically loyal to Yahweh.

As the reader stands looking over the narrator's shoulder while Yahweh interprets past and future for Samuel, he has no doubts about who is shaping the course of events. Whatever happens, Yahweh is responsible.

Yahweh's presentation of his punishment for the Elides aims at an appearance of just retribution. As Stoebe observes, v. 14 seems an appropriate denial of expiation to the Elides (1973:125). They 'kicked' at Yahweh's *zebaḥ* and *minḥâ* (2.29), which were instituted for sin (*me'awon*) /7/. As their punishment, therefore, they are denied the use of *zebaḥ* or *minḥâ* to expiate their sin (*'awon bêt-'elî*). What could be more just than such measure for measure punishment?

Verses 15-16

Samuel lies down until morning and then opens the doors of Yahweh's house /8/. Bourke, alone, seems to have noticed the symbolic significance of this gesture. Citing 2 Paraleipomenon 28f, where good King Ezechias opens the temple doors closed by his wicked father, he suggests that Samuel's act symbolizes the restoration of God's word to Israel (1954:86). Samuel, associated with the still-burning lamp in v. 2, floods the temple with the light of morning; 'good has prevailed over evil, and light over darkness' (1954:86).

As his ignorance did before in vv. 4-9, Samuel's fear introduces a tension into the narrative. Will

Samuel tell Eli what he knows? The narrative highlights the similarity of the two situations by using
the same call and reply scheme used before: Eli calls
Samuel, 'Samuel my son,' and Samuel says, 'Here I am.'
Samuel's simple reply shows his submission to Eli
and perhaps his reluctance to say anything at all.

Verses 17-18

Eli wants all the details and seems to assume that
it is bad news. The oath formula that he uses to encourage Samuel to 'tell all' - 'May God do so to you
and more also, if you hide anything from me of all
that he told you' - is only coercive if the content of
the message is actually bad. Eli seems to have drawn
the conclusion that the divine message to Samuel is
about his termination as priest. Eli could reasonably
suspect this both because of the message he himself
had received in 2.27-36, and because Yahweh had chosen to avoid him and had spoken instead to the young
temple servant.

Eli's response to Samuel's news has usually been
understood as an expression of resignation and even
pious submission to the will of God (e.g. Keil &
Delitzsch 1880:51; Hertzberg 1964:42; Willis 1971:
291; Stoebe 1973:126). McCarter's translation (1980:
95) exemplifies the pious reading, 'He is Yahweh. Let
him do what seems best to him!'

On the other hand, it seems odd that Eli, who of all
people should know that Yahweh's claim that he did not
try to stop his sons was not true, should capitulate so
easily to a spurious condemnation /9/. Admittedly he is
dealing with Yahweh, and so has no higher authority to
turn to, but he could at least try to save his reputation.

I would suggest that Eli does not simply lie down,
but his only sympathizers are those who share his knowledge and so appreciate the ironic ambiguity of his
answer to the message delivered to Samuel: 'He is Yah-

weh, he does as he pleases.' Eli's reply is an expression of despair. How can man resist God? Since Eli does not know that we readers are out here listening, our impression of the tragic isolation of his situation is strengthened. Certainly the innocent, but now indoctrinated Samuel could not appreciate the despair contained in Eli's ambiguous reply. For Samuel, like the majority of commentators, Eli's remark would only seem to be a humble acceptance of just punishment.

Eli's remark is in agreement with 2.25, in which the omniscient narrator reveals the hidden divine intention. Yahweh wants to slay Eli's sons and he is going to do it. Eli's remark also casts an ominous shadow over the unknown future. If Yahweh is so concerned with the proper punishment of the sons of Eli that he allows his anger to outstrip his sense of justice - his ability to discriminate between guilty persons and innocent bystanders - then anyone who is associated with or even in the vicinity of the Elides is in danger. Yahweh's treatment of Eli is a harbinger of things to come.

The alternative reading of Eli's reply to Samuel as pious submission can be seen as a reflection of Eli's realization that Yahweh is answerable to no one. Fearing a fate worse than death, Eli hides his cynicism about Yahweh beneath the guise of piety and submission to the Almighty. It is, therefore, not a question of favouring either one or the other reading, but of realizing the ambiguity and including both as mutually interacting opposites /10/.

Verse 19

The placement of a note that Yahweh is with Samuel at this particular point highlights the fact that Yahweh has confirmed Samuel as the replacement for Eli. As always, Yahweh's presence with Israel, or an Israelite, is to be considered as a sign of divine favour and blessing (cf. Exod 3.12; Josh 1.5; Zimmerli

1978:70-81). The description of Samuel's growth is paralleled by 2.21, but there is a difference that underlines the fact that Yahweh has now chosen Samuel as Eli's replacement:

2.21   wayyigdal hanna'ar šemû'el 'im-yhwh
3.19   wayyigdal šemû'el wyhwh hayâ 'immô

Samuel was growing with/under the influence of Yahweh. Now, he has grown and Yahweh is with him. Yahweh's choice of Samuel is highlighted both by the contextual contrast provided by 2.21, and by the fact that Yahweh is the subject of *hayâ* in 3.19, which implies volition on his part.

Most commentators have observed that the expression, 'he did not allow his words to fall to the ground,' indicates that the information conveyed by Yahweh to Samuel and by Samuel to Eli accurately describes subsequent events (e.g. McCarter 1980:99) /11/.

This observation from the narrator takes the reader once again behind the human scenes to the place of hidden divine activity. Yahweh has indoctrinated his apprentice with an interpretation of what will happen to the Elides, and now he ensures that events are made to correspond to that interpretation. When the narrator tells us that Yahweh 'did not allow his words to fall to the ground' we can only believe that Yahweh shaped the course of events to agree with the words. The narrator's 'back-stage' observation assures the reader that disaster will overtake the Elides at the same time that it reveals the divine hand moulding Samuel into a believer by shaping events.

Verse 20

The description of Israel's recognition of Samuel's status as a 'reliable' prophet of Yahweh presupposes a message that Samuel gives, and which proves to be true

/12/. Both here and in v. 19, the narrator makes a point of anticipating the fulfillment of the judgement on the Elides. The people of Israel, recognizing its fulfillment, come to a knowledge of Samuel's prophetic capabilities.

That the people's recognition is narrated prior to the event and even prior to Samuel's publication of his message (4.1), is neither a sign of a dislocated text nor of a misreading of v. 20. Only when the reader requires that the text proceed step by step, with narrative event, comment, or description proceeding in exact chronological order, do such problems arise.

W. J. Martin has recognized and described several instances of what he calls 'dischronologized' narrative, in which events, as related in narrative sequence, are not in chronological sequence. He suggests that such 'dischronology' can be understood by analyzing its literary effect (1968:186). As Chatman says:

> Its [Plot's] order of presentation need not be the same as that of the natural logic of the story. Its function is to emphasize or de-emphasize certain story-events, to interpret some and to leave others to inference, to show or to tell, to comment or to remain silent, to focus on this or that aspect of an event or character (1978:43; cf. Sternberg 1978).

In the case of v. 20, the focus of attention is not on Israel's perception of the fulfillment or even on their reception of Samuel's word. Rather, what all Israel - from Dan to Beersheba - comes to understand is that Samuel is 'reliable' or 'confirmed' (*ne'eman*) as a prophet for Yahweh. Like v. 19, v. 20 is a description from the narrator. In v. 19, he revealed that Yahweh shaped events to confirm Samuel's words, thereby confirming Samuel as his apprentice. Now, in v. 20, the narrator directs the reader's attention to the public reaction to Samuel's prophecy. He focuses on Israel's perception of Samuel, and not the events since

their course is a foregone conclusion. All Israel understands the prophecy and fulfillment as a visible manifestation of the close relationship between Samuel and
Yahweh. Samuel is *ne'eman* to prophesy for Yahweh;
whatever Samuel prophesies will come true by virtue
of Yahweh's backing. Samuel has proven himself as the
mouthpiece of God. As such he is to be respected and
perhaps even feared. As A. Jepsen suggests, the people's·recognition that Samuel is *ne'eman* to Yahweh
emphasizes their perception of a rare closeness between Samuel and God (1977:296).

As in vv. 19 and 21, the narrator's concern is not
with chronology in v. 20; rather, he traces Yahweh's
steps to legitimate Samuel as a prominent theocratic
mediator. Samuel proves himself to be and is recognized as a reliable replacement for the priests in the
office of mediator. Verses 19-20 trace the enactment
of the two aspects of legitimation necessary to any
official mediator in Israel. First, the individual,
Samuel, is chosen and supported by God, and then he
is recognized by the people as capable of functioning
in the mediatory office, in this case to prophesy for
Yahweh (cf. Soggin 1967:6). It is this concept of sacral and secular legitimation that explains the order
of the text here /13/. Yahweh has chosen Samuel,
equipped him, and obtained public recognition for
him. Samuel, mediator *par excellence*, has arrived.

Verse 21

With Samuel's 'arrival,' the break in communication between Yahweh and Israel caused by the Elide defection is repaired. Buber, pointing to the three connected occurrences of the verb *glh* in 2.27; 3.7, 21,
suggests 'the old priestly mediators of revelation,
who had become unworthy, are replaced by the new,
worthy, prophetic' (1964:820). Buber's suggestion is
supported by the structure of ch. 3. In vv. 1f, the
scarcity of the word of Yahweh and the vision is

associated with Eli's failing sight. Now, in v. 21,
contact is restored, and Yahweh reappears in Shiloh.
The self-revelation of Yahweh to Samuel restores the
word of Yahweh to Israel (Péter-Contesse 1976:314).
This reappearance of Yahweh is a result (indicated by
kî) of his self-revelation to Samuel by his word
(Noth 1963:399) /14/.

The structure of v. 21 consists of two parallel
sentences with a final preposition tag added to the
second. The repetition of 'in Shiloh' emphasizes that
the renewal through Samuel reaches to the very heart
of the damages done by the Elides, for it was in the
cult at Shiloh that they carried on their priestly
malpractise. The final prepositional clause, *bidbar
yhwh*, when not emended (e.g. Buber 1956:125 n.5),
or deleted (e.g. Ehrlich 1910:181) stands outside
the parallelism of the previous sentence and is thereby foregrounded. As in v. 7, it is through the word of
Yahweh that Yahweh himself is revealed to Samuel.

The inauguration of Samuel as Israel's new mediator is begun, therefore, with the message of doom to
the Elides. The reappearance of Yahweh occurs once
Samuel has received this message. The new era is based on the revelation of the old era's passage. Verse
21, far from being 'somewhat posthumous' (Wellhausen
1971:54) or 'tautological' (Smith 1899:30), offers a compact summary of the major development of chs. 1-3 (cf.
E. Robertson 1944:189f). It is through the announcement of the passage of the Elide era that the new mediator receives his authorization, and with that
authorization Yahweh reopens the lines of communication. The goal towards which the divine initiative
(cf. 1.5) was moving has been reached. The Elides are
doomed and Samuel has been equipped and accepted as
a replacement. The imbalance caused by priestly excess
has apparently been righted - the lack of divine communication is ended. All seems well in Israel once
more.

One small item of business remains to be concluded

before the transition in mediators is completed. The destruction of the Elides remains undone. The narrator moves on to describe Yahweh's operations towards that end in ch. 4. The reader has been prepared for ch. 4 in numerous statements and suggestions throughout chs. 1-3.

What the reader is not totally prepared for are the disastrous side-effects that the punishment will bring with it. It is those side-effects and their implications that will occupy the centre of attention in chs. 4-6. The principal result of this first section of the narrative (chs. 1-3), namely Samuel's installation as prophetic mediator, will remain unaffected by the events of chs. 4-6; in fact, it is Samuel as mediator who will serve as the principal agent for repairing the damages caused by the side-effects of the Elide punishment.

PART FOUR

1 SAMUEL 4

Verse 1

The first sentence in v. 1 picks up the temporal development of the narrative, which was briefly set aside in 3.19-21. Those verses gave a short summary of a large time-span, even including events from the narrative's future (the fulfilled prophecy). The summary described what happened when Samuel prophesied in order to show how Yahweh went about legitimating Samuel; it was not concerned with the temporal sequence of the events. With 4.1, the narrator returns to a consecutive rehearsal of events.

The content of the word of Samuel, spoken to 'all Israel,' is not specified by the narrator. The reader has already been told, though, that 'all Israel' recognized that Samuel was a reliable prophet on account of Yahweh fulfilling his words (3.19f). Since the only word that Yahweh has revealed to Samuel is the message of doom against the Elides, it is probable that this message is the implied content of the word in 4.1. Chapter 3.19-20 summarized the subsequent course of events as it concerned Samuel's prophetic capacity. Those events are now presented in detail in ch. 4.

Willis has made a study of similar summaries in 1 Sam calling them 'comprehensive anticipatory redactional joints.' He suggests that a redactor uses such summaries to introduce major themes that are revealed in the *following* traditional complex or unit (1973: 295). One might also add that, as in 3.19-21, the an-

ticipatory summary incidentally provides the reader
with a rudimentary map by which to follow the events
subsequently narrated. Such literary maps are especially useful in cases where subsequent events are
complex and do not appear to follow logically from
their antecedents. Since this is the actual reading
experience of some readers of ch. 4 (e.g. Campbell
1975:200), the placement of 3.19-21 can be taken as
evidence of the good literary sense of the narrator.
Hence in chs. 4ff the reader expects a narrative description of what is summarized in 3.19-21. Chapter
4.1 rewards this expectation by describing how Israel
came to know of the prophecy against the Elides -
Samuel told them (against Ehrlich 1910:181).

Once he has shown Samuel actually transmitting
the unspecified message to Israel (did Samuel, in fact,
tell them everything?), the narrator moves directly to
a description of events that led to the destruction of
the Elides. Many commentators have regarded 4.1b as
abrupt and lacking connection to 4.1a (e.g. Schicklberger 1973:25) /1/. Following LXX, they suggest MT
has undergone haplography through homoioteleuton
(e.g. McCarter 1980:103) /2/. As Campbell notes, what
is at stake in the differences between LXX and MT is
not only the question of literary style, but also the
question of who began the hostilities - the Israelites
or the Philistines (1975:58)?

While text-critical debate continues over this
verse, there is no basis, from a literary point of
view, for preferring one version to the other. Chapter 4.1b of MT is neither too abrupt nor does it
require the additional material of LXX for logical
consistency. Chapter 4 presents a new scene in the
narrative. The shift in characters and backgrounds
does not imply literary disjunction anymore than a
cut and shift to a new scene is a result of something
having 'dropped out' in film production. As in any
narrative medium, perspectival presentation sometimes shifts abruptly, focusing on certain aspects of

separate scenes so as to accent specific connections
without the intervention of long, and unnecessarily
tedious, logical or causal connections /3/.

The LXX reading is neither better connected to
the preceding context nor a better introduction to the
following battle with the Philistines by making them
the aggressors in this scene. Schicklberger suggests
that MT's statement that Israel went out to meet the
Philistines presupposes mention of a Philistine de-
ployment (1973:26). From the perspective of literary
response, however, the narrative could assume the
Philistine advance and leave it as an 'indeterminacy'
to be filled by the reader (cf. Iser 1978).

On the other hand, MT does not even require us to
assume an indeterminacy. The statement, 'Israel went
out to meet the Philistines /4/ for battle,' only requires that the reader understand that there is going
to be a fight. Neither Israel nor the Philistines are
specifically labelled as the aggressor because it is irrelevant. The balanced initiative is indicated by the
parallel statements of vv. 1 and 2:

1. Israel goes out to meet [liqra't] the Philistines for battle.
2. The Philistines get ready to meet [liqra't] Israel.

Each group is equally active. Verse 1 focuses, therefore, not on who started it, but on the simple fact
that a battle is brewing.

The description of the Israelite camp's location
will be important later in the narrative, when Israel
defeats the Philistines in the very location where it
is defeated here in ch. 4 (cf. 7.12).

Verses 2-3

The battle is 'joined with a clash' and Israel is
smitten before the Philistines /5/. The use of the
passive Niphal, *wayyinnagep,* to describe Israel's
losses is important. Already the narrator is hinting

that the Philistines are merely agents of destruction, which originates from a higher authority. Israel is smitten 'before' (*lipnê*) the Philistines. When the narrator follows this description with the active Hiphil, *wayyakkû*, he does not modify his previous interpretation of the defeat. The Philistines are still agents; the narrative merely continues with a description of the details of the event /6/. About four thousand men from Israel's ranks are killed.

In v. 3, the interpretation of the battle suggested by the narrator in v. 2 is supported by the participating Israelites' interpretation of their defeat. The narrator's verbal description, 'they were smitten,' (*wayyinnagep*) now becomes active with Yahweh as subject: 'Why has Yahweh smitten us (*negapanû*) today before the Philistines?' There is no question of Philistine responsibility; the elders immediately assume that Yahweh has smitten them 'before the Philistines.'

The basis of this assumption lies, of course, in the Israelite view of war /7/. Yahweh had established his covenantal kingship over Israel by defeating Egypt in the great battle that occurred when Moses led Israel out of Egypt (Exod 15; cf. P.D. Miller 1973:83; 113-17, 174f). Yahweh and Israel agreed that the basis of the covenantal relationship between them was divine protection in war on the part of Yahweh and obedience to Yahweh on Israel's part (Exod 19.3-8). Israel's obedience to Yahweh's commandments guaranteed his protection in war, and hence, victory in war (Exod 23.22-24). Only one thing could ever defeat Israel in battle, namely its own sin (e.g. Josh 7f). Warfare for Israel was not a contest between opposing forces but strictly an indicator of the state of covenantal relations between Israel and Yahweh (cf. Campbell 1975:65). Judg 2.14f supplies the classic expression of the Israelite view of defeat. Israel's enemies are only victorious on account of Yahweh's will to defeat Israel.

Only two interpretations of the defeat at the hands

of the Philistines are possible for Israel: either
Israel or an Israelite has sinned, or Yahweh has reneged. Miller and Roberts agree that only two interpretations are possible, but see an ambiguity in the
question: was it Yahweh who put the Israelites to rout
or were they (and consequently Yahweh) simply defeated by a mightier nation (and god) (1977:64, 70-75)?
According to Miller and Roberts, ch. 4 suggests that
the Philistines and their god have defeated Israel and
its god (1977:71). This reading of the chapter is, however, in direct contradiction to vv. 2 and 3. There is
no question in Israel's mind over Yahweh's responsibility for the defeat (v. 3), and the narrator implies
in v. 2 that the Philistines are not ultimately responsible for Israel's defeat. The question, rather, is
what to make of Yahweh's action - '*Why* has Yahweh
smitten us before the Philistines?' (cf. Smith 1899:
32).

The response of the elders suggests that they place
the blame for the defeat on Yahweh (cf. Schulz 1919:
72; against Mauchline 1971:70). The elders say, 'Let
us get from Shiloh, the ark of the covenant of Yahweh.'
Their proposal presupposes two things: 1. Yahweh has a
covenantal duty to fight Israel's enemies. The ark of
the covenant is called for as a reminder to Yahweh
of those duties /8/; 2. The elders do not say 'What
have we done?,' or 'Who sinned?' (cf. Budde 1902:34).
They can only think that Yahweh has momentarily forgotten his covenantal responsibility, because they are
aware of no sin on their part.

The elders' neglect of the possibility that human
sin has brought on the defeat is a reflection of the
narrative's concern, which is not with the question
of the relationship between the sins of the people and
defeat. The narrator does not, after all, contradict
the elders' omission of such a possibility; in fact he
does everything he can in preceding scenes to present
the people as without sin. Since the narrator appears
to accept and agree with the elders' attribution of the

cause of the defeat, an attribution that is strikingly
unique in narratives about Israelite defeats in battle
(contrast e.g., Josh 7; Judg 2-16; 2 Kgs 21.12-14), the
reader must also accept it. Refusal to do so is simply
a refusal to accept the conventions of the narrative,
whereupon the reader becomes the writer of another
story.

The purpose for bringing the ark into Israel's midst,
on the battlefield, is not simply to bring Yahweh into action as a result of the presence and imperilment
of his palladium; nowhere does v. 3 imply that the
summons of the ark will automatically bring Yahweh
to deliver Israel (so, for example, Rössler 1966:119;
Willis 1971:301f; Campbell 1979:36). Yahweh is already active in the battle *before* the elders decide
to summon the ark. The point of bringing the ark of
the covenant of Yahweh (the name of Israel's covenantal God) is to remind Yahweh that his actions do not
agree with his covenant. He is supposed to smite Philistines, not Israelites.

Another aspect of the elders' suggestion is seen
in the explicit mention that it is to be brought from
Shiloh. This association of the non-performing Yahweh
with Shiloh, where the non- or mal-performing Elides
are, may suggest that the elders perceive some connection between the military defeat and the misdeeds of
the Shilonite priests. (One recalls that Samuel's word
in 4.1 may have been the word about the punishment on
the Elides.) In any case, the mention of Shiloh does,
as Willis notes, presuppose the prior description of
the ark at Shiloh (1971:302). The literary link invites
the reader to form his own conclusions about the relationship between Yahweh's anomalous military performance and the previously described situation at
Shiloh. The reader may recall from 3.2ff that Yahweh
revealed his plan for punishing the Elides in the
temple, where the ark was. At least, the link makes
room for the reader's speculative anticipations of
what the presence of the ark will do for Israel.

The final sentence of v. 3 - 'He/it will come into
our midst and deliver us from the hand of our enemies' -
can be read with either the ark or Yahweh as subject.
Since the elders know that it is Yahweh who has smitten
them, it is probable that Yahweh should be understood
as the subject of this sentence. Reminded of his covenant by the ark, Yahweh will come into the Israelites' midst and from there, deliver them from the Philistines /9/.

Verse 4

Acting on the elders' decision, the people send for
the ark, which receives an even longer title in this
verse. Despite the many different attempts to break
this ark title down into separate components, Jackson
is right when he observes that MT needs no correction
(1962:116). This is the most ceremonious title given
to the ark and Yahweh, 'God of hosts,' is characterized
in his martial aspect (Hertzberg 1964:48) /10/. The
divine symbol is brought on stage dressed in all its
glory. The elders decided to remind Yahweh of his duties with the 'ark of the covenant of Yahweh'; what
they get instead - courtesy of the narrator - is the
'ark of the covenant of Yahweh of hosts who sits on
the cherubim.'
Only the reader is privy to the narrator's characterization of the ark that is brought from Shiloh. So
far as Israel is concerned, they are bringing 'the ark
of the covenant of Yahweh' as planned. The narrator's
perspective on the ark sheds a different light on its
arrival in the Israelite camp. Emphasizing as it does
the tremendous power and divinity of Yahweh, the narrator's description of the ark reminds the reader of
who it is that is being reminded of his duties. This
God is not to be trifled with. If Eli could say of
Yahweh, 'He is Yahweh and does as he pleases' (3.18),
then so much the more so for the God whose ark gets
this regal title.

Accompanying the ark of this awesome God, the narrator tells us, are Eli's two sons, whose presence with
the ark is indicated by the words, 'And there' (*wešam*)
(cf. 1.3; Wellhausen 1871:55; McCarter 1980: 102f). As
Stoebe suggests, the association plays on the foreboding doom announced first in chs. 2-3 (1973:132). In
1.3, the identical introduction (*wešam*) to Eli's sons
tells us that they are priests to Yahweh. Chapter 2 describes their priestly abuses and the consequent punishment assured to them by Yahweh's desire (2.25). By re-
introducing them in the same way as 1.3, the narrator
points out that these corrupt priests are now not simply 'there' at Shiloh but 'there' with Yahweh of hosts,
who desires to kill them.

The structure of v. 4 stresses the ominous conjunction of the sons of Eli and Yahweh by repeating it
twice. The order of repetition is significant. It traps
the two sons of Eli 'there,' between two references to
Yahweh's/God's ark:

> . . . the ark of the covenant of Yahweh of hosts . . .
> and there are the two sons of Eli
> with the ark of the covenant of God,
> Hophni and Phinehas.

The two outside references name the adversaries - Yahweh of hosts versus Hophni and Phinehas; the two inside descriptions contrast them as humankind and God -
the sons of Eli versus God (*ha'elohîm*). The reader,
already aware of Yahweh's desire and intention to
slay the sons of Eli (2.25), is alerted by this ominous
companionship to the likelihood of the Elides' forthcoming demise; syntactically trapped between Yahweh
of hosts and God, there is no escape for them.

Verse 5

Neither Israel nor Eli's sons seem to be aware of
the threat hinted at by the narrator and thus seen by

the reader. The ark is again described simply as 'the ark of the covenant of Yahweh,' to which the people respond with a great shout.

The resumptive use of this title for the ark can be viewed as the narrator's return to a non-revelatory mode of description with which he indicates that he is returning to a simple description of the chain of events after the revealing insights of v. 4. The reader, favoured with the privileged information of v. 4, however, knows that it is not simply the ark of the covenant of Yahweh that goes with Eli's sons. The Israelite welcome for 'the ark of the covenant of Yahweh' is a product of their misunderstanding of the reason for the first defeat. Although they attempt no specific explanation for Yahweh's behaviour, the Israelites' summons for the ark and their great shout upon its arrival indicate that they see no reason for continuing failure. They give vent to the great shout (terû'â gedôlâ), suggesting that they expect Yahweh to turn the battle in their favour.

P. Humbert has suggested that the terû'â was 'the primitive but ritual acclamation of Yahweh, king, guide, (and) . . . warchief, he who revealed his power in the exodus' (1946:34) /11/. Whether the Israelites shout simply because they believe their troubles are over, or as a further attempt to goad Yahweh into action on their behalf, is not made explicit by the narrative. Given that the ark is called as a reminder to Yahweh, it is possible that the terû'â, while expressing a sense of relief and hope, was also employed as a further reminder to spur Yahweh on to combat and victory at the head of his Israelite troops.

Verses 6-9

The Philistine reaction to the ark's arrival affords the narrator a further opportunity to point out to the reader the important implications of the impending Israelite defeat (cf. Stolz 1972:49; Campbell 1975:

67). The Philistines deduce that the Israelite gods
have come into the enemy camp /12/, fearing this new
turn of events not because of the presence of the ark,
but because they have heard of the power of these gods
/13/.

The Philistines wrongly assume that their previous
battle with Israel was waged in the absence of Israel's
gods. 'Woe to us; it wasn't like this before' (v. 7).
Their despair reveals to the reader that they are the
unwitting instruments employed by Yahweh in his
dealings with Israel, and more particularly Israel's
priests. The narrator, the reader, and even the Israelite elders know that it *was* like this before (v. 3),
only 'Israel's gods' acted in a way perplexing to
Israel and totally misleading the Philistines.

The Philistines' recollection of the Israelite
gods' victory over Egypt in the wilderness is an obvious example of the narrator's use of a character's
voice to draw the reader's attention, unobtrusively,
to important theological-political considerations.
(Cf. Smith 1899:34, and Hertzberg 1964:48, who sense
something odd about the Philistines' comment, but are
not quite sure what to make of it.) It was Yahweh's
victory over Egypt that began the covenant relationship formed between himself and Israel in the wilderness /14/. As a result of Yahweh's military victories
over their enemies, the Israelites came to see him as
their king (Exod 15.1-18; Deut 33.5; P. D. Miller
1973: 174f).

The Philistine question, 'Who will deliver us from
the hand of these terrifying gods [of the exodus]?'
(v. 8), is rhetorical - at least from the Israelite perspective if not the Philistine. Only if the exodus gods
themselves allow it can the Philistines be delivered. Hence, both from the Israelites' understanding of
the previous battle (v. 3) and the Philistines' fear of
Israel's gods, the reader is given to understand that
any subsequent Philistine victory is willed by Yahweh,
god of the exodus. As Buber observes, the question

that is raised by the inclusion of these exodus recollections is, what has become of the covenant formed
on the basis of the exodus (1964:823)?

The Philistines' exhortation to be strong and to
act manly (v. 9) is understood by Stoebe as an attempt
to preclude any misunderstanding that the subsequent
loss of the ark was due to Yahweh's inferiority to the
Philistine gods (1973:132). The Philistines rely on
their human capacities and not their gods in their battle against Israel's god. As the reader knows from
1 Sam 2.4, 9f, however, human strength cannot defeat
Yahweh. As a prelude to the battle report in vv. 10f
then, the Philistine exhortation in v. 9 again directs
the reader to regard any subsequent Israelite defeat
as the intention of Yahweh. Verses 8f set up a battle
between the mighty gods of the exodus and the Philistine men. This contrast is highlighted by the descriptions of the opponents:

	v. 8	v. 9
1.	ha'elohîm ha'addîrîm	'anašîm pelištîm
2.	ha'elohîm hammakkîm 'et-miṣrayim	ta'abdû la'ibrîm

The Philistines are mere men, potential slaves, fighting the awesome gods who destroyed mighty Egypt /15/.
Clearly the Philistines do not have a chance if they
really have to fight Yahweh (cf. Schicklberger 1973:
31).

Verse 10

The unexpected, which by now the reader expects,
occurs: the Philistines fight; they are subject of
the verb *wayyillaḥamû* indicating, perhaps, their
dominance over the Israelites (cf. v. 2). Israel, on
the other hand, is subject only of *wayyinnagep*, 'they
were smitten,' an indication of their poor showing in
the battle. Obviously Yahweh has not been constrained
by the reminders of his covenant. The people of the

gods that devastated Egypt (*hammakkîm 'et-miṣrayim bekol-makkâ*, v. 8) are themselves devastated (*wattehî hammakkâ gedôlâ*) by the Philistines, mere men. The entry of the ark into the Israelite camp saw Israel united in giving expression to the *terû'â* (*wayyari'û kol-yiśra'el*) (v. 5). The second Philistine victory destroys this re-grouping, which was centered on the ark's presence, and the Israelites flee separately, each to his own tent (v. 10; cf. McCarter 1980:107).

Israel's expectations, or at least any hopes for a reversal in military fortunes, are disappointed by the second defeat. This reversal of Israel's hopes, which were justifiable on the basis of Yahweh's covenanted commitment, fulfills the prophecy of 2.32. Yahweh had promised Eli that he would see affliction because of sin in what should be good for Israel /16/. Now, in the course, of events leading up to Eli's sons' punishment, Israel experiences a terrible defeat instead of the expected, and covenantally assured victory. The subsequent fulfillment of the predicted sign (2.34) confirms that it is indeed the sin of the priests that has brought defeat upon Israel.

Verse 11

The ark of God (*'elohîm*) is, like the Israelites in v.10, subject of the passive; it is taken (*nilqah*) by the Philistine army.

The loss of the ark in battle (*nilqah*) is the ironic counterpart to the elder's decision to bring (*niqhâ*, v. 3) the ark into the camp as a reminder to Yahweh of his military duty (noted by J. P. Fokkelman in a letter). God (*'elohîm*) seems to have been overpowered by man (*'anaśîm*, v. 9) /17/. The reader is well aware of the fact, however, that the Philistine victory is engineered by Yahweh, who has his own purposes, the accomplishment of which is now described.

Yahweh allows his ark to be captured and so allows Eli's sons to be killed. He has finally executed his

heart's desire to kill them (*lahamîtam*, 2.25). The
conjunctive description of the capture of the ark and
the death of Eli's sons, without any mention of the
Philistine agency, focuses attention on the connection,
known to be causal from the previous context, of these
two incidents.

An interesting structural parallel between v. 11
and v. 4 supports the latter observation. Ranged side
by side, the correspondences highlight one important
difference. Both sentences are prefaced with a mention
of the ark; in v. 4 it is brought by the Israelites
into their camp on the advice of the elders (*niqhû*)
and in v. 11 it is taken (nilqah) by the Philistines.
Then follows each of these sentences:

v.4	v.11
wešam šenê benê-'eli	ûšenê benê-'elî
'im-'arôn berît ha'elohîm	metû
hopnî ûpînḥas	hopnî ûpînḥas

Verse 11, in place of a note about the presence of
Eli's sons with the ark, inserts a verbal description
of their death; their presence with the ark is transformed into their death.

The description of the ark as the *'arôn 'elohîm*
is important not only for the contrast it provides
with the Philistine victors, who are mere 'men' and
unlikely conquerors of gods; it also helps the reader
to avoid misinterpreting the second defeat as the Israelites and Philistines do. Israel had summoned the
ark of the covenant of Yahweh. When the ark is captured, they can only believe that the covenant is broken and that Yahweh has abandoned them (4.21-22). Yet
the reader knows that it is not the ark of the covenant
of Yahweh that is taken. Rather it is the ark of God,
the tool of him who allows men to 'defeat' him and so
to further the divine aims.

As Campbell notes, the simultaneous death of Hophni

and Phinehas is the sign, comprehensible to Eli and the reader, that the prophecy of 2.27-36 has been set into action (1979:35). In as much as the description of the battle culminates with the sign, the narrative presents the death of Eli's sons and not the capture of the ark, which is only an important contributing factor, as the final, and most important consequence of the battle (cf. Miller & Roberts 1977:65). That the entire conflict between Israel and the Philistines culminates in the fulfillment of the prophetic sign is a further indication, available to Eli and the reader, that Yahweh has had the guiding hand in these events.

The death of Hophni and Phinehas resolves the problem of wicked priests, at least from Yahweh's point of view (Miller & Roberts 1977:66). Yet the elimination of Eli's sons has brought with it dire consequences. Innocent Israelites have also been injured, even killed, as Israel's theological-political covenant has, from Israel's vantage, apparently been revoked.

Against Miller and Roberts it should be noted that the second defeat does not call into question the power of claims of Yahweh (1977:70-72). Israel is well aware that their defeat is willed by Yahweh (v. 3) and the capture of the ark does not change this one bit. Just as Yahweh operates without the ark in the first battle, so he uses it in the second battle as the instrument of Hophni's and Phinehas' perdition. The reader, knowing that Yahweh was responsible for the first defeat which resulted in the call for the ark of the covenant (and Eli's sons), and that Yahweh desired to kill Eli's sons and promised to do so, can only regard their deaths in the second defeat as Yahweh's doing. The issue raised by the second defeat is the same as that raised by the first; it is not Yahweh's power that is questioned, but his covenantal faithfulness.

The reader, privileged with information unavailable to Israel, knows that Yahweh has not annulled the covenant but only appears to have done so. At the same time, the reader is able to appreciate the problems

posed for Israel by the defeats. The narrative, therefore, poses separate questions with regard to the covenantal relationship - one to the reader and another,
within the story, to Israel.

For the reader the problem is not Yahweh's abandonment of the covenant but the justice of Yahweh, 'who
does as he pleases,' and the weakness of the theocratic
political system as a practical government for the Israelite nation. Yahweh may have cause and even precedent (e.g. Josh 7) for his drastic means of punishing
Eli's sons, yet the injustice of his actions and the
political uncertainties inherent in the theocracy are
underlined in this narrative. Campbell, who wants to
say that the defeats are not aimed at punishing the
Elides, is a good example of a reader impressed by the
political dangers posed by the theocracy.

> Yet the disproportion between the deserved disgrace
> of the Elides and concomitant disaster for Israel is
> glaring. The loss of the ark, two defeats and the
> death of 34,000 men is a steep price to pay for the
> punishment of two or three errant priests. Can this
> be justified by the central role of these priests in
> the nation? (1979:35).

Is Yahweh's covenantal justice just? Is the covenant
along with its mediators of real value to Israel,
given that Israel in fact suffers because of it?

The question raised for Israel, on the other hand,
is the question of Yahweh's allegiance to his covenant
with his people. The call for the ark of the covenant
of Yahweh was a call for responsibility on his part.
The second defeat suggests, not that Yahweh is weak,
but that he has abandoned Israel. As subsequent interpretations of the second defeat suggest, Israel takes
the defeat as a signal of the end to the special relationship between Yahweh and his people.

Verses 12-18

The fulfillment of prophecy continues. The literary links between vv. 12-18 and 3.2-18 confirm that the defeats are Yahweh's doing as he goes about punishing the Elides:

3.2	**4.13**
Eli lies in his place.	Eli sits on his chair.
3.2	**4.15**
Eli cannot see.	Eli cannot see.
3.4	**4.10-11**
God calls Samuel to tell him what he is about to do (the ear-tingling event) (cf. above on 3.11).	Israel is defeated.
3.5	**4.12-13**
As a result, Samuel runs [wayyaroṣ] to Eli.	A Benjaminite runs [wayyaroṣ] to tell news.
3.11-14	**4.14-15**
Yahweh reveals his plans to Samuel. (Eli does not know what God says because he is 'blind' and does not receive visions.)	Eli does not know what has happened because he cannot see.
3.16-17	**4.16**
Eli, wanting to know what God said, calls Samuel [šemû'el benî] and asks what God said [mâ haddabar].	Eli asks for the news [meh-hayâ haddabar benî]
3.18	**4.14**
Samuel tells all [wayyaged-lô šemû'el 'et-kol-haddebarîm].	The messenger tells Eli what happened [wayyagged le'elî].
3.18	**4.17**
Contents of Samuel's message: everything (including what Yahweh had previously said in 2.27-36 according to 3.12).	Content of message: Israel fled, great losses, Eli's sons dead, and the ark taken.

The appearance of the messenger alone is enough for anyone seeing him to know that Israel was defeated (v. 12, Campbell 1975:78). Eli is unable to see the facts, however, and must ask. The description of Eli in v. 13 is paralleled in 1.9, with the difference that Eli is no longer called 'the priest' and he no longer sits at the doorpost of the temple. Instead, he sits atop the gate, watching because he was fearful on account of the ark /18/.

Eli's fear has been the subject of some debate. Campbell, who sees the loss of the ark and the interpretation of that loss as the primary concern of ch. 4, suggests that the text's explicit statement requires that we understand Eli to be fearing for the ark, and presumably, its safety (1979:37). P. R. Davies, on the other hand, notes that hrd does not mean to be concerned or worried, but rather to be fearful and trembling (1977:12; cf. BDB 'terrify,' p. 353). According to Davies, Eli is afraid *of* the ark and *for* his sons, because of their sins and, one might add, because of the prophecy. The disagreement extends to the understanding of the focus of ch. 4: for Campbell it is the loss of the ark, for Davies it is Eli and his family.

In fact, both Campbell and Davies are correct insofar as it is possible to have a 'correct' interpretation. The chapter is concerned with the punishment of the Elides, but that introduces a new problem, the loss of the ark (cf. Miller & Roberts 1977:66). It is likely that Eli fears both this loss and the potentially dangerous situation of his sons, who are accompanying it. We may take it that Eli shares the elders' assumption that Yahweh was responsible for the first defeat, especially in view of Yahweh's last message to Samuel. Knowing that death is promised his two sons and that Yahweh was acting very weirdly towards Israel, Eli could be expected to entertain fears for his sons' safety and misgivings about the possibility that his sons had brought this evil on Israel (cf. 2.32; 3.12, and the interpretation above).

It is important to note that when the ark, accompanied by his sons, goes out the battlefield, Eli does not worry about the danger of the situation for the ark or his sons; his fear is explicitly focused on the ark alone. Eli's attention, attuned by the prophetic messages of chs. 2 and 3, is drawn to a single aspect of the situation, the presence of the ark and what that might portend. Further detailing of his concern is left to subsequent verses.

The scene at the entrance of the ark to the Israelite camp is tragically mirrored by the messenger's entrance to the city. In v. 5, all Israel (*kol-yiśra-'el*) had voiced an earth-shaking *terû'â* on the ark's arrival in the camp. In v. 13, the whole city (*kol-ha'îr*) cries out at the messenger's report. The Philistines, hearing the sound of the *terû'â* ask 'What is the meaning of this great *terû'â*' (v. 6). The narrator tells us that they realized that the ark had arrived. Eli, on the other hand, when he hears the sound of the outcry and asks, 'What is the meaning of this outcry (*hehamôm*),' (cf. v. 5, *wattehom*) has to be told. Instead of offering a comment to the effect that Eli realizes what has happened (as in v. 6), the narrator tells us that he was an old man (lit. 98 years old) who could not see. As previously (3.2), Eli's blindness is more than physical and the narrator uses it to compare him unfavourably, first with Samuel and now with the Philistines /19/. As Dorn observes, v. 15 does provide general background to the narrative (1978:318f), but more importantly, it renders a subtle judgement on Eli, who is even less perceptive than the Philistines. As in ch. 3 where he has to ask what Yahweh said (v. 17), now Eli has to ask what Yahweh has done (v.16).

The messenger's perception of the climax of the second defeat differs from the narrator's (cf. vv. 10f). Instead of placing the death of Eli's sons last, the messenger regards the capture of the ark as the final blow. The difference is significant and indicative of the gradual change of focus in ch. 4. The narrator's order in v. 11 places the military defeat first, which leads to the capture of the ark, which leads to the deaths of Hophni and Phinehas. The list follows the causal sequence that Yahweh uses to kill the Elides. The messenger's list, on the other hand, is an expression of an interest in the consequences of the defeat for Israel. The list gives these consequences in ascending order of importance: first the people are destroyed, then the priests are killed, and finally, the ark of God is taken /20/. What will become of Israel?

When Eli hears the last item in the messenger's list, he falls off his chair and breaks his neck (v. 18). The narrator's explanation of the cause of Eli's death, 'for the man was old (*zaqen*) and heavy (*kabed*),' places Eli's death alongside his lack of control over his sons as a consequence of old age. Though Eli's death fulfills Yahweh's prediction that there would be no old man (*zaqen*, 2.32) in his house, the narrator ensures that the reader will remember that Eli's punishment is for the 'crime' of becoming old and feeble. By tying Eli's death explicitly to his age and decrepit condition (*kabed*), the narrator emphasizes the correspondence of his death with his 'crime' and plays down the actual cause of death, the broken neck. The expositional intrusion suggests that the narrator is more concerned that the reader recall why Eli is dying than he is with the actual circumstances of the death. The death of the old man reminds the reader of the injustice of the whole scene, which is directed by the a-rational divinity, 'Who does as he pleases' (3.18).

Commentators have often taken Eli's reaction in v. 18 as confirmation that Eli was fearful for the ark's safety in v. 13 (e.g. Campbell 1979:37). Hertzberg, for example, says that 'it is the news that the ark has been captured and not that his sons have been killed, that is the direct cause of the old man's death' (1964:

49; cf. Smith 1899:30; Campbell 1975:80, 1979:37; Miller & Roberts 1977:66; McCarter 1980:116).

Careful attention to what the narrator tells us in v. 18 suggest an alternative. What Eli hears, according to the narrator, is everything up to and including 'the ark of God.' The narrator explicitly states that when the messenger mentioned 'the ark of God' Eli fell and died. Whether or not Eli actually heard the word *nilqaḥâ*, 'was taken,' is debatable; the point made by the narrator is that immediately upon hearing the words, 'the ark of God,' mentioned after the message about the defeat and the death of his sons, Eli fell to his death. It may be that Eli had already guessed what had happened to the ark on hearing of the defeat and his sons' deaths. But the narrator's obvious omission of the word *nilqaḥâ* from his description of what Eli heard before his death serves primarily to link the death of Eli's sons with 'the ark of God.' Having heard that his sons were dead, Eli recognized the fulfillment of the sign (2.34). Upon hearing the words 'the ark of God' Eli surely recognizes God's hand in all of this and is so overcome that he falls to his death.

Hence although Campbell is correct to observe that the messenger's list presents the capture of the ark as the most important consequence of defeat, he is wrong to see Eli's death as confirmation of this (1975:80). Eli and his sons are solely catalysts of the problem they create for Israel and are not concerned with the consequences of the lost ark. The ambiguous v. 13 will, at this point, be reinterpreted by the reader in light of the unambiguous v. 18 (cf. Perry 1979:46-48). Eli fears on account of the ark of God in v. 13, since he knows that the ark's God is going to kill his sons. In v. 18, he is not interested in the ark *per se*, but only with the mention of it in connection with his sons' deaths.

The note that Eli judged Israel for forty years is often passed over with the comment that it is of

deuteronomistic provenance, designed to incorporate
Eli's career into the framework of the book of Judges
(e.g. Smith 1899:36; McCarter 1980:114). While this
redactional hypothesis may be true, it does not app-
rehend the function of the notice in the narrative.
Hertzberg faces this question and decides that the
notice shows the damage done to Israel's social and
political institutions by the loss of the ark (1964:
50). This interpretation can be expanded.

First, it is not *because* the ark is lost that Israel experiences this blow to its leadership. Rather
it is the corruption of the priestly leadership of
Eli's sons that provokes Yahweh to arrange this defeat
and to allow the loss of the ark. Viewed in the light
of the role played by previous judges in Israelite
history, the conclusion of Judge Eli's career and its
effect on Israel is ironic /21/. The reader's attention
is directed to this ironic contrast by the formulaic obituary notice, which follows the examples of obituary
notices about other judges in the book of Judges. Such
obituary notices were usually prefaced with a description of how the judge delivered Israel 'from the hand
of their enemies' (e.g. Judg 2.18; 3.31; 8.28). Eli's
obituary notice, on the other hand, comes immediately
after a detailed description of how Israel was delivered into the hands of its enemies because of the sin
of its priestly leaders. The system of theocratic
mediators seems to have backfired.

Verses 19-22

The news of the ark's capture and the death of her
father-in-law and her husband causes Phinehas' wife to
go into premature labour, and the delivery of the boy
brings about her death (*ke'et mûtâh*, v. 20). She
takes neither interest nor satisfaction in her accomplishment. Her only action with respect to her son is
to name him and even this act reveals that her thoughts
are elsewhere (cf. McCarter 1980:115). The name she

gives to her child, Ichabod, means 'Where is the glory?' or, 'Alas, the glory!' (McCarter 1980:115f).

Like Eli, Phinehas' wife is mortified by the news of
the battle. She too hears a list of three items, which
are summarized by the narrator in the following order:
the capture of the ark of God, the death of her father-
in-law (Eli), and the death of her husband (observed by
Fokkelman in a letter). In her case, the news brings
on her labour pains (v. 19). She gives birth to a son,
but dies soon after.

Phinehas' wife presents an interpretation of the
crisis that reveals that she either has not, or refuses
to come to grips with the implications of the connection between the defeats and the word of Samuel given
in 4.1a. To her the second defeat is disastrous because
'glory' has departed from Israel. Her two separate but
parallel statements on the departed glory (vv. 21f)
seem contradictory and have given rise to emendations
and excisions to remove the conflict (cf. Schicklberger 1973:38-42, Stoebe 1973:135). The seeming contradiction can be resolved, however, by paying close
attention to the differences between the two verses.

The first statement (v. 21) is a narratorial description of how she knows that glory has departed from
Israel. 'She said glory has departed from Israel with
respect to (*'el*) the captured ark, her father-in-law,
and her husband.' Campbell (1979:37) has suggested
that 'glory' refers to the loss of the ark, but this
interpretation neglects v. 21, which emphasizes equally the ark and the priests. Davies makes the opposite
mistake, suggesting that 'glory' refers primarily to
Eli and Phinehas (1977:12). P. H. de Robert comes
closer to the mark when he suggests that 'glory' refers
both to the ark, Israel's esteemed divine symbol, and
Eli and Phinehas, Israel's honoured priests (1979:
352f). These prestigious symbols and honoured figures
are supposed to be Israel's glory. The difficulty with
de Robert's suggestion is that only the ark has left
Israel; Eli and Phinehas are dead and in Israel.

Schulz takes an entirely different approach. Citing Jer 3.16ff; 14.21; and 17.12, he suggests that *kabôd* without the definite article may be a circumlo-
cution for Yahweh (1919:83f) /22/. Elaborating, one
might note that the ark was the physical symbol of
Yahweh's presence with Israel (cf. vv. 3-7; Num 14.39-
45). The priests were installed by God as operators of
the sacrificial cult (1 Sam 2.28), the purpose of which
was to remove the impurities caused by sin (2.29).
These impurities were believed to attack both man and
God, the latter in his sanctuary (Milgrom 1976:766).
The pollution of the sanctuary by human sin drives
God out from the midst of his people (cf. Num 5.1-4;
Deut 23.9-14). The priests are, therefore, agents of
the presence of God in Israel. The narrator suggests,
in v. 21, that Phinehas' wife sees the divine presence
as having left Israel /23/, pointing to the capture of
the ark and the deaths of the priests as indications
thereof (cf. Gutbrod 1956:41). Without these instruments and tokens of the divine presence, she assumes,
God can no longer be present with Israel.

The second statement (v. 22) is a 'tagged quotation'
of this view of the divine presence. If we translate
kî as 'in that,' then the verse seems to suggest
that the capture of the ark was the first visible manifestation that the presence had left. The deaths of
the priests are comprehensible because Yahweh is no
longer around to defend them. His absence is inferred
from the capture of his ark. Were he present, he would
not allow such a thing. If, on the hand, we read *kî*
causally, the verse becomes a strong expression of the
view that Yahweh's presence is tied to the ark. The
presence left Israel because the ark was captured.

The picture of the distraught wife of Phinehas
offers a contrastive parallel to that of Hannah. In
ch. 1, we see a barren woman who, thanks to the intervention of God, gives birth to a son and celebrates
the divine action by naming her son in honour of God.
For Hannah, the birth of Samuel is a jubilant affair,

a time for praise of God and celebration of his aid to the faithful (2.1-10). For the reader, the birth of Samuel was the first in a series of events being shaped in accordance with some obscure divine plan. The birth of Phinehas' wife's child stands as the concluding event of that plan. In contrast to Hannah, Phinehas' wife's comment on divine intervention is full of despair. Ichabod, 'Alas, the glory,' is a living reminder of the undesirable effect that Yahweh's intervention (or lack of appropriate intervention) can have, even on his own people. Hannah was typically overjoyed at the birth of her son, yet Phinehas' wife, who should also be happy, pays no heed to the news of her accomplishment, overcome as she is by the news of the disaster (v. 20).

The contrast between these two child-bearers is clear and it reveals that events in Israel have taken a turn for the worse. Since in both cases it is divine intervention that provokes the mothers' reactions, the reader might anticipate a third intervention that will again restore the favourable reaction.

By allowing the wife to voice her own interpretation of the disaster, the narrator creates an opportunity for the reader to reflect on the course of events from yet another vantage, namely that of a human character who sees things from the limited horizons of her existential position within the story world. The reader has been privileged to know the true cause of defeat and shares few if any of the wife's thoughts about Yahweh's supposed absence from Israel. Neither she nor the elders (v. 3) seem to have linked the defeats with the word of Samuel. Instead, they think in terms of God's abandonment of (v. 3) or departure from (v. 22) Israel. What is a simple punishment of sin from Yahweh's perspective is experienced by Israel as a religious and existential crisis.

The reader is forced to consider the two perspectives on the defeat and to integrate them. Knowing the real cause, he or she yet sympathizes, as a human being, and perhaps as an Israelite, with the wife's and elders' interpretation of defeat. An omniscient perspective on the entire episode allows the reader to see the injustices of the slaughter, bringing agreement with the elders, who view the defeat as a failure of Yahweh to do what he promised (vv. 3-4). This sympathy for Israel is strengthened by the impression, gained from the narratorial intimation in 2.25, that the entire episode could have been avoided had not Yahweh desired the death of Eli's sons.

What emerges for both the reader and Israel is the unpredictability of Yahweh, and for the reader alone, the apparent irrationality and even the injustice of Yahweh's means of punishing the priests. The narrative displays the potential danger of having a god living amongst men and serving as their minister of national defence. The controls and insurance against disaster in this situation are the priests and the cult. When these means of insulating the community against the awful powers of the divinity fail there is no back-up system (cf. 2.25). The narrative exposes a weakness inherent in the theocratic polity, namely the fallible human mediator(s) between God and man, and the consequent danger to the community from the unleashed wrath of the punishing God, 'who does what he pleases.'

As B. A. Levine points out, Yahweh's wrath knows no distinctions and is uncontrollable when unleashed (1974:71). Yahweh is portrayed as a 'demonic' power, dwelling in the innermost sanctuary and requiring that his worshippers defend themselves from his wrath. Israel was willing to risk the dangers of divine immanence in order to gain the blessings thereby made possible (1974:71). The episode in 1 Sam 2-4 questions the viability of the political system established to accommodate the divine presence. Problems between the priests and Yahweh interfere with the nation's defence, due to the constitutionally based lack of distinction between the sacred and profane aspects of national existence. Similarly, Israel experiences an existential and

religious crisis when it is defeated in war due to this
same lack of distinction.

The reader is left waiting for a resolution of the
difficulties created by punishing the Elides. Yahweh
has estranged himself from Israel. How will he repair
the damage done to his relationship with them? The
process of reconciliation is described in chs. 5-7.

PART FIVE

1 SAMUEL 5

*Excursus on Perspective and
Knowledge in 1 Sam 5.1-6.11*

The events of 5.1-6.11 are reserved for the eyes of the
narrator and his reader. The defeated Israelites in the
story are not allowed any insight into the reasons for
the return of the ark in 6.12, nor do they know what
Yahweh or the ark have been doing during the time of
the ark's sojourn amongst the Philistines. By limiting
access to these events the narrator illuminates the
meaning of Israel's defeat for his reader, while leaving Israel in the dark. The revelation of Yahweh's
superiority to Dagon and the Philistines is a clear
testimony to Yahweh's intentions in the Israelite
defeats (Gutbrod 1956:44; Miller & Roberts 1977:71).
The reader is granted absolute certainty regarding
the real causes and results of the Israelite defeat
in ch. 4.

At the same time, however, the reader is aware
that the Israelites share neither the unrestricted
view nor the certainty about the meaning of their
defeat. Even though the narrative states that 'the
word of Samuel was (broadcast) to all Israel' (4.1),
the problem of correlating that prophecy with specific events remained. While the reader is privileged by
the narrator with corroborating details such as 5.1-
6:11 Israel sees only the bare facts and only some of
those. The reactions of the city-dwellers (4.13) and
of Phinehas's wife (4.20-22) illustrate the initial

confusion over the significance of Israel's defeat.

The reader sees all and knows all, but is reminded of the uniqueness of his or her vantage by the presence in the story of an Israel that cannot share this view. Since the reader is also aware that normally he or she would share Israel's limited perspective, this privileged access to narrative events also become a privileged opportunity for reflection on the encounter in history between God and humankind, and on the implications of the normally limited human access to an intelligible perspective on divine action. Though not himself explicitly engaging in such reflection, the narrator does encourage the reader to do so by allowing him or her the temporary use of the omniscient point of view.

It is also important to be aware of the reverse side of the unconditioned perspective. Just as the narrator can use his 'omniscience' to create an opportunity for reader reflection on the problems of human limitations in knowledge, he can also give his readers an experiential grasp of those problems by denying them a share in the knowledge that is always available to the narrator. So in 6.19, for example, the narrator resigns the reader to a view of divine action 'from below,' thereby cultivating a fuller appreciation of Israel's perspective on that particular action /1/.

As the majority of commentators have observed, 5.1-5 demonstrate Yahweh's complete superiority to Dagon, the Philistine god. Only on the basis of this demonstration is it usually inferred that Yahweh was responsible for the Israelite defeat (e.g. Campbell 1975:92; Miller & Roberts 1977:71; McCarter 1980:124f). Miller and Roberts suggest that vv. 1-5 are a vindication of Yahweh's power in response to the doubt cast thereon by the Israelite defeat (1977:70f). As Campbell intimates, however, Israel was never in doubt about Yahweh's role in the battle - the question they asked was *why* Yahweh had smitten them, not whether he had (1975:92). In addition, one might add that the reader has few doubts

about Yahweh's responsibility, given his prior knowledge of Yahweh's intent gained from chs. 1-4. For
whom, then is this demonstration? The only answer is
that it is for the Philistines. Israel is unaware of
the events in the temple at Ashdod and the reader is
in no doubt about Yahweh's abilities, but the Philistines appear to have been in a position to misunderstand their success. From 4.9 it should be recalled
that the Philistines plunged into battle as 'men' a-
gainst the powerful and mighty gods of the exodus.
Their apparent victory might be taken by them as an
indication that they had conquered those mighty gods.

As in the case of King Nebuchadnezzar, who was reduced to an animal existence for thinking that he was
responsible for his success rather than God (Dan 4.20-
37), the Philistines are made to remember their proper station whether they have forgotten it or not /2/.
Their god is shattered and they themselves are strick-
en with a plague of tumors. Perhaps the best comment
on ch. 5 is contained in a line from Hannah's song,
'man cannot prevail by strength' (2.9). The episode is,
however, not so much a vindication of Yahweh's powe-
ers as it is a glorification of them. The keynote of
Yahweh's adventures among the Philistines is glorification amongst the nations (6.5f; cf. Exod 9.15-16).

Verse 1

Verse 1 introduces a new scene in the chain of events consequent to the Israelite defeat (cf. Schicklberger 1973:100; against Campbell 1975:83f). The positioning of *pelištîm* first in the sentence emphasizes
the Philistine initiative as subject. At the same time
the syntax of v. 1 also serves to distinguish this new
scene from the preceding scene in ch. 4 (Miller & Roberts 1977:41; cf. Budde 1902:39; Schulz 1919:84).

The emphasis on the Philistine initiative is also
seen when v. 1 is compared with 4.22. In 4.22, the ark
is subject of the passive 'was taken' (*nilqaḥ*), but

in 5.1 the Philistines take over as subject of the same verb (*laqeḥû*). Ehrlich notes that *laqaḥ*, in this incidence 'means not simply "to take" but as previously (4.11, 17, 21, 22) "to capture"' (1910:183). The point of such emphasis is, as in the following verses, to show that the Philistines deserve the punishment they get. They act presumptuously, as though *they* had won the victory and are bringing home their trophy (Miller & Roberts 1977:42f).

Verse 2

The repetition of a large part of v. 1 in v. 2 is reminiscent of certain aspects of poetic parallelism and need not be taken as a redundancy to be explained by the text's compositional history (Wellhausen 1871: 58; Miller & Roberts 1977:41; against Dhorme 1910:55; Stoebe 1973:138; Campbell 1975:84f; cf. Kugel 1981: 59-95). Verse 2 specifies exactly where in Ashdod they brought the ark. The emphasis on the Philistine initiative continues in v. 2; they are the subject of all three active verbs, while the ark is mentioned three times only as object of the verbs. The Philistine manipulation of the ark, so strongly highlighted in vv. 1f, is soon to end /3/.

Verses 3-4

The significance of Dagon's fall continues to be debated. Does the verse depict a battle of gods? Is it Yahweh or the ark that brings down Dagon? Is Dagon worshipping Yahweh or is he lying at his feet in defeat? In the two verses themselves these sorts of consideration are not given special prominence. No conflict is described. The contest is really no contest. Yahweh does not act and the ark is impassive. Only Dagon does anything, and he simply falls to his face before the ark /4/.

The reader is allowed to see only the results of

the nightly activity. The activity itself is intentionally disregarded. The scene of the morning after
is set forth in a simple, matter-of-fact description
that evokes neither surprise nor excitement in the
reader. There is no hint that either Yahweh or the
ark has lifted a finger in this 'contest.' Dagon, the
inferior, naturally falls with his face to the ground
before his superior (cf. Miller & Roberts 1977:44)
/5/.

The first fall of Dagon turns the tables on the
Philistines. In vv. 1f they took (*wayyiqhû*) the ark
and brought it to the house of Dagon, setting it next
to Dagon. When Dagon falls from his former estate,
it is he who the Philistines have to take (*wayyiqhû*)
and return to his place. The reversal of fortunes,
indicated by the parallel and contrastive verbs describing actions with the ark and Dagon as objects,
indicates that it is simply the *presence* of the ark
that brings about Dagon's downfall. When in the presence of a superior, an inferior god quite naturally
shows deference.

As v. 2 is a development of v. 1, so v. 4 develops
the implications of v. 3. The first half of v. 4 virtually repeats the first half of v. 3, while the second
half contains a new development. This time Dagon
seems to be broken up by his fall. His head and the
palms of his hands are severed on the threshold of
the temple leaving 'only Dagon on him' /6/. Against
Miller and Roberts (1977:45), one must maintain that
Dagon is not 'slaughtered by Yahweh.' The mythological
parallels that they adduce as a possible context for
understanding Dagon's dismemberment, while interesting, make Yahweh's involvement explicit when the text
leaves it implicit. (Cf. Gutbrod 1956:43, 'To this
point in the narrative the action of Israel's Lord is
read only between the lines.')

Granted that the narrator leaves the determination
of the agent of Dagon's demise to the reader, and Yahweh is the only logical choice, the narrator's formu-

lation focuses on the simple fact that Dagon lies dis-
membered before the ark. Yahweh's absolute supremacy
over Dagon is thereby demonstrated without any explicit struggle or effort on Yahweh's part, thus making
the feat more remarkable.

Verse 5

In this etiological note, the narrator supplies the
reader with empirical confirmation of the truth of
what is told in vv. 3-4, citing 'factual evidence'
from outside the narrative (cf. Miller & Roberts 1977:
46). The reader is reminded that the events did occur
and did bear consequences still felt 'until this day.'
Viewed from a literary perspective, this etiology
appears as a rhetorical technique supportive of the
narrative /7/. Since the Philistines are supposed to
have been the only viewers of Dagon's calamity, the
narrator adds an etiology both as proof of his story
and as a reminder to the reader of his privileged
perspective.

Verse 6

Although Yahweh's activity and responsibility for
Dagon's downfall is purposefully left implicit, the
narrator does reveal the divine hand (*yad-yhwh*) when
it moves against the Philistines themselves. When it is
a god with whom Yahweh contends the narrative carefully avoids any appearance of activity on Yahweh's or
Dagon's part.

The only thing that reveals Dagon's inferiority is
that each morning the statue of Dagon is found lying
face down before the ark, cultic symbol of Yahweh. Yet
even in that change of position, we are prevented from
seeing any activity. Dagon's submission to Yahweh is
a state, without beginning, and not a process.

When it is merely the Philistines that are the objects of Yahweh's offensive actions, however, there

can be no question of Yahweh's vast superiority. His total mastery of the situation is denoted in the playful, almost comic way that he defeats the Philistines (Bentzen 1948:46; Hertzberg 1964:53; Stoebe 1973: 144).

The specific ascription of the Philistines' sufferings to 'the hand of Yahweh' is also significant in view of the fact that Dagon's hands (palms) are cut off (v. 4, Miller & Roberts 1977:48). The intended contrast is exhibited in the verb conjugations: Yahweh's hand is subject of the active verb *wattikbad*, while Dagon's palms are governed by the passive, *kerutôt*; Yahweh acts, Dagon is passive.

Miller and Roberts suggest that the use of plague as a machine of war is part of Israel's divine warrior idealogy (1977:49). They see the divine warrior as a primary image that binds all parts of the narrative together - the defeats of Israel, Dagon, and the Philistines - demonstrating that the power of Yahweh, the divine warrior, is the key to what the narrative is really about. One can agree with this suggestion insofar as the narrative does illustrate Yahweh's complete control of the situation from beginning to end. The instance of the plagues and their association with the divine warrior idealogy is a further example of the narrator's efforts to impress upon the reader the fact of Yahweh's supremacy.

The insuperability of Yahweh is, however, only a key to the meaning of the narrative. The point of illustrating at such great length (chs. 5-6) that Yahweh was in control is not simply to affirm Yahweh's superiority over the enemies of Israel and their gods (e.g. Miller & Roberts 1977:68). Rather Yahweh's obvious superiority is given centre stage to evoke a question in the mind of the reader.

If Yahweh is so obviously superior to the Philistines that one must assume his *total* control over the Israelite defeat, why did the defeat have to take place on such a grand scale? Could not the sinful priests have been exterminated more economically (cf. Campbell 1979:35)?

Verse 7

The Ashdodites' recognition that Yahweh is behind their misfortunes parallels that of the Israelites in 4.3. The difference between the Philistines and the Israelites is that the former see the elimination of the ark's presence among them as the way to relieve their suffering while Israel, Yahweh's people, regarded the presence of the ark as the guarantee of their deliverance (4.3). In future, however, Israel will come to share the Philistine antipathy to the ark's presence (cf. 6.20).

Campbell has drawn attention to a recurring pattern of interaction that begins here in vv. 6f (1975:96-99; cf. Schicklberger 1973:155-59). Yahweh is shown plaguing the Philistines in the vicinity of the ark, and they respond by passing the ark along to someone else /8/. The pattern is partially unified through a chiastic structure that shapes vv. 6-7. The structure, in outline, is:

The hand of Yahweh is heavy on the Ashdodites	he smites them (Ashdod and precincts /9/) with tumours
The men of Ashdod cognize their situation	they say that his (Yahweh's) hand is hard on them and their god

The pattern is important. Its repetition firmly impresses upon the reader the way that Yahweh treats his enemies and the recourse that they have to his attacks. When the ark is finally received by Israel (6.19-7.1), Yahweh's similar treatment of Israelites and their similar response are clear indications to the reader that the disturbing effects of the Elide affair have not been remedied.

Verse 8

Like the Israelites in ch.4, the Philistines are
now faced with their first 'defeat,' and the apparent
inability of their god to do anything for them. The
Philistine princes convene to decide what to do with
the ark of Israel's god in view of their situation,
just as the Israelite elders met and together decided to summon the ark in view of their defeat (4.3).
The operation of this technique of scenic parallelism
has often been observed operating in other narratives
(e.g. the wife-sister motif in Gen 12, 20, and 26).
Robert Alter suggests that 'narrative analogy' (his
term) is an important feature in much biblical narrative, through which 'one part of the text provides
oblique commentary on another' (1981:21). The parallel between Israel in 4.3 and the Philistines in 5.8
highlights the difference in the response to known
defeat by Yahweh. Israel calls for the ark to remind
Yahweh of his covenantal commitment, while the Philistines, who have no contract with Yahweh, pass it on.
The narrator will use this Israelite/Philistine parallel again in 6.19-21 with a definite difference in
Israel's response, which is in obvious contrast to the
parallel here in v. 8.
The Philistine decision to send the ark around to
Gath indicates their unrepentant will to retain Israel's God's ark and affords further opportunities
for exploiting the effect of Yahweh's show of power
on the reader's understanding of the narrative. (Cf.
Schicklberger 1973:155-58, who discusses the repeated
incident in terms of 'Intensification' [*Steigerung*]
and 'Dramatization' [*Dramatisierung*] and their effect
on the reader.)

Verse 9

The pattern established in Ashdod (vv. 6-8) is repeated in vv. 9-10; the Philistines' suffering is inten-

sified as a result of the ark's continuing presence amongst them. The hand of Yahweh results in a 'great confusion' in the city /10/. Yahweh makes use of his divine implements of war to do what he would not do when called upon by Israel in ch. 4.

The second sentence of v. 9 reinforces this reading of the *mehûmâ*. The objects of the divine warrior's attack are specifically the men of the city, 'from small to big.' The detailed description of the human object of the divine attack emphasizes the insignificance of Yahweh's 'opponents.' Again Yahweh is shown to have been in full control of Israel's defeat; at the same time, however, the inappropriate grandiosity of his methods is highlighted. As he engineered a defeat of the entire Israelite nation to kill the sons of Eli in ch. 4, Yahweh now brings his divine armament to bear on the men of Gath in order to show them who is really responsible for victory and defeat. Both his sense of proportion and his timing seem skewed /11/.

Verses 10-11

The men of Gath respond to Yahweh's attentions with greater speed than the Ashdodites. Without a convention of the Philistine leaders, the ark is immediately dispatched to Ekron (Campbell 1975:98). The Ekronites, however, have already heard of the misfortunes of those to whom the ark is sent. They object to the ark's presence in their town /12/. Fearing for their lives in view of Yahweh's prior exhibitions, the Ekronites reconvene the Philistine princes. Unlike the Ashdodites (v. 8), they finally know exactly what to do with the ark and demand that it be sent back to Israel. As in the final plague in Egypt (Exod 12.29-33), it is the *mehûmat mawet*, which brought death to the Ekronites, that convinces the Philistines to send the ark back:

Exod 12	1 Sam 5
wattehî ṣe'aqâ gedolâ [v.30]	wayyiz'aqû ha'eqronîm [v.10]
qûmû ṣe'û mittôk 'ammî [v.31]	šalleḥû 'et-'arôn . . . [v.11]
'amerû kullanû metîm [v.33]	lahamîtenî we'et 'ammî [v.10;
	cf. 11)/13/

Yahweh's affliction of the Philistines can get
no worse, since he has intensified his efforts from
plaguing them to killing them. The intensification is
highlighted by repeated vocabulary taken from vv. 6-9:

wattikbad yad-yhwh [v.6]	kabedâ me'od yad ha'elohîm [v.11]
mehûmâ gedôlâ me'od [v.9]	mehûmat-mawet [v.11]

Verse 12

David Daube (1963:75) notes that the idea that
those who escape one peril are smitten by another is
also found in the exodus narrative (Exod 10.5, 12,
15). Driver also makes the exodus connection when he
observes that *šaw'â* is paralleled in prose only by
Exod 2.23 (1913:53). It would seem, then, that the vocabulary of v. 12 has been employed to remind the reader of the exodus event. Daube especially has drawn
attention to numerous parallels between the events in
1 Sam 5-6 and the exodus (1963:73-88; cf. Bentzen
1948:45-47; Bourke 1954:96-99; Fretheim 1967:120f).
Chs. 5-6 should be read in the light of the exodus
story and the latter's significance for Israelite
thought /14/. In v. 12, however, the narrative has only begun to draw attention to the exodus motifs, so
that the reader's consideration of such allusions is
just developing.

In view of 4.9 the description of the cry of the
city 'mounting up to heaven' is especially interesting.
In 4.9, the Philistines are exhorted to fight brave-
ly so as not to become slaves to the Hebrews as the
Hebrews are slaves to the Philistines. Now in 5.12,
however, the Philistine city utters the same cry for

help (*šaw'at ha'îr*) that the Israelites cried to
God when they were slaves in Egypt (Exod 2.23).
Though they won the battle, the Philistines' existence under the heavy hand of Yahweh seems to have
become as oppressive as that of the Hebrew slaves.

The captivity of the ark, which is also to say the
Israelite defeat, has resulted in the Philistine degradation in 'slavery.' Hence it is not only Israel that
experiences loss from the battle. The Philistines too
are subject to the experience of defeat. Are there any
winners? Yes, one; 'By withholding his hand from the
Philistines at Ebenezer, Yahweh had created an opportunity not only to remove his ark from Shiloh and its
wicked priests but also to demonstrate his power in
the land of his enemies' (McCarter 1980:126).

The whole series of events from the defeat of Israel, to the deaths of the Elides, to the Philistine
devastation portrays men as pawns in the hand of Israel's God. With them Yahweh plays a deadly game in
which he eliminates those who have sinned against him,
simultaneously affording himself the opportunity to
display his power to the Philistines. The narrative
follows the movement of the ark from town to town to
show Yahweh in action, revealing his gradual intensification of the Philistines' devastation. Yahweh's
personal motivation is the same as his purpose in
devastating the Egyptians in Exodus. He sends minor
plagues at first, not wanting to crush 'the opposition'
straightaway so that he can give an extended demonstration of his power. God's ultimate aim, of course,
is to spread his reputation (cf. Exod 9.15f; Lev 26.45;
Num 14.13, 15; Josh 2.9-11; Kaufmann 1972:297). While
the narrator has not put such an explicit avowal as
that of Exod 9.14-16 in the mouth of Yahweh here, he
has made the divine intention clear in the structural
parallels between this scene and the exodus narrative.

Yahweh's hand in the Israelite defeat was not explicitly mentioned. The reader knows of it from chs.
1-3, and Israel assumes it in 4.3, but Yahweh accom-

plished his first purpose in secrecy. When it comes
to his self-vindication amongst the Philistines, however, he plays his hand in full view (ch. 5) /15/.

The divine character obviously wishes to be associated only with the victory over Israel's enemies. Since
he later exhibits no qualms about proclaiming his own
active role in Israel's greatest defeat, the exile, the exile
may be that he realizes that his role in the defeat of
ch. 4 is indefensible. The divine justification for the
exile was the extent of Israelite sin, and so God could
publish his role as a just act of retribution. Without
such justification, however, he remains silent, working
only behind the scene in ch. 4.

The reflective reader is hard-pressed to find reassurance in the tale of Yahweh's vengeful rampage in
captivity (as according to McCarter 1980:126). If Yahweh was always in control of the situation why could
he not have simply stricken the Elides with the deadly
plague that killed the Philistines? When David wanted
Uriah dead, he simply arranged for him to be deserted
in the frontlines of a battle (2 Sam 11.14-17). Miller
and Roberts are right that the might of Yahweh is the
red thread of ch. 5 (1977:49), but they are wrong when
they suggest that the narrative is an 'early theodicy'
that vindicates Yahweh's actions by giving the reader
an insight into the larger purposes of Yahweh (1977:
73).

Far closer to the mark is Campbell who sees the
narrative as an expression of 'an overwhelming conviction of the absolute freedom of Yahweh' (1975:206).
As Eli said, 'he is Yahweh and does as he pleases'
(3.18). Rather than providing reassurance, the narrative exposes the frailty of the theocracy in the weak
link of its human priests, and the a-rationality of
Israel's God, whose purposes are not always compatible with the well-being of his people.

Granting all these negative considerations created
in and by the narrative, there is an as yet unexplored,
positive possibility in ch. 5 (and 6). The exodus assoc-

iations in ch. 5 have been observed by several readers, most of whom have suggested that chs. 4-6 describe a new or second exodus by which Yahweh demonstrates his desire for renewed affiliation with Israel (Bentzen 1948:46; Timm 1966:525f; Fretheim 1967:120-22; Campbell 1975:200-7).

Campbell offers an example of a reader who is guided by the exodus associations in chs. 5-6. He perceives the end of ch. 4 as the end of an epoch in Israel's history (1975:199f). The covenantal relationship established at Sinai on the basis of Yahweh's saving deeds in the exodus, seems to have been dissolved (Timm 1966:522, cited with approval by Campbell 1975:199). When, in the course of chs. 5-6, Yahweh is seen engaged in a second exodus, the reader is led to entertain the belief that Yahweh is establishing a new basis for renewed relationship with Israel. Campbell is careful to point out that this second exodus does not lead *automatically* to Israel (1975: 205). His caution at this time is, however, a product of his inclusion of the conclusion of the next scene (6.19-21) in the reading of ch. 5. That is to say, his reading of ch. 5 is made after the fact of having read the entire narrative.

For a reader following the step by step unfolding of the narrative, the exodus associations are more seductive. The prospect of renewed relationship between Yahweh and Israel on the basis of this second exodus is brought to the reader's attention by literary parallels that recall the exodus and its theological-political significance (Fretheim lists 15 parallels, 1967:120.). The similarities between the Philistine and Egyptian devastations lead the reader to expect similar conclusions. The rhetoric of the exodus parallels, therefore, leads the reader to believe that though Yahweh may have botched the Elide affair he is, in the new exodus, showing a desire and intention for reconciliation with Israel. The new relationship will be based on the second exodus which indicates Yahweh's will to act for Israel against its enemies (cf. Fretheim 1967: 121).

As will be seen in the conclusion of the voyage of the ark, however, the new exodus does not result in a renewal of Yahweh's relationship to Israel. The opposite occurs. The narrator uses the exodus parallel to set up his reader for a great disappointment at the end of ch. 6. The reader's disappointment is focused squarely on Yahweh, who seemed to be engineering a new exodus leading to a renewed covenantal relationship.

This elicitation of reader disappointment encourages the reader to sympathize even more with the suffering Israelites, who are ignorant of all the processes and events the reader has seen. The narrator seeks to establish the bond between the reader and suffering Israel just as his protrayal of Yahweh tends to alienate the reader from Yahweh. The narrative establishes these polarities in preparation for ch. 8, in which the story of Israel's rejection of Yahweh will be told. In order to preclude any automatic pious judgements on Israel's request in ch. 8, the narrator has equipped the reader to understand the reasons for Israel's action; the reader will thus be able to consider, seriously, the validity of Israel's claim. The presentation of chs. 4-6 neutralizes the theological-political prejudices of the reader (that God rightly and justly rules Israel) so that the reader can approach the request in ch. 8 with an appreciation of its legitimacy. Without the background provided by chs. 1-7, the reader is almost inevitably dominated by theological prejudice and the overpowering rhetoric of Samuel and Yahweh in ch. 8. The reactions of commentators who read chs. 8-12 separate from chs. 1-7 testify to this predisposition.

CHAPTER FOUR:
PART SIX

1 SAMUEL 6

Verse 1

Verse 1 follows naturally on the description of the
final plague that breaks the Philistine determination
to keep the ark. It is not 'late' (Stoebe 1973:151)
nor does it displace an expected conclusion of the
account concerning Ekron (Smith 1899:42, followed
by Budde 1902:42). The Ekronites' resolve in 5.11 is
firm - the ark must be sent back. Chapter 6.1 is a
summarizing chronological note, a flashforward or
prolepsis, indicating the total duration of the ark's
stay in Philistine territory /1/.

The insertion of a chronological summary at this
point indicates, beforehand, that the ark will definitely be sent out of Philistine territory and so
serves as a fitting conclusion to the description of
the plagues. What follows v. 1, therefore, is presented as a detailed retrospect of the final moments
that led up to the ark's departure (against Campbell
1975:108).

The proleptic vision afforded by v. 1 diverts the
reader's attention away from the simple chronological
sequence of the ark's departure and towards the significance of the departure. This deictic function of v. 1
supplements the emphasis placed on words and meaning
throughout vv. 1-16. Schicklberger has noticed that,
in contrast to ch. 5, ch. 6 focuses on the spoken word
rather than on events or actions. Even from a purely
quantitative point of view it is a conversation develop-

ing into a sermonic address that constitutes the better part of this chapter (1973:168).

Verse 2

The double question of the Philistines has provoked much scholarly discussion about literary-critical implications (see Campbell 1975:108-12). Any difficulties can be obviated, however, by the simple observation that the multiple questions of the Philistines exhibit both their anxious desire to get rid of the ark and their self-confessed ignorance of how to go about that needful task. The point is not how many questions are asked, but a realistic depiction of the distraught Philistines, who are anxious to relieve themselves of the ark.

The same impression is conveyed by the summons to the priests and diviners, specialists called in to deal with the technical problem at hand (Ehrlich 1902:186; Hertzberg 1964:57). The narrator's note that the Philistines call priests and diviners to get answers to their questions demonstrates that the situation is beyond the means of ordinary people (cf. Gutbrod 1956: 46).

Bourke notes a parallel to v. 2 in Exod 8.19 (1954: 97; cf. Fretheim 1967:120); again the reader is reminded that this narrative is proceeding along the lines laid down in the exodus narrative. Will Yahweh and Israel be reunited?

Verse 3

The advice of the priests and diviners makes it clear that the Philistine difficulties require a cultic resolution. A solution is proposed in terms of an 'asam offering, indicating that the Philistines acknowledge that they have committed an inadvertent trespass against Yahweh by their capture and retention of the ark /2/.

The significance of the cultic solution lies in the nature of the action, which is an appeal for divine forgiveness and a halt to punishment. The Philistines are forced to recognize their actual position with respect to Yahweh, and to assume a proper posture of submission. There is no other option. God will be glorified.

Daube notes that the priestly instruction in v. 3 resembles the casuistic 'if/then' legislation of Deuteronomy (1963:80). The Philistines, according to Daube, appear to have come under the rule of religious legislation that obliges them to propitiate Yahweh in recognition of the authority of Israel's God. Yahweh's grip on the Philistines is tightening as it did on Egypt. In the course of the plagues, Pharaoh was also forced to submit to Yahweh, and requested that Moses make supplication to Yahweh on his behalf (Exod 8.4, 24; 9.27f; 10.16f; 12.32). Similarly, the Philistine priests' advice that the ark must not be sent away empty (*rēqam*) is paralleled by Israel's despoliation of Egypt, commanded by God himself (Exod 3.21f [*lo' telekû rēqam*]; 11.2f).

The narrator uses such exodus parallels to demonstrate the complete success of Yahweh's operations amongst the Philistines, and even more so, to increase the reader's expectation of a future reconciliation of Yahweh and his people. After all, was it not the case in Egypt that when Pharaoh and the Egyptians recognized Yahweh's authority (e.g. Exod 9.27f), Israel was soon allowed to leave Egypt and join Yahweh on non-Egyptian territory? The only difference in the present situation is that it is Yahweh who will soon be allowed to leave Philistine territory to make the expected reunion with his people Israel.

Verse 4

All Philistines are represented by the *'ašam* to Yahweh, which takes the form of five golden tumors

and five golden mice. The introduction of the mice at
this point has proved troublesome to scholars, who
have offered various literary-critical explanations.
Hertzberg suggests that the mice are a natural cause
for the plague and hence their appearance is contrary
to the purpose of divine glorification in the narrative (1964:58; cf. Stoebe 1973:151).

But the Philistines are uncertain about how to interpret the entire incident. They do not know what they
did to deserve their plague, and they do not know
how to stop it (v. 2). The priests' religious explanation of the plague depends on the success of the
'asam; only if they are healed will they know why
Yahweh afflicted them ('az terape'û wenôda' lakem,
v. 3). Even the act of returning the ark, the material
'admission' that Yahweh was responsible, is a test
to determine whether it was Yahweh or chance that
brought the plague to the Philistines (v. 9).

Miller and Roberts point out that there are no
known, exact, ancient parallels to the Philistine
procedure of making golden tumors and mice, but suggest, on the basis of a Hittite ritual, that a plague
could be attributed to an enemy god and that an end
was sought by placating the god with gifts (1977:55;
cf. Gaster 1969:453). Stoebe says the inclusion of
five golden mice, even though no mice have been previously referred to, is based on the prior knowledge of
instances of plagues of mice (1973:151). Though all
are agreed that we cannot be certain about the exact
significance of the golden mice, it seems possible
that these golden offerings were included as a kind
of insurance policy, in case the plague had some connection with mice. Whether the Philistines thought
Yahweh had sent the mice, or whether they thought of
them as a separate, natural cause, is not specified.
The fact that the mice are included in the offering
sent along with the ark, however, suggests that the
mice were connected to the action of Israel's God.

It is not necessarily contrary to the narrator's

attribution of the plagues to Yahweh, then, for the
Philistines to be uncertain about the cause of the
plague. Instead, it is a further reflection of the Philistine priests' human uncertainty about the causes
and meanings of the plague. They are simply playing
it safe and covering all possibilities, including the
chance that the plague is somehow connected with mice.
The mice need no explicit introduction in the previous
narrative; their introduction here, as the product of
Philistine uncertainty, is another instance in a continuing series of situations where man is not certain
how to respond to Israel's God's interventions in human affairs.

Verse 5

The exhibition of the Philistine uncertainty continues in v. 5. The fabrication of the golden tumors
and mice is a separate act virtually unconnected with
Israel's God, to whom the priests only say 'honour'
(*kabôd*) must be given. As commentators have observed, the images seem capable of two functions
(Mauchline 1971:78). They are both an *'ašam* presented to Yahweh, and homeopathic objects designed to
draw off the ill-effects of the objects they represent (cf. Hertzberg 1964:58; Num 21). The Philistine
vacillation is further illustrated in the participial
adjective, 'the destroyers of the land' (*hammašḥîtim
'et-ha'areṣ*), that modifies the images of tumors and
mice. Here the priests seem to view the destruction in
terms of its limited physical causes rather than as a
result of the divine hand. Of course they suspect the
hand of Yahweh (v. 3), but at the same time, as one
might expect of Philistines, they lean towards other
possibilites.

McCarter notes that the final sentence in v. 5
makes the priests and diviners seem even less confident than in v. 3 (1980:134; cf. Campbell 1975:113).
According to BDB (p. 19), the preposition *'ûlay* ex-

presses hope, fear, or doubt. In all cases an element of uncertainty prevails. To the Philistine religious experts Yahweh's divine acts in history are an uncertain quantity, not easily reckoned with. They are anxious and willing to respond, but uncertain about how to respond because they are uncertain about how to interpret what has happened to them. One gives honour to Yahweh in hope (*'ûlay*) that he will lighten his hand on people, god, and land, while at the same time, making apotropaic images as an insurance policy. Although there is some relation between the two acts, even the syntax of v. 5 separates them into distinct sentences, each with its own verb.

Within the compass of the entire Israel-Philistine episode, the Philistine uncertainty over Yahweh's part in their misfortune is yet another expression of the sub-theme of human uncertainty about divine action that runs throughout. Just as Israel did not know why their own God would allow them to be defeated (4.3), the Philistines are not certain what they have done to displease Israel's God, nor even certain that he is displeased. The narrator emphasizes this gap between human understanding and divine action, only temporarily bridged for the reader by the narrator's unrestricted point of view, because it is of central importance to the developments in Israel's political thought in ch. 8. In that chapter, Yahweh's undependability in conjunction with Israel's uncertainty concerning the divine mind provide Israel with justification for a new political structure.

Verse 6

This warning against hardening of the heart is not at variance with the fact that the Philistine priests were in some doubt about the exact cause of the plagues. Their doubts were not denials, and the possibility that Yahweh was responsible warranted an unhedged response (Keil and Delitzsch 1880:64).

Both Thenius (1864:25) and Campbell (1975:114) have noted that the Philistines voice no reluctance to which v. 6 may be seen as a priestly reponse (cf. Rost 1926:13). The explicit recollection of the exodus events seems, rather, to be somewhat akin to an aside, delivered in the presence of the Philistines (who have no need of it), yet directed mainly to the reading audience. Bourke comments that 'one cannot avoid the impression that at this point the writer is putting a central idea of his own into the mouths of his characters' (1954:96).

This reference to the exodus reminds the reader of Israel's origins in 'salvation history' (Timm 1966: 525). What we see, we are told, is a new exodus, a new basis for relationship between Israel and Yahweh. In view of the fact that the relationship was disrupted in ch. 4 (cf. 3.30-32) the narrator indicates the significance of Yahweh's actions during his stay among the Philistines. Like the Philistines' question in 4.8 (a reminder about the covenantal significance of the upcoming battle for Israel), v. 6 directs attention away from simple events to the theological and political significance of those events. 4.8 served as the theological-political key for understanding the crisis engendered by Israel's defeat (cf. Timm 1966:521). Now 6.6 serves a similar purpose; in contrast to 4.8, though, it points to a hope for covenantal renewal by directing attention to the similarity of the ark's departure from Philistine land to Israel's departure from Egyptian territory.

Finally, it should be said that although v. 6 is not a response to any preceding obstinacy amongst the Philistines, it is not altogether inappropriate in the context of events. In v. 5, the priests recommend that Israel give 'honour' (*kabôd*) to Yahweh. It is exactly this, giving honour, that the priests themselves do in v. 6. As Hertzberg observes, there is a paronomastic link between vv. 5-6 based on the words *kabôd* (v. 5) and *tekabbedû, kibbedû* (v. 6) (1964:59).

Verse 6 gives glory to Yahweh by correctly evaluating his power and advising the proper response of submission. It was in order to elicit such recognition, both in Egypt and world-wide, that Yahweh performed his mighty deeds in Egypt (Exod. 7.4f; 9.14-16). By acquiescing to Yahweh and pointing out the folly of the Egyptian resistance, the Philistine priests give honour to Yahweh in hopes of not becoming the object of Yahweh's 'sporting activities' (hit'allel).

Verses 7-9

The instructions for the return of the ark and its booty are a continuing expression of the Philistine uncertainty. The plans exhibit an effort to show reverence and respect to Yahweh, but at the same time they exhibit some disrespect by designing a test to determine whether Yahweh is really responsible. The two motives are especially visible as concatenated in v. 7. The new cart and the unworked milch cows are signs of respect for the ark's sanctity and a desire to avoid further profanity towards it (Keil & Delitzsch 1880:65). Yet the fact that the cows are unbroken to yoking and their calves are separated from them also makes them tests to see if Yahweh can take this unlikely carriage home (Hertzberg 1964:59). Like the story of a doubting Thomas (John 20.24-29), this trial of Yahweh's cart driving abilities offers the narrator an opportunity to display the divine wonders (cf. Keil & Delitzsch 1880:66).

In v. 8, the Philistines are given instructions for the ark's removal from Philistine territory. Several parallels between v. 8 and v. 2 reveal a remarkable change in the Philistine attitude toward the ark:

v. 2	v. 8
The Philistines took [wayyiqhû] the ark of God.	Take [ûleqahtem] the ark of Yahweh.

They brought [wayyabî'u] it to the house of Dagon.	Put [ûnetattem] it onto the cart.
They installed [wayyaṣîgû] it next to Dagon.	Set [taśîmû] the golden objects, rendered as an 'ašam, in the box /3/ beside it (the ark).

In the first parallel a change is seen in the motivation for the same verb; *lqḥ* in 5.2 describes the Philistines taking the ark home as booty, while in 6.8 it is an order from the Philistine priests telling how to get rid of the ark. The same contrast is seen in the verbs of the second parallel, albeit using different verbs. Also in 5.2 they bring the ark to the sanctuary of their own god, Dagon, but in 6.8 they put the ark into the cart, a new 'sanctuary' constructed to house the ark alone. Finally in the third parallel we see a clear contrast between the ark, set beside Dagon as a trophy in 5.2, and the golden *'ašam* set beside the ark as a propitiatory going-away present in 6.8. The distinct change of heart evidenced by the comparison of these two verses supplements statements such as v. 6, which demonstrates the effect of Yahweh's mighty deeds on his enemies.

As Fretheim notes, v. 8 also offers a parallel to the exodus story in the mention of the golden objects (*kelê hazzahab*) that are given to the departing captives by their repentant captors (1967:120; cf. Exod 12.35). The common despoliation motif is yet another encouragement to the reader to identify Yahweh's exit as a new exodus, and so to expect a renewal of the covenantal relationship inseparably associated with the exodus.

Miller and Roberts correctly surmise that v. 9 reveals some uncertainty on the Philistines' part, but wrongly conclude that their concern in the test 'is obviously due to the consideration that if Yahweh was not responsible, then some other power was, and they would have to keep searching for the correct deity to appease before the plague would abate' (1977:56). The priests explicitly state that if it was not Yahweh that had perpetrated the calamity, it was simply 'chance' (*miqreh*). The narrator's concern is not to explore the various theological explanations for war or plague in the ancient near east. His aim is, rather, to demonstrate Yahweh's control over the Philistine situation and to follow that demonstration with an examination of its implications for Israel (6.13ff).

Verses 10-12

The plan is put into effect with the result, predictable from the reader's perspective, that the cows and cart head straight for Beth-Shemesh without deviating. As Driver notes, the emphasis in v. 12 falls on the straightness of the cows' route (1913:56). The narrator has the Philistine princes follow the ark on its homeward journey so that there is no doubt, even amongst the Philistines, about the significance of the journey.

Verses 13-14

The reader's attention is now directed to the Israelite reaction to the ark's return. The Philistines and their doubt have served their purpose and so are retired, temporarily, with the note in v. 16.

This view of Israel is the first offered since ch. 4, where the reader was left with the picture of an Israel lamenting the departure of Yahweh. Any uncertainty over what Israel's response to Yahweh's return would be is quickly removed. After presenting a view of Israel going about its yearly agricultural activities (v. 13), and hence in no dire strait requiring Yahweh's aid, the narrator describes Israel's reaction to the return of their God.

Recalling that Israel had questioned Yahweh's beha-

viour in 4.3 and that it was possible for an Israelite
to think that Yahweh had abandoned Israel (4.22), Israel's response is amazing. One would expect at least
a hint of reproach, yet there is none. In three short,
uncluttered, verbal descriptions their undivided joy
over the return is depicted - 'they looked up, saw the
ark, and rejoiced at the sight'/4/. The description
focuses exclusively on Israel's visual reception of
the ark, indicating thereby that 'just the sight (of
it)' made them happy. They have gained nothing from
the ark's return. They know nothing of the conditions
of its return. The fact that they are harvesting the
wheat crop indicates that they are getting along very
well without the ark. Yet their reaction to the mere
sight of it is spontaneous and positive. Again, Israel
comes out spotless in the narrator's presentation. The
people seem to have forgiven and forgotten.

The actual dinner reception ('olâ) for Yahweh is
described in v. 14. The cart goes into the field of a
certain Joshua and stands there. The cart itself is the
subject of the verbs in v. 14. The reader, well aware
that carts are without volition, will no doubt see
the hand of Yahweh at the reins of the cart. The description leaves Yahweh behind the scenes once more
and lends an aura of weirdness to the cart's movements, as was the case in v. 12. The divine cart-driver
has stopped at a specific spot (šam) where (šam),
it so happens, there is a large stone /5/.

The name of Joshua, the man in whose field the cart
stops, recalls another more famous character who was
chosen to lead Israel into the promised land when Moses was barred entry (cf. Num 20.12; Josh 1). Once
again an allusion to the exodus story is used to indicate the significance of these events. In this particular example, the ark's passage onto Israelite soil
in the field of a certain Joshua recalls Israel's own
entry into the land under the leadership of another
Joshua. From the perspective of Israel's history, the
return of the ark into Joshua's field after the des-

truction of Israel's polity in ch. 4 would seem a perfect portent for the renewal of that selfsame polity.

The second Israelite response, after seeing the ark
and rejoicing, is to offer a holocaust to Yahweh, using as material the spoils of his travels among the
Philistines (Hertzberg 1964:59f). The response is
immediate, following right after the description of
the cart's stop by the big rock. The offering of an
'olâ by Israel with materials provided by the
Philistines is appropriate. The 'olâ was, among
other capacities, both an expression of thanksgiving
(Lev 22.17-19; Num 15.1-16) and an expiatory sacrifice
(Lev 1.4; Milgrom 1976:769). Here the Israelites express their thanks, and at the same time unwittingly
perform an expiatory sacrifice on behalf of the Philistines, who had supplied the sacrificial materials.

Verse 15

Most commentators have viewed v. 15 as a late insertion designed to correct any misimpressions about
the manner in which the sacrifice of v. 14 was carried
out (Stoebe 1973:148; McCarter 1980:136). The Levites
are described taking the ark and the box of gold articles down (hôrîdû) and setting them on the
great stone. As Stoebe observes, however, the cart has
already been burnt so that the description is out of
chronological sequence (1973:148). The difficulty can
be resolved by attention to the rhetorical emphasis
and structure of vv. 14f.

In v. 14, the description of Israel's reaction is
presented as immediate and spontaneous. An 'olâ is
offered the moment the cart stops. The description of
the Levites' activities in v. 15 can be understood as
a narratorial aside, not intended as a chronologically
subsequent event to v. 14. The concern of v. 15a is to
show that the ark was not mishandled /6/. Rather, it
was dismounted and set on the great stone by the Levites, the only Israelites consecrated to handle the

ark (Num 4.4-15; Deut 10.8). The people of Bethshemesh do not make Uzzah's mistake (cf. 2 Sam 6:6f).

That v. 15a is not intended as a continuation of the
chronological sequence is indicated by two factors: 1.
The breaking up of the cart on which the ark sat is
narrated already in v. 14 in *chronological* order. 2.
In the second half of v. 15 the narrator makes use of
'resumptive repetition,' a rhetorical technique used
to resume the chronological sequence of a narrative by
an aside.

> By cutting the thread of a story at a convenient or
> even not quite so convenient, juncture, then inter-
> weaving other matter of a different narrative cha-
> racter, and again resuming the first account by
> means of repeating the verse, phrase, or even the
> word, at which the cut-off occurred, the author
> safeguards the linear continuity of the narration,
> and at the same time permits the listener or the
> reader to become aware of the synchroneity of the
> events related (Talmon 1978:17).

Verse 15b resumes v. 14 by repeating the words *he'elû
'olôt . . . lyhwh*, 'they offered holocausts to Yahweh.'
The rhetorical need for the device of resumptive repetition is created in v. 14, in which the narrator underlines the swift and *immediate* sacrificial response of
Israelites, the unspecified subjects of the verbs, to
Yahweh. Immediately thereafter (v. 15a), in narrative,
syntactic - not chronological - sequence the narrator
takes pains to show that no trespass was committed by
the unsanctified against the ark. Finally, in v. 15b,
the narrator returns to describe the unreserved sacrificial response.

In the resumptive repetition in v. 15b the subjects
of the sacrificial verbs are specified - the Bethshemeshites - an important development in view of the
subsequent incident. In addition, the narrator adds
that they also made sacrifices (*zebaḥîm*) to Yahweh
as a further indication of their unstinting welcome

for Yahweh. The temporal determinant - 'on that day' -
serves to link the action of v. 15b with that of v. 14,
a further support for the device of resumptive repetition.

Verse 16

At the same time that Israel is celebrating Yahweh's
apparent return, the Philistine chiefs are observing
the proceedings. The temporal simultaneity of their
observation is indicated by the repeated temporal determinant, 'on that day,' in both vv. 14 and 15. In
contrast to the Bethshemeshites, who rejoiced after
they saw (*wayyir'û*, v. 13) the ark, the Philistines
leave when they see (*ra'û*) the proceedings. The repeated verb *ra'â* functions as a *Leitwort*, directing the reader to connect the two occurrences and compare them (cf. Buber 1964:1131; Alter 1981:92-96). In
this instance both Philistines and Israelites are 'seeing' the return of Yahweh to Israel. The return sparks
a joyful celebration in Israel; the Philistines, on the
other hand, simply return home to the now devastated city of Ekron. The parallel is important because
it shows that Israel responds to Yahweh's return far
differently than the Philistines. Israel greets him as
their God. The Philistines just walk away. Obviously
Israel holds no grudge against Yahweh for his part in
their defeat in ch. 4. Yahweh's response to their
welcome will soon change this attitude, however, and
Israel will come to view Yahweh and the presence of
his ark just like the Philistines.

Verses 17-18

The verses, as Campbell observes, add an element
of verisimilitude to the narrative 'by associating it
with concrete and verifiable objects' (1975:120; cf.
McCarter 1980:137; above on 5.5)/7/. The narrator
opens his address, which is directed to his reader,
with the words 'and these' (*we'eleh*) as though he

had the very things he lists sitting in front of him.
He uses this rhetorical device to create the impression in his readers that he does have the items and, in
turn, that the events described did happen. Supplementary to his reference to the golden tumors and mice, he
points to the great stone which sits 'to this very day
in the field of Joshua, the Bethshemeshite' (v. 18) as
a 'witness' ('ed) to the truth of what he has depicted /8/.

Perhaps the emphasis on the reality of the events under description is made with a view to the subsequent
events. All through chs. 5-6 the narrator has encouraged the reader to see the ark's sojourn and return in
terms of the paradigmatic exodus story. With the return and joyous celebrations of ch. 6 the reader is
led to believe that the problem of the captured ark
and the foreboding covenantal implications of that
occurrence have been not only ended, but even have a
certain value. Once more Yahweh has had an opportunity to display his awesome abilities to the nations and
to reaffirm his choice of Israel as he had in the first
exodus. Now, with Yahweh back with Israel, surely the
bad times are over. Could any further misfortune really come to Israel?

Verse 19

Nothing could be more unexpected, either by the
Israelites in the narrative, or the person reading
the narrative, than the response of Yahweh to the
attentions of the Bethshemeshites. Confronted with
the startling presentation of MT in v. 19 - standing
in such clear tension with the preceding context, says
Stoebe, that it cannot be the organic continuation but
must be an individual tradition (1973:153) - the majority of scholars follow LXX or some reconstruction
based thereon. Unfortunately the LXX reading has its
own contextual difficulties /9/.

N. H. Tur-Sinai lists the main difficulties of MT

as follows: 1) The predicate verb *wayyak* appears twice, the first time without an explicit subject; 2) The description of the numbers of the smitten also occurs twice - 70 men and 50,000 men - in asyndetic combination; 3) The larger number - 50,000 - is difficult to accept for a small town like Bethshemesh; 4) The smaller number - 70 - is unexpectedly small in a legend about 'a great slaughter' (1951:277). Tur-Sinai fails to mention the further difficulty seen by most readers in the 'justification' supplied for Yahweh's action, 'because they looked in/on (*b*) Yahweh's ark.'

The opening sentence of v. 19 describes Yahweh's response to the inhabitants of Bethshemesh, who were last seen in v. 15 offering both *'olâ* and *zebaḥ* sacrifices to Yahweh. 'And he struck down (*wayyak*) some of the men of Bethshemesh because they looked at the ark.' What kind of way is this to treat the people who rejoice at the mere sight of his ark? Yahweh's treatment of the Bethshemeshites is similar to his treatment of the Philistines (5.6, 9, 12) - both are stricken by God (Willis 1971:296). The connection between the two incidents of divine assault against human objects is foregrounded by the repetition of the verb *nkh* in the same form, *wayyak* (v. 19; cf. 5.6, 9). The omission of 'Yahweh' as the explicit subject of the first occurrence of *wayyak* in v. 19 contributes to this linkage with the previous incidents, where the verb also appears without the addition of an explicit subject.

When the reader recalls that Yahweh's previous assaults on the Philistines were cast in the mould of the exodus pattern, designed to exalt Yahweh in the course of his saving deeds performed on Israel's behalf, the repetition of the same divine behaviour amongst his own chosen people changes the meaning of the ark's 'new exodus' entirely. Instead of a dual purpose event, with both divine and human dividends, it becomes solely an opportunity for an overbearing display of divine power. If, instead of leading up to

Israel's renewal of relationship with Yahweh, the 'new exodus' leads up to a situation in which Israel is also subjected to the divine assault and self-glorification, the entire spectacle becomes an occasion for realignment. Instead of Israel and Yahweh against the nations, we see Israel and Philistia (representing 'the nations') against Yahweh.

This realignment of Israel is particularly evident when we recall that 6.19-21 is the third incidence of a 'narrative analogy,' in which Israel or the Philistines respond to a divine action in connection with the presence or absence of the ark. In the first instance Israel, seeing itself submitted to defeat by Yahweh (4.3), calls for the ark's presence to remind Yahweh of his covenantal commitment to Israel (4.3-4). In the second case, the Philistines convene after their evident 'defeat' at Yahweh's hands, and decide that the ark must be sent on to someone else (5.8).

Now in the third incidence Israel's attitude is seen to have undergone a remarkable shift. Their response to Yahweh's action and the presence of the ark is like that of the Philistines who have no covenant with Yahweh, and unlike that of the Israelites in 4.3f. The latter still operated within the covenantal guidelines and attempted to call Yahweh to order. Israel in 6.20f, seeing no rationale for Yahweh's behaviour, makes no claims based on the covenant, and simply tries to relieve itself of the burden of the ark's presence. Without mutual understanding, there are no grounds for relationship. The parallel to the Philistine response in 5.8 offers convincing evidence that Israel has become 'like the nations' (cf. 8.20) as a result of Yahweh's disregard for his people.

The narrator seems, nevertheless, to supply some mitigation for Yahweh's attack on the Bethshemeshites in the explanation that he did it because they looked 'at the ark of Yahweh' (*ba'arôn yhwh*) /10/. But what kind of mitigation is this? The narrator has already given the reader a direct description of the

Bethshemeshites looking at the ark (*wayyir'û 'et-ha'arôn*, v. 13) including an unambiguous description of their mental state at that time - they were overjoyed at the sight (*wayyismehu lir'ôt*, v. 13)/11/.

The simplest solution to the seeming contradiction between the joyful seeing in v. 13 and the seeing in v. 19, for which Yahweh assaults the Bethshemeshites, is to regard the mitigation as ironic. Yahweh's response is made to appear totally incomprehensible by the narrator. It is as though Yahweh assaults the Bethshemeshites for simply looking at the ark. The mitigation is, ironically, a concealed criticism of Yahweh's conduct towards his people. Both before (ch. 4) and after the new exodus of the ark they suffer at his hands for no just cause. The rationale for Yahweh's actions is now hidden not only from the people in the narrative, as seemed to be the case for some in ch. 4 (e.g. 4.3). The irony of the mitigation is shared by the omniscient narrator with his reader, who is now numbered among those who do not see the purpose of Yahweh.

'Recourse to irony by an author carries an implicit compliment to the intelligence of the reader, who is invited to associate himself with the author and the knowing minority who are not taken in by the ostensible meaning' (Abrams 1981:90). In this case, the narrator invites the reader to share an ironic jab at Yahweh that underlines the Bethshemeshites' perplexity over Yahweh's ungrateful response to the joyous visual reception. The ironic explanation also promotes the reader's sympathetic identification with the Israelites in the story. At this juncture, he or she actually does share in their ignorance of the divine motivation. Knowledge of the ironic mitigation causes the reader to reflect on the distance between the purposes of God and the cognitive possibilities of humankind.

The question still remains why the narrator chooses to say that the Bethshemeshites looked *ba'arôn* in

v. 19 instead of *'et-ha'arôn* as in v. 13 if he was
intending only ironic justification of Yahweh's assault. A rhetorical justification may be seen in the
fact that the preposition *b* occurs four times in v.
19. The use of the preposition *b* after the verb 'to
see' (*ra'â*) parallels the latter to the smiting (*nakâ*)
performed by Yahweh. The parallel usage of *b* to
introduce the objects of both verbs draws attention
to the contrast in the type of action done by each subject:

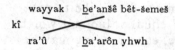

kî

wayyak ḅe'anšê bêt-šemeš

ra'û ḅa'arôn yhwh

The chiastic structure highlights the incongruity of
Yahweh's response by drawing attention to the parallel
and reciprocal action of the Bethshemeshites; their
looking was joyful; his response is wrathful.

The second problem that Tur-Sinai saw in MT was
that the repetition of the words 'and he smote the
people' (*wayyak ba'am*) seemed to indicate a disturbed, unnatural text. In conjunction with the emphasis
on the reprehensibility of Yahweh's action, however,
the repeated emphasis on the smiting is suitable. The
narrator repeats the word *nakâ* four times in the
verse, forcibly recalling the parallel with the Philistine devastation (cf. 5.6, 9, 12) and focusing attention on Yahweh's unfriendliness.

The first occurrence of *nakâ* has 'the men of
Bethshemesh' as object; the second has 'the people.'
The change in object recalls the fact that the Bethshemeshites are a people, or more specifically, 'the
people' of Yahweh. He smites some of 'the people'
(cf. Exod 6.7) just as he smote the Philistines. The
repetition, therefore, emphasizes the overwhelming
nature of Yahweh's smiting and at the same time introduces the anti-covenantal aspect of the deed by the
subtle change of objects in the second occurrence /12/.

In Tur-Sinai's list of four difficulties in v. 19, the asyndetic numbers, 70 and 50,000 men, comprise three of the four. The asyndetic syntax is thought to show that 50,000 is a gloss (cf. Schulz 1919:109). The first number, 70, is unexpectedly small, while 50,000 is too many for a small town such as Bethshemesh (Tur-Sinai 1951:277). But the two numbers can be understood as examples of what Talmon has called 'double readings' (1975:231). Such double readings may result from the insertion of marginal glosses into the text together with the readings they were intended to supersede, or they may be the attempt of a scribe to preserve two variant readings of equal value and worth (p. 231). From this perspective, each reading may be examined to determine its effect on the narrative without the influence of the prejudicial label 'gloss' being attached to either.

When such separate readings are made, the difference between the two variants is small in terms of the effect on the narrative. Seventy men would represent the elimination of a complete complement of men. As Umberto Cassuto observes, 'This number - seventy - commonly indicates the perfection of a family blessed with offspring, both in the pre-Israelitic and in the Israelite traditions' (1967:8; cf. 1961:12f). The number seventy in v. 19 points to the severity of the divine assault in that the 'perfect number' of men are destroyed /13/. The second number, 50,000, is not that different, rhetorically speaking; it too emphasizes the severity of the damages done to Israel in the divine attack. Since the two readings are rhetorically synonymous, it is understandable why they were both preserved. In the present form of the text, the repetition of the numbers slain is in accord with the repeated verbs of Yahweh's smiting; the enormity of the devastation is foregrounded and impressed on the reader.

Yahweh's return to his people, signaled by the reappearance of the ark, made them happy (v. 13). His response to their reception has now changed their joy

to sorrow and they mourn their dead (*wayyit'abbelû*,
cf. Baumann 1977:46). Once more the narrator focuses
on the ill-effects of Yahweh's return to his people.
When Yahweh deserted Israel in ch. 4 he left them to
be defeated before the Philistines (4.3). The result
of that desertion is given in 4.10 - 'there was a great
slaughter' (*wattehî hammakkâ gedôlâ*). Having
achieved his purpose (the death of the Elides) in that
escapade and having shown the Philistines who really
controlled that battle, one would expect Yahweh to
return home and make amends for the incidental injustices to his people. Instead, Yahweh personally
makes yet another great slaughter amongst 'the people'
(*hikkâ yhwh ba'am makkâ gedôlâ*).

The narrator seems to be doing his best to point
out certain imbalances in the relationship between
Yahweh and Israel. Thus far the pattern of interaction
has been: 1. Israel offers sacrifices to Yahweh (2.13-
17; 6.14f); 2. Yahweh 'responds' with great slaughters
(4.10; 6.19).

Though Yahweh may have been justified (cf. 2.25) in
what he did to the Elides, he was not justified to include so many of the people in the punishment; though
Yahweh is justified to punish sanctum trespass, there
is no trepass in 6.19. The question mark that the narrator's portrait of Yahweh's behaviour places over the
viability of the covenant relationship is openly stated
in v. 20.

Verse 20

The questions posed by the Bethshemeshites are paralleled by two questions put by the Philistines during the course of their dealings with Yahweh. The
first question, 'Who can stand before Yahweh, this holy
God?,' is similar to the Philistines', 'Who can deliver
us from the power of these mighty gods?' (4.8, Willis
1971:296). The second, 'To whom might he go up from
upon us?,' is preceded by the Philistines', 'What

should we do with the ark of Yahweh? What shall we send back with him?' (6.2). The simple fact of the parallel itself reveals a remarkable affinity between Israelites and Philistines in their attitudes to Yahweh. Both attitudes are brought about by the warring actions of Yahweh, the divine warrior, against his enemies and against his people.

'The inability of the Bethshemeshites to stand before "this holy God" points to the primitive ideology of holy war, according to which an enemy could not stand before Yahweh' (Stoebe 1973:153; cf. Judg 2.14). Stoebe has correctly noted one implication of the Bethshemeshites' question: it is an expression of the conviction that no one, not even his own people, is safe from the warlike attacks of Yahweh. Israel, in coming close to the Philistines in the expression of this attitude, has become distant from Yahweh.

A second implication of the question, 'Who can stand before Yahweh, this holy God?,' is noted by Ehrlich, who suggests that the Bethshemeshites are expressing their inability as unsanctified people, to render properly sanctified treatment to the ark (1910:191; cf. Schulz 1919:111). More recently McCarter has adopted this view in conjunction with his emendation of the mitigation in v. 19 ('no members of the preisthood joined in') and the belief that the mention of levitical activity in v. 15 is a late insertion (1980:136f). Citing examples, he notes that the expression 'to stand before' connotes 'attend upon' and is often used of priests attendant on Yahweh or his cult. The Bethshemeshites, accordingly, are simply admitting their guilt in profaning the ark and suggesting that they find a suitable attendant.

While touching upon an important sense of the phrase 'to stand before,' McCarter's suggestion must be rejected for two reasons: 1. It depends upon an unconfirmed emendation of LXX in v. 19, and upon a hypothesis about the literary history of v. 15 that, in turn, depends on debatable literary-critical observations. 2. If the Bethshemeshites had admitted culpability for their misfortune and were simply seeking a proper priest to attend to the ark, why would they want to get rid of it? Why would the ark be derelicted to the care of a person who was not a member of a priestly family (cf. 6.21; 7.1)? Why would all Israel mourn Yahweh as though he were dead (7.2; cf. Buber 1956: 118)? Surely there was at least one proper priest in Israel.

The value of McCarter's observation about the phrase 'to stand before' is that it reveals yet another side to the Bethshemeshites' exasperation. Reading the chapter as it stands, v. 15 indicates that the ark was handled by licensed personnel, the Levites. The question of v. 20 may, therefore, be rhetorical. If those sanctified to handle the ark are not able to stand before Yahweh, who can? Only from this perspective on the cultic side of the Bethshemeshites' question do the subsequent question and events make sense (against Schicklberger 1973:128). If the Levites cannot deal with Yahweh and his ark, no one can. The ark goes into 'cold storage' and Israel mourns Yahweh.

Finally, there is a third side to the first question of v. 20. Not only is the phrase 'to stand before' used with reference to priestly service of Yahweh, itself a prominent aspect of covenantal intercourse between Yahweh and Israel; the phrase is also used both of covenantal intermediaries and of Israel standing before God in covenantal ceremonies /14/. In view of its context, then, the question of v. 20 is also rhetorical in a covenantal sense. No one can covenantally stand before this holy God who makes great slaughters (4.10; 6.19) amongst his people for no apparent reason.

The addition of the phrase 'this holy God' is a sarcastic comment on Yahweh's unapproachability and incomprehensibility. Hertzberg, who does not see any sarcasm in the phrase, still get the same impression and cites Eccl 5.2, 'God is in heaven and you upon earth,' as a parallel (1964:61). A covenant with such a totally 'other,' whose behaviour admits of no rationale from an Israelite perspective, is impossible. The question, then, is an expression of Israel's alienation from a God who will not be approached.

That the answer to the question, 'Who can stand before Yahweh, this 'holy' God?' is 'no one,' is confirmed by the second question, which contains an implicit answer to the first. The only way to deal with this God, as the Philistines well knew is to unload him on someone else. The use of the prepositional phrase 'from upon us' (*me'alênû*) characterizes the renewed presence of Yahweh with Israelites as a burden, wearisome to its bearer.

Verse 21

Like the Philistines, the first step the Israelites take when they decide to get rid of the ark is to send (*wayyišlehû*, cf. 6.8, 11) for outside help. The narrator continues to point out that Israel has been forced into the ignominious role of behaving as if they were Philistines on account of Yahweh; he has, in fact, modelled the entire Israelite encounter with Yahweh on the previous Philistine encounter. In outline form, the parallels are:

	Philistines	Israelites
1.	Take possession of the ark (5.1).	'Repossess' the ark (6.14).
2.	Install the ark in the cultic sanctuary (5.2).	Perform cultic acts celebrating the repossession (6.14f).
3.	Yahweh stikes the Philistines and creates a 'great confusion' [mehûmâ gedôlâ] in the city (5.9).	Yahweh strikes the people with a 'great smiting' [makkâ gedôlâ (6.19).
4.	The people cry out (5.10,12).	The people mourn (6.19).
5.	The people demand that the ark be sent away (5.11).	The people ask to whom they may send the ark (6.20).
6.	The ark is sent to Israel in a specially dedicated	The ark is taken up to Qiryath-ye'arim, and a guard

vehicle along with propiti-   is sanctified to keep it (7.1).
atory offerings (6.7-12).

Hertzberg asks the important question why the ark was
not sent to one of the more important, well-known
sanctuaries, instead of putting it into 'cold storage'
in a back-water like Qiryath-ye'arim (1964:61f). He
suggests a plausible historical reason, but misses the
reason implied in the narrative. The ark is now seen
as a dangerous burden, one not to be kept where many
people would be exposed to it. The choice of an out-
of-the-way hamlet is, therefore, quite natural.

The Bethshemeshites, aware that no one would take
the ark if they knew the true story of its return,
conceal the facts and make the description of the
ark's return as matter of fact as possible. They say
'the Philistines have returned Yahweh's ark,' failing
to mention the peculiar manner of the ark's return.
They are also deceptive in their instrucions to the
inhabitants of Qiryath-ye'arim. 'Come down and take up
the ark to you.' As Driver observes, Bethshemesh was
at a lower altitude, hence 'come down' and 'take up'
are geographically appropriate (1913:59f). But the
instructions also contain a hidden significance that
appears only when they are compared with the second
question of v. 20:

v. 20   we'el-mî ya'aleh me'alênû
v. 21   ha'alû 'otô 'alêkem

The Bethshemeshites conceal their real concern, that
Qiryath-ye'arim take on the burden, in a geographical
subterfuge.

CHAPTER FOUR:
PART SEVEN

1 SAMUEL 7

Verse 1

The men of Qiryath-ye'arim seem to see through the
Bethshemeshites' deception or to have some clues about
the dangers posed by the ark and its God. They come
and take the ark, but do not install it in a sanctuary
as would be expected (cf. Hertzberg 1964:61). Instead
the ark is brought to the home of a private citizen,
Abinadab, whose son Eleazar is consecrated to guard it.
The means by which the men of Qiryath-ye'arim came
to know the truth about the ark is left as a 'gap' or
'indeterminacy' to be filled in by each reader in his
or her own way (cf. Ingarden 1973a under 'concretization'; 1973b under 'indeterminacy'; Iser 1978:172-82).
That they do know that Yahweh has apparently rejected the services of the Levites is apparent from their
consecration of a secular person to a sacral task.

Chapter 7.1 describes how the ark was put into cold
storage, out of harm's way. As Ehrlich notes (1910:
192), the people cannot make priests or levitical at-
tendants for the ark (cf. Schulz 1919:111); the latter
are chosen and sanctified directly by Yahweh (Num 4.4-
15; Deut 10.8; 1 Sam 2.27f)/1/. Keil and Delitzsch, faced
with this difficulty, suggested that Abinadab was probably a Levite 'because otherwise they would hardly
have consecrated his son to be the keeper of the ark,
but would have chosen a Levite for the office' (1880:70).
This suggestion, wrong as it is, clearly reveals the emphasis of 7.1. Eleazar is a commoner elected to watch over

the ark, which along with its absentee levitical atten-
dants, no longer plays a role in the active religious
life of Israel. Nothing at all is said of Eleazar's belonging to a priestly family or tribe (Smith 1899:50).

Verse 2

Verse 1 cannot, therefore, be regarded as any kind
of resolution of Israel's difficulties with Yahweh. It
is only a temporary measure designed to bring sympto-
matic relief of the troubles associated with the ark's
presence. That the care of Eleazar is not a cure for
the ills in Israel's relationship with Yahweh is shown,
in part, by the chiastic structure governing 6.19-7.2:

6.19	The people mourn because Yahweh has made a great slaughter.
7.1	The men of Qiryath-ye'arim bring the ark home.
7.2	The ark stays twenty years at Qiryath-ye'arim.
7.2	Israel mourns Yahweh.

The removal to Qiryath-ye'arim has brought no perceptible change in Israel's behaviour or relationship with
Yahweh. The only difference that twenty years of dere-
liction has made is that Israel mourns Yahweh rather
than its own dead, killed by him.

Gutbrod has noted the presence of much summary
in ch. 7, in contrast with the preceding six chapters
(1956:51). Verse 2 offers a good example in which a
period of twenty years is passed over with a simple
temporal description. The only descriptive content that
the narrator attaches to that whole period is that of
Israel mourning Yahweh as though he were dead (cf.
Ezek 32.18; Mic 2.4; Jer 9.9, 17-19; Amos 5.16; Buber
1956:118; against Seebass 1967:166 n.3). The reader
is thereby directed to think in terms of a long period
of mourning and hence of a state of serious disrepair
in covenantal relations between Yahweh and Israel (cf.
Willis 1971:304; 1979:209; against Miller & Roberts

1977:20, 59, 66, 69). The ark, and by implication Yahweh, is interred in Qiryath-ye'arim, and Israel obviously sees no hope for renewal.

That v. 2 provides the last view of the ark, sitting
in storage (*šebet*), has troubled some scholars who
seem to require that all characters and important
objects such as the ark continue to occupy a place in
every scene if a narrative is to be judged and interpreted as a unity. Press, for example, says '7.2, no
doubt, attempts to create a transition from the 'history of the ark,' but leaves unanswered the question
of why in the following chapter the existence of the
ark is no longer mentioned. In addition on considerations of context and style 7.2 is not a suitable
transition' (1938:192). Apparently the possibilities
that the role of the ark is taken over by someone else
(cf. Stoebe 1973:172) such as Samuel, and that the
narrative has been purposefully moving toward that
transition are overruled by the vague considerations
of 'content and style,' which are left unspecified by
Press.

The note that a period of twenty years passed during
the ark's stay in Qiryath-ye'arim is usually taken to
be a later deuteronomistic insertion (e.g. Blenkinsopp
1969:143 n.1; Veijola 1977:31; McCarter 1980:142).
Even if the attribution were acceptable - it is debatable on the grounds that someone other than the deuteronomist may have had use for temporal descriptions /2/
- the contribution of such redaction labels to an understanding of the narrative is questionable. Do we
learn what the deuteronomist was trying to say in his
literary montage by examining what we think are his
fingerprints on the tape that holds the separate pieces
together, or by making a careful study of the literary
effect of the montage (cf. Alter 1981:140)? Even when
there are clear indications of a vocabulary and theology that permeate all the books of the deuteronomistic history, it is only through detailed examination of
the contextual literary impact of each 'deuteronomis-

ticism' that the reader will ever come close to an understanding of deuteronomistic literature.

This is not to say that it may not be helpful to correlate the usages of specific 'deuteronomisticisms' so as to form a general understanding of deuteronomistic usage which may then be applied to the individual occurrence. Although there is a good amount of circularity in such an approach, it is the circularity attendant upon the study of the relationship between any single phenomenon and its wider context, and cannot be avoided. What can and should be avoided is the act of simply labelling any phrase or unit as deuteronomistic and thinking that such is explanation enough for a 'late redactional element.'

Verse 3

The sudden reappearance of Samuel along with the implication that Israel's subjection to the Philistines is a result of its idolatry and defection has prompted scholars to think in terms of source or redactional conflicts in the text (e.g. Budde 1902:48f; Blenkinsopp 1969:148 n.19). In chs. 4-6, the Israelite defeats are caused by Yahweh's desire to kill the Elides, and the ark plays a central role. Samuel does not appear in those chapters. Now Samuel reappears, the ark disappears, and a causal connection seems to be implied between the Philistine domination and Israelite idolatry. Is there any other explanation for such contradiction and shifting focus than a source-critical or redaction-critical analysis?

Taking the matter of Samuel's sudden reappearance first, it should be noted that Samuel makes his second debut with a plan for renewal and victory exactly at a point when all hope seems to have vanished. Israel's attempts to converse with Yahweh, whether by using the ark as a reminder to him (4.3-5), or simply in sacrificial response to the ark's reappearance, have failed miserably. Thereafter the ark is interred in a hamlet with a common person ordained as its keeper. Samuel's sudden reappearance could not be more perfectly timed /3/.

Furthermore, the words used to reintroduce Samuel provide a link back to 4.1, the place at which Samuel was last seen (Schulz 1919:114). In 4.1, Samuel gave out the prophetic word to Israel, presumably a word related in some way to the visit he received from Yahweh. Now in 7.3 he returns after the disaster with a plan for repairing the resultant damages. Both his exit and his entrance show Samuel speaking to Israel, attempting to guide it through and out of the crisis precipitated by the Elides. Samuel takes over exactly where the 'failed' ark leaves off, and he has a plan that should bring about what Israel thought the ark could be used to effect, namely responsible divine action.

Could Samuel have timed his reappearance for this important point so that if all goes according to plan, he will be established as the new centre of mediation between Yahweh and Israel? If his mediation is successful in ch. 7, he will have accomplished what could not be accomplished through priest and ark in chs. 4-6. Buber, especially, has seen this side of Samuel's succession to the place held by the ark in 4.3-4. Samuel's prophetic idea is to have divine guidance without an ark as a substitute for the priesthood - cause of all the trouble - and the cult. No more ark; no more inflexible cultic bonds; no more pilgrimages to material oracles. Replacing all that is the itinerant man of God to whom Yahweh speaks and to whom he is able to make known his divine will (1964:836).

Samuel does not appear in chs. 4-6 and so he is not associated with the failure of preceding mediatory institutions. He appears only after those institutions have failed. He steps in after a lengthy period of depression about the disastrous meeting at Bethshemesh and offers a plan for rehabilitating the relationship. No politician could have timed his campaign better than

Samuel. Israel is obviously ripe for anything that can give them hope for renewed ties with Yahweh whom they have been mourning for twenty years. In such a state of mind they could be expected to do almost anything that Samuel would suggest.

The second problem in v. 3 is the apparent connection between Israelite apostasy and the Philistine domination. That the people have served other gods and that this apostasy has brought on the Philistine crisis is silently presupposed, but we have thus far heard nothing about it. In addition chs. 1-3 made the house of Eli solely responsible for the same Philistine crisis (Budde 1902:49).

The problem resolves itself when close attention is paid to what Samuel says. He does not say that the Philistine victories were *caused* by Israelite apostasy, but only that a future victory over the Philistines may be had if the people will repent and return to the sole worship of Yahweh (Willis 1971: 303). The narrative is very definite that the Elides, and no one else, were responsible for Israel's defeats.

If one asks when, following the defeat, Israel might have turned to other gods in the face of Yahweh's apparent defection, only one answer is possible. Prior to Yahweh's action in 6.19 the Israelites appear still faithful to Yahweh (e.g. 6.13-15). Following 6.19, however, they voice a Philistine-like objection to the presence of Yahweh and the ark (6.20); they put it (and him) in cold storage (6.21-7.1), and they mourn Yahweh's passing. With Yahweh dead and gone, Israel might well have turned to the reluctant worship of other deities.

Though the narrator does not himself tell us when Israel turned to these substitute deities, he does confirm (v. 4) the fact that Israel did turn to other gods. Given their unstinting devotion to Yahweh, even after the disaster in ch. 4 /4/, it seems that they turned to these other gods out of desperation.

Samuel attaches no blame to his exhortation in

v. 3. He simply states that if Israel will return to Yahweh, the latter may give them victory over the Philistines /5/. Those who suggest that v. 3 is based partly on a pattern found in Judg 10.6-16 have usually not seen the essential difference between the two passages (e.g. McCarter 1980:143, 150). In Judges, the peoples' apostasy provokes Yahweh to abandon them. In 6.19-7.3, on the other hand, Yahweh's apparent abandonment of the people provokes them to apostasy. The deuteronomistic idea of 'return' may be present, but this does not automatically incorporate the incident into the deuteronomistic theology of history with its pattern of apostasy, punishment, repentance, and deliverance (against McCarter 1980:143). Rather, the sequence in which v. 3 is incorporated is: unwarranted punishment, apostasy, exploratory repentance, and deliverance.

A question may arise in the reader's mind at this point about why Israel should be desirous of a victory over the Philistines. The answer is to be found in Israel's continued mourning for Yahweh (v. 2), which is a result of catastrophic disturbances in the relationship with Yahweh. It will be recalled, and Israel needed no reminder of this fact, that the disorder of the relationship first appeared in the battle against the Philistines. Seeing that Yahweh was against them Israel had called out the ark of the covenant, a reminder to Yahweh to deliver Israel from the hand of its enemies (*weyoši'enû mikkap 'oyebênû*, 4.3). Yahweh ignored the reminder and since then things had gone from bad to worse. Now Samuel proposes a plan to reverse the bad turn taken in ch. 4. If the Israelites will take the first step by eliminating their newly adopted religious practises, Yahweh will deliver them from the hand of the Philistines (*weyaṣṣel 'etkem miyyad pelištîm*, 7.3). Obviously, to an Israel that mourns Yahweh for twenty years, nothing could be more desirable than an opportunity to get back to a normal relationship with Yahweh.

Samuel has promised a reversal of the effects and the covenantal implications of the defeat in ch. 4. The question that arises for both Israel and the reader is whether Yahweh, whose behaviour has been anything but normal or comprehensible, will do as Samuel suggests. The narrator makes use of this question in the mind of his reader to increase tension and narrative interest as he traces events up to the crucial moment when the promised action is required of Yahweh.

Samuel has asked Israel to give Yahweh one more chance. They are required to take a gamble since they must first return to Yahweh before he will act again on their behalf. The significance of Israel's initiation of the rapprochement will appear in ch. 9, where Yahweh launches a second reconciliation. In both cases it is the injured party that must make the first move towards covenant renewal. If the injured party is not desirous of reconciliation, nothing can be done to repair the relationship.

Verse 4

Israel's response is immediate and unequivocal. They turn out their adopted religions and worship Yahweh alone. There is no question about Israel's continued desire for normal relations with Yahweh. Obviously they turned to other gods only because Yahweh was acting so strangely towards them. As soon as an opportunity arises, Israel turns back to its covenantal God without hesitation. Israel's forced apostasy is, therefore, mitigated from the reader's perspective.

Verses 5-6

Samuel enjoins all Israel to congregate at Mizpah where, he says, he will intercede on their behalf in prayer. Israel, as ever in this narrative, responds immediately to Samuel's direction (v. 6). It has been suggested that the actions of v. 6 indicate a ceremony for community purification necessitated by Israel's defection to other gods (McCarter 1980:144). The confession of sin also points to a parallel in 12.19 (cf. 12.10, Buber 1956:158), where a similar confession is part of a process of covenant renewal (Seebass 1965: 294f; McCarthy 1978:217).

Given the immediate context of v. 6 it is possible that these rites should also be viewed as rites of covenant renewal (cf. Weiser 1962:15 n.1). First Israel engages in acts of symbolic contrition and confession, and then Samuel, the new intermediary, judges Israel.

Weiser also suggests a covenantal function for Samuel's judging. The concluding sentence, 'And Samuel judged all Israel in Mizpah,' is part of the author's presentation of Samuel going about the business of re-ordering Israel's disturbed relationship with Yahweh (1962:15; cf. Budde 1902:49).

Although Samuel's judgeship is not specifically described, the context makes Weiser's suggestion plausible /6/.

Verse 7

The Philistines, last seen heading back to Ekron (6.16), hear of the Israelite assembly in Mizpah and come back up to Israel. The Philistines' speedy response to the news is the author's gift to Samuel, affording him and Yahweh the opportunity to set things right at the critical moment, when Israel has just confessed its sin.

The attitudes of the Philistines and Israelites are linked and contrasted by the repetition of the verb, 'they heard,' for both. When the Philistines hear (*wayyišmeʻû*) they aggressively advance against Israel. Apparently they have not connected their devastation by Yahweh with their prior defeat of Israel. On the other hand, when the Israelites hear (*way-*

yišme'û) of the Philistine advance, they fear the
Philistines. Samuel's promise of divine aid, by itself, is not enough to allay their fear. Israel has
no more confidence in Yahweh's intentions towards it.

   This description of aural response is also contrasted with an earlier scene paralleling the present
one (cf. Willis 1979:211). In schematic form the parallels appear as follows:

	4.6-7	7.7
1.	wayyišme'û pelistîm	wayyišme'û pelištîm
2.	a great noise in Israel's camp	that Israel had reassembled
3.	They knew that the ark of Yah-Yahweh had arrived in Israel' in Israel's camp.	The Philistine heads go up to Israel.
4.		Israel hears [wayyišme'û benê-yiśra'el] that the Philistines are coming.
5.	The Philistines fear [wayyir'û] Israel's gods.	Israel fears [wayyir'û] on account of the Philistines.

Verse 8

   Israel's acceptance of Samuel's role as the new mediator is evidenced by the parallel between 7.8 and
4.3. In the latter instance, Israel calls for the ark, symbol of the covenant, when faced with the continued
threat of the Philistines following the first defeat.
With the ark in their midst, they believe that 'he will
deliver us from the hand of our enemy' (*weyoši'enû mikkap 'oyebênû*) /7/. In 7.8, on the other hand, Israel expresses its faith in Samuel's unceasing intercession
to stir Yahweh into action, *weyoši'enû miyyad pelištîm*.

   As Hertzberg points out, the expression 'to cry'
mizze'oq indicates the urgency, and one might add the

helplessness, of Israel's situation (1964:68). It is
the same word used to describe Israel's oppressed cries
to Yahweh in Egypt (cf. Exod 2.23; 3.7), and is also
followed in Exod 3.7 with the expression 'to deliver
them from the hand of the Egyptians.' It would appear
that once again an ensuing battle is framed in terms
of the exodus. The reader is led to interpret a victory on Israel's part as a new divine saving deed upon which a renewed covenant may be based. Thus far,
though, the narrative has given no indication as to
what Yahweh's response, if any, will be. The Philistines are approaching; Israel is getting nervous. The
narrator prolongs the increasing tension by describing,
in detail, Samuel's sacrificial ministrations at this
crucial hour.

Verse 9

The animal offered is not simply a lamb, but a
'single milk lamb.' Samuel not only offers a 'whole
burnt offering'; it is a 'complete whole burnt offering to Yahweh' /8/.
The narrator's descriptions of sacrificial procedures slows the narrative's progress towards resolution
of the increasing tension. Momentarily diverting the
reader's attention away from the pressing circumstances of the Israelites, the narrator's attention to the
details of the sacrifice recalls the initiation of
this entire series of events through the performance
of sacrifice. Eli's sons' abuse of the sacrificial system provoked Yahweh and he arranged for them to
be killed in battle. Now, some twenty years later,
Samuel takes care to offer a proper burnt offering to
Yahweh. Again the outcome of a battle is linked to a
sacrifice. Will a proper sacrifice have a better effect on Yahweh? The inclusion of the retardatory
details on Samuel's sacrifice is doubly designed to
increase tension and suspense about Yahweh's role in
the up-coming battle (cf. Buber 1956:119). It slows

the reader's progress towards the crucial details
while at the same time increasing the suspense about
how Yahweh will respond to sacrifice.

Finally, the narrator turns to the matter of immediate interest to both Israel and the reader. Samuel's intermediary role is foregrounded in the description of his cry; it is to Yahweh on behalf of Israel. Having arrived at the peak of expectation, the
narrator wastes no more superfluous words: 'And Yahweh answered him.' This is Yahweh's first positive
action towards Israel or an Israelite since he answered Hannah's petition in 1.19. In both cases, Samuel
is inextricably involved - once as the positive answer
and once as the intercessor requesting and receiving
the positive answer. In between, Yahweh's treatment
of Israel is totally conditioned by the presence of
the wicked Elides as Israel's priestly intercessors,
and his desire to eliminate them.

Verse 10

Characterization by way of contrasts revealed in
dialogue is a favorite technique of biblical narrative
(Alter 1981:84f, 123). Verse 10 offers an example of
contrastive characterization created by juxtaposing
the different characters' simultaneous acts. The reader
sees the pious Samuel offering up a sacrifice. At that
very moment the sneaking Philistines are moving in for
the kill. The simultaneity of the two actions is expressed syntactically by a *yqtl-qtl* structure; *wayehî
šemû'el ma'aleh . . . ûpelištîm niggešû* (cf. Talmon
1978:11f; Driver 1913:65).

The whole of v. 10a is recognized by McCarter as
a parenthetic discursion supplying the reader with
incidental information (1980:145; Nowack 1902:33).
He wrongly suggests, however, that it obscures the connection between Yahweh's 'answer' in v. 9 and 'thunder' in 10b (p. 145). The reader of biblical narrative
familiar with the convention of parenthetic discursions

would recognize its function and appreciate its apt placement. Just before Yahweh lets loose with his thunder the reader is treated to a picture of the stealthy Philistines whose sacrilegious designs on the pious Israelites are so richly deserving of punishment. Far from obscuring the connection between v. 9 and v. 10b, v. 10a makes it so much more appropriate.

What failed to materialize in 4.5 when Israel gave vent to its great earth-shaking shout is now accomplished with ease by Yahweh's loud thunder against the Philistines:

4.5	wayyari'û kol-yiśra'el	terû'â gedôlâ wattehom ha'areṣ
7.10	wayyar'em yhwh	beqôl-gadôl . . . wayehummem

Israel's shout gets an echo; Yahweh's thunder gets action. As before (5.9) Yahweh's attack on the Philistines throws them into a confusion (*wayehummem*). Most commentators have noted that Israel steps into the battle only after it is already decided by Yahweh (e.g. Smith 1899:53; Stoebe 1973:174). Yahweh's overthrow of the Philistines thereby becomes a solid basis for renewed relationship between himself and Israel /9/. It is an unambiguous indication of the divine will to be with and for Israel against its enemies (cf. Hertzberg 1964:68). It is also a reversal of Yahweh's previous contraventions of his promise to make Israel's enemies his enemies (cf. Exod 23.22; 1 Sam 4.2f).

The final sentence of v. 10 describes an obvious reversal in Israel's fortune at war. In 4.2, Israel is smitten (*wayyinnagep*) before the Philistines (cf. 4.10; Veijola 1977:37f; Willis 1979:211). Now however, Yahweh honours his agreement and it is the Philistines who are properly smitten (*wayyinnagep*) before Israel. In both cases, it should be noted that the action is described with the defeated as subject of a passive verb, 'x was smitten before y,' indicating Yahweh's responsibility for the outcome of both battles. Whether it is Israelites or Philistines that

win, Yahweh alone determines who will be smitten before whom. The reversal is another assurance of Yahweh's renewed good will towards Israel. Samuel's
promise (v.3) is thus made good by Yahweh. A new
effective and beneficial team of God and mediator has
been tried and proven true.

Verse 11

Continuing his description of the symmetrical reversal of Israel's previous defeat, the narrator now shows
the Israelites going out from Mizpah in pursuit of the
Philistines. The contrast with 4.10 is striking:

4.10   wayyanusû 'îš le'ohalayw
7.11   wayyeṣe'û 'anšê yiśra'el min-hammiṣpâ wayyirdepû

The first noticeable difference is in the verbs. In
defeat each man flees whereas in victory they pursue
their enemy. In defeat, it was every man for himself
and each was not even described as an Israelite, perhaps an indication of the devastating political consequences of military defeat for Israel. In victory,
however, it is the men of Israel, now united by their
God-given victory, who pursue their enemy (against
Ehrlich 1910:193). Finally, one might note that in
defeat each man returns to his own tent, a measure of
the disunification caused by defeat. In contrast, the
men of Israel go out from Mizpah, their base, indicating the security brought by victory, which allows
them to venture out of their own territory.

Verse 12

The stone set up by Samuel is a tribute to the renewed aid given by Yahweh to his people /10/. Given
the memorial name *'eben ha'azer,* 'stone of help,' the
stone also serves as another indication that Israel's
victory constitutes a complete reversal of its pre-

vious defeat, for it was exactly at Ebenezer (4.1)
that Israel had been defeated (cf. Willis 1979:210f;
McCarter 1980:146).

Contrary to Buber, Samuel's expression 'as far as
here' ('ad-hennâ) does not imply 'and for the
moment heaven's help will not go further' (1964:731).
Verse 13, which Buber disallows as integral to the
original narrative, states quite clearly that Yahweh's
hand was on the Philistines throughout Samuel's life.
Instead, one must seek a meaning for 'ad-hennâ
that agrees with its present context.

Both Samuel's actions and words in the preceding
sentences of v. 12 are centered on the commemoration
of the particular place to which Israel pursued its
victory (cf. Gutbrod 1956:55). The name that Samuel
gives to that place just happens to be identical to the
name of the place where Israel was first defeated, that
is, Ebenezer. In view of the strong emphasis on symmetrical reversal of Israel's previous misfortune in
vv. 10-12, it is likely that the final sentence of v.
12 also contributes something to that aim. When Samuel says, therefore, that Yahweh has helped them 'as
far as here' or 'up to here,' and 'here' (hennâ) refers to Ebenezer, it would seem that he is making two
points, one geographical and one theological. Yahweh
has helped them back to Ebenezer and has there reversed the ill-effects of the previous disaster; he has
helped the Israelites back 'ad-hennâ, to the place
where they were undone and their relationship with
Yahweh seemed at an end.

Samuel's 'ad-hennâ is a fitting summary and
conclusion to the entire battle report. The battle
brings Israel back to Ebenezer in victory and, thereby, Yahweh back to Israel. The point by point reversal of Israel's defeat is the means that Yahweh chooses
to right his wrongs and to show Israel that he desires
reconciliation with them. It should be noted that it
is only after the Elides are dead and Samuel has taken
over as leader and covenant mediator that Yahweh moves

to renew relations. Before Samuel's appearance and
intervention there were no indications of any such
desire. Hence the victory not only expresses Yahweh's
renewed concern for Israel; it also legitimates Samuel, firmly establishing him as the new mediator chosen (cf. chs. 1-3) and designated by Yahweh.

Verses 13-14

The legitimation of Samuel as mediator continues
in vv.13-14 (cf. Good 1965:60f). In contrast to chs. 5-
6, where the heavy hand of Yahweh on the Philistines
was of no benefit to Israel, the hand of the Lord on
the Philistines during the period of Samuel's judgeship brings peace to Israel. Again the difference is
due to Samuel's assumption of the role of renewer (v.
6) and maintainer (v. 15) of the relationship between
Israel and Yahweh. The connection between the lack
of a Philistine presence in Israelite territory and the
influential presence of Samuel is explicit in v. 13.
The state of affairs therein described exists 'all the
days of Samuel.'
All territories lost to the Philistines are regained by Israel and there is even peace with the Amorites
on the eastern front (v. 14) /11/. Once again the narrator shows how the accession of Samuel to the mediating office results in a return to normal patterns in
Israel with divine protection from external forces. The
description of recaptured cities on the western front
(Philistine) and peace on the eastern front (Amorite)
expresses the completeness of the peace on all fronts
achieved under Samuel (cf. Keil & Delitzsch 1880:75;
McCarter 1980:147; against Hertzberg 1964:69).
Verses 13-14 summarizes Samuel's 'military' career
in a formulaic pattern known from the book of Judges
(McCarthy 1973:402; McCarter 1980:147). The summary
is designed to convey the impression of a lengthy
period of peaceful existence in Israel under the
judgeship of Samuel. 'The consequence of the battle

was *šalôm* roundabout' (Stoebe 1973:175). During this period, the narrator tells the reader nothing about the people or their reactions to the renewed protection of Yahweh under the auspices of Samuel's judgeship. It is as though having been brought back to a normal state of covenantal existence, they have no further interest in the matters being described, that is, matters of state. So long as there is peace in Israel, with no threat of recurring political disaster such as the Elide affair, this is how the people continue to behave.

Verse 15

As Weiser observes, vv. 15-17 lay great emphasis (three occurrences of *špṭ*) on Samuel's role as judge over all Israel (1962:10). Against Noth's assertion that Samuel the judge is a deuteronomistic fiction, Weiser suggests that the emphasis on Samuel's judgeship is more elegantly explained as a true historical reminiscence born by the old tradition upon which vv. 15-17 are based (p. 10; cf. Wildberger 1957:464; Seebass 1965:292; V. Fritz 1976:351; and Noth 1967:55).

The emphasis on Samuel's judgeship, whatever its historical basis, fulfills certain important literary functions in its immediate context. Verse 15 says that Samuel judged Israel 'all the days of his life.' The description of the duration of his period in office parallels the description in v. 13, a description of the period when Yahweh's hand was against the Philistines, 'all the days of Samuel.' By means of this repeated temporal definition, the narrator draws attention to the contemporaneity of Samuel's judgeship and the absence of a Philistine threat to Israel /12/.

The obvious implication of this link between vv. 13 and 15 is that when Samuel is judge in Israel, *Yahweh* effectively wards off external dangers. Samuel and Yahweh make a successful administrative team. Samuel

judges Israel, maintaining internal affairs, while
Yahweh keeps his part of the bargain in his defensive
activities against the Philistines /13/. M. A. Cohen
agrees that Samuel's judgeship should be understood
in terms of political leadership:

> Samuel's importance derived not from his role as a
> *shofet* or military leader or from his role as a
> prophet, but from his actual position as the Shilo-
> nite seer-priest. As such he was the legitimate
> spokesman for Yahweh and the embodiment of the
> idealogy that united the tribes in what might be
> called today a religious federation (1965:66f; cf.
> Press 1938:193).

Willis has observed that v. 15 makes Samuel the
immediate successor to Eli's office as judge (1971:304;
1979:211; cf. 4:18). With a good judge in this office
Israel experiences the positive side of covenantal
existence under Yahweh. The contrast between Israel's
experiences under bad judges and good is highlighted
by the link between these descriptions of Eli and Samuel, both of which are written as formulaic summaries.
Eli's summary is placed at 4.18, immediately following
the catastrophic defeat brought on by his sons' misdeeds. Samuel's summary, on the other hand, follows
immediately after the reversal of Israel's defeat,
a reversal produced and engineered by Samuel in his
role as judge.

By means of these structural parallels linked by
the formulaic summaries, the narrator draws attention
to the effect that good and bad judges have on the
theological-political fortunes of Israel. A bad judge
brings about political destitution and an apparent end
to the relationship with Yahweh (4.22). A good judge,
on the other hand, is capable of reversing the ill-
effects of any predecessor's mismanagement. The lesson
taught by these parallels is that Israel's fortunes are
determined, to a great extent, by the degree of its

judges' rectitude. Without a good mediator in place
Yahweh is too unpredictable (cf. 3.18), too holy (cf.
6.20) for a regular, normal relationship with Israel.

Verses 16-17

The portrait of Samuel on his regular yearly rounds
as Israel's circuit-judge serves to give an impression
of restored regularity to Israel's existence /14/.
Samuel's conscientious application to his duties is
emphasized by the threefold repetition of the words
'he judged Israel' in v. 17. Thereby the impression of
regularity and a lengthy period of peace in Israel is
directly tied to Samuel's performance in office.

The summary format of vv. 15-17 also contributes
to the impression created by vv. 15-17. By compressing
a large span of story time into a short narrative description, the narrator is able to characterize the
whole period uniformly (cf. 7.2). In this particular
case the result is an unblemished and lengthy period
of peace under the all-encompassing judgeship of Samuel.

The final portrait of Samuel's leadership in Israel
seeks to combine all aspects of his career and to use
this combination as a culminating characterization of
his function in Israel and of the results thereby accru-
ing to Israel's profit. Samuel returns home following
his rounds, suggesting a time of peace when Israel's
judge can retire to his own home. The peaceful scene
is explained, as previously, by the covenantal maintenance performed by the judge. Samuel judges Israel in
Ramah, thereby preserving the social and political
order required by covenantal law. He also builds an
altar to Yahweh so as to maintain proper relationship
with Yahweh by means of expiatory sacrifice, 'given
for sin' (see above on 2.29). Samuel, as apparently Eli
before him (cf. 1.9; 2.28; 4.18), unites the sacral and
secular aspects of mediation in one person.

In all this time the reader does not hear of Israel,

save as the object of Samuel's judging. No complaint is voiced during the entire period of Samuel's office. Trivial as this observation may seem, it is very important in view of suggestions that have been made as to the purpose of ch. 7. McCarter, for example, suggests the following reading of ch. 7:

> All is well in Israel. Yahweh rules by his prophet. The land is secure. We have seen a major crisis met and surmounted under Samuel's leadership. Our narrator would have us believe that at this point in history the people of Israel could perpetrate no greater breach of trust, no more arbitrary exercise of self-will, no more senseless deed of vanity than to demand for themselves a human king (1980:151).

These are strong words, but do they accurately describe the effect of ch. 7 when seen in conjunction with ch. 8? The reasons that the elders supply for their request in 8.5 are, in fact, based on developments that arise subsequent to the situation in ch. 7. Hence ch. 7 can no more be used to defame Israel's request than the Elides' predecessors' good behaviour could be used to criticize Yahweh's decision to eliminate the Elides. Things change and from ch. 7 to the time of the elders' request in 8.5 great and portentous changes have occurred.

Chapter 7 cannot, then, be viewed as an attempt to predispose the reader to a negative valuation of the request for a king in 8.5 (against Schulz 1919:121; Boecker 1969:97; Stoebe 1973:175). It may in fact do the opposite in that the people voice no complaint at all until situation demands it. McCarter is right to see all well in Israel in ch. 7. Apparently the people of Israel agree. It should be recalled that even though they were wrongfully spleened by Yahweh in 6.19, not to mention ch. 4, they are the first to make a move towards reconciliation. Having achieved the state they so anxiously desired, it is not surprising that they do not complain. All is indeed right in Israel at the end of ch. 7. From 7.17 the reader knows that Samuel is at home judging Israel; Israel is doing no other thing than being properly judged by Samuel; and Yahweh is presumably in heaven, ready and willing to accept the sacrifices offered by his chosen servant, Samuel.

PART EIGHT

1 SAMUEL 8

Verse 1

A new scene is begun with a circumstantial clause (cf.
Andersen 1974:79 #5.1.1). At the same time, the new
scene contains recurring elements from preceding
scenes. A state of affairs is described that will
trigger a sequence of events ending only in ch. 12.
It is important to note that this description (vv. 1-3)
comes from the omniscient narrator himself and is,
therefore, not controvertible by anything a character
might say or a reader think.

Attention is drawn to Samuel's age by placing the
predicate adjective, *zaqen,* before the noun, 'Samuel.' The prominence that the narrator gives to Samuel's
age supports the weight subsequently laid on it by the
elders in their request (v.5).

More importantly, however, the foregrounding of Samuel's age draws the reader's attention to the picture
of an aged judge with two sons. The reader struck by
the emphatic position of *zaqen* cannot fail to recall
the importance attached to Eli's age in preceding
scenes (cf. 2.22, 32; 3.1f; 4.15, 18). Moreover, this
associative recollection of the Elide affair is supported by the second sentence, which describes Samuel
installing his sons as judges for Israel: the aged Eli
also had his sons working under him as priests (1.3;
2.11-13, 22-25; cf. E. Robertson 1944:193).

The reader of v. 1 will recognize, therefore, that
the narrative has moved on to a new scene on account

of the introductory circumstantial clause. Initial reaction to the new scene is likely to be one of foreboding because of the associations with the Elide
affair. Perhaps under Samuel's firm leadership, however, events will not take the bad turn that they did
under the aged Eli.

Verse 2

Scholars reading v. 2 have suggested that it, along
with v. 1, stems from an old, genuine tradition (Wildberger 1957:457; Weiser 1962:30; Noth 1967: 56 n.7;
Birch 1976:26). The straightforward presentation of
the names of Samuel's sons, along with their place of
occupation seems to convey to these readers, at least,
verisimilitude. Perhaps the narrator has supplied these
details to lend realistic background to the new scene;
but there is an even more important function for the
names. As Dhorme notes, the manner of presentation
of Samuel's sons is reminiscent of that of Eli's sons
(1910:70; cf. 1.3). Even the simplest introduction is
used to reinforce the association of the sons of Eli
and Samuel /1/.

The statement that the sons occupy themselves in
Beersheba - possibly an authentic, southern Samuel
tradition (Weiser 1962:30), or an effort to extend
the narrative's geographical focus to all of Israel
(cf. McCarter 1980:156) - establishes an important
difference between the situation of the corrupt sons
of Eli and that of the equally corrupt sons of Samuel.
Eli's sons engage in their wrong doing in the very
same temple that Eli presided over so that Eli was
implicated, and even charged by God as complicit in
his sons' sins (2.29). By placing Samuel's sons in
Beersheba, approximately 80 km. south of Ramah, Samuel's home (7.17), the narrative physically removes
Samuel from any reproach that might fall on his sons
/2/.

Verse 3

The narrator reinforces the geographical separation of Samuel and his sons by inserting his own comment to distinguish them. The first sentence of v. 3 characterizes the misdeeds of the sons as the opposite of their father's behaviour. Samuel serves as the standard of uprightness against which his sons are measured and found wanting. Samuel is placed above the wrong-doing of his sons; the narrator puts him beyond reproach.

The misdeeds committed by Samuel's sons are similar to those of Eli's sons, excepting specific differences attendant on variations between the offices of priest and judge. Samuel's sons turn aside after personal gain and take bribes - abusing the mediatory office (cf. McCarter 1980:156) and evidencing an attitude that places self before others in an office where self-denial is part of the occupation. Eli's sons are no different (cf. Kellermann 1977:208): they pursue their own ends in sacrifice, callously neglecting the needs of their people and transgressing the rights of God (2.12-17).

By repeating the verb *natâ* twice in v. 3, an equation is made between 'turning aside (*wayyiṭṭû*) after gain,' and 'perverting (*wayyaṭṭû*) justice.' The equation indicates that the pursuit of selfish gain is an abuse of the office that creates the opportunity. The maintainers of justice (*šopeṭîm*) have become perverters of justice (*mišpaṭ*) (cf. Weinfeld 1977:87).

This description of the sons' misbehaviour is the first sign of trouble since the great reconciliation of ch. 7. Significantly the fault lies on the side of the theocratic administrators as opposed to the common people. The situation duplicates the previous priestly sin which was contrasted with the innocence of the common people (as in 2.12-17). And as the people complained of their priestly mediators' misbehaviour there (2.22-24), they will now complain to Samuel about his sinful sons.

Verse 4

The last assembly was described in 7.6, where all Israel assembled (*wayyiqqabeṣû*) to make confession for sin as the first step towards reparation of the rift in their relationship with Yahweh. Though they were the injured party, the Israelites made the first move towards reconciliation. Now in v. 4 we see a re-assembly (*wayyitqabbeṣû*).

A difference between the assemblies of v. 4 and 7.6 is immediately apparent in the assembling group; in v. 4 it is 'all the elders of Israel' and in 7.6, 'all Israel' (7.5). The last time the elders conferred they voiced a concern over the outcome of a battle and decided to call out the ark as à reminder to Yahweh of the covenant (4.3). Now in v. 4 the elders are reassembling for a related, but different purpose. As Gutbrod suggests, the elders seem to act whenever there is a matter that affects Israel's status as the covenantal people of Yahweh (1956:58). The description of their assembly before they go to Samuel at Ramah already indicates that they are united as a group with a singular purpose even before going to see him. Israel, as a body, is to confer with Samuel, Yahweh's mediator.

Verse 5

The reasons the elders give for their request for a king are supported by the narrator's description in vv. 1-3. Samuel's age and the sins of his sons constitute the sole basis for their request. Some have seen this narrow support as an attempt by the narrator to cast aspersions on the request (e.g. Buber 1964:728; Good 1965:60, 'The fact of incompetent incumbents is no reason to throw over the whole institution of judgeship'). Others have seen it as an indication that Israel was beginning to awaken to political realities and the insufficiency of the judge system (e.g. Ishida 1977:35). Yet another view is expressed by Weiser, who regards the reasons as plausible and an indication that the narrative, at this point, is not anti-monarchic (1962:30; cf. Veijola 1977:68f).

Given the narrator's support, the reader knows that the elders' evaluation is accurate. The reader also knows that it was an identical state of affairs that earlier brought Israel to grief, through the Elides and Yahweh's desire to punish them. The elders, aware of potential disaster in the offices of their mediators, are determined at all costs to avoid a repetition /3/.

The fact that the elders come to Samuel, the designated mediator, and ask him to establish a king to take over the office of judge indicates that they regard their complaint and request as legitimate and justifiable in terms of the existing covenantal constitution (cf. Willis 1972:52). The request is a product of a defect in the theocratic system, a defect lying wholly on the side of Yahweh and his chosen mediators. What the request amounts to is a formal petition, calling for an end to the theocratic system with its fallible mediators and its holy God.

The request for 'a king to judge us' has posed a problem in determining the meaning of the word 'to judge.' For Press the meaning is determined by v. 20; 'The king is supposed to establish justice for his people as the victorious leader of his wars' (1938:197; cf. Boecker 1969: 24 n. 2). Speiser, on the other hand, states that the obvious meaning is not 'to judge' but 'to govern' as the preceding context would lead one to expect (1971:282).

It is probable that both meanings are represented by the verb 'to judge.' As Hertzberg intimates, the verb 'to judge' is used of the requested king to show that the office of judge is replaced by that of king (1964: 72; cf. Stoebe 1973:183f citing W. H. Schmidt 1966: 39f in support). Buber notes that such a reading of 'to judge' in v. 5 is exactly what the repeated use of *špṭ* in chs. 7-8 would lead one to expect. The sixfold repetition of the root *špṭ* in the immediately preceding context in the sense of 'to judge,' 'a judge,' and 'justice' has so thoroughly conditioned the reader that on encountering the seventh and eighth occurrences he or she can hardly understand it otherwise (1964:728). But Buber disallows that the king takes over the functions of the judge on the grounds of 7:15-17, which states three times that Samuel judged Israel. Since in ch. 8 the mediatory office of judge continues, it cannot be that activity which the people desire of the requested king.

Buber's rejection of the reading demanded by the repetitions of *špṭ* is, however, more a product of his own reconstructed narrative, than of the narrative found in MT. The elders' request for a king 'to judge' is a pointed rejection of the existing judgeship. The unusual role requested of the future king is intended to show that a king will obviate all the functions that the judge has performed in chs. 7-8. As Buber says, the word *špṭ* and its significance as a description for Samuel's mediatory activities has been pounded into the reader so that its recurrence in a request for a king cannot be understood as anything else than a replacement of the office of judge by that of king. When we recall that the primary function of all of Samuel's judging activities in ch. 7 was to act out the role of covenant mediator, renewing and maintaining the relationship, we can appreciate the seriousness of the elders' request for a replacement. But what is the point of the switch? Why is it necessary and what does it accomplish?

Only with the last three words of the request does its full implication becomes clear. The elders seek a new government that will make Israel a state like any other pagan nation. The key lies not in Deut 17.14, to which the request is certainly related, but in the implications of an expressed desire to be 'like the nations' /4/. Hertzberg notes that the word for nations, *haggôyim*, stresses the 'non-Israelite, heathen element,' and correctly concludes that the elders express a desire to depart from the special political status of a nation chosen and ruled by God in order to become simply one among many ordinary nations (1964:72).

Israel had been created as a people with a theocratic political system as a result of Yahweh's special action. Israel was Yahweh's people (*'am yhwh*) chosen from out of all the peoples of the earth to be Yahweh's special possession (Exod 19.5f; Lev 20.26; Deut 7.6; 14.2; 26.18f; 32.8f; 1 Sam 12.22). 'Israel's social existence was founded on the premise of being distinct from all peoples by virtue of divine election' (Talmon 1979:6). The covenant between Israel and Yahweh distinguished Israel, elevating it above all the nations of the earth (Deut 4.6-8). The request of Yahweh's people (*'am yhwh*) to become like the nations (*kekol-haggôyim*) in political structure is, therefore, not only a rejection of the theocracy and its judges, but even more it is a rejection of the covenant /5/. 'The fundamental thing threatened by Israel's action was the covenant relationship' (McCarthy 1973:412).

Some have regarded the request, subsequently correctly interpreted by Yahweh as apostasy (v. 8) and rejection of his rule (v. 7), as an overreaction (Good 1965:60) or as out of sorts with its subsequent context (Press 1938:196f). Recall, however, that this is a response, not simply to one instance but to recurring instances of corrupt leadership leading Israel to disaster and an apparent end to the covenant (cf. 4.22; 7.12), and the elders' drastic request seems entirely appropriate. Rather than requesting new judges and leaving themselves open to further disaster, they attack the roots of the problem - the theocratic system. Before Yahweh can respond to the corruption of Samuel's sons as he did to that of Eli's sons, the elders ask that the whole problematic system - with

its judges, its covenant, and its 'holy God' (6.20) -
be done away with. It is in fact a timely nipping of
another theocratic disaster yet in bud. The lack of
continuity that Press sees between a request for a
king on account of sinful judges, and Yahweh's interpretation of the request in vv. 7-8 as a rejection of
divine kingship and covenantal rebellion, is only apparent and disappears when the sins of Samuel's sons
are viewed in the context of chs. 2-7. Rather than allowing Yahweh to create another national disaster that
would again seem to be an end to the covenant (cf.
4.22; 6.20), Israel will end the relationship less
painfully by simply installing a king in a secular government. Yahweh will then have neither cause nor justification to foist another national disaster on Israel
on account of his officials' misdeeds.

On a structural note, one observes that v. 5 constitutes the beginning of a balanced dialogue between
Yahweh and Israel, with Samuel, true to his profession,
acting as go-between. The structure constitutes a remarkable network of correspondences and reversals in
the roles of speaker and addressee; its complexity
cannot be explained as a redactional pastiche of
sources, traditions, and redactional insertion:

v.5	People to Samuel: 'give king.'
v.6	Samuel to Yahweh: prayer.
v.7-9	Yahweh to Samuel: 'listen; declare the manner of the king.'
v.10f	Samuel to people: description of the manner of the king.
v.19	People to Samuel: 'No - give king.'
v.21	Samuel to Yahweh: reports people's refusal.
v.22	Yahweh to Samuel: 'listen; make a king.'
v.22	Samuel to people: 'Go home.'

At the centre of this balanced inversion we see that

the opposition between two groups is really between Samuel and the people - not between the people and Yahweh as would be expected. The structural opposition supports and confirms a fact that appears during the course of the unfolding dialogue: Yahweh, though not liking the request, does not deny it; instead, he simply subverts it (cf. Buber 1964:734f).

Verse 6

Scholars have often spoken of a perspectival division between vv. 1-5 and vv. 6ff (e.g. Wildberger 1957:467). Verses 1-5 are regarded as positive, or at least neutral with respect to the suggested monarchy. Veijola calls the request 'a thoroughly understandable Plan in view of the growing abuses' (1977:55; cf. Weiser 1962:30; Stoebe 1973:182). Nevertheless, according to Veijola, vv. 6-22a, the product of one (DtrN) of two deuteronomistic redactors (DtrN and DtrG), voice an absolutely negative judgement on the proposition (1977:55). While in vv. 1-5 the reason for the request is stated to be the abuses of Samuel's sons, vv. 6ff. attribute the request to Israel's stubbornness (Wildberger 1957:457). Furthermore, from v. 7 on, the confrontation over the issue of the monarchy takes place between all the people and Samuel, whereas in vv. 4-5 the elders alone bring forward the request (Veijola 1977:55).

Impressive as this argument for redactional divisions in the text may be, there is a case to be made for a unified reading, which at the same time calls into question the validity of the anti-monarchic label attached to 8.6-22 if not all of ch. 8. Both redactional analysis of the chapter and the more generally accepted opinion that ch. 8, and hence the compiler/narrator of ch. 8, is expressing an anti-monarchic point of view depend on a total disregard of the 'voice structure' of ch. 8.

> In the analysis of a speech or literary composi-
> tion, nothing is more important than to determine
> precisely the voice or voices presented as speak-
> ing and the precise nature of the address (i.e.,
> specific direction to a hearer, an addressee); for
> in every speech reference to a voice or voices and
> implication of address (i.e., reference to a process
> of speech, actual or imagined) is a part of the mean-
> ing and a frame for the rest of the meaning, for
> the interpretation of which it supplies an indispen-
> sable control (La Drière 1953:441f).

The simple act of attention to the question 'Who
says what?' soon reveals who the real anti-monarchist
is in ch. 8, and he is definitely not the narrator.

The description of Samuel's reaction to the request
is the first indication that the narrator holds a different view than Samuel. The proposed monarchy (*haddabar*) displeases Samuel, not the narrator and not
Yahweh (cf. McCarthy 1973:403, 'it is Samuel's dis-
courses during the assemblies which attack kingship,
while the stories are positive toward it'). That Samuel, groomed from before birth to be Yahweh's agent,
should be displeased is neither surprising nor expressive of narratorial anti-monarchism.

Samuel's personal dislike for the request receives
additional emphasis in the narrator's description of
what specifically bothered Samuel about it: 'The matter
displeased Samuel because (*ka'ašer*) they said, "Give
us a king to judge us".' Pointedly left out is the
crucial information about the covenantal implication
of the request (*kekol-haggôyim*) in order to show
that Samuel's interest is, at this point, focused on
the personal import of the request (against Talmon
1979:10). Samuel is concerned *only* with the administrative switch from judge to king /6/. As Schulz
says, Samuel's resentment is 'a genuinely human
portrayal' (1919:123; cf. Gutbrod 1956:59; Weiser
1962:33; C.P.W. Gramberg 1830:74, cited by Boecker

1969:25 n.1) /7/.

Samuel's personal involvement has initially prevented him from seeing the larger implications of the
request (cf. Stoebe 1973:184). Even though intimately
involved in the Elide affair, knowing both its causes
and consequences, he is unable to see the justice and
necessity of the elders' request as an attempt to prevent a repetition of the previous disaster. Neither
does he yet appear to have fully perceived the covenantal implications, the termination not simply of the
judgeship, but of the whole theocratic enterprise.
Poor old Samuel, he is human after all.

Returning to the supposed split between vv. 5 and 6,
it is difficult to see how Samuel's resentment can be
read as 'an absolutely negative judgement on the
people's scheme' (Veijola 1977:55; cf. Hylander 1932:
118; Soggin 1967:32). Smith provides an example of
how scholars can misunderstand narrator's purpose by
taking a protagonist such as Samuel as the unquestionable mouthpiece of the narrator. Commenting on vv.
6-9 he says:

> The view of the author is evidently that the theo-
> cracy is the divinely appointed constitution for
> Israel, and that the substitution of another form is
> treason to God. He does not seem to recognize that
> Samuel was chargeable with fault in not correcting
> the abuses of his sons' government, not does he tell
> us how Yahweh would give them relief (1899:56).

What Smith fails to recognize is that it is the narrator himself who presents the misdeeds of Samuel's
sons as legitimate cause for the Israelites' request.
It is the narrator who has constructed chs. 1-7, in
which the basis for the request is established. It is
Samuel and not the narrator who fails to recognize
his sons' shortcomings.

Naturally if the reader assumes that the narrator
is publishing his own views through each character's

thoughts and speech, then it is also necessary to assume a multiplicity of narrators to account for the varying viewpoints expressed by the different characters. Once it is allowed that a narrator can and will let his characters voice contradictory opinions over which the narrator and reader stand as observers, shifts in opinion such as that between the elders in v. 5 and Samuel in v. 6 can be seen in their proper literary perspective. They are the integral parts of the narrative's dialectic. Verse 6 explicitly limits dissatisfaction to Samuel and only with respect to the king as a replacement for a judge.

Verse 7

Samuel takes his problem to the Lord in prayer, and Yahweh replies with an astute observation about Samuel's personal involvement: 'Listen to the peoples' voice, *to everything that they said* (*lekol 'ašer-yo'merû 'eleyka*); (*kî*) they haven't rejected you but me from reigning as king over them' (cf. Gunn 1980:59). Yahweh has a much more profound understanding of both the nature of the people's request and the nature of Samuel's displeasure, in contrast to Samuel's clouded vision /8/. The narrator has nicely used the deity's omniscience, which is unquestionable, to reveal the true import of the request in an unerring evaluation.

Yahweh tells Samuel that he is getting side-tracked by a relatively minor implication of the request, because he has not really listened to *all* of it (Cf. Weiser 1962:35). At issue is not simply the fate of particular judges, but the entire theocratic enterprise. As Driver observes, Yahweh emphasizes the difference between Samuel's misinterpretation and the realities of the request with the emphatic syntactic positioning of the contrasting phrases introduced by *kî*: *kî lo' 'oteka . . . kî-'otî* (1913:67).

Yahweh's statement that the people reject his kingship, in conjunction with the cause of the rejection in the recurrence of sinful mediators, indicates that Yahweh's actions in chs. 1-7 are to be understood as actions of the divine king. The people now reject him as king because they do not want a repetition of such actions on the part of the divine monarch. They reject him and his government because of the inherent dangers and weaknesses of the theocratic constitution.

According to Crüsemann, the function of the opposition between divine and human kingship in v. 7 is to label the request as reprehensible (1978:74). He regards v. 7 as the most extreme critique of the monarchy from the pre-deuteronomistic elements in 1 Sam 8 and 12. In v. 7 the inauguration of a monarchy 'signifies a practising atheism' (1978:84).

Similarly Boecker, who places emphasis on the interpretation of v. 7b (the 'Alternativformel') in the context of its prehistory rather than its existing literary context, suggests that the pre-monarchic history of Israel was decidedly anti-monarchic (1969:26). The deuteronomist uses an 'Alternativformel' from the pre-monarchic period and so purposefully incorporates the early anti-monarchic political thought into his history (1969:25f).

Is v. 7 any more an anti-monarchic expression of the narrator than the request in v. 5? Already in v. 5 the reader was made aware of the covenantal implication of the request - a profane, non-covenantal status for Israel as one among many nations. The reader is also well aware that the request is justified by the recurrence of sinful mediators. When Yahweh corrects Samuel's misimpressions in v. 7, therefore, he is doing nothing more than accurately expounding the implications with respect to his own sovereignty over Israel. His correct apprehension of the aim of the request should not be taken as the narrator's attempt to cast aspersions on it. The fact that Yahweh uses the verb *ma'as* to describe the rejection does not characterize the narrator's evaluation but Yahweh's (against

Veijola 1977:55f; cf. Gunn 1980:59). That Yahweh is disturbed is well within the bounds of expectation. The narrator, it should be observed, refrains from commenting on Yahweh's assessment, a strange silence if he agreed with Yahweh and was trying to show that the requested monarchy was a bad thing for Israel.

Verse 8

Verse 8 presents great interpretational difficulty because it contradicts v. 7; in v. 7, Yahweh tells Samuel it is not Samuel but Yahweh that the people reject, but in v. 8, Yahweh tells Samuel that they are forsaking (*'azab*) Samuel and serving other gods as they have been doing to Yahweh since the exodus. As Buber especially has noted, the conflict is irreducible. 'Here Yahweh speaks as though the people's treason really applied to Samuel. He compares their action to what Israel had often done to himself, their God, through the worship of other gods' (1964:733). Buber's remark touches on the other major difficulty, namely the incongruity of equating the rejection of Samuel, only a man after all, with Israel's previous religious defections from the worship of Yahweh.

Taking the second difficulty first, one should note that the described sin of Israel is not simply religious, but covenantal, as the parallels in Deut 29.25f clearly indicate (cf. 1 Kgs 9.9):

	1 Sam 8.8	Deut 29.24-25
1.	Mentions the exodus, the divine act of deliverance on which the covenant is based.	Cf. 29.1f, 15.
2.	Recalls the period between the exodus and the present.	Cf. 29.3-5, 15-17.
3.	Israel forsook Yahweh [wayya'azbunî] and served other gods [wayy'abdû 'elohîm 'aherîm].	Israel is punished because they forsook ['azebû] the covenant of Yahweh . . . and went and served other gods [wayya'abdû 'elohîm 'aherîm].

In v. 8, the deeds that Yahweh compares to what Israel is now doing 'even to Samuel' are of a covenantal nature and constitute a rebellion of Israel against its sovereign Yahweh /9/. Samuel is, however, a most unlikely candidate for sovereignty. Are we really expected to believe that Yahweh, having just told Samuel that Israel is not merely rejecting a judge, but its divine sovereign, now tells him that he is experiencing the rejection that Israel customarily gives to its sovereign?

A solution by way of a small, justifiable emendation has been proposed by S.L. Harris. Not only does Harris' solution clear up v. 8, but it also reveals clear parallels (and gains support therefrom) between v. 8 and 10.18f and 12.6-12, both of which also give a past history of Israel's covenantal transgressions, and both of which, like v. 8, conclude with a divine 'affirmation' of the monarchy. Harris suggests that the last clause in v. 8 has undergone the haplography of *m* after *g*, so that it should read 'so they are also making a king' (*ken hemmâ 'ośîm gam-melek*[!]) (1981:79). The emended text is then eminently agreeable to its context, and simply constitutes an expansion of the theme stated in v. 7. The final clause is not compatible with the previously mentioned deeds of v. 8; the act of making a king is, like all previous defections (*kekol-hamma'aśîm*), a rejection of Yahweh (*wayya'azbunî*).

Harris' emendation neatly removes the contradiction between vv. 7 and 8. Yahweh does not change his mind over who is rejected in v. 8. Both vv. 7 and 8 interpret the request as a rejection of the divine king.

The parallels cited by Harris support his emendation. In 10.18f, a history of Yahweh's saving deeds is given, followed by a description of the request for a king as the rejection of God. The verses conclude with the adverb *we'attâ*, and a description of mak-

ing a king follows (10.19-24). Chapter 12.6-12 follows
the same pattern; the past history (vv. 6-10), the rejection of Yahweh as king (v. 12), and the conclusion,
introduced by *we'attâ*, describing the new human
king. In 8.8f, we see the past history, the making of
a king characterized as a rejection of Yahweh, and the
acquiescence to the wish, again introduced by *we'attâ*,
(Harris 1981:80).

In all these examples, the prefacing of a recollection of Yahweh's mighty acts of deliverance before
the description of the rejected divine king (and his
human replacement) indicates that it is the saving
deeds that constitute the basis of Yahweh's kingship
(cf. Exod 15.18). The covenant at Sinai was established
on the basis of those deeds and hence, as Buber notes,
they should be seen as basis for relationship with
Yahweh as king and Israel as his people (1967:39; cf.
P. D. Miller 1973:174). Like v. 5, then, v. 8 draws attention to the covenantal significance of Israel's request, which repudiates any claim based on the exodus
events.

The links between verses 7 and 8 are strengthened
by alliterative connections between the verb for rejecting Yahweh in v. 7 and those for rebellious deeds and
king-making in v. 8:

v.7 ma'asû . . . ma'asû
v.8 hamma'aśîm . . . 'aśû . . . 'ośîm /10/

It has been observed that v. 8, widely agreed to
contain deuteronomistic vocabulary, incorporates the
present incident into the deuteronomist's historio-
graphic pattern of cyclic apostasy (e.g. Weiser 1962:
33f; Veijola 1977:56f; McCarter 1980:157). The recapitulation of Israel's past failings does little, however, to support the anti-monarchic label attached
to ch. 8. It should be noted that it is not the narrator but Yahweh, the divine king whose abdication is
demanded, who compares the request to past apostasy.

The narrator refrains from inserting his own views.

Yahweh's interpretation of the request, while an accurate assessment of the covenantal implications, may also contain an ironic revelation about Israel's past defections, referred to here. If the reader can see justification for the present defection, might not there also have been mitigations for past apostasies, which Yahweh finds comparable to the present? This question about Yahweh's reading of Israel's past defections is a result of the direct conflict between the narrator's voice and Yahweh's voice. The narrator supports the justice of the present request by his narrative in chs. 1-7 and by his description in 8.1-3. Yahweh, in contrast, impugns it by associating it with previous defections from the theocracy. Since the narrator's voice is the ultimate authority in the narrative world that he creates, and since the narrator's voice contradicts and overrules Yahweh's in the evaluation of the request for a king, doubts are also cast on Yahweh's interpretation of past defections - which he himself has chosen to compare to the request /11/.

Within the context of the voice structure of the whole narrative, therefore, Yahweh may voice antimonarchic sentiments in v. 8, but his views, because they are subordinate to the narrator's, are to be regarded as expressions of personal opinion, not statements of fact. Seen from the narrator's perspective Yahweh's comparison suggests that perhaps past defections were somewhat more complex too. Could Israel actually have had valid reasons for rebelling in the wilderness? Such an implication is not beyond the possible for the narrator who created an incident such as that of 6.19f.

Verse 9

In all three parallel occurrences of the adverb *we'attâ* (cf. 10.19; 12.13) the word introduces a new possibility, 'now,' as opposed to the immediately

preceding past, the exodus events. The adverb signals
the dawning of a new political age in Israel. In contrast to v. 7, where Yahweh placed emphasis on Samuel's audition of *all* that the people said, he now
tells Samuel simply to hearken to their request:

v.7 šema' beqôl ha'am lekol 'ašer-yomerû . . .
v.8 šema' beqôlam . . .

Yahweh's capitulation to the request, immediately
after he has voiced his opinion that it is a breach of
covenant, seems odd (Birch 1976:23). One would expect
him to put up some resistance. In fact, that is exactly what he does - the immediate compliance is only apparent, limited as it is by the expression *'ak kî,*
'howbeit.' As Buber observes, the *'ak kî* presupposes
that the request *will* be honoured, that is, a king
will be made (1964:736). But the *'ak kî,* places a re-
striction on the act of making a king by laying down
guidelines for Samuel to follow. 'The *ak kî* means:
that, nevertheless, it will not be a monarchy such as
all the nations have, but rather might style itself as
a vicariate of God, not simply reporting to heaven,
but really a government held accountable to the higher
authority and so replaceable by it' (Buber 1964:738;
cf. Weiser 1962:38).

Yahweh's first condition is that Samuel must 'stipulate the stipulation against them' (Israel) /12/. Although the reader is not given to know whether this
'stipulation' is drawn from the old theocractic covenant or a new one created explicitly for the monarchy,
it is obvious that Yahweh has not renounced his role
as creator and legislator of Israel's political system. He commands Samuel to lay down the legal framework for the establishment of a monarchy. This action
alone should indicate to the reader that the king to
be installed will not be a king like those of other
nations, but a king that stands under 'the stipulation'
(*ha'ed*) of Yahweh.

Buber calls attention to the fact that Samuel is to stipulate the stipulation *against* Israel (*bahem*) (1964:737f). Yahweh understands that the stipulation is contrary to the wishes of the people. Hence it must be stipulated 'against them.'

Samuel's second task is to declare the 'manner' (*mišpaṭ*) of the king that will be established /13/. Both the 'stipulation' and the 'manner of the king' in v. 9 are to be proclaimed by Samuel on behalf of Yahweh. The declaratory force of both verbs is emphasized - both are given in the Hiphil form. As Buber points out, the 'manner of the king' is not a constitution 'from below' but one 'from above.' The king will be completely answerable to Yahweh, his irremovable predecessor (1964:737).

At this point, though stating his intention to remain in control, Yahweh does not specify the content of the stipulation or the manner of the king. His vagueness leaves room for misinterpretation on both Samuel's and the reader's parts.

Yahweh's conditional acquiescence is in accord with his perception of the request as characteristic of Israel's covenantal behaviour. As many times as Israel had expressed its dissatisfaction and thrown off the yoke of the covenant, Yahweh had responded with a solution to repair the damage and pacify Israel (e.g. Exod 15-19; Num 11; 14). So now when Israel tries to escape the covenantal relationship, Yahweh tries to appease them by giving them a king, but not such as they desired.

Verse 10

The narrator informs the reader that Samuel repeats 'everything' (*kol-dibrê yhwh*) that Yahweh said to the people. The people are thus *potentially* made aware of Yahweh's grasp of the implications of their request and of his intention to maintain a hold on Israel and its king. Due to the vagueness of Yahweh's response, and Samuel's own misinterpretation of Yahweh's directives (a fact revealed in v. 11), however, it seems that the people do not perceive Yahweh's intention until it is unveiled in 10.24f. When they finally understand, there are mixed reactions, with some vocal opposition (10.26f). It seems that Samuel's simple re-telling (*wayyo'mer*) of what Yahweh said is not powerful enough to carry the imperative directive force of Yahweh's 'stipulate' (*ta'îd*) and 'declare' (*wehiggadta*).

The people to whom Samuel tells all are explicitly described as 'those asking a king from him (Samuel)' /14/. With this description the narrator highlights the fact that the request is not a simple rebellion or apostasy, contrary to what Yahweh might say. The people pursue their case legitimately through the institutions open to them in the theocratic political structure. Unfortunately for them, that structure places all power and authority in the hands of Yahweh and his mediator; the people must make their case to the very individuals whom they wish to oust. We see the same political principle at work in our own time, when the Canadian people had to take their request for constitutional reform to the Queen of England for her approval, even though she was the very person whose authority over Canadian political affairs was finished with her assent to the new constitution. Like the Canadians, the Israelites went about the business of securing reform in a proper, law-abiding manner.

Verse 11

Conspicuous by their absence from Samuel's conversation with the people in v. 10 are the stipulation that he was to stipulate (*ta'îd*) and the manner of the king that he was to declare (*wehiggadta*). Instead, Samuel simply told (*wayyo'mer*) the people what Yahweh said. Although one might infer that such stipulating and declaring are subsumed by the verb *'mr* in v. 10,

it would seem that the peculiar usage of *'mr* with a
definite object is specifically intended to highlight
the difference between what Yahweh commanded and
what Samuel did /15/. Neither does Samuel make the appropriate declarations in v. 11: again he simply 'says'
(*wayyo'mer*) 'this will be the manner of the king that
will rule over you.' Yahweh tells Samuel to *prescribe*
'the manner'; instead Samuel *describes* it /16/. As a
result of his misunderstanding of Yahweh's directive,
Samuel proceeds with a lengthy description of what he
perceives as the prospective disadvantages of the
monarchy /17/.

The request for a king that would unseat him as
judge seems to have unsettled Samuel. First he missed the more important and larger implications of the
request (vv. 6f), and now he misses the regulative
intention of Yahweh's reply in v. 9. Thinking that
Yahweh has simply acceded to the demand, Samuel
seems to interpret Yahweh's instructions as warnings
to Israel. He presents the 'manner of the king' not
as a divine directive, but as an analysis of possible
monarchic abuses /18/. Buber, who regards vv. 11-18
as a redactional insertion comes, nevertheless, to a
similar reading of the difference between 'the manner
of the king' in vv. 9 and 11. For Buber, though, it is
the redactor who inserted the tendentious exegetical
pamphlet now seen in vv. 11-18 who misunderstands
Yahweh, and not Samuel (1964:738).

The misunderstanding is, nevertheless, appropriate
to Samuel and serves to illustrate further his personal
anxieties over the request. He has heard nothing Yahweh has said and seeks only to dissuade the people from
their purpose. His arguments, as we shall see, seek to
persuade the people of the favourability of the theocratic regime, under Samuel and Yahweh, over the monarchy. Samuel assumes the role of rhetorician, speaking
his own thoughts, rather than the role of Yahweh's authoritative mediator commanded to make specific declarations on the 'manner of the king.' Ironically it is

the very fear of losing his role as mediator that prevents Samuel from fulfilling that role. He begins his skillful speech with a hard-hitting description of how a monarchy will encroach on the individual Israelite families. As Weiser notes, the fourfold repetition of the verb 'he will take' (*yiqqaḥ*) stresses the burdensome aspect of the monarchy (1962:40; cf. Veijola 1977:60). Samuel attempts to emphasize the negative in everything that the monarchy will do. The list of things that the king will take begins with the most important of possessions, the sons (v. 11), and proceeds in descending order through daughters (v. 13), real estate (v. 14), and income tax (vv.15-17a). Each description is introduced by placing the affected object first in its sentence - an emphatic position (Driver 1913:67) intended to impress on the audience these major areas that will be affected by the monarchy - family, land, and wealth. Nothing will be left untouched. The cost of kingship is very great, says Samuel. Will Israel be willing to pay, asks the reader?

At the same time that he lists the evils of the monarchy, Samuel unwittingly reveals positive aspects - aspects that have provoked some scholars to find a promonarchic tradition lying behind vv. 11f (e.g. Press 1938:197; Stoebe 1973:186f). As Talmon notes, of fundamental importance to any stable ancient near eastern monarchy are the creation and organization of an army and the internal administration of the kingdom (1979:13). The inclusion of these aspects in Samuel's criticisms is not so much the result of a combination of sources as it is a necessity of the speech. If Samuel wants to criticize the monarchy for pressing Israelites into military service, he is forced to mention the good of a monarchic army, a necessity for national defence. Similarly to criticize the monarchy for taxation necessitates mentioning the good of a centralized administration.

In order to appreciate the rhetoric of Samuel's speech, we must follow it through in its given sequence. The royal expropriation begins with 'your sons.' The first blast strikes uncomfortably close to the persons of the audience, emphasizing the high personal cost of establishing a royal army. The descriptions of the sons' duties are intended to emphasize the service that the people will render to the king. The king appoints them to *his* chariot, to *his* cavalry, and they will run before *his* chariot. 'The entire piece is based on a conscious distancing: you, the people - he, the king' (Crüsemann 1978:69). From Samuel's description one would hardly think that a national army could benefit anyone other than the king. Yet the most important aspect of any army is defence and enforcement of external policy.

Verse 12

Even high-ranking officials are made to do the menial tasks of farming the king's estate by Samuel (cf. Smith 1899:57; de Vaux 1965:124) /19/. Not even those in positions of authority have anything to gain from Samuel's king.

Verse 13

The second assault on the audience's purposes exhibits a slight weakening in that it is only daughters who are taken. Samuel begins to prepare his audience for a devastating grand finale by gradually lessening the importance of the affected item; he leads his audience to believe that the worst is over with the sons. The same tactic can be discerned in the descriptions of the tasks to which the daughters are put - they are now simply perfumers, cooks, and bakers rather than *his* perfumers, *his* cooks, and *his* bakers.

Verse 14

The lulling effect continues with the transition

from families to possessions. Samuel makes his criticism elegantly, using contrasting verbs and pronominal suffices: 'He will *take* your best fields, *your* best vineyards, *your* best olive groves and *give* (them) to *his* servants' /20/.

Verse 15

The neat structure of the three preceding cases breaks down in vv. 15-17. Crüsemann notes the inconsistency, especially in v. 15, and suggests that v. 15 and the asses in v. 16 be omitted as obvious additions disturbing the clear structure of vv. 11-17 (1978: 67f). It is possible, however, that the disturbed structure is the narrator's way of showing the growing emotion and forcefulness of Samuel's presentation, which comes, as often in speeches, at the expense of order and precision. The same impression is conveyed by the principle of linking words (*Leitwörter*) that does organize vv. 15-17. Growing animation brings Samuel to present his arguments in an associative concatenation rather than a logical, structured order.

Verse 15 is connected to the preceding verse by the repetition of the words 'your vineyards.' 'Both *your* grain crops and *your* vineyards he will tithe and give them to *his* officers and *his* servants.' The use of contrasting verbs and pronominal suffixes continues to emphasize the negative side of the monarchy. Also continued is the diminishing severity of each item. In contrast to the expropriation of the best vineyards (v. 14), only the tenth part of the produce is taken in v. 15.

Verse 16

Verses 15 and 16 are linked by the word 'servants.' In this case, the connection itself serves to make a point about the cost of kingship. 'He will give (the

tithes) to *his* servants (v. 16), but *your* servants . . . he
will take and put to *his* (own) works.' The king pays
his own servants with the taxes and on top of that,
conscripts Israel's servants to do his own work - a further development of taxation (cf. Talmon 1979: 14f).

The list of expropriations in v. 16 reflects the
rhetorical pattern of the entire speech; it proceeds
from the most important to the least of the losses to
the king: slaves, maidservants, 'cattle' /21/, ending
with asses. Although the mention of the asses following the adjective *haṭṭôbîm* does seem incongruous
(Dhorme 1910:72), its position can be understood as
an indication of Samuel's growing excitement as he
nears his punch line.

The mention of the tithe on the flocks is linked to
v. 15 by the verb *ya'śor* and to v. 16 by the parallel
categories of possessions (cattle, asses, flocks). The
associative logic and appearance as an afterthought
contributes to the impression of Samuel's growing
fervor.

Verse 17

As commentators have noted, the mention of the
tithe on the flocks appears as an anti-climactic afterthought (Stoebe 1973:186). It is, however, precisely
on account of its anti-climactic aftertone that it
should not be seen as a late redactional expansion.
As with the whole of vv. 11-16, Samuel uses this final
afterthought to accommodate his audience to the costs
of kingship. Certainly Samuel's audience would also
have been impressed with the incongruity of his concluding remark, which is remarkably similar to Yahweh's final words to Jonah, 'and also much cattle?'
(Jonah 4.11).

Samuel's assumption of the appearance of a scatter
brain is only a ruse designed to lower the defences of
his audience. Having given them a growing sense of ease
with the descriptions of what would happen to their

families and possessions, Samuel fires a parting shot aimed squarely at the persons of his audience. Such is the emphasis supplied by the opening *we'attem*, 'And you,' of v. 17b, following, as it does, after all the 'your' openings: your sons, your daughters, your fields, your vineyards, your olive groves, your seed crops, your vine crops, your slaves, your maidservants, your cattle, your asses, your flocks, *you* (cf. Driver 1913:68). Having gradually accustomed his audience to the adjustments in lifestyle under a monarchy by the rhetorical pattern that governs his speech, Samuel blasts his unsuspecting audience with the most devastating description of all /22/.

'And you will be slaves to him.' The line has a familiar ring to it that Israel would easily recognize from its past, and which the reader also recalls from the latter part of 2.27, 'when they (your fathers) were in Egypt "to the house of Pharoah".' Samuel is using the same methods as the book of Deuteronomy to dissuade his audience from what he sees as their wrong purpose: 'Remember that you were a slave in Egypt' (Deut 5.15; 15.15; 16.12; 24.18; 22). The election of a king will return Israel to the slave status from which Yahweh originally freed them. Samuel's purpose is clear, especially when v. 17 is set beside Deut 6.21, an explanation of the significance of Israel's covenantal laws:

8.17   we'attem tihyû-lô la'abadîm.

Deut 6.21 'abadîm hayînû lepar'oh bemiṣrayim

          wayyôšî'enû yhwy mimmiṣrayim beyad ḥazaqâ.

Israel's anti-theocratic request will lead them back to the state from which Yahweh rescued them. 'Thus "the manner of the king" as it is stigmatized in 1 Sam 8.11-18, could just as aptly have been labelled in that context "the Egyptian manner"' (Speiser 1971:283). Since they cannot cope with the freedom (and uncertainty) of political life under the theocracy, they will have to live as slaves under the overbearing, monocratic rule of a human king. The change cannot be from the freedom under theocracy to a freedom under a monarchy, but only from freedom to bondage.

Samuel's characterization of the wish for a king as, in fact, a desire for renewed slavery parallels certain facets of the murmuring traditions in the Pentateuch. In both the request as interpreted by Samuel, and the murmurings in the wilderness, Israel rejects the freedom of life under Yahweh and his mediator in favour of the life of slavery in Egypt, under a king (cf. Exod 16.2f; 17.3; Num 11.4-6; 20.3-5; 21.5; Ps 78:18-22). The rationale for the choice is that life 'in Egypt' is free from the uncertainties and insecurity of the free life under Yahweh; 'a live dog is better than a dead lion' (Eccl 9.4).

Verse 18

Samuel, having been corrected by Yahweh in vv. 7f, now correctly interprets the anti-covenantal intent of the people. Yet his interpretation is not neutral, but polemical; he tries to emphasize the ills of the people's request for an 'Egyptian' lifestyle. Verse 18 combines the memories of Egyptian slavery with the more immediate memory of deliverance under Samuel in order to call the wisdom of the request into doubt.

Samuel notes that the life of slavery under a king will undoubtedly lead to cries for help (*ûze'aq-tem*), just as in Egypt (cf. Exod 3.7). Yahweh, however, will not answer because it was Israel's choice to reject their divine king and covenant. They chose, instead, to elect a human king (*behartem lakem*).

Verse 18 also contains specific recollections of the crucial moment in 7.8f, when Samuel cried (*wayyiz'aq*) to Yahweh on Israel's behalf, and Yahweh answered him (*wayya'anehû*). The rejection of the existing covenant will mean that Israel will no longer have a mediator to convey its cries to Yahweh; without a mediator,

there can be no answer such as there was in 7.9. The
options are clear: slavery under a human king, or deliverance under Yahweh and Samuel.

Verse 19

The people unhesitatingly reject Samuel's argument.
The narrator's description of their refusal 'to listen
to Samuel' (*lišmoaʿ beqôl šemûʾel*) reminds the
reader of Yahweh's previous instructions to Samuel to
listen to the people (*šemaʿ beqôlam*, v. 9). Samuel
has not listened to Yahweh, so the people do not listen
to him. His words from v. 11 on lack the authority of
the words given to him by Yahweh in v. 9. Instead of
declaring the manner of the king and stipulating the
stipulation, Samuel presented the people with his own
estimation of their alternatives. Accurate as it may
be, Samuel's evaluation of the monarchy is an inef-
fecual restatement of facts already contained in the
request and in Yahweh's own evaluation (vv. 7f). Contrary to Samuel, however, Yahweh did more than evaluate: he moved swiftly with a declaration, as reigning
king, to cut off his people's insurrection.

The people brush off Samuel's alternatives as the
irrelevant redundancies they are (cf. Gunn 1980:60)
/23/. They remain firm in their decision to opt out of
the theocracy: 'their insistence even in the face of
Samuel's objections indicate[s] that the negotiations
were conducted on the basis of clear knowledge of the
obligations and privileges that went with the monarchy'
(Talmon 1979:15).

The fact that the people prefer even the despotic
monarchy described by Samuel is also a clear indication
of the degree to which they fear another disaster such
as that brought on Israel by the Elides. Samuel's description of the change their choice involves is welcomed: from Israel's point of view it is a positive
change from the uncertainties of theocracy to the cer-
tainties of monarchy. The price that Samuel names

is apparently counted as small against the benefits received.

Verse 20

The people reaffirm their wish to be like the nations with a non-covenantal political structure. Their emphatic declaration, '(Yes) even we shall become like all the nations,' is an unambiguous repudiation of their special status as Yahweh's own possession, a priestly kingdom and a holy nation (cf. Exod 19.5f). As in Ezek 20.32, Israel's desire to become 'like the nations' is a proclamation of independence, a vocal manifesto ending allegiance to the divine king. 'The author of 1 Sam 8 tries to capture in a single phrase how Israel repudiates the special position ordained for her by God, and wishes to assimilate her own special constitution to the profane constitution of the states in the heathen world around her' (Eichrodt 1970:277). Yahweh said, 'You shall be to me a priestly kingdom, a holy nation' (Exod 19.6), but Israel says 'But we, yes we (*gam*) will be like the nations.' As their subsequent reasons show, the people view monarchy and theocracy from a much different perspective than Samuel; they also have memories, recalled in v. 20, which extend back to the exodus, and more recently, to the events of ch. 4.

The king will take the place of both Yahweh, the present king, and Samuel, the present judge - 'our king (*malkenû*) will be our judge (*ûšepaṭanû*)' (cf. North 1932:9; Whybray 1962:138). The king will go out before Israel (*weyaṣa' lepanênû*) in battle as Yahweh had once gone out before Israel (cf. Judg 4.14; Boecker 1969:32f). The king is supposed to fight Israel's battles, which are specifically described as '*our* battles' rather than 'Yahweh's battles,' the usual, and covenantally grounded description of Israelite warfare (cf. Hertzberg 1964:74; Boecker 1969:34; Stoebe 1973:189). The king is expected to take on the role that Yahweh promised to play - but did not (cf. ch. 4).

As Buber notes, v. 20 is a development of v. 5, a response to the recurrence of an 'Elide' situation amongst the judges. Of v. 20, Buber says: 'Behind it stands the experience, which was gained in the military undertakings against the Philistines, of sacred shrines and personnel' (1964:739). In the people's view, Yahweh had unquestionably reneged on his covenantal obligations in the battles of ch. 4. Now, with the recurrence of an 'Elide' situation amongst the judges, Israel chooses to have a human king whose military activities will not be affected by these, or any other theocratic concerns. The people prefer the stability and reliability of a human king and their own devices to fight *their* wars, rather than helpless dependence of Yahweh to fight a 'Yahweh war.' As a profane political unit there will be no sacral complications to interfere in either the internal or external affairs of state; at least military defeats will be produced only by Israel's own military deficiencies.

Over against Samuel's alternatives, the people set their own. Israel's request for a king is a decision on a national level to take its fate into its own hands, with one of its own people at its head where Yahweh used to be.

Verse 21

The narrator informs the reader that finally Samu-'el does hear 'all the words' (*'et kol-dibrê ha'am*, cf. v. 7), the implication being that he finally realizes fully what Israel's request for covenantal reform really means. Israel's polemical rebuttal of his remarks about the monarchy is what finally brings Samuel to this understanding of what lies beyond the merely personal implications of their request. As before (v. 6) he brings what he considers as news to Yahweh.

There is a difference between Samuel's two conversations with Yahweh (cf. Press 1938:198). The first
time Samuel speaks of the request it is in a prayer
concerning his own replacement as judge (v. 6). In v.
20, however, Samuel has finally realized the full import of the request and so relates this 'new' development to 'Yahweh's ears,' an expression chosen, perhaps,
to indicate that Samuel relates a discovered secret to
Yahweh.

Verse 22

Yahweh's response to Samuel's news is simply to
reiterate his previous command to Samuel to listen
to the people (*šema' beqôlam*, cf. v. 9; Stoebe 1973:
189). Samuel's discovery has changed nothing and
Yahweh tells him to get on with his job. As in v. 9,
Yahweh's instructions indicate that he is not abdi-
cating. Samuel was to 'stipulate the stipulation'
(*ha'ed ta'îd*), 'declare the manner of the king'
(*wehiggadta lahem mišpaṭ hemmelek*), and now he is
to 'make them a king' (*wehimlakta lahem melek*), all
Hiphil verbs indicating that Yahweh still controls
Israel's politics even in the matter of kings (cf.
Cohen 1965:69; Payne 1972:323).

Once again, however, Samuel balks at the command.
Instead of making a king straight away he sends every
man to his city. Samuel was unable to follow Yahweh's
instruction, even when only aware of the instability
of his own position. Now, aware of the covenantal implications of the request, he cannot bring himself to
do as bidden /24/. His act marks a failure to obey out
of a sense of loyalty to Yahweh and the covenant concept. It will take some further explaining on Yahweh's
part before Samuel understands the divine plan and
joins in its enactment. This failure to obey reveals
the human side of Samuel; he is faithful to his own
perception of what should be done (the maintenance of
the covenant) and will not obey even Yahweh when the

command seems to contradict his allegiances. Samuel's loyalty to the theocratic covenant is immaculate.

Verse 22 does, as most commentators have noted, prepare for the description of Saul's anointment (e.g. Smith 1899:59); but it is not the simply redactional link that it is often said to be. McCarter for example comments *'Exeunt omnes.* The prophetic narrator dismisses the people' (1980:159). It is not the narrator who dismisses the people, but Samuel, who thereby reveals something of his character and understanding of the situation to the reader. Samuel does not immediately make the king because he does not know what kind of king Yahweh has in mind, and he refuses to make the kind of king that the people have in mind. The dismissal of the people does 'make room' for Yahweh's leading of Saul to Samuel in ch. 9, but not simply as an artificial redactional link. Since Samuel has not caught on, Yahweh himself has to choose a man, Saul, bring him to Samuel, and tell Samuel exactly what he has in mind. The room made for ch. 9 is not redactional and artificial, but vital and integral to the narrative. Samuel's inability to follow orders creates an opportunity for Yahweh himself to move to centre stage. As will be seen in ch. 9, his orchestration of Saul's journey to the throne leaves no doubt about his conception of an Israelite monarchy.

PART NINE

1 SAMUEL 9

*Excursus on the Context
of 1 Sam 9.1-10.16*

Past literary analysis of ch. 9 is emblematic of the
analysis of chs. 8-12 as a whole - no single dissection
of the text is generally accepted /1/. The predominant
approach to these scenes, in which Saul is selected to
be *nagîd* by Yahweh, is evident in a comment by
Wolfgang Richter. He observes that the most reliable
criterion by which a narrative may be divided - doublets - is lacking in 9.1-10.16. 'This does not guarantee the unity of the passage, on the contrary one must
be on the look out for further criteria' (1970:13).

Contained in Richter's advice is one of the most
widespread and fundamental of historical-critical assumptions: biblical narrative is composite and can be
shown to be so, appearances to the contrary. It is held
to be methodologically unsound to draw exegetical
conclusions, either historical or literary, prior to
the isolation of the atomic unity ('die Kleine Ein-
heit') (Richter 1970:13 n. 3).

It is exactly this order in historical-critical analysis that has prevented scholars from reaching any
kind of agreement concerning the historical content
of 9.1-10.16 (cf. L. Schmidt 1970:59). Since it is the
principal aim of such criticism to achieve a historically accurate understanding of biblical narratives,
the methodological sequence is self-stultifying. L.
Schmidt's own attempt to resolve the inconclusive de-

bate is to provide yet another analysis - and that has subsequently been added to Kegler's list (1977:67f). In turn, Kegler continues the tradition with his own unique analysis and historical conclusions (1977:70-7).

A relatively untravelled path around the morass created by such division and redivision of 9.1-10.16 is the narrative itself, when read in its existing consecution /2/. One would be short-sighted not to anticipate the objection that such a holistic reading is itself just another analysis to be added to the existing pile of disagreements. While it is true that there are no compelling arguments in favour of final-form readings, other than the possibility of achieving more interesting readings of the narrative itself rather than the history behind it, the approach does have one important advantage: at least when readings are all based upon the same text, rather than various segmentations of the text, a major variable and source of disagreement is eliminated.

From a contextual perspective, most of the literary phenomena that historical criticism has used to divide the narrative appear as integral components in an episode which is itself an integral component in a larger pattern. One recalls that certain aspects of ch. 8, notably the recurrence of a particular state of affairs in the offices of Yahweh's mediators (8.1-5) and the consequent request for a king to fight Israel's battles (8.20), appeared to parallel or react to the precedent-setting events of chs. 1-7. It should come as no surprise, given the narrator's previous use of the literary technique of scenic parallelism, that 9.1-10.16 might also correspond to certain aspects of the events of chs. 1-7 and reacts to others.

Verse 1

As scholars have observed, Samuel's refusal to listen either to the voice of the people or the command of God opens the door to the events described in chs. 9-10

(e.g. Veijola 1977:73) /3/. When Samuel refuses to carry out Yahweh's commands, the counter-measures to
Israel's request, the reader expects Yahweh to respond,
perhaps by taking matters into his own hands. Hence
any subsequent events that exhibit the slightest hint of
divine intervention on the human plane will be scrutin-
ized by the reader on the lookout for Yahweh's response
to Samuel's refusal.

The reader is immediately provided with some hint of
what is to follow by the introduction of Saul, which,
as most commentators have noted, is similar to that of
Samuel (Budde 1902:58; Nowack 1902:39; Schulz 1919:
128; Hertzberg 1964:80; Stoebe 1973:193; McCarter
1980:172). As in 1.1, the opening in 9.1 (*wayehî 'îš*)
marks a new scene following the pattern of previous
introductions (e.g. Judg 13.2; 17.1; 19.1; cf. Richter
1970:30). The parallel encourages a recollection of
Samuel's birth story and alerts the reader to watch
for any further similarities.

The genealogical information about Saul consists of
a list of unimportant ancestors known otherwise only
from the books of Chronicles (1 Chr 8.33; 9.39) /4/.
These connections, like Samuel's, are incapable of
providing any legitimate claim to superior office or
status in Israel (cf. above on 1.1). Considering that
it is the normal function of a linear genealogy such as
v. 1 to provide social, religious, or political legitimation (Wilson 1977:40-45, 155, 164), the lack of any such
potential in Saul's genealogy should be regarded as an
intentional manipulation of conventions. The genealogy
without legitimation, used as a prelude to the story of
Saul's anointment, indicates that any successful elevation of Saul is not a product of familial connections.

Like Samuel, Saul begins as a nobody who will become a somebody as a result of Yahweh's decision to
make use of him. The unusual function of both Samuel's
and Saul's genealogies creates a conspicuous parallel
between the two. With Samuel in mind, therefore, the
reader may begin to formulate some hypothetical frames

about the connection between the new character, Saul, and Yahweh's plans for the Israelite monarchy.

The description of Kish as a *gibbôr ḥayil,* a 'man of means' (Eising 1980:351; McCarter 1980:173), might seem to contradict the suggested function of the genealogy. The reader is, however, not certain about Kish's role in the story and so cannot make any firm conclusions. All he or she knows is that a new scene has begun and that a relatively unimportant man of means has been introduced.

Verse 2

The explicit introduction of Saul into the story by-passes his birth, a circumstance that has fueled speculation that Samuel's birth story may have been stolen from Saul (e.g. Hylander 1932:11-39). The connection between the two stories is, in fact, literarily reinforced by v. 2 as well as by the links already seen in v. 1. Placed side by side, the correspondences and differences are evident:

1.1-2	9.1-2
1. Introductory formula [wayehî 'îš 'eḥad]	Introductory formula [wayehî 'îš] /5/
2. Geographical note	Geographical note
3. Name: Elqanah	Name: Kish
4. Genealogy	Genealogy
5. Introduction of wives [welô šetê našîm]	Introduction of Saul [welô hayâ ben]
6. (Miraculous birth)	(Miraculous anointment)
7. Introduction of Samuel	

The introduction of Saul contrasts with that of Samuel in passing over the birth story. Saul's career as an instrument of Yahweh is not one pre-ordained before birth, but one to which he is adapted. Samuel and Saul are miraculously enlisted in the divine service, but Saul's career begins only later in life,

entailed as it is by the unforseen demands of the people for a king. The lack of a birth story in the episode describing Saul's rise to kingship is congruent
with the immediacy of the demand and the fact that
Saul's career as a servant of Yahweh is not one that
Yahweh had intended from before his birth. The un-
planned choice of Saul develops into complications
that reveal the danger of forcing Yahweh to make
spur-of-the-moment choices (1 Sam 15.11).

An even stronger association between Samuel and
Saul comes in the form of Saul's name, which appeared
several times in verbal form (*š'l*) in ch. 1. Though
I have argued against the position that Samuel's birth
story originally belonged to Saul, the use of the verb
š'l in ch. 1 does link Saul with Samuel by association. After reading the miraculous birth story of Samuel and being told several times that Samuel is
'asked' (*š'l*) from God (1.17, 20, 27) or granted to
God (1.28), the reader cannot fail to associate 'Saul'
with the story of Samuel's birth. The question that
remains unanswered at this point is the meaning of
the association. Is 'Saul' (*ša'ûl*) perhaps an answer to
Israel's request (*haššo'alîm*, 8.10) (Gunn 1980:123)? Is
he another of Yahweh's dedicated servants (cf. 1.28)?
The narrator is not telling yet, so the reader can only
hypothesize and wait for subsequent expositional clari-
fication.

Saul's description as a handsome, tall young man,
taller and better looking than any other in Israel,
also suggests that Yahweh may have decided to go even
further to please the people with his choice for a king
/6/. Far from being an inconspicuous, unlikely choice,
Saul stands head and shoulders above any other Israelite. Though the reader is far from certain that Saul is
indeed the man that Yahweh has chosen to make king,
the parallels with the Samuel birth story encourage
that hypothesis /7/.

Again the reader is led, by the narrator's description, to wonder whether Yahweh is choosing more accor-

ding to how Israel would choose - by appearance - than according to how the divine should choose, by character (cf. 1 Sam 16.7; Stoebe 1973:193, 201) /8/. Whatever the answer to this complication, the questions posed to the reader remain to influence the reading of the narrative. Why might Yahweh choose the greatest instead of the least? Would such a choice prove felicitous? The reader must wait until 9.16 and then 10.23f before understanding the divine logic in the choice of Saul (cf. Buber 1956:115). And due to the complete lack of narrative exposition at the beginning of ch. 9, making explicit that Saul is Yahweh's future king, the reader must certainly wait until vv. 15f before being able to confirm or reject any hypotheses (frames) about the connection between chs. 8 and 9.

The introduction to Kish, Saul, and the subsequent tale of the asses is, at first glance, a simple case of retardation for increased suspense. At a crucial moment the narrator switches from the matter of monarchy to this pastoral scene. 'One of the prime means of creating, intensifying, or prolonging suspense consists in the author's temporarily impeding ('suspending') the natural progression of the action, especially its onward rush towards some expected climax, by the interposition of more or less extraneous matter' (Sternberg 1978:159) - which observation might have been written to describe the transition from ch. 8 to ch. 9.

On account of the parallel between the introductions to Samuel and Saul, however, the reader is led to suspect some connection, however slim, between past and present descriptions and hence between the matter of the monarchy and the story about Saul. Similar hints of an implicit connection between past and present are offered throughout vv. 1-14 of ch. 9. It is these that keep the reader's interest alive in the first 14 verses and which also make these verses more than a simple retardation: they indicate that the tale of the lost asses may be an integral part of the ongoing events, as in fact, turns out to be the case.

Verses 3-4

The accidental loss of some asses becomes the occasion for a journey by Saul to find them /9/. Familial relations, already established by v. 2, are foregrounded by the redundant descriptions of Kish as 'the father of Saul' and Saul as 'his son.' Explanation of this foregrounding is to be found in the contrast between Kish and Saul and previous fathers and sons, Eli, Hophni, and Phinehas; Samuel, Joel and Abijah. In previous cases, the sons either disregard their father's instructions or fail to follow his exemplary actions in office.

Relations between Saul and his father are different. Kish issues a simple command, 'Take a servant, and go search for the asses.' The command is even softened by the word *na'* after the imperative (Smith 1899:60). Saul's response is lightning quick: Kish has only just finished speaking when we see Saul crossing over to the Ephraimite hill country (v. 4). Recalling that Israel's previous misfortunes in ch. 4 and the standing request for a king in ch. 8 were predicate to the situation of disobedient or wayward sons, Saul's unquestioning, immediate obedience becomes an important characterization. Disobedient sons have been rejected by God and man; might Saul be an obedient replacement?

The search is described first generally - 'he crossed the Ephraimite hill country' - and then in detail in three specific locales (McCarter 1980:174). Although scholars have generally preferred to follow LXX and Vulg. in reading all verbs in the plural, MT does exhibit an ordered pattern of singulars and plurals:

1. General overview: singular, wayya'abor
2. Specific descriptions:

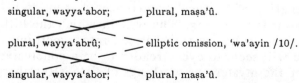

singular, wayya'abor;   plural, maṣa'û.

plural, wayya'abrû;   elliptic omission, 'wa'ayin /10/.

singular, wayya'abor;   plural, maṣa'û.

Though it is difficult to derive semantic import from the patterning, it does indicate that MT is not entirely random, and hence, that it need not be regularized.

Regarding the topography and significance of the places visited, Mauchline's conclusion is safe, and reflects the rhetorical effect of the description: 'We can conclude without hesitation that a wide search was made of the hill country between the range of Shechem in the north and well nigh Jerusalem in the south' (1971:94) /11/. Despite a thorough search, the asses are not found. Could someone have hidden them? The text does not say, but the extent of the search leads the reader to entertain the thought.

Verse 5

Saul receives further characterization as a devoted son who is concerned for his father's well-being (cf. Gunn 1980:61). As most commentators have noted, the search has brought Saul to the land of Zuph, which the reader associates with Samuel on the basis of 1.1. McCarter, for example, says 'providentially (v. 16) Saul's wanderings have brought him to Samuel' (1980: 175; cf. Buber 1956:124). Saul's presence in the territory associated with Samuel prompts the reader to wonder whether there will be a chance meeting between the two, or whether the loss of the asses and the search for them have perhaps been engineered to bring Saul to this locale. Though refraining from any explicit exposition about these possibilities, the narrator has provided the associations that allow the reader to speculate.

Saul's choice of a location in which to express his doubts about continuing the search is the second in a concatenation of 'chance' occurrences that guide his steps towards anointing. 'The way in which the hitherto negative results are transformed into something positive will seem to every reader to be a conclusive proof of the mysterious workings of fate' (Hertzberg

1964:81). As such coincidences continue to mount, the reader's initial inkling that the story of Saul might be another story of divine choice and election, such as Samuel's, is nurtured.

Having read chs. 1-7, in which Yahweh is often at work behind the scenes, the reader has already been acquainted with the divine modus operandi. The narrator's notable restraint in withholding explicit identification of Yahweh's hand in all of this earns the dividend of increased reader interest and active participation in the unfolding events at the negligible price of some initial uncertainty over the connection between chs. 8 and 9 /12/.

Verse 6

The servant's speech is another invitation to speculation. 'He said to him, 'But there is a man of God in this city. He is an honoured man, and everything he says comes true . . .'.' This servant seems to know a lot about the man of God, whose identity he, nevertheless, does not reveal. The narrator employs the servant temporarily to divulge this important information at a point when Saul was threatening to turn back, thus ending the journey and frustrating the reader's own search for its significance. Though the servant drops some important clues about the identity of the man of God, he is not allowed to destroy the narrator's veil of mystery. His advice to Saul itself exemplifies the narrator's secretiveness: the servant is used to provide Saul with information that allows for the continuation of the journey, and at the same time, provides the reader with hints about the identity of the unknown man of God.

The servant speaks of an honoured man of God whose predictions always come to pass. The reader will recall that Samuel is the only prior example of someone whose words always come true (3.19f; cf. Schulz 1919:131). Although Samuel is called a prophet in ch. 3, unlike v.

6, the reader's suspicions are roused by the claim of accurate prediction for both individuals.

The problem that historical criticism has found in the contradiction between vv. 6-10 (which speak of a 'man of God'), vv. 11, 18f (which speak of a 'seer'), and vv. 14-17, 19 (which identify both 'man of God' and 'seer' as Samuel) can be resolved, as Buber noted, by paying close attention to the rhetorical impact of the variations (1956:124f) /13/. Weiser observes that the obscure identity of the man of God creates curiosity in the reader. The narrator reveals only gradually the specific details of his tale as the chain of events requires. Nevertheless the details about the man of God do not exclude the subsequent identification with Samuel (1962:50).

The narrator is able to disguise his deliberate suppression of the identity of the man of God by introducing him through the mouth of Saul's servant, who need not know Samuel's name. To Saul's servant, the adviser is important for their predicament only as a man of God who can make their way known to them. His lack of concern for the man's name is realistically motivated by his focus on the problem at hand. Whether or not the servant knew of Samuel, or should have known of him on account of the latter's prominence, is debatable (against e.g. L. Schmidt 1970:71). It is sufficient that the usage of the generic appellation is con-sistent with the situation in the story /14/.

The narrator plays on the indefiniteness of 'man of God' to contribute to the sense of marvellous coincidence in the journey: his characters go in search of a man of God and find, instead, a Samuel (Hylander 1932:243, citing G. Hölscher). That the servant should expect simply a man of God in the city, yet encounter a Samuel there, illustrates yet again the divine engineering so dominant in 9.1-10.16 (cf. e.g. Gressmann 1921:34; McCarter 1980:184f).

As first noted by Buber, the young man's speech also introduces an element of irony to the quest

(1956:126, 142; cf. McCarter 1980:176). The young man says 'Let us go! Perhaps he will advise (*yaggîd*) us about the journey we have undertaken' (McCarter's translation). The suggestion that the man of God will 'declare' (*yaggîd*) introduces a number of repetitions of words based on the same root as *nagîd* (vv. 6, 8, 16, 18, 19; 10.1), an office to which Saul is being divinely directed. To the reflective reader of ch. 9, the young man's innocent description of the forthcoming 'advice' is a remarkable verbal irony based upon a repeated *Leitwort* (cf. Buber 1956:126). The man of God will 'declare' (*yaggîd*) their way and the result is that Samuel anoints Saul as *nagîd* /15/.

The narrator supplements the irony with the young man's account of what it is that the man of God will do for them. In view of the fact that they are out searching for the lost asses, it is rather surprising that the man of God is expected to tell them of 'the path that we have taken' instead of the whereabouts of the asses /16/. Surely they knew the path they had taken! Viewed in the context of what the man of God actually does, however, the significance of the strange suggestion - and the irony in the naive young man's utterance - becomes clear. Samuel does, in fact, tell Saul about the immediate cause of their journey (v. 20), and also, through his subsequent actions, about the ultimate reason for their taking a path that led to him and the office of 'nagîd' (9.19-10.1). The reflective reader will see the narrator's irony behind the young man's words: the latter expects some sort of solution to his immediate difficulties, while the narrator hints at a somewhat different significance for the path that the two characters have taken /17/.

Verses 7-8

Saul points out a complication for the servant's proposal - they do not have the means to pay the man of God for his advice. The mysterious appearance of the quarter shekel in the young man's hand seems to be another of the narrator's subtle hints that events are being guided from behind the scenes. 'Fate rapidly works its way into the pattern of events: the young man would have turned back but for his servant's chance find of money to provide a gift for the seer' (Gunn 1980:61). The unusual expression *nimṣa' be-yadî*, 'there is found in my hand,' rather than the more common *yeš lî*, 'I have,' is conspicuous, and emphasizes that the money comes from a source other than Saul or the servant (McCarter 1980:176). The sudden materialization of the shekel in the young man's hand creates a gap in the narrative by leaving the natural question, 'Where did it come from?' unanswered. The reader will, of course, formulate some provisional answers, but expects to find some authoritative answer later in the narrative.

Verse 7 offers a further hint about the identity of the man of God by juxtaposing the words *nabî'* and *'îš* and then underlining the juxtaposition by repeating it in a modified form, *lehabî' le'îš ha'elohîm* (Buber 1956:126). The verb *nabî'*, 'we bring,' is a homonym of the noun *nabî'*, 'prophet.' Though the syntax prevents any ambiguity about the meaning of *nabî'*, the similarity of the roles of 'man of God' and prophet is enough to bring the juxtaposition to the attention of a careful reader such as Buber. Though no explicit equation is made in Saul's unconscious juxtaposition, the man of God is related to prophecy, as he was in v. 6.

These subtle intimations about the identity of the anonymous man of God function as goads, prodding the reader on in hope of an authoritative identification of the man of God that will fill in the gap (indeterminacy) created by his anonymity (cf. Sternberg 1978: 311 n.31). It should be recalled that this gap is created first to show that neither Saul nor the servant knows who the man is, and second to add to that aura of mysterious purpose enveloping the entire search for the asses.

The curiosity excited by this gap and the glimmer-
ings of a mysterious purpose shaping the search capture the reader's attention. Were it not for such literary techniques, the seeming lack of connection between
the issue of monarchy, unresolved in ch. 8, and the
matter of lost livestock might serve as a distraction
to the reader, and perhaps suggest that the stories
were unrelated /18/. The disjunctive effect of the *in
medias res* beginning of ch. 9 is ameliorated by the
mystery of the search and the smaller gaps of the identity of the man of God and the question of where the
coin came from in v. 8 /19/.

> In fact, however, the reader's attention is not
> drawn immediately to this single large gap as a
> whole but rather to a series or system of smaller,
> successively opened gaps subsumed by it . . . For a
> soon as the initially propelled situation and the
> characters figuring in it have caught his attention,
> the reader becomes aware - and this awareness can
> easily be heightened by a suitable manipulation of
> gaps - that he will not understand them fully or at
> all as long as he lacks certain information about
> the period preceding the beginning of the subject
> . . . The very sketchiness of the information thus
> unfolded renders these gaps even more prominent
> and proportionately stimulates his curiosity even
> further (Sternberg 1978:53f).

Verse 9

As others have noted, v. 9 is a gloss, a narratorial intrusion into the ongoing tale /20/. It is addressed directly to the reader, and though often transposed
to a position between vv. 10 and 11 (e.g. McCarter
1980:165), or between vv. 11 and 12 (e.g. Smith 1899:
61), it is also appropriate in its present location
(cf. Hylander 1932:139f; Seebass 1967:158 n.16).

Before he explains the history of the words 'seer,' and 'prophet,' the narrator characterizes the proposed visit to the man of God as an 'enquiry of God' (*drš*) (Stoebe 1973:195, 203). He thus indicates that the conversation about going to the man of God for information has shifted the focus of the journey; it began with Saul seeking (*baqqeš*) the asses, but now it has come to seeking (*lidróš*) God. The synonymous verbs, *bqš* and *drš*, are narratorial confirmations to the reader who perceives more than a simple search for livestock in the trek.

Yet the narrator does not offer this authoritative description to his reader without camouflaging it with another meaning - the explanation in v. 9b - and so preserving the ambiguity of the search. As Stoebe notes, v. 9b shifts attention away from the nature of Saul's quest (1973:203). He suggests that it is a further (and presumably later) expansion of the gloss in v. 9a. Recalling, however, that there have been prior allusions to the relationship between prophets and men of God (vv. 6f), a similar allusion, albeit between seers and prophets, might not be totally out of context.

Verse 9b opens with the words *lekú wenelekâ,* which hark back to the servant's words, *yabó . . . nelekâ* (v. 6), and Saul's *nelek* (v. 7), and look forward to Saul's *lekâ nelek* (v. 10). Each occurrence has as its end an audience with the man of God. The narrator thus equates the actual visit to the man of God with a hypothetical visit to the seer, as do Saul and the servant in v. 11. Seer and man of God are synonymous in this narrative.

The narrator goes on to tell his reader that the seer is the same as a prophet, that is, the two words describe the same office. Again the narrator is offering the reader hints about this man of God. The difference expected in an explicit authorial comment such as v. 9 is that the equation is clear and specific: man of God = seer = prophet (cf. Buber 1956:125f). As

in v. 9a, the narrator partially conceals his explicit
clues in the guise of an antiquarian linguistic comment. The hidden message of v. 9, which is intended to
be discovered, is that Saul is really seeking God and
really going to a prophet.

The insertion of a comment of this nature offers
some positive reinforcement to the assiduous reader
who has struggled through the abrupt beginning of ch.
9, and the gaps along the way. The comment encourages
speculation about the ultimate meaning and goal of the
journey by confirming that there is a hidden significance to it. Having momentarily drawn back the veil,
however, the narrator quickly replaces it and covers
the partial revelation with the antiquarian tone of v.
9. The brief respite over, the reader is plunged back
into the ongoing flow of events.

Verse 10

Saul voices his agreement to the servant's plan.
The narrator then tells his reader that Saul and the
young man went off to the city where the man of God
was. The narrator's use of the descriptive term 'man
of God' (previously used only by Saul and the young
man) immediately following his equation of Saul's visit
with a visit to a seer/prophet reveals that he uses the
terms as synonyms, interchanging them as he sees fit.

Verse 11

The situation of a young man meeting a young woman, or a group of women at a well is a 'type-scene' frequent in the Genesis narratives (cf. Exod 2.15ff; John
4; Culley 1976:41-43; Alter 1981:51-62). Alter characterizes a 'type-scene' as 'the recurrence of the same
event - the sameness being definable as a fixed sequence of narrative motifs which, however, may be presented in a variety of ways and sometimes with ingenious variations' (1981:181). Verse 11 alludes to that

type-scene and the complex of associations and expectations included with it in order to add further information about the nature of Saul's approaching encounter
with the seer. Press reaches a similar conclusion from
a historical perspective: 'If we ask about the historical facts that 9.1ff. presupposes, [we see] that it is
not by chance that the two folktale motifs, the search
for the asses and the woman at the well before the
gate, serve only to give prominence to the meeting of
Samuel and Saul in Ramah' (1938:201).

The betrothal type-scene, as summarized by Alter
(1981:52) is as follows:

1. The future bridegroom (or surrogate) journeys to a foreign land.
2. He encounters a girl, usually described as a na'arâ, at a well.
3. Someone, either the man or the girl, draws water from the well.
4. The girl(s) rush home to bring the news of the stranger's arrival
   (the verbs 'hurry' and 'run' are emphasized here).
5. A betrothal is concluded between the stranger and the girl, usually
   after he has been invited to a meal.

When Saul's encounter with the women is compared,
noticeable differences appear:

1. Saul journeys to a foreign land in search of the lost asses.
2. He encounters the ne'arôt coming out to draw water.
3. No one draws water.
4. The girls tell Saul to hurry [maher] to the city if he wants to find
   the seer.
5. Saul meets Samuel, he is invited to dine at the head of the table,
   and he is anointed nagîd over Israel.

On being cued to the convention by the first two
items of the list (vv. 1-11), the reader familiar with
it forms certain expectations about what will happen.
The modification of the typical consummation by replacing the union of male and female with the events
leading to Saul's anointing, his entrance into theocratic service, is another means the narrator uses to show

that Saul's journey is no ordinary journey. Though the
reader does not yet know that Saul will be anointed in
v. 12, the deviations from the conventional type-scene
are sufficient notice that something unusual is happen-
ing. The importance of Saul's appointment with the seer
does not allow him to dally with the maidens, who speed-
ily send him off to meet his destiny.

The question put by Saul and his servant to these
women, while plausible in itself, affords the narrator
the opportunity to place some well-chosen words in the
mouths of the latter. As Richter notes, 'in answer [to
the question of v. 11b] an explanation of where he was
and how he could be found would have sufficed' (1970:
23). The rather lengthy response is more a provocation to
the reader than a pertinent response of the maidens to
Saul and servant /21/. The narrator preserves his un-
intrusive mode of narrating the journey by getting his
characters to supply the reader with important information (cf. 6.6).

Verse 12

Saul's arrival could not have been better timed by
the narrator: as the maidens tell Saul, the seer has
arrived 'just ahead' (*lepaneyka*) /22/ of him, another
in the chain of fortunate coincidences (Gunn 1980:61).
The repeated temporal explanation of the seer's presence (*kî hayyôm . . . kî zebaḥ hayyôm*) emphasizes
the uniqueness of the occasion /23/. The article with
yôm is demonstrative - 'today' (cf. R. J. Williams
1976:19 #87; GKC #26ab). Like Saul and his servant,
the seer has only come to the city for a special reason
- they, to receive his explanation of their journey,
and he, because there is a sacrifice for the people on
the high place.

The sacrifice is specifically described as 'for the
people' (*la'am*) /24/. The last time the people were
seen they had been sent home after requesting a king.
Now they reappear as the beneficiaries of a sacrifice.

Is there any connection? Have the people forgotten
their demand? Has the demand been filled in the mean-
time? Do these people even know about the request?
These and other questions are created by the reappearance of 'the people,' who so far are the only characters explicitly common to both chs. 8 and 9. The fact
that the sacrifice is 'for the people' also introduces
a commonality between the two chapters in which the
people are benefited or potentially benefited by the
actions of a prophet or seer.

Verse 13

The seeming superfluity of the continued response
is not simple revelry in detail (so Stoebe 1973:203).
Rather it supplies the reader with additional important
information: the seer plays a central role in the sacrifice and the people will not eat of it until this
seer comes and blesses it. As Wildberger notes, however, sacrificial duties are not the usual province of
a seer, or even a prophet (1957:462). This seer seems
to have a wider range of duties and authority than
that of any ordinary seer. Yet this information, as
before, serves only to increase the awareness of the
seer's anonymity and of the gap which that creates.

After the seer blesses the sacrifice, it is 'the
invited' (*haqqeru'îm*) and not simply the people
who eat /25/. This description of the eaters seems to
imply that they have been summoned especially for this
occasion (Buber 1964:740). Like all of the other hints
dropped by the narrator, however, the *qeru'îm* contribute more to the mystery and mounting tension than
to any new illumination /26/. The reader sees the mysterious confluence of Saul and servant, the seer, and
the invited eaters all converging on the city and then
the sacrifice; yet there is still no certainty about
the meaning of the meeting.

One might recall Sternberg's observation that
such expositional information is usually intentional-

ly sketchy, serving to spark curiosity and force the reader onward (1978:53f, quoted above on vv. 7f). The fact that there is a noticeable increase in such hints (exposition) towards the latter part of the tale is an indication that the narrator is aware of the danger of losing his reader's interest, and so includes proportionately more of these goads to curiosity.

The final sentence on v. 13 places emphasis on two things: first, on the necessity for Saul and the young man to get going right away, and second on the fact that they will find *him*, (the seer). The emphasis on timely departure and meeting is conveyed by the words *we'attâ* and *kehayyôm,* and on the anonymous person they are to meet by the repeated *'otô* /27/. The impression is one of a unique opportunity that can be lost if Saul and the young man are late. (On the ironic parallel between this scene and the sacrifice in chapter 13, through the motif of urgency/delay, cf. Gunn 1980:62.)

Verse 14

The most important contribution of v. 14 is, of course, the narrator's identification of Samuel as the mysterious man of God/seer. To the historical critic, Samuel's presence in v. 14 represents an indisputable key to the separation and analysis of the components and prehistory of 9.1-10.16. For the close reading of the story it is an important break in the shroud that covers almost every aspect of the search for the lost asses. The reader who had correct suspicions as to the identity of the anonymous holy man is rewarded and encouraged to continue thinking and hypothesizing about the narrative. Attention is now shifted completely to the significance of the journey and the encounter between Saul and Samuel, both of which remain as gaps in the reader's understanding. The meeting with Samuel momentarily becomes another of those expositional elements that gives a little information while demand-

ing larger and larger amounts of attention and curiosity as payment from the reader (cf. Sternberg 1978:
86-89).

Samuel last appeared in 8.22, where he sent the people home instead of installing a king over them as Yahweh had commanded. The problem of the monarchy was
left in suspension at that point, in order to tell the
story of Saul's search for the asses. The revelation
that it is Samuel to whom Saul has come for enlightenment about his journey is certainly intriguing to the
reader, especially in view of the previous reticence
about the seer's identity. Without further information,
however, the reader is reduced to speculation about the
meaning of journey and meeting, and must wait upon
the narrator for any real understanding.

Verses 15-16

Finally the narrator reveals the information that
will make sense of the events. Turning back the clock
for a moment and allowing his reader to listen in on
Yahweh's private revelation to Samuel, the narrator
finally confirms those suspicions that the events on
the human plane were somehow being moulded by divine guidance. All the coincidences and intimations
of the narrative about the journey are confirmed by
Yahweh's explication to Samuel (cf. Gunn 1980:61).

The sense of mystery and the many uncertainties
that prodded the reader towards this moment of revelation were not, however, purely means of stimulating
the reader's attention. Such responses were aroused by
narrating the journey largely from the viewpoint of a
detached human observer with no knowledge of any larger purpose or meaning in these events (cf. N. Friedman 1955:1174f on 'witnessing' and point of view). The
aura of mystery functions both outside the story as a
literary technique to spark attention and interest,
and inside the story as a pervasive description of the
atmosphere surrounding the journey. None of the charac-

ters knew of hidden purpose or significance. There is
no intentional human complicity in the engineering of
this concatenation of events. God, alone, has brought
these things to pass /28/.

The revelation to the reader opens significantly
with the words 'Yahweh revealed.' The keynote for both
reader and Samuel is revelation. Yahweh returns to the
stage giving his first communication to Samuel since
he told the latter to make a king. Samuel had refused
that task and the reader was led to expect a divine
response. Yahweh proceeds to explain what he has been
doing, how he has begun his response, and what that
response actually entails.

The strayed asses were simply the means that Yahweh has chosen to send (*'ešlah*, v. 16) Saul to Samuel.
The predictive aspect of the revelation in v. 15 is an
important characterization of the entire journey as
divinely engineered. Yahweh is able to predict the
future course of Saul's journey because he has directed
it all along.

Yahweh's revelation is indeed a response to Samuel's failure to make a king in 8.22. Though Yahweh
had implied that he would maintain theocratic control
of Israel and its monarchy (8.9, 22), Samuel did not
understand and so, did not make a king. Instead of
choosing a man and installing him as king, Samuel had
sent all the people home. In immediate response, as we
now see, Yahweh took Saul from his home and brought
him directly to Samuel. Saul's journey from home to
Samuel is the divine summons that reverses the effect
of Samuel's dismissal of the people. Having directed
Saul's steps to Samuel's doorstep, as it were, Yahweh
now gives a fuller explanation of the role that this
future monarch will play.

Yahweh tells Samuel that he is to anoint Saul as
nagîd. The act of anointing itself indicates that
Samuel is in a position of authority. The fact that
Samuel is commissioned by Yahweh to invest Saul
with the commission of *nagîd* reveals the lines of

authority /29/. The theocratic structure remains, as ever, God over mediator over Israel, or in this case, over Saul the *nagîd*. Yahweh's command for Samuel to anoint Saul is a specification of the manner in which Samuel was to 'make a king' (cf. 8.21). Yahweh's explanation reveals, or should reveal, to Samuel that the theocratic structure will remain in place. If Samuel proceeds to carry out Yahweh's commands it will indicate that he refused to do so previously on account of his misunderstanding Yahweh's original intention.

The subjugation of the 'king' to the theocracy is also indicated by the name of the office for which Saul is anointed /30/. The etmological derivation of *nagîd* is uncertain (Fritz 1976:351f; Mettinger 1976:158f; Ishida 1977:35 n.8). Tomoo Ishida suggests that the term was originally the title of a person designated, either by Yahweh or a reigning monarch, to be ruler (1977:45). Mettinger narrows the meaning of *nagîd* in 1 Sam 9 even more. He sees this instance as the product of prophetic circles in Israel (the northern kingdom) (cf. Mayes 1978:14):

> [They] introduced the idea that YHWH, the Supreme King, could take one of His own people and designate him *nagîd*. It is tempting to see in the choice of this terminology for divine designation a tacit criticism of the secular institution of a human king designating his successor: God Himself and no one else was to decide who was to sit on the throne (1976:168; cf. Richter 1965:77f; Fritz 1976:352).

Both Mettinger and Ishida agree that the term describes a person who is designated to perform a task, usually of leadership (Mettinger 1976:182; Ishida 1977:48; cf. McCarter 1980:178f).

When Yahweh prescribes an anointing as *nagîd* for Saul, the combined meaning of the words *ûmešahtô lenagîd* is clearly and uncompromisingly theocratic. The man is chosen as the official 'designate' of Yah-

weh, to be invested in office by Samuel, the theocratic
mediator (cf. Kegler 1977:74). Yahweh has now clearly
delineated what he left implicit in his previous instructions for inaugurating the monarchy /31/. Samuel's
refusal to make a king provides the occasion for Yahweh's entrance and an unambiguous statement on what
kind of king (*mišpaṭ hammelek*, 8.9) he will stipulate
(*wehiggadta*, 8.9). Samuel's misinterpretation of Yahweh's words in 8.9, detailed in 8.11-18, is now corrected by Yahweh. Yahweh had said 'Designate (*wehiggadta*) the kind of king' (8.9), and now he has brought the
man to be anointed as 'designate' (*nagîd*). Saul's rise
to the office of 'king' is, therefore, Yahweh's doing
from beginning to end.

The people had demanded that a king be established
over them (*'alênû*, 8.19) so that they, the people
of Yahweh, could be 'like all the nations' - the phrase
was Israel's declaration of independence. In response,
Yahweh now issues his theocratic declaration: 'Anoint
a designate over (*'al*) my people Israel (*'al-'ammî
yiśra'el*).' A clear denial of the people's declaration
resounds in Yahweh's command. The one who will be
over (*'al*) Israel is Yahweh's designate; the reason -
Israel is Yahweh's people. Buber's description of Yahweh's counter-declaration is accurate:

> Yahweh's actual answer to the people's request is
> voiced in the command to Samuel, namely the deci-
> sive transformation of the concession. For the nar-
> rator this process signifies the divinely decreed
> *supersession of the primitive, immediate theocracy
> by the mediated*. (1956:128, Buber's emphasis).

Yahweh's description of the task for which Saul is
anointed places the new designate well within previously established theocratic bounds. 'He will deliver
my people from the hand of the Philistines.' W. F.
Albright, among others, sees the description as a
statement that Saul was anointed only as a military

leader of the tribal confederation (1969:163; cf. E. Robertson 1944:183; Langlamet 1970:191f). Yahweh's statement is in pointed opposition to the people's idea that their new monarch would make them 'like the nations.' The 'king,' as designate, will instead widen and maintain the gap between Yahweh's people and the nations such as the Philistines.

The reader familiar with the exodus narrative in the book of Exodus recognizes that Yahweh is quoting himself in v. 16. That he spoke almost identical words to Moses when preparing to bring Israel out of Egypt (cf. Exod 3.7-9) indicates that Yahweh regards the present situation as similar to that of the exodus /32/. He also sees parallel outcomes. Saul is to be a new Moses, delivering Israel from the Philistines as Moses delivered them from the Egyptians (cf. Exod. 3.10) /33/.

Smith (1899:62) correctly observes that Yahweh's suggestion of a Philistine threat contradicts 7.11-14 and on this ground Buber (1956:114-20) labels the end of 7.9 as a gloss along with the description of victory in 7.11-14. He suggests that only with the revelation of 9.15f does Yahweh answer Samuel's cries of 7.9 (Buber 1956:128).

An alternative arises from the observation that it is Yahweh who seems to contradict the events of 7.10-14. Either he has forgotten - unlikely - or his statement is more complex than it first seems. One recalls that v. 16 is a response to the request for a king by way of defining what that king will be. The request in turn was provoked by the reappearance of a situation (cf. 8.1-4) threatening catastrophe as in ch. 4. The people feared bad judges (theocratic mediators) because Yahweh had previously allowed the Philistines to defeat Israel in order to punish errant priests (also theocratic mediators). Thus their request for a king could be 'interpreted' by Yahweh, whose judgement is obviously prejudiced by personal involvement, as an expression of their fear of a recurring Philistine disaster.

Yahweh leaves out any mention of his own part in the disaster both because he has no one to answer to and because he is concerned to place the request in a new light. He ignores the request's implication that he has misgoverned as he 'forgets' his own role in the disaster. Yahweh redefines the request as a plea for divine aid within the theocratic structure. All anti-covenantal emphasis simply evaporates beneath Yahweh's forceful reassertion of national covenantal idealogy.

Yahweh's response to the request characterizes him as a powerful, domineering God. The nearest he comes to an admission of guilt is his installation of Saul as *nagîd*. The fact that he gives in even halfway to the request indicates that its justice requires Yahweh to recognize it. Far from expressing the noble sentiment that it did in Exodus, however, Yahweh's self-quotation becomes the sarcastic response of an unmoving, all-powerful God who will not admit his mistakes /34/. As Eli said, 'he is Yahweh and does as he pleases' (3.18).

Israel requested a *melek* and political independence; Yahweh responds with a *nagîd* and an emphatic 'my people' (3 times in v. 16). Yahweh's reliance on the exodus and its significance to respond to Israel's request for a king reminds the reader of his prior reenactment of the exodus in chs. 5-6. In both instances, Yahweh resorts to the exodus typology because his status as a mighty divine warrior and Israel's king has been called in question. Israel's defeat in ch. 4 seemed to suggest to the Philistines that they and perhaps their god Dagon had defeated Yahweh, the fearsome god of the exodus (cf. 4.8; 5.1-2). Similarly, Israel's request for a king was justified with the statement that a king would go out before Israel to fight Israel's battles (8.20). Since the request was made in view of Israel's past defeat in ch. 4, the clear implication of 8.20 was that Yahweh, who was covenantally committed to Israel's defence, had failed to live up to his commitment and so forfeited his kingship over Israel.

Both times Yahweh responds by 'rehearsing' some aspect of his actions in the exodus. Apparently Yahweh regards the exodus events as fundamentally establishing his sovereignty over Israel and as clear signals to the nations that he is the mightiest divine warrior. In res-ponse to the Philistines' apparent victory, he reenacts the exodus using the ark as his new Israel. The result is that his reputation cleared. Similarly, when Israel itself questions his right to rule them, Yahweh calls out a new Moses to lead them to safety. He uses the exodus events to overrule any objection that Israel might have to his rule, and simply reas-serts the covenantal dogma: they are his people and he is their divine king.

The parallels that the narrator has drawn between these exodus allusions are part of a broad parallelism that he has constructed between chs. 1-7 and chs. 8-12. If the reader remembers what Yahweh's prior exodus recollection did for Israel - nothing - the implicat-ions for Israel's requested monarchy are not good. The one most likely to benefit from Yahweh's new Moses is Yahweh himself.

Samuel, alone amongst the human characters, is giv-en to know the specifics of Yahweh's response. No one else is allowed to know the true nature of the monarchy and the divine response until after the new arrangement is ratified and made law (10.25). By giving the reader access to the details of Yahweh's plans for the monar-chy the narrator exposes another reason for the sense of mystery surrounding Saul's journey, and for the secrecy attendant on his subsequent anointing. If any-one else were to know the true nature of the new mon-archy, it would be immediately rejected. The entire affair is, therefore, concealed from start to finish. Even Saul and his servant have no idea about the true nature of their quest. The air of conspiracy that Wildberger detected in ch. 9 is there, but it is a con-spiracy perpetrated by Yahweh and Samuel, rather than Samuel and the elders (Wildberger 1957:454).

The reader's access to the revelation functions as an important interpretive guideline for the remainder of the narrative. With it the reader will be able to penetrate the appearances staged by Yahweh and Samuel, and so understand the realities of their inauguration of the Israelite monarchy. Having attuned the reader to the realities of the divine plan, the narrator will proceed to present an ironic picture of Israel as it welcomes Saul, the people's 'king' who is really Yahweh's designate.

Verse 17

The narrator resumes his description of the flow of events that is carrying Saul towards kingship. He left off his narration with a view of Samuel from Saul's perspective. The revelation to Samuel is bracketed with the temporal description that it came the day before (v. 15). The return to the time frame of Saul's arrival is indicated in v. 17 by a description of Samuel seeing Saul.

The sequence of perfect verbs suggests the simultaneity of the actions in v. 17. As soon as Samuel saw Saul, Yahweh answered, 'Behold the man . . .' (McCarter 1980:179; GKC #164b.) /35/.

The verb *ya'eṣor* in the last sentence of v. 17 has not yet been successfully shown to mean 'will rule,' despite many citations of cognates in other languages and post-biblical Hebrew (cf. Smith 1899: 64, and examples in Stoebe 1973:196).

McCarter, noting that *'aṣar* usually means 'restrain, hinder, retain, shut in' suggests that Yahweh is referring to Saul's activities in mustering Israel's forces, hence 'to retain' (1980:179); 'This one shall muster my people!' (McCarter 1980:165). There is, however, quite a difference in meaning between 'restrain' and 'muster.'

An alternative reading for which the normal sense

of *'aṣar* is quite sufficient, appears when Yahweh's
sarcasm is appreciated. Yahweh does not himself see
any need for a king to defend Israel. Instead, he is
installing a *nagîd* precisely because he wants to
restrain Israel from its admitted goal of becoming
'like all the nations.' In v. 16, Yahweh tells Samuel
that he intends to maintain the theocracy and the covenant by installing a *nagîd*, which in this context
might be translated 'puppet king.' In v. 17, then, one
should translate *'aṣar* as usual: 'Behold the man of
whom I spoke to you. This one ought to stop my people.'
/36/ Yahweh's explicit statement about the purpose of
the new *nagîd* thus continues his sarcastic comments
about his 'capitulation' to the people's request for a
king. Certainly Samuel, who was not willing to give in
to the people, would appreciate Yahweh's vitriolic description of the designate's function.

Verse 18

When Saul comes asking Samuel where the nameless
seer is, he shows his innocence of any complicity in
the plan revealed by Yahweh. He does not even know
who Samuel is.

As Buber observes, Saul's question, 'Can you tell me
. . .?' (*haggîdâ*) is another instance of the narrator's
subtle structural ironies by way of word-play (1956:
126, 141f). Saul still seeks the seer whom he hopes will
explain (*yaggîd*, cf. vv. 6, 8) their course. It is his
quest for explanation that brings him to ask (*haggîdâ*)
Samuel the seer's whereabouts. The irony is that
his quest is really a summons to become *nagîd* (cf.
McCarter 1980:179).

Verse 19

If there was any doubt left in the reader's mind
that Samuel was the seer, it is now dispelled by Samuel's answer, 'I am the seer.' Saul seems neither to

recognize Samuel nor to know of his role in Israelite politics. Saul appears as the naive country boy from Benjamin, out of touch with national concerns. In terms of Yahweh's subterfuge, he could not have chosen a better subject for his designate: under his and Samuel's conniving tutelage, Saul will be easily moulded to suit their purposes.

Samuel can also engage in the verbal irony of which the narrator is so fond; 'I'll send you off in the morning and explain (*'aggîd*) everything on your mind.' One can almost see Yahweh and Samuel winking at one another /37/.

Verse 20

Samuel proves himself as seer by telling Saul that the lost asses have been found even before Saul makes any mention of them. That, having done, so Samuel should then have him up to eat and to stay overnight, indicates that more important issues than lost asses are at hand (cf. Hertzberg 1964:83).

Samuel's veiled explanation of why Saul should not worry about the asses 'is obscure to Saul as it is clear to the audience' McCarter 1980:179). The word *ḥemdat*, usually translated as 'desirable' (objects) or 'riches,' also contains an ambiguity that reveals Samuel's continuing disgust at Israel's request for a king. According to G. Wallis *ḥmd* can be negative, neutral, or positive (1980:455f). On the face of it Samuel appears to say that Saul need no longer worry about such silly things as asses when all the riches of Israel are at his disposal. But this windfall is only available because Israel requested a king, a request that Samuel regarded with open disfavour (ch. 8). Wallis notes that *ḥmd* can be negative when the desire is viewed in conjunction with a disreputable act (1980:455). Samuel's comment plays on the ambiguity of *ḥmd* to voice another criticism of Israel's 'base desire' for a king. Edwin Good also observes this ambiguity in Samuel's rhetorical question and suggests that, on the basis of ch. 8, 'Israel's desire (*chemdah*) amounts to a rejection of Yahweh' (1965:62). Samuel leaves no doubt in the reader's mind about his stance on the monarchy. Even though he knows that Saul will only be another theocratic official, Samuel still resents the request.

Verse 21

The narrator continues to develop his characterization of Saul as a modest country boy. Saul protests that his background does not warrant such lofty promises as Samuel has given. The reader knows why Samuel has spoken as he has and is assured by Saul's reaction that the boy has not the slightest inkling about contemporary political issues /38/.

Anyone who knew about the request and Samuel's important involvement in the transactions of ch. 8 would easily understand his meaning - and recognize him, moreover, as scholars have frequently noted. Since Saul gives no evidence of any such knowledge, the reader sees him entering into his anointed office innocent and unsuspecting.

The point is stressed because Saul's simplicity plays an important role in the scheme that Yahweh and Samuel use to gain legal acceptance of their puppet king /39/. Saul is Yahweh and Samuel's dupe; the success of their operation depends on their total control of him. As soon as Saul shows signs of going his own way (ch. 15) he is rejected as unfit for office:

> For rebellion is as the sin of witchcraft,
> and stubbornness is as iniquity and idolatry.
> Because thou hast rejected the word of the Lord,
> he hath also rejected thee from being king.
> (1 Sam 15.23 KJV)

Verse 22

Observing Saul's puzzlement and hesitation, Samuel personally leads Saul and his servant to the banquet hall /40/. Saul is a good catch that must not be allowed to escape. Samuel continues to honour him in a way that is mysterious to the characters but transparent to the reader.

The reader's privileged perspective - all the more appreciated now because denied in the first suspenseful half of ch. 9 - allows a clear view of the theocratic conspiracy. Samuel and Yahweh are revealed in all their manipulative nakedness. Nor does the sudden lifting of the previously troublesome veil leave the reader with an unbiased view of these characters' machinations. Having been subject to the mystifications thrown round Saul's journey to kingship, the reader has been educated to sympathize with the unsuspecting Israelites (cf. above on 6.19f).

But the narrator's goals are far more complex than the simple alliance of the reader with Israel. Only in ch. 12, where Yahweh and Samuel face Israel openly with their subterfuge, does the narrator present his reader with a conclusive position in which the whole issue of theocracy and monarchy is resolved. Whether it is a satisfactory resolution remains to be seen.

That Samuel honours Saul at a public banquet indicates that Yahweh's scheme is now put into action. The people at the banquet are themselves being prepared for a reception of what they think is their new king. Nothing is mentioned about any *nagîd* or king, however, indicating that the banquet is used as a preparatory step: Saul is made to feel that Samuel *and the invited guests* are united in purpose, and the guests are given the impression that Samuel has honoured Saul in accordance with a preconceived plan. What the plan and purpose are, however, is left ambiguous for the guests and Saul. Samuel, like a good narrator, leaves his audience to fill in the indeterminacy /41/.

His purpose at this time is best achieved by allowing all participants to close the ambiguous gaps with their own expectations.

Verses 23-24

Samuel's instructions to the 'butcher' (*laṭṭabbaḥ*) make it seem as though he had prepared for Saul's presence. Richter observes that any preparation for this moment contradicts v. 12 (1970:24) - a contradiction resolved, however, by v. 15, which takes place before v. 12 in narrative time (the day before). Samuel was prepared for Saul's coming and apparently arranged with the butcher to have a special portion set aside for the man Yahweh was sending.

The text of v. 24 is corrupt and, as the most recent textual treatment has suggested, has not yet been explained (McCarter 1980:170f; cf. Driver 1913:75-77). It is, however, comprehensible (excluding the obscure *he'aleyha*) as far as the word *le'mor*, and describes the butcher bringing out the thigh which has been set aside for Saul's consumption /42/.

In the butcher's address to Saul the latter is again given to understand that his arrival and presence have been anticipated. He is made to feel that his destiny has been guided and pre-arranged, leading him to this meeting (cf. Gunn 1980:61). Obviously such psychological manipulation is of great utility to Samuel who uses the meal especially to convince Saul of his destiny (against Hertzberg 1964:84). The butcher, whose own understanding of the situation is left undetermined, is only a tool in Samuel's hands to shape Saul's perception of things.

The shock of experiencing such pre-arrangement of his life takes obvious effect on Saul. No longer questioning the incredible behaviour of others towards him, Saul's response to the butcher's speech is simple and passive - he eats what is set before him. The narrator's description reveals that Samuel's staged sacrifice has achieved its goal: 'And Saul ate *with Samuel* on that day.' Saul has become Samuel's accomplice; he simply complies with the situation and its requirements. The conspiratorial sacrifice has transformed Saul into Samuel's compliant eater, who, for a time, swallows everything that Samuel feeds him.

Verses 25-26

Most scholars since Thenius have preferred the reading of LXX in vv. 25-26. Driver notes that the sequence of verbs in MT is so incongruous compared to LXX's natural and suitable sequence that there can be little doubt that LXX is the 'true reading' (1913:77; cf. Thenius 1864:38, who comments on LXX, 'thus everything in beautiful order'). Nevertheless, Stoebe (1973) follows MT, which is comprehensible even if incongruous. Since both the readings of LXX and MT accomplish more or less the same function - to get Samuel and Saul to bed and back up again in the morning - I shall 'harden my heart' with Keil (so Smith 1899:66) and follow MT in accordance with the interpretational principle of reading with the primary text whenever possible.

The topic of Samuel's discourse on the roof-top is not disclosed by the narrator /43/. Instead, he focuses on the simple fact that Samuel and Saul converse, indicating thereby that they become more closely acquainted. Since it is Samuel's goal to make an obedient theocratic servant out of Saul, the detail is not without significance.

According to Keil & Delitzsch, the temporal description 'it was sunrise' following the verb 'they rose' (*wayyaškimû*) is simply a more precise definition of the verb (1880:94 n.1). The night's activity - sleeping - and the preparations for it, all described by LXX, are passed over and left indeterminate by MT. In defence of MT, Keil and Delitzsch offer the pertinent comment that both bed making and sleeping were 'matters of course, and there was consequently no necessity to mention them; whereas Samuel's talking with Saul upon the roof was a matter of importance in relation to the whole affair, and one which would not be passed over in silence' (1880:94 n.1).

The final three sentences of v. 26 are important for the light they cast on the relationship between Samuel and Saul. First the reader sees Samuel issuing a command: 'Get up and I'll send you off.' The immediacy of Saul's response is visually conveyed by making the very next word a description of Saul's response - "Get up (*qûmâ*) and I'll send you off'; and he (Saul) got up (*wayyaqom*).' One recalls that Saul demonstrated such obedience previously in response to his father's command to go and find the asses (vv. 3f). Yahweh's choice of an obedient young man is already paying dividends. The order of dominance has been unquestionably established: Samuel commands and Saul obeys.

The relationship is not entirely stratified, however, as we see from the final sentence of v. 26. 'And the two, he and Samuel, went out.' The impression conveyed by this description is one of solidarity between the two, an impression based on the grammatically redundant double subject (*šenehem hû'ûšemû'el*) which serves to emphasize the unity of the pair /44/. This description is the final member in a chain showing the convergence of Samuel and Saul: first we saw Saul eating with (*'im*) Samuel (v. 24), then the latter speaking with (*'im*) Saul, and finally the two of them going out together. They may have arrived by separate paths and for individual reasons, but, following the revelation to the one and the banquet for the other, they leave town as a pair. They are united by the single purpose of which the reader and Samuel are aware, and by which Saul is obediently governed.

Saul has shown himself fit to become *nagîd* by his obedience; the morning on which Samuel told Saul he would tell (*'aggîd*, v. 19) everything has arrived (v. 26; cf. L. Schmidt 1970:71). The reader now awaits an account of the anointing which must follow.

Verse 27

The moment for Saul's enlightenment arrives, but the word of God is for his ears only and so the servant is directed by Saul to travel on ahead. Once again the chain of command is presented: Samuel commands Saul to tell the servant to go ahead, and the servant goes ahead, the implication being that Saul followed Samuel's directive. No one but Saul himself is allowed to see or hear what Samuel is going to tell him, nor is Saul allowed to tell anyone (see below on 10.16).

Contrary to Weiser, the reason for the secrecy is not the simple result of 'the peculiarity of legendary representation, its origins, and its intent' (1962:51). Rather the secrecy has a function within the story. The true nature of Israel's new monarch and his subordination to Samuel are hidden from all; only after the people have accepted Saul does Samuel reveal the secret of the anointing.

PART TEN

1 SAMUEL 10

Verse 1

Verse 1 continues the description of Saul's anointing. In 9.27, Samuel tells Saul to send the servant ahead and then he will proclaim to him the word of God (*we'ašmî'aka 'et-debar 'elohîm*). Thus he prepares the innocent young Saul to hear and accept the political idealogy he is about to reveal. The official sounding announcement (cf. Birch 1976:37f) is designed to make the deepest impression on the young country boy. Whatever Samuel is going to say or do, Saul is supposed to take it as official and irrevocable.

Samuel breaks the vial of oil on Saul's head, kisses him, and explains why (*halô' kî*) he has performed the ritual. Like the earlier announcement (9.27), the ceremonial anointing and kiss (Blank 1962:39) are calculated to impress. After such treatment, Saul should be all ears to anything Samuel says. The anointing should have much the same effect on Saul as the banquet did (cf. above on 9.24).

As it stands in MT, Samuel's explanation of the anointing is a terse reformulation of the revelation that he received in 9.16 /1/. As always when a piece of information is repeated by any character, additions and deletions are important (cf. Alter 1981:97).

Samuel repeats only the command portion of Yahweh's revelation to Saul:

9.16 ûmešaḥtô lenagîd 'al-'ammî yiśra'el

10.1 kî-mešaḥaka yhwh 'al-nahalatô lenagîd

One notes, first, differences in syntax. Yahweh's order of emphasis was first Samuel's role as anointer, then Saul's position as designate, and finally Yahweh's own intention to keep a hold on Israel, 'his people.' Samuel, on the other hand, directs Saul's attention first to the fact that the anointer is Yahweh, then to the condition of anointing - it is over his (Yahweh's) 'property' - and lastly to Saul's status as designate. Yahweh sought to show Samuel that he still has a theocratic role to play and to explain the constraints that would be placed on the monarchy /2/. Samuel seeks to awe and overpower Saul with the information that Yahweh anoints him /3/, while at the same time downplaying Saul's subordinate status as designate. Both Yahweh and Samuel take advantage of the primacy effect (better known as first impressions) in their speeches /4/.

Samuel also changes Yahweh's description of the group over which Saul will be designate. Yahweh called it 'my people, Israel,' but Samuel calls it 'his possession'/5/. Yahweh affirmed the covenantal aspect of his relationship, as does Samuel, but Samuel's choice of the word 'possession' emphasizes the fact that Saul is being set over a group that belongs to Yahweh (cf. Buber 1956:132). Through syntactic construction and vocabulary Samuel seeks to combine an overpowering sense of subordination with the fact of political elevation.

Omitted altogether are Yahweh's ironic comments about the intended function of the designate. Saul is to be a puppet king and so is not taken completely into Samuel's confidence. Anything that might cue Saul to the real purpose of his new position is discreetly left unmentioned (against Seebass 1967:159 n.21). The goal is to make of Saul a loyal theocratic designate; all efforts are directed exclusively to that end /6/.

Verse 2

If the sacrificial meal was orchestrated to convince Saul that his destiny lay in the guiding hand of God, Samuel's prediction of the course of Saul's return journey is doubly so. Each of the three predicted incidents corresponds to a specific event on the journey that led Saul to Samuel (Buber 1956:133-34). The most important persuasive element in Samuel's description is the fact that he knows what will happen before it happens. This predictive aspect, in combination with the uncanny correspondence of each incident to a prior occurrence, constitutes an overpowering mechanism by which Saul is to be throughly convinced of his destiny. The miraculous correspondences show Saul the power and authority of Yahweh who guides his every step, and Samuel's predictions of these events bear witness to his own intimate relationship with Yahweh.

The first incident involves a meeting with two men who repeat Samuel's disclosure that the asses are found (cf. 9.20), and confirm Saul's own fear that his father would forget about the asses and begin to worry about him (cf. 9.5; Smith 1899:67). As Saul heard Samuel describing the future, he would no doubt recall the past and his own worries about his father. This first description would not, however, lead him much beyond the recollection of the past and a marvelling at Samuel's predictive abilites. He might recall that it was his worrying that had sparked the decision to seek the seer's advice and hence had helped to bring him to become designate and to stand there listening to Samuel's prediction. For the moment, however, the narrator leaves Saul's reactions as an undetermined gap.

Verses 3-4

The second incident involves an encounter with three men who just happen to be going up to God at Bethel.

Their gift of bread to Saul as they go up to God recalls Saul's own lack of bread when he wanted to go to a city to inquire of a man of God (Hertzberg 1964:85). But now a pattern begins to appear. As in the first prediction, Saul has changed places in these parallels to his previous journey. Before, he was the one who suggested that his father might worry about him; now, it is Saul who listens while someone else tells him the same. Before, Saul was the one who had no bread to give to the man of God; now, having visited Samuel, bread is given to him. The correspondences appear to point to a significant change; could it have something to do with the fact that Saul has been anointed by Yahweh as designate /7/?

Verses 5-6

The final incident and recapitulation of Saul's journey to Samuel and the office of *nagîd* takes the form of a meeting between Saul and a band of prophets coming down from the high place /8/. As Buber notes, the encounter with this group of prophets matches Saul's previous encounter with Samuel, who was just going up to the high place when Saul met him. '. . .the meeting with them (10.10a) [The prophets] is carried out with the same words as the prior meeting (9.14b), and what was begun at one *bama* is completed at another' (Buber 1956:135; cf. 9.14).

The parallel to which Buber draws attention also serves to highlight a major difference. In the second encounter with prophets at a high place, Saul is overcome by the spirit of Yahweh and actually joins in the prophetic activity. Samuel's prediction that Saul will 'become another man' is a perfect description of the desired effect of all these incidents - Saul will become a convert - presented in the guise of a portrayal of Saul's prophetic condition. Unlike his first encounter when he went to the prophet Samuel seeking information, Saul now joins the company of prophets

and prophesies with them. Between the two incidents
lies the event that explains the change, namely Saul's
induction into the theocratic service as *nagîd*.

Verse 7

The purpose of Samuel's predictions and the astonishing correspondences with Saul's first journey is
suggested by Samuel's description of the future incidents as 'signs' (*'otôt*). "*Oth*, "sign," is an object, an
occurrence, an event through which a person is to recognize, learn, remember, or perceive the credibility
of something'; a sign works to support an understanding or to motivate behaviour (Helfmeyer 1977:170f,
quoting Gunkel).

Samuel suggests that Saul is to respond to the
signs with action - 'Do whatever your hand finds' - for
the signs convey the knowledge that 'God is with you.'
Samuel thus supplies Saul with their correct interpretation: their purpose is to convince Saul that God is
with him by showing him his new position within the
theocratic regime in contrast to his former position
outside /9/. The means to this end are the contrasting
parallels: when Saul sees the actual change that the
anointing has brought about, he will be certain that
God is now with him, the new designate, and that his
steps and actions are all directed by God.

As Irwin suggests, Samuel's advice that Saul do
whatever comes to hand is closely bound to the fulfillment of the signs (1941:124; cf. Buber 1956:137).
When it is recalled that the final event in these three
incidents is Saul's conversion to another man, it is
clear that Samuel's instruction is directed to the
changed Saul and not to Saul as an ordinary person.
Hence the freedom granted to Saul in v. 7 is not
completely unconditioned. Furthermore, L. Schmidt
concludes from a study of the expression to do 'what
comes to hand' that it does not mean unlimited personal freedom. Rather it emphasizes that a person has

been enabled to perform a task (1970:77).

As the divine guidance had led Saul in the past, without his awareness, so it will continue to lead him. The signs do not enable him to know the entire course of his destiny. On the contrary, they give him only the assurance that his steps are indeed divinely guided and that whatever actions are required of him by circumstances are in fact ordained by God. Samuel alone knows how God will direct Saul's path as designate - he demonstrates this knowledge in his predictions of vv. 2-7. The signs themselves are also examples of how Saul's divinely guided career will proceed: in all three examples, Saul is a passive respondent to the circumstances into which he is led.

Verse 8

Samuel's instructions to Saul in v. 8 are primarily preparatory to the events of ch. 13, but need not therefore be regarded as contradictory to v. 7 (against e.g. Buber 1956:137-39; Richter 1970:19). Samuel has just finished predicting a series of events, fulfillment of which was to be a sign to Saul of a divinely guided future both in these events and beyond. The content and sequence of incidents subsequent to the prophesying is left undetermined, described only as 'whatever comes to hand.' Following this predicted blank, however, Samuel continues his decription of future events.

The resumption of the prediction is indicated by the waw-consecutive perfect verb, 'You will go down' (*weyaradta*), which continues the series of such verbs in vv. 2-6 /10/. What Samuel says in v. 8 is no less predictive or prescriptive than what he said in vv. 2-6. The difference between v. 7 and v. 8 is that v. 8 leaves the future course of events undetermined.

To say this is not to say say that events are left to be determined by Saul. Rather, Samuel seems not know precisely what is to happen; thus he leaves it open and tells Saul to improvise. Why Samuel should do such a thing at the very time when he and Yahweh are seeking to establish strict control over Saul's loyalty and action is left undetermined by the narrative. The reader, at this point, can only speculate about Samuel's reasons. Perhaps there are some conditions that cannot be predicted for that particular period. Could it be that Samuel and Yahweh are not yet certain of how the people will respond to their choice for a king? Or has Samuel got some ulterior motive? The answer to this question lies in subsequent scenes.

This reading of the banquet (9.22-24), the anointing (9.27-10.1), the signs of vv. 2-6, and the subsequent prediction of v. 8 as the scheming efforts of Yahweh and Samuel to form Saul into an obedient and loyal designate is supported by the events of ch. 13 which are dependent on v. 8 /11/. At the first sign of independence from Saul, when he deviates from the passive role assigned to him by Samuel (v. 8; cf. 13.8f), Samuel predicts a premature end of Saul's monarchy (13.14) (see Gunn 1980:66f, 124f).

Verse 8 need not, therefore, be regarded as diametrically opposed to its context (so Crüsemann 1978:58f) /12/. To recapitulate: Samuel predicts events and prescribes Saul's responses (vv. 2-6); fulfillment will constitute a divine sign, in the knowledge of which Saul may continue to do 'whatever his hand finds to do,' assured that his steps are still divinely guided (v. 7) /13/. Finally, sometime in the future, Saul is to go to Gilgal and wait seven days for Samuel whereupon the latter will come and make known Saul's future undertakings /14/.

Verse 9

Samuel has done what he can to indoctrinate Saul; now God takes over. No sooner does Saul turn to leave Samuel than God gives Saul another heart. The narra-

tor's description emphasizes the immediacy of this
divine intervention (cf. Nowack 1902:47). Listening
to Samuel in v. 6, the reader has been led to expect
that Saul will not be a changed man until he joins in
the prophesying with the band of prophets /15/. Why
does the narrator now contradict Samuel?

Various solutions have been sought to explain the
apparent prematurity of the conversion. Keil and Delitzsch rationalize, suggesting that the change did
not come early but on the same day as the signs were
fulfilled. 'As he left Samuel early in the morning,
Saul could easily reach Gibeah in one day . . .' (1880:
104). Smith demythologizes, suggesting, 'it is psychologically quite comprehensible that the impulse should
anticipate the predicted order of events' (1899: 70;
cf. Dhorme 1910:86).

More recently Helfmeyer has suggested that the
changed heart was given to Saul so that he might gain a
clear and proper understanding of the subsequent signs
(1977:185). Citing parallels, Helfmeyer suggests that
only when Yahweh gives an 'understanding heart' is it
guaranteed that a sign will be properly understood.
Helfmeyer fails to observe, however, that unlike Deut
29.3, which speaks of the need for Yahweh to give an
'understanding heart' (*leb lada'at*), v. 9 speaks only
of a 'changed heart' (*leb 'aher*).

The problem resolves itself, however, as soon as
one pays attention to the question of who says what to
whom. In v.6, it is Samuel who tells Saul that he will
be a changed man when the spirit takes him and he prophesies. In v. 9, on the other hand, it is the narrator
who reveals to his reader that God intervenes at the
very moment that Saul turns to leave Samuel. Certainly Samuel told Saul that he would be changed after or
during the prophesying. But God, as the narrator so
kindly shows us, has no qualms about speeding up the
change in Saul as an insurance against any slip-up;
he makes the change straightway.

'When he turned to leave Samuel, God transformed

his heart.' No entrance is left for accidental influ-
ences to deflect Saul from the course on which Samuel
and God have set him. From what Samuel told Saul, it
would be the signs given by the three incidents that
would objectively show him that God was with him.
The reader now knows, however, that God has exercised his divine prerogative, intervening to ensure that
Saul is properly affected. Welcome Saul, automaton.

The third sentence in v. 9 is the narrator's matter-
of-fact summary: all the signs came to pass on that
same day. By recounting in one sentence what it took
Samuel roughly sixteen detailed sentences to describe,
the narrator brings the reader back to the reality of
the situation. Given God's direct intervention to
change Saul's heart, the narrator indicates that it is a
matter of course, requiring a little attention, that the
signs are fulfilled. The reader's attention is diverted
away from the astonishing correspondences and meanings of the signs, towards God and Samuel in action.
Save the rhetoric and fulfilled signs for Saul - both
narrator and reader already know that God is 'with
Saul' /16/.

Excursus on the Structure
of 1 Sam 9.1-10.16

Buber has noted a significant pattern exhibited by the
events of 9.1-10.16 (1956:142). First Saul is the centre of action as he makes his unknowing way towards
Samuel (9.1-14). Then Samuel takes over in the actions
leading to Saul's anointing and induction into the theocratic service (9.15-10.9). Finally, Saul returns to
centre stage on his return journey (10.10-16). Three
parts to the story of Saul's designation may also be
labelled according to the reader's perspective.

First we travel with Saul, experiencing and understanding the journey solely from the limited perspective of the human character. Although the narrator
sprinkles hints about some larger significance through-

out vv. 1-14, they are not enough to afford the reader the opportunity to climb out of this limited access.

In the second stage, where Samuel takes over as the principal actor (though Yahweh's part should not be ignored), the narrator reveals the hidden significance of Saul's journey and the true nature of the office that Yahweh bestows on him. Through the narrator's omniscience the reader is allowed to listen in on the revelation to Samuel, and to peek behind the scenes as God implants a new heart in Saul.

Finally, Saul sets out on his return journey. In contrast to the outbound journey, however, Saul is now *nagîd,* and the reader now knows what that designation really means. The narrator focuses on two events, both illustrating the reception that the new designate receives from his fellow countrymen and from his immediate family. The reader watches with interest, as we may assume Yahweh does, to see if Saul will be detected or give away his secret. Once again, the narrator presents events primarily as they are seen on the human plane, that is, from a limited point of view. Saul is presented as he appears to other characters and their reactions to him are recorded. The reader, noting that he or she was formerly in the same state of ignorance as Saul's onlookers and interlocuters are in vv. 10-16, is able to appreciate both the ignorance of the human characters and the advantages that Yahweh holds over the people who demand a king.

Verse 10

Most scholarly readers of v. 10 have been troubled by the omission of the first two signs from description, or conversely, with the description of the third sign when v. 9 has already told of the fulfillment of all the signs. Smith suggests that two signs may have 'dropped out' (1899:70f; cf. Budde 1902:69; Driver 1913:82). McCarter, accepting the integrity of the narrative, regards v. 9b as a summary that replaces

the first two signs (1980:183). But why does it not replace all the signs? Stoebe answers that question with
the suggestion that the third sign receives special
mention because of its greater important (1973:208; cf.
Hertzberg 1964:86 who regards the emphasis as an
accident of transmission rather than a reflection of
intention).

An examination of v. 10 soon reveals, however, that
the narrator is not simply relating the fulfillment of
the third sign. 'The description of the prophetic succession is not as complete here as in v.5' (Schulz
1919: 151). Only a summary is offered, with only those
elements essential to the reader's understanding of the
people's reaction. Were description of the fulfillment
of the third sign the narrator's intention, the failure
to mention Saul's change to another man - the climax
of the third sign according to v. 6 - would be especially peculiar.

When we accept the narrator's statement that the
matter of the signs and their fulfillment was finished
in v. 9, however, v. 10 poses problems neither of redundancy nor omission. Instead, it presents an example of
Saul's reception by the people who are allowed to
glimpse the first manifestations of his new position
within the theocracy. Keil and Delitzsch are on the
right track with their explanation: 'The third sign is
the only one which is minutely described, because this
caused a great sensation at Gibbeah, Saul's home'
(1880:104). If vv. 10-13a may be taken as a complete
scene, without change in place or break in temporal
continuity (Abrams' definition of scene, 1981:2), it
is obvious that the topic is the people's reaction to
Saul's new position amongst the prophets.

This reading of the function of v. 10 as a prelude to
vv. 11f rather than a fulfillment of vv. 5f is also congruent with the subsequent encounter between Saul and
his uncle. In both meetings Saul, the new theocratic
designate, is exposed to contact with ordinary people
who question his behaviour - known by the reader to be

be an exhibition of Saul's new status - ask him about his journey - of which the reader knows the real significance - and ask about his conversation with Samuel - in which the reader knows that more than asses were discussed. Both meetings are tests: the first tests the people's ability to discover Saul's secret; the second, Saul's desire to keep it, and hence, his loyalty.

Verse 11

The reader knows that Saul's prophesying is a manifestation of God's presence with him, of his new position within the theocracy as *nagîd*. The narrator now presents the view from outside, that is from a human perspective. He draws attention to the people's perception that Saul's behaviour differs from what it had *formerly* been (cf. Keil & Delitzsch 1880:104). Those commenting on his radically new mannerisms are 'everyone who knew him previously.' Moreover the people now see him in a new group: twice Saul is described as 'among the prophets' (*'im-nebi'îm, bannebî'îm*). The people's double question, 'What has happened to the son of Kish? Is Saul also among the prophets?,' reflects their awareness of a change in him and raises the question of its cause; 'the implication is that his former life had been of a very different kind from theirs [the prophets]' (Smith 1899:70).

Nowhere in v. 11 or the immediate context is any indication afforded the reader who wishes to know whether the people approve or disapprove of Saul's new prophetic talent, or his new-found companions. One recent study suggests that the proverb central to the incident is misunderstood in its present aetiological narrative context and so antedates it (Sturdy 1970: 208f). Read in isolation the proverb turns out to be critical of Saul. An equally conjectural 'setting in life' is created as a new context for it and the ultimate result is that it is seen as Davidic propaganda against Saul (p. 213). Sturdy's study provides a modern

parallel to midrashic exegesis in which a word or a
phrase is taken out of context and made to serve as the
basis from which new, interesting stories and anecdotes
are created. With respect to the interpretation of 1
Sam 10.11, however, it is almost totally irrelevant.

The meaning of v. 11 is quite simple in context.
Saul has been inducted into the theocratic service,
and his prophetic activity is a visible manifestation -
a sign, in itself neither positive nor negative - of
his new role. His former acquaintances witness his
prophetic display and ask themselves if Saul is also
now a prophet. They have come rather close to the
true meaning of Saul's activity, but only accidental-
ly, because the prophets were also considered to be servants and mouthpieces of God. Saul's participation in
this group's activities is only an ambiguous evidence
of his new status.

In fact, however, the people's guess is no more
than an expression of surprise, an exclamation, in
which they simply restate what they see in the form
of a rhetorical question. They have no answer to their
own question. Though they are presented with a visible,
indubitable manifestation of Saul's new association,
they do not comprehend its significance. The point is
not that they should understand, but rather, that it is
impossible for them to know what Yahweh has done to
Saul, their future king, even when the latter publicly
displays his theocratic association. The verbal reaction to Saul's behaviour is, therefore, neither a
negative (e.g. Wildberger 1957:454) nor a positive
(e.g. Ishida 1977b:44) evaluation, but a simple rhetorical question.

The question asked by Saul's acquaintances, unanswerable by them yet easily answered by the reader, can
be viewed as another example of the narrator's frequent
irony, this time dramatic /17/. The people express the
proposition that Saul is among or with the prophets,
but their use of the question format indicates their
uncertainty and incredulity over this state of affairs.

The reader shares the narrator's knowledge that they have correctly stated Saul's new association, however, making their question dramatically ironic. Saul, as they shall soon find out - to the dismay of some - stands with the prophet Samuel; he is a living rebuttal to the demand for a king.

Verse 12

Supplementary (*wayya'an*) to the general expression of surprise at the incongruous sight of Saul prophesying amongst the prophets, a local man (*'îš miššam*) adds another question of similar import, also conspicuously unanswered. Who, he asks, is the 'father' of the group? The word 'father,' in contexts where it describes a person who heads or is honoured by a group, is usually regarded as a title given to the leader or master (Ringgren 1977:8; cf. Lindblom 1962:69 n. 39; Wilson 1980:141).

This second question like the first comes close to comprehending the significance of Saul's act. If they knew who the leader of the band of prophets was, the people might have a better idea of what Saul was doing in the band. Yet the question is also an admission of failure to know.

The reader, on the other hand, at least knows that Samuel was able to predict the movement of these prophets and that it is likely that Yahweh has, as previously, orchestrated the entire meeting. Subsequent events and the recurrence of the proverb about Saul will confirm the reader's suspicion that Samuel is indeed the head of the band of prophets (1 Sam 19.20-24). Thus the second question, like the first, strikes very near to the heart of Saul's appearance among the prophets. The second question may also be regarded as an example of dramatic irony, with the reader knowing both the answer to the question and the significance of both question and answer. The last sentence of v. 12 is a narratorial comment addressed directly to the reader.

It suggests that 'for this reason (*'al-ken*) it became a proverb, "Is Saul also among the prophets?".' The bare facts of what has just been narrated do not, however, explain why the question became a proverb, and so scholars have attempted to supply historical contexts that might explain the proverbial status of the question (e.g. Sturdy 1970; L. Schmidt 1970:118).

An alternative is available, however, arising from the observation that both questions are examples of dramatic irony. Both the narrator and his reader know the significance of Saul's action, and the answer to the questions. As they watch Saul's fellow Israelites struggling to come to grips with Saul's unusual behaviour, the narrator knows and the reader suspects that Israel will soon know what Saul's activity signified when Saul is publicly installed in the office of designate. At that point, those Israelites who asked these ironic questions will share in the irony. For this reason - the irony of the situation - (*'al-ken*) it became a proverb, 'Is Saul also among the prophets?.'

It is perhaps unnecessary to point out that the suggestion about the ironic origin of the proverb is purely literary and only intended as a description of the contextual significance of the proverb and of the narrator's statement about the proverb. Whether, in fact, there ever was such a proverb, and if there was, the questions of how it came to be and what it meant are beyond the concerns of this reading. One might add that such questions are also beyond the *known* concerns of the narrator, whose only *known* interest in the proverb comes to expression in his narrative. As a proverb, 'Is Saul also among the prophets?' is not a matter of fact, but a matter of biblical literature.

Verse 13

The secret of Saul's anointing has passed the first test: no one was able to penetrate the truth even when

the sign of God's presence with Saul was manifest.
Without pause the narrator stops Saul in his prophetic
tracks and moves him quickly on to the next scene, the
encounter with the uncle. Obviously the narrator does
not regard causal continuity as a necessary feature of
narrative representation.

Saul comes to the high place, the definite article
suggesting that it is the high place that Samuel mentioned in v. 5 (cf. Buber 1956:140) /18/. Saul moves
into that period in which Samuel told him to do what
came to hand, Samuel's predictions and directions having ended with the prophesying (against Ap-Thomas
1961:242). The point is important to the following
scene in which Saul's loyalty to his new affiliation
is tested. Since he is now more or less on his own his
actions should reflect his own position on what has happened to him (cf. L. Schmidt 1970:115f).

Verses 14-16

How did Saul's uncle happen to be at the high place?
How did he meet Saul? Why is it Saul's uncle that questions Saul, and not his father? These and similar questions have provoked some scholars to regard vv. 14-16
as a disconnected traditional fragment (e.g. Birch
1976:41). Ap-Thomas attempts to integrate the scene
by giving a new meaning to the word *dôd* - usually
translated as 'uncle' - namely '(Philistine) governor'
(cf. 10.5): thus Saul conceals his anointing from the
enemy (1961). Were this the intention of v. 14, one
might wonder why the text would call this person
'Saul's governor' (v. 14) instead of 'the Philistine governor.' Moreover, why would the same words not
be used as in 10.5 (*neṣibê-pelištîm*) to describe
this governor?

A simpler solution to the problem of why the uncle
poses the questions to Saul may be had by observing
what literary gains result. First, if Saul's father had
asked the questions, he could not have asked 'Where

were you?' and received the evasion, 'Looking for the asses' /19/. He knew where Saul had gone (9.3). Since the narrator apparently wishes to show how Saul evades any questions that would disclose his secret anointing, the uncle is a good choice. (An even simpler explanation [which I owe to Alan Cooper] of why Saul's father does not question Saul is that he simply was not around - in the narrator's story - when Saul came back.)

Saul's answer to his uncle's first question is truthful, even if it does omit the most important events of Saul's journey. At the comment, 'When we saw that they were nowhere to be found, we went to Samuel,' the reader is led to entertain the thought that Saul might disclose the contents of his conversations with Samuel. Tension mounts. Will Saul give it away?

The uncle's second question especially opens the door to disclosure and so heightens the tension of the moment. Saul, we know, was secretly anointed as *nāgîd*. When the uncle says, 'Tell me (*haggîdâ*) what Samuel said to you' (v. 14), it seems to the reader (and so, the reader must think, to Saul) as if he somehow must know about this great secret, and is only asking Saul to confess it. The apt choice of words also tests Saul's loyalties to the limit. This is the moment of truth for Yahweh's entire scheme: one word from Saul about being the new *nāgîd* over Yahweh's property, and Yahweh's 'messianic secret' will be ruined.

The narrator increases the suspense even more in v. 16 by continuing the paronomastic play and having Saul use the root *ngd* twice more: 'Saul said to his uncle, 'He told (*hagged higgîd*) us that the asses were found'.' Yet Saul says nothing of *nāgîd*: 'he did not say (*higgîd*) a word to him about the kingdom.'

Why Saul kept his counsel is answered for us by a narratorial comment on Saul's answer. The final three words of v. 16 are usually read as a relative clause modifying 'kingdom,' that is, 'the kingdom of which (*'ašer*) Samuel had spoken.' Were this the case, one would expect the relative clause to follow immediately after the noun that it modifies /20/. BDB (p. 83 8e), however, suggests that *'ašer* can be equivalent to *ka'ašer*, 'as,' citing Jer 33.22; Isa 54.9; and perhaps Jer 48.8; Ps 106:34. In its present position, separated from the noun *hammelûkâ* by the verb, *'ašer* is easily associated with the verb, not so with the noun.

Saul makes no mention of the kingdom because Samuel told him to keep quiet about it. 'But he did not tell him anything about the kingdom, as Samuel had said.' As past readers have observed, Saul's reasons for silence are not found in the text when *'ašer* is connected to 'the kingdom' (McCarter 1980:184). Connect it to the verb, however, and Saul's reasons are clear, while Samuel's instructions are in accord with his previous efforts to keep the subject under wraps (9.27).

The introduction of the word 'kingdom' (*hammelûkâ*) here is conspicuous. The word is used to describe the secret arrangements surrounding Saul's anointing as *nagîd*. The narrator thus introduces the reader to 'the kingdom' as a description of the theocratically subordinate institution that Yahweh has planned in response to the people's request for a king 'like all the nations.' Since it is the narrator himself who so characterizes 'the kingdom' (*hammelûkâ*) the reader is obliged to understand that that is what the word means in this narrative.

The narrator's comment that Saul did not let out the secret of 'the kingdom,' while an important summary description of Saul's silence on this topic, is even more important as a preparation for the description of Samuel's subsequent public unveiling of 'the kingdom' (10.25). When the reader hears what Samuel proclaims in that verse, his prior acquaintance with the word *melûkâ* and its significance help him to understand the reaction of Samuel's audience.

Saul's return to public view bearing the visible signs of his new status (10.10) and even speaking about

his journey and visit with Samuel (10.14-16) is successful. No one suspects what has happened to him and Saul
has demonstrated his own fidelity to the theocratic
cause. The stage is now set for Saul's public acclamation as king. Too late Israel will discover that they
acclaim Yahweh's *nagîd* as their king.

Verse 17

The beginning of a new scene in v. 17 is indicated
by the temporal and geographical disjunction between v.
16 and v. 17. According to Weiser, the disjunction 'is
due to the non-existence of any further traditions with
which the redactor could fill the interim' (1962:62).
While it is possible for the reader to suggest many
events or 'traditions' that might fill this temporal
gap in the narrative, one need not conclude that something has been left out and that the narrative is defective. All literary creations are based upon a selection of events from the sum total of available real or
conceivable events. 'We can say that, with regard to
the determination [exhaustive representation] of the
objectivities represented within it, every literary
work is *in principle* incomplete and always in need of
further supplementation; in terms of the text, however,
this supplementation can never be complete' (Ingarden
1973b:251, my emphasis). With respect to the disjunction of v. 17, then, the reader should respect the
narrator's decision as to what he wishes to represent
and accept the disjunction as an indication of a new
scene.

A *nagîd* has been made (9.1-10.10) and his loyalty proven (10.11-16). Samuel will now set in motion
processes to obtain public support and acclamation for
Saul. The secrecy that has enveloped Saul's designation
continues to play a fundamental role in this new scene,
which stretches from v. 17 to v. 27. Buber describes
this continuing role of the secret with respect to the
interchange between Saul and his uncle:

The uncle's question and this answer are supposed to
make it totally clear that everything hitherto was
only a matter between God and Saul. That is the *presupposition* for what follows, but not it anticipation. Symbolically the elders have already experienced the completed choice, but that means: as, for the
moment, a potential silence ['als vorerst schweigen
Sollende'], the people are to know nothing of the
intent ['Kürung'] (1956:141, Buber's emphasis).

The secret of Saul's theocratic affiliation will not
be revealed until after Israel has irrevocably accepted
him as king.

10.17-27 is also linked to chs. 8-10.16 in another
respect, namely Samuel's change of heart regarding the
installation of a king over Israel. Samuel, who had
refused to make a king in ch. 8 and had, instead, sent
the people home (8.22), finally recalls them. He is
able to carry forward his task of making a king only
because of the intervening developments of 9.1-10.16,
and because he now knows exactly what Yahweh means
when he says 'Make a king for them' (8.22; cf. 8.9;
9.15f). Hence the scenes of 9.1-10.16, far from being
unrelated or even contradictory to 10.17-27, are absolutely essential to the reader's understanding of Samuel's change of heart, not to mention the reality behind
Saul's public installation (against e.g. Press 1938:
198f; Weiser 1962:62; Hertzberg 1964:87; McCarter
1980:191, 194).

Verse 17 draws attention to parallels between the
new scene and the assembly in ch. 7, both located at
Mizpah /21/, by repeating words used in the narration
of the previous meeting:

10.17	ch. 7
wayyaṣ'eq šemû'el	wayyiṣ'aq šemû'el (v. 9)
('et-ha'am)	(be'ad yiśra'el, v. 9)
'el-yhwh	'el-yhwh
hammiṣpâ	(hammiṣpatâ, v. 5) /22/

The Mizpah meetings are also parallel in purpose: both convocations are called to deal with covenantal matters, the first to renew the relationship, and the second for its supposed annulment.

Mizpah is, therefore, an appropriate place at which to hold the second convocation, for it was there that Yahweh and people had been reunited after Yahweh's apparent abandonment of Israel in the Elide affair. Israel and Yahweh will now meet again at Mizpah, apparently to undo the work done at that prior meeting. The second meeting, like the first, looks back to the Elide affair and the disaster it caused for Israel; in order to avoid such consequences, the second meeting at Mizpah is convened to replace the old theocracy and its fallible mediators with a new, profane kingship.

Included in the parallels between the two meetings is a shift in the way words from the account of the first meeting are used in that of the second. The intervening request for a profane king explains the shift. In ch. 7, Samuel had cried *to* Yahweh on the people's behalf, because Yahweh had apparently left them. Now, Samuel cries *to* the people and calls them to Yahweh, the implication being that they have departed from him. In ch. 7, Samuel called out to Yahweh on behalf of the people, who had made amends and wished to renew relations. In 10.17, on the other hand, Samuel cries to the people on behalf of Yahweh, who has made a *nagîd* and wishes to maintain his grip on Israel /23/.

Both meetings are initiated by Samuel on behalf of the covenantal partner who has been spurned or openly rejected. The major difference is that the second meeting appears, initially, not as a covenant renewal but as an annulment /24/. The people are led to believe that their rejection of Yahweh has been acknowledged (v. 19) and that their request has been granted (vv. 19-24). Only when the pact is concluded does Samuel reveal the meeting's true meaning (v. 25).

Verse 18

Samuel initiates the proceedings with a formal recitation of Yahweh's past saving deeds, deeds that had inaugurated and served as the constitutional foundation for Israel's theocratic policy (cf. Boecker 1969:38f). He prefaces his remarks to the assembled people with the official-sounding statement, 'Thus says Yahweh, God of Israel' - what he is about to say comes from Yahweh, and not himself. The people must be convinced of the formality and seriousness of the procedures to follow.

Samuel's introductory words may be contrasted with his previous address to Israel on the matter of the requested king. In 8.10f, where Samuel disobeyed Yahweh's instructions because he misunderstood them, he did not say 'Thus says Yahweh.' Instead, he simply related what Yahweh said and went on to give his personal reflections on the disadvantages of monarchic government. In 10.18, on the other hand, he has finally come to understand Yahweh's intention and so he is able to represent Yahweh's position officially.

As the sympathetic mouthpiece of Yahweh, Samuel returns to what Yahweh really told him (8.7f), and delivers that word to the people. He emphasizes the covenantal role of Yahweh as Israel's God in the first sentence of the historical recitation. Speaking now for Yahweh in the first person, he says 'I brought *Israel* up from Egypt.' Only in the next sentence does Samuel address his audience in the second person plural. The reason for his initial impersonality is, of course, to emphasize the covenantal significance of the exodus. The nation Israel was formed on the basis of this act: 'Israel from Egypt' is an important recollection of the national political significance of the exodus.

Samuel's second sentence recalls the continuing covenantal fidelity of Yahweh from the exodus on. Israel's God delivered it from Egypt and all other oppressive kings /25/. Boecker, commenting on the significance of

the verb *he'elêtî*, also notes the emphasis on Yahweh's
continuing acts of protection on Israel's behalf (1969:
42). The emphasis in v. 18 is on the magnanimity of
Yahweh towards Israel. He did all these things for
Israel without compulsion.

Verse 19

The new sentence, begun with the pronoun 'But you'
(*we'attem*) in the emphatic position, contrasts Israel's
response to Yahweh with what Yahweh has done for
Israel (Driver 1913:83). In gratitude for Yahweh's be-
nevolence, Israel rejects its God. Speaking for Yahweh
Samuel correctly characterizes the request for a king
as a rejection of God. Samuel rehearses God's saving
deeds and then immediately repeats the people's words
from 8.19, 'No, /26/ but you will set a king over us,'
as though the people were asking for a king because of
the acts of salvation (cf. Boecker 1969:43). In place
of the expected response of fealty and obedience to
Yahweh's acts of deliverance Samuel places, in direct
contradiction, the request for a king. Rather than
honouring and respecting the divine king Israel re-
quests his replacement. Israel's request is made to
appear as a vile repudiation of its national God and
its foundational myth, the exodus.

Samuel obviously recognizes that the basis of Israel's request lies in its previous defeat at the hands
of the Philistines, but refuses, along with Yahweh, to
admit the validity of the request. Like Yahweh (8.7f),
Samuel totally ignores the disaster at Aphek, refusing
even to mention it. Samuel presents the final theocratic position on the requested monarchy: Yahweh has
been completely faithful to his obligation, and the request is legally (covenantally) groundless (cf. Weiser
1962:64).

As presented by Samuel and Yahweh, the request
might appear totally arbitrary. Thanks to the narrator,
however, the reader sees Samuel's speech in a wider

perspective from which the usual description of 10.17-19 as an anti-monarchic tradition appears highly questionable. There are, as we have seen, good reasons for the people's request - reasons clearly presented by the narrator. The only anti-monarchists in vv. 18f are Samuel and Yahweh.

The narrator, therefore, stands over against Samuel whose anti-monarchic tendencies reflect only the personal tendencies of a character in a story, not of the narrator outside the story. In view of the blatancy of the anti-monarchic bias of vv. 18f it may even be that the narrator is anti-theocratic. By allowing both Yahweh (8.7f) and Samuel (10.18f) to voice their bigoted descriptions of the request, the narrator lets them convict themselves, for the reader knows that the people have not rejected Yahweh on account of any saving actions such as Samuel has just rehearsed.

Rather than reading vv. 18f as the anti-monarchic vilifications of an isolated tradition (Weiser 1962: 63) or redaction (Veijola 1977:41, citing support in n.18) that is inconsistent with the subsequent election of Saul, these verses must be read and understood from the perspective of Samuel's rhetorical purpose. Samuel seeks to convince his audience that they are getting what they asked for - a king that replaces Yahweh and the theocracy - while at the same time denying the validity of the request. He must deny its validity because Yahweh does not intend to dissolve the theocracy and so cannot admit any failing on his own part. To admit to past covenantal failing would be political suicide for Yahweh and, therefore, for Samuel too.

Nevertheless, while denying its validity, Samuel must convince the people that their request has been granted so that they will formally accept Saul as their new king. He therefore correctly summarizes the request as a rejection of the theocratic covenant and acts, subsequently, as though Saul were the king that fits the bill of a new, non-theocratic state.

Samuel's brief restatement of the anti-covenantal

implications of the request for a king seems to be agreeable to Israel. Nobody protests that Samuel has misunderstood the implications of the request. Since this is the first occasion for the theocrats to convey their understanding of the request back to Israel, it is also the appropriate point for Israel to correct any misimpressions that Samuel or Yahweh might hold about the request. Israel's silence indicates that Yahweh and Samuel do correctly understand and represent the request as anti-covenantal.

Several scholars have suggested that vv. 17-19 take the form of a judgement oracle, with the ceremonial lottery to find a king taking the place of a specific judgement or punishment (Birch 1976:48-54, citing also Richter; Kegler 1977:77f; McCarter 1980:191f, 195). Even granting this categorization, the resulting negative presentation of the transition to a monarchy expresses Samuel's attitude and not the author's. It is part and parcel of Samuel's rhetorical endeavour to convince his audience that they have no right to ask for a king and that from the theocratic perspective, the installation of a monarchy is a judgement on Israel.

As readers we sit in the privileged position granted us by the narrator and look over Samuel's shoulder as he puts his audience through its paces. His apparent anger and indignation (expressed in the form of a prophetic judgement) at the request and at the task of making a king are designed to lead his audience to believe that they are getting what Samuel seems not to want (cf. 8.6, 11-18), namely a profane king.

The employment of the prophetic judgement oracle has two sides: 1) To Samuel's audience it is a sign that their request is grudgingly being fulfilled; 2) To the reader it is an ironic intimation of the true nature of the monarchy to be installed. The installation of theocratic designate in response to the request for a secular monarch is, indeed, a judgement and punishment of the people who only want freedom from the uncertainties of the theocratic polity.

The discord between Israel and Yahweh has been ceremoniously recapitulated by Samuel; the resolution
of the problem is now dramatically introduced by the
particle *we'attâ*, 'And now . . .' (Birch 1976:50). This
introduction is more than dramatic, and serves as in
other covenantal contexts to introduce the stage in the
proceedings where Israel is called upon to participate
in something that will affect the covenantal relationship thereafter (cf. Exod 19.5; Deut 4.1; 10.12; Josh
24.14, 23; 1 Sam 8.9; 12.7; Muilenburg 1959:355, 363;
Weiser 1962:65; Stoebe 1973:216) /27/. Samuel uses
it, in conjunction with the solemn call to assemble
before Yahweh in their tribal groupings, to impress
upon his audience the seriousness of what they have
done and are about to do. Playing upon Israel's manifest belief that the demand for a king was just and
lawful, and hence to be pursued through the existing
judicial system of the theocracy (8.4-6), Samuel accents the formality of what will take place. The people will be bound by what they say and do.

Verses 20-21

The sham continues with Yahweh now joining directly in the operations of the lottery. To the participating
Israelites all appears normal, which is to say that
the lottery is completely unpredictable. To the reader,
however, it is no surprise to watch the successive
lotteries closing around Saul until he is finally
taken. Yahweh is obviously working behind the scene.

Stoebe misses the point when he suggests that this
scene presupposes neither Saul's meeting with Samuel,
nor his anointing 'following which a choice by lot
would be not only superfluous but sacreligious' (1973:
214). The lottery is staged by Samuel and Yahweh solely
for the benefit of the unsuspecting Israelites, who are
led to believe that the divine will is being formulated
and made manifest before their very eyes, and in res-

ponse to their request for a replacement for Yahweh /28/. Weiser observes that the use of a lottery to find the new king was also intended to show that the lottery was fair (1962:65). Though the Israelites in attendance may have been expected to believe in the equity of the lottery, we readers of 9.1-10.16 are certainly not.

Hertzberg comes closer to the contextual significance of the lottery when he says it is a 'miraculous confirmation' of the events of 9.1-10.16 (1964:88). In view of Yahweh's ultimate purpose (stated in 9.15f), however, the choice of Saul by lot is neither surprising, nor miraculous to either the reader or, apparently, Saul.

Saul seems to anticipate the results of the final throw: when he is taken, he is nowhere to be found. Scholars have found Saul's absence troublesome. In lot-casting, it is pointed out, the only answers that could be given were yes, no, or silence; Saul must have been present when taken and so it is nonsensical to say that he could not be found (J. Lindblom, cited by Birch 1976:44). It is also suggested that beginning with the words 'They sought him' (v. 21), we are faced with a new tradition - in a separate literary strand - according to which the means of election is determined by the physical superiority of the candidate rather than by lottery (Eissfeldt 1931:7; a list of subscribers to this view is given in Mettinger 1976:180 n.73).

It is possible, however, that our narrator did not know exactly how the lottery worked in practice, and even that he was not so concerned with a historical representation of Israelite lottery practices as he was with constructing an interesting story (cf. Weiser 1962:65f). Pursuing this possibility, one must ask what is gained by Saul's absence when he is chosen by the lottery. The answer lies in v.22, in which the significance of Saul's absence is probed.

Verse 22

From the Israelite's point of view, the fact that
the lot has fallen to someone who is absent and cannot
be found suggests that there may yet be another, as yet
unidentified, person to come forward. Since the mechanism of the lottery seems to have malfunctioned, they
inquire directly of Yahweh, 'Is there still (i.e. besides ourselves) any one come hither?' (Driver's translation, 1913:84) /29/. In the absence of the one designated, the people look for 'anyone' (אִישׁ without
article) to fill the gap; they are completely at a loss
and depend entirely on Yahweh for the choice of their
king.

The reader, at this point in the narrative, is no
more certain about Saul's whereabouts or the reason for
his absence than the human characters in the story.
The text leaves these things completely undetermined.
The reader knows that Saul was predestined by Yahweh
to be Israel's leader, so Saul's absence and the people's apparent confusion pose no immediate jeopardy
to the theocratic scheme. What emerges most clearly
from the people's question is their total passivity
in the choice of a monarch. When the lottery 'before
Yahweh' seems to fail, they do not even think to make
their own choice, but go straight to Yahweh for a resolution. The people, as always in the entire narrative,
remain under the authority of their existing king -
Yahweh - and make no insurrectional moves, even
when opportunities, such as the apparent failure of
the lottery, arise.

Aside from reinforcing the passive, law-abiding
characterization of the people, their question and
Saul's absence afford Yahweh another opportunity to
demonstrate his control over the whole situation; his
determination to install his designate Saul as Israel's
new king is brought home again to the reader (cf.
Weiser 1962:66; Stoebe 1973:218). To the Israelites
in attendance, Yahweh's directions for finding the

hidden Saul in response to their indefinite question show that Saul is 'abundantly confirmed and without doubt the chosen favourite of Yahweh' (Gressmann 1921: 42). They had asked simply for an *ʾîš*, any man, and Yahweh had responded in affirmation of the choice of Saul by lot: 'He (*hû'*) has hidden . . .'

The obvious question, asked by almost every published reading of v. 22, is why did Saul hide? His action presupposes that he knew the lot would fall to him, and hence that he had made the connection between his anointing and the matter of the monarchy (Keil & Delitzsch 1880:108). The text, however, supplies no indication as to his motives for hiding so that readers have had to fill that gap, usually with some suggestion about Saul's modesty and self-effacement (e.g. Smith 1899: 73; Ishida 1977:46).

However this gap is filled, McCarter is probably right when he says that to seek Saul's motive is to miss the point (1980:196) /30/. The gap in the text - Saul's motivation - cannot be filled conclusively on the basis of the prior context, nor will it be filled immediately in the subsequent context; it is what Sternberg calls a permanent gap:

> No reader can afford to disregard them, but he will look in vain for pat explicit answers. Only through a close analysis of the text can he evolve an hypothesis of a set of hypotheses by which these gaps can be filled in with some degree of probability (Sternberg 1980:51).

An entrance to such a hypothesis is provided by the fact that Saul's action was manifestly taken in the knowledge that he would be chosen: why else would he hide? His action reveals, in a small way, a certain will for self-determination, and hence the potentiality for this meek and mild designate to frustrate Yahweh's designs. To hide when Yahweh has chosen him may be a futile act on Saul's part, but it does reveal a side to his character that becomes increasingly important later in his career (e.g. ch. 13).

In summary, v. 22 is primarily a verse of characterization: of Israel in the question, Yahweh in the answer, and Saul in the baggage.

Verses 23-24

Upon hearing the whereabouts of Yahweh's chosen, the people run and get him. Once more, Israel's forthrightness - they *ran* and got him - shows that they willingly accept the condition that Yahweh alone decides who his replacement will be.

The description of Saul standing head and shoulders above all the people around him harks back to 9.2, where it prefaced the description of Saul's secret designation. In v. 23, on the other hand, it plays an important part in his public acclamation. While it has often been suggested that 9.2 is a redactional connector based on 10.23, and aimed at linking a disjointed narrative, closer examination demands a reconsideration /31/.

As noted above in the discussion of 9.2, the reader is given to wonder about the significance of Saul's size, especially as it might relate to his possible involvement in the proposed monarchy. The description in 9.2, as it stands in context, opens a gap in the reader's understanding of the information about Saul's stature as it relates to previous events and the ongoing story. What, if any, is the connection between this Saul and the request for a king? What about his great size? The expositional gap is only temporary, however, and is now closed by the description of the use to which Samuel puts Saul's size.

The narrator directs the reader's attention to this closure of the gap, the answer to those previously unanswerable questions, by means of repeating words from the verse that created the gap. Buber is an example of a reader sensitive to this use of *Leitwörter:* 'Here at last Samuel pronounces the decisive word, which the *bachur* of 9.2 foreshadowed, but which since then, re-served by the careful expositional strategy of the nar-rator, had been kept waiting. Saul is *bachar* because Yahweh has chosen him' (1956:145). The repetition is not limited to *bḥr*, however; also repeated are *miš-šikmô wama'elâ gaboah mikkol-ha'am*, and with some variation, *we'ên 'îš mibbenê yiśra'el ṭôb mim-mennû*. The reader is thus invited to renew the attempt to understand the significance of these descriptions using their second occurrence as a context.

Samuel commends Yahweh's choice to the people by pointing to his size /32/. Keil and Delitzsch unknow-ingly put their finger on the strategic reason for the choice of the giant Saul: 'Such a figure as this was well adapted to commend him to the people as their king (cf. ch. x.24), since size and beauty were highly valued in rulers, as signs of manly strength' (1880:87; cf. Gressmann 1921:42).

Knowing Samuel's (and hence Yahweh's) deceptive in-tentions, one of the reasons for the choice is clearly that Saul would be attractive to the people. They had requested a king who could fight their battles, going out before them to war (8.20). Who would seem better suited to this task than the biggest man in the land? Samuel even implies that Yahweh's choice was made in view of Saul's incomparable size (*kî 'ên kamohû*) /33/.

That Yahweh had Saul's attractive size in mind from the very start of his operation to subvert the proposed monarchy is evident from 9.2, which the reader of Sa-muel's speech in v. 24 now sees to fit into the total maneuver; the size of the giant is the bait that, when taken by the people, will spring the trap of the *nagîd* on the unsuspecting victims.

The literary dynamics of this particular example of a temporary gap may be summarized as follows: 1) A gap is created in the reader's understanding of the nar-rative by supplying a detail, Saul's size, that seems

important, but has no immediate contextual significance; 2) Following a lengthy plot development, the
gap is closed by placing the detail in a new context
in which the importance of its previous occurrence is
explained by its second contextual connection.

The author did not explain the significance of
Saul's size at the first occurrence for two important
reasons: 1) The withholding of exposition creates reader interest and curiosity, making a more compelling
tale; 2) On account of the sense of mystery and unseen
purposes which he seeks to create in 9.1-14, the author
could not afford to explain that, in consideration of
Saul's size, Yahweh would choose him for a king. Such
preliminary exposition would totally destroy the literary artistry of both 9.1-4 and that now created by
the delayed exposition in 10.24. As it is, the reader,
watching Samuel present the bait to Israel and recalling that prior mention of Saul's size, says 'Of course,
how diabolically clever!' By allowing his reader to
'discover' the explanation for 9.2, the author creates
a more satisfying reading experience.

The proceedings of vv. 17-27 are a trap set up to
trick Israel into accepting Saul, the *nâgîd*. In
order to be successful, however, the trap must have
also teeth, some means of compelling Israel to abide
by their acceptance, if they should give it.

Throughout the narrative, the people have been the
model of covenantal fidelity. Even when they have
justifiable cause to reject Yahweh, they do so only
through existing covenantal channels, which is to say
through Samuel and Yahweh. Playing on this characteristic uprightness, Samuel engineers the proceedings so
that Israel commits itself to Saul *before* he reveals
the constitutional basis of the monarchy (*mišpaṭ hammelukâ*, v.25). Samuel has set a serious, ceremonious
tone for the proceedings from the beginning (v. 19).
Using the form of a prophetic judgement, he leads the
people to believe that their request is being acceded
to. Now, in v. 24, Samuel asks the people if they will

'appoint' (*hare'îtem*) Yahweh's choice /34/. What he is hoping for is a binding agreement to accept Saul.

The response is immediate. *All* the people (*kol-ha'am*) send up a great shout (*wayyari'û*). The acclamation is unanimous and so binding on all Israel.

The acclamation of Saul has two separate vocal parts, the 'great shout,' and the exclamation 'Long live the king!' (Mettinger's translation of *yeḥî hammelek*, [1976:132]; cf. Humbert: the great shout 'was the ritual acclamation of Yahweh as king and war leader, who revealed his prowess in the exodus' [1946: 34]). The people's use of this means to voice their approval of Saul as leader is particularly appropriate, revealing their conception of what is taking place. Yahweh, their past king, their military leader, the one who led them in the exodus, is replaced by Saul as the one acclaimed by the great shout. Everything symbolized by the expression in the past is now transferred to the new, supposedly profane monarchy. Yahweh had failed them before, even though they had greeted the arrival of his ark with a 'great shout' (4.5). The acclamation of his replacement with the same sound can, therefore, be taken as a communal recollection of the reason for their installation of this new king. Significantly this is the first and last time that Israel acclaims a new king with this shout, normally reserved to recognize Yahweh as king.

The second part of the acclamation, *yeḥî hammelek*, occurs six times in connection with the investiture of a king (De Boer 1955:225; Mettinger 1976: 132f; Ringgren 1980:335f). Though the exact translation of the phrase is disputed, it is agreed that it expresses recognition of the new king's authority and consent to submit to it (de Boer 1955:231; Mettinger 1976:135f; Ringgren 1980:336).

The alert reader will see in Israel's first response to Saul (the great shout) dramatic irony based both on the verb *wayyari'û*, previously occurring in 4.5, and on the parallelism of scene, character, and character

expectations between the two occasions /35/. In 4.5,
the people send up a great shout when they see the ark,
expecting its arrival to turn the battle in their favour. In fact, the exact opposite takes place. Now in
10.24 they send up a similar shout expressing their approval of the new king, who they think will lead them
as a profane nation into new conquests, uncomplicated
by the problems of theocratic political existence
(8.19f). As the reader knows, however, they are actually expressing their approval, not of a king to make
them like all the nations, but of a *nagîd* whose only real commission is over Yahweh's 'inheritance'
(10.1) /36/.

Verse 25

The bait taken, the trap sprung, Samuel lays down
the law concerning the new monarchy. Z. Ben-Barak
(1979) has presented a detailed comparison of v. 25
with two well-known tribal covenants - at Sinai (Exod
19-24), and Shechem (Josh 24) - concluding that v. 25
is also a description of the ceremonial formalization
of a covenant (1979:32f; cf. Stoebe 1973:218, who
cites Baltzer's work on Josh 24 and Exod 19ff; Mettinger 1976:136). In view of the emphasis on acclamation
and commitment in v. 24, Ben-Barak's judgement also
appears sound from a contextual perspective. Samuel's
actions in v. 25 bind the people to the king in a
'covenant document' that is legally inescapable /37/.
If the people continue in their law abiding ways, they
will do so with Saul as their king.

Besides the legal aspect of v. 25, there is yet another revelatory side to Samuel's management of the
covenantal installation. Samuel describes the 'manner,'
'type,' or 'law' (constitution) of the monarchy (*mišpaṭ hammelukâ*) to the people, prompting various suggestions about the content of this constitution: it is
identical or related to the *mišpaṭ hammelek* described in 8.11-18 (e.g. Smith 1899:74; Budde 1902:72;

Dhorme 1910:90); it is unrelated to 8.11-18 which is
not a constitution, but a critical evaluation of the
weaknesses of monarchy (e.g. Keil & Delitzsch 1880:
108; Birch 1976:51f; Mettinger 1976: 87f; McCarter
1980:193f); it is related to the description in 8.11-
18, but may (Stoebe 1973:218f) or does involve further
considerations than the purely negative valuations of
8.11-18 (Hertzberg 1964:88; Langlamet 1970:187); it
presupposes, or relates to the law of the king in Deut
17.14-20 (Nowack 1902:49; Talmon 1979:13).

There are four textual features that can help to
resolve this problem. Against the identification with
8.11-18 is the people's differing reactions to each
mišpaṭ. The people find nothing objectionable in 8.11-
18, insisting that they will have a king, no matter
what he may do. In response to the *mišpaṭ* in v. 25,
on the other hand, there are mixed feelings. Those
'whose hearts God had touched' accept Saul, and so
the conditions described in the *mišpaṭ* (v. 26). Other
untouched persons - *benê belîya'al* - however, reject Saul as a king that cannot benefit them (v. 27);
and since everyone (*kol-ha'am*, v. 24) accepted Saul
before mention of the *mišpaṭ*, one must conclude that
it is the monarchic constitution and not Saul per se
that has upset these particular people. Thus the two
mišpaṭîm of 8.11-18 and 10.25 cannot be the same.

The second point to consider is the treatment accorded to this new *mišpaṭ*, which is written in a covenant document and installed before Yahweh. As with
the example of the great stone in Josh 24.26, the implication is that Yahweh will watch over and guarantee
the fulfillment of its stipulations and, if necessary,
punish any infractions. 'One would deposit this document in Yahweh's presence as a sign of the new monarchy's dependence with regard to the national deity'
(Langlamet 1970:198; cf. Weiser 1962:67; Thornton
1967:420; Boecker 1969:56). In view of the people's
intention to sever the ties between 'church and state'
it is altogether understandable that there should be a

negative reaction to Samuel's news. The installation before Yahweh also stands, therefore, against the linkage of the *mišpaṭîm* of 10.25 and 8.11-18.

Regarding the third point, we can recall that there was an important difference in ch. 8 between what Yahweh said - 'Declare the manner of the king to them' (v. 9) - and what Samuel did (8.11-18). Instead of declaring the 'manner of the king,' Samuel had tried to dissuade the people by describing, in the worst light, 'the custom of a king.' Could Samuel now be fulfilling Yahweh's command by unilaterally laying down this new constitution on the basis of what he has learned in ch. 9? Certainly the two passages would seem to agree with regard to the question of whether or not Israel could have a monarchy which did not lie under the direct governance of the theocracy and its agents. In 8.9, Yahweh commands Samuel to take immediate regulatory control over the implementation of the request, and in 10.25, Samuel places the new monarchic constitution squarely before Yahweh, a clear indication of its theocratic subservience.

One seeming difficulty posed by the suggested connection is the difference in terminology. Yahweh had said 'Declare to them the manner of the king' (*wehiggadta lahem mišpaṭ hammelek*, 8.9), but here Samuel simply 'tells' the people what the constitution is (*wayedabber 'el-ha'am 'et mišpaṭ hammelukâ*). As H. J. Boecker has noted from a somewhat different perspective, the solution to this problem is to pay close attention to the contextual frame of each occurrence (1969:52). In 8.9, Yahweh seeks both to still Samuel's fears about losing his position to the new king, and to tell him what action to take in response to the request. The words Yahweh uses are specifically suited to that immediate need. In 10.25, on the other hand, Samuel, no longer fearful for his position, is engaged in the public proclamation and installation of a constitution to go with the already accepted king. Though what he does is in essential accord with Yahweh's command, Samuel's public proclamation has a different rhetorical emphasis (cf. Boecker 1969:56) /38/.

The fourth and conclusive indication of the identity of this 'monarchic constitution' is the word *melûkâ*. The reader will recall that this word has occurred only once previously, in 10.16. There the narrator himself introduced the reader to this word, which in context, could only be taken to refer to the secret arrangements that Yahweh and Samuel had made to install a theocratically subordinate designate over Israel as king. That introduction provides the reader with a ready understanding of the *mišpaṭ hammelukâ* in v. 25, and of the mixed reactions resulting from Samuel's announcement. The meaning of the word established by 10.16 is also in accord with the installation of the constitution before Yahweh: it is, after all, his creation.

The combined weight of these four considerations is, in my opinion, sufficient to establish the meaning of the *mišpaṭ hammelukâ*. It is 'the monarchic constitution' that subordinates the monarchy to the theocracy. It is installed before Yahweh as a sign of his continuing political supremacy and as a warning that he is the warden who will ensure that Israel, the committed 'signatory,' lives up to this new constitution.

According to McCarthy the final sentence of v. 25 is comparable to Josh 24:28, a formal phrase of dismissal counterpart to the call to assembly in Josh 24.1 (cf. 1 Sam 10.19) (1978:224). Samuel leaves no room for protest at his deception. The people are dismissed and explicitly told to go their separate ways (*'îš le-bêtô*), perhaps to prevent insurgent assemblies from forming.

Verse 26

The first thing the reader is told after Samuel dismisses the people is that 'even' (*gam*) Saul went to his home. The emphasis is placed on Saul's response because his action is the first of the inaugurated monarch - an obedient response to the command of Samuel, the theocratic mediator. Saul, in exemplary fashion, leads the way for his subjects. His obedience is, of course, a result of his conditioning and heart-changing experience in ch. 10.

Not surprisingly, as our narrator points out, those who go along with Saul - thus expressing their acceptance of him as king under the new constitution /39/ - are also persons whose hearts are touched by God. As God changed Saul's heart in 10.9 to ensure compliance so now he touches the heart of the army, making them Saul's supporters /40/. Again God appears as the divine enforcer of what Samuel has begun; Samuel sends the people home separately to avoid rebellious mobs, and God (who must have read Thomas Hobbes! /41/) provides the force to keep the monarchy in place. The future of the new monarchy is now guaranteed by a constitution and the means to enforce it.

Verse 27

Not all of the people are touched by God; the unaffected openly question the utility of Saul's monarchy. They were looking for a king freed of disaster-prone theocratic entanglements, someone dependable to to fight for them (8.19f). The new theocratically orientated monarchy is, therefore, useless. Truly King Saul cannot deliver them from the theocracy.

It may seem odd that the narrator who has been sympathetic to Israel's plight should now characterize these dissenters as *benê belîya'al*. This descriptive term has been used twice before in the narrative; once in Hannah's protest to Eli, who thinks she is drunk in the temple, not to take her for a *bat-belî-ya'al* (1.16), and once in a description of Eli's sons as *benê belîya'al* who do not know (*yd'*) Yahweh (2.12). Both examples relate to possible or actual cultic abuse (Otzen 1977:135f). 10.27, on the other hand, seems to be related to juridical abuses since these persons refuse to honour their expressed commitment to Saul as king (cf. Otzen 1977:134). In all three cases, the translation 'renegade' captures the essential significance.

The narrator's critical evaluation of these renegades, however, should not be taken to indicate a turnabout in his attitude towards the people or their case for a profane monarchy (Cf. McCarthy 1973:411, 'From the tone of things one might even wonder whether the opponents of Saul in 10.27 are not in the right!'). Rather, the term *benê beliya'al* should be understood: 1) as an accurate, and so not completely condemnatory, description of someone transgressing against an existing statute /42/; 2) as an indication that the narrator places a high value on the virtue of honouring one's commitments, a trait already revealed in his negative presentation of Yahweh and positive presentation of the people; 3) as an indication that the narrator believes Yahweh's concession of Saul to be a necessary compromise in view of the ultimate meaning and value of Israelite existence as the people of Yahweh. This last consideration, which will predominate in ch. 12, is obviously at the forefront of the narrator's evaluations of either covenantal partner's action. When Yahweh disregarded his commitment, the narrator sympathized with the people. And now that Yahweh has made the conciliatory gesture of a monarchy under the theocracy, which the people have legally accepted, he tenders a criticism of those individuals who cry foul play. Though they have been duped, everyone acclaimed Saul (v. 24) so that any subsequent rejection of him automatically marks the protestors as 'renegades.'

A similar emphasis is also seen in the second sentence of v. 27, 'And they spurned him.' M. Görg notes that the verb *bzh* is sometimes used when a 'sacral legal relationship' is contravened (1977:62f). Saul, it will be recalled, is Yahweh's anointed and

so any slight against him is also a slight against
Yahweh. The choice of the verb *bzh* also harks back
to those previous *benê belîya'al* who, Yahweh implies, are despisers of Yahweh (*bozay*, 2.30). In both
cases, as both epithet and verb used of their action
suggest, the offenders have broken a covenant with
Yahweh.

The verse and the chapter are concluded with a description of Saul's personal reaction to these rebellious dissenters. The narrator introduces the change of
focus by switching from the general covenantal implication of the dissent to its particular expression. The
benê belîya'al show their disrespect by not bringing
any 'tribute' (*minhâ*) to the new king /43/. Saul's
response is described as silence, 'as being deaf' /44/.

Saul's reaction, while not qualified by the narrator, can be judged by the reader as astonishment,
or inexperienced inability to respond, or forbearance,
or perhaps all of these. The reader must wait, however,
for further events and narratorial comment before being able to gauge accurately the new king's behaviour
towards his subjects. In terms of narrative technique,
then, Saul's silence opens a gap in characterization
that may or may not be filled in the subsequent narrative. His silence is, nevertheless, the third significant characterization of Saul (cf. 9.21; 10.21) and
supports the impression that he is meek and mild.

PART ELEVEN

1 SAMUEL 11

Many readers of ch. 10 have noted that the final
scene closes on an inconclusive note (e.g. Mettinger
1976:84f; Veijola 1977:40). The doubts expressed by
some of the people go unanswered by Saul himself with
the result that the reader looks ahead for a resolution
of the question about Saul's monarchy (cf. Noth 1967:
59; McCarthy 1973:411; Crüsemann 1978:55f).

Saul's public inauguration has been performed, and
the new constitution publicized and installed before
Yahweh. And yet, as Wellhausen says, 'then everyone
goes home and everything is as of old' (1899:241).
There is no indication of any accord between Yahweh
and his people. The imbalance created by Israel's request has obviously not been corrected by the installation of a monarchy whose constitution is dictated by
the theocratic representative.

The reader will recall that in the previous Mizpah
meeting (ch. 7), which consisted of a ceremony in which
Israel tried to bridge the gap between itself and Yahweh, the reunification of the two partners was sealed
in a battle against a common enemy, the Philistines.
When Israel saw Yahweh once again fighting on its
behalf, it became clear that Yahweh had accepted the
contrite plea for renewed relationship. As the reader
will soon discover, the new scene, about to unfold in
ch. 11, runs parallel to the battle scene that followed
the first Mizpah rapprochement. When the Israelites
see just how well their new king is able to save them
from an outside enemy, they will unite in their accep-

tance of him, and hence in their agreement to a renewed relationship with Yahweh. As Israel remained unsure of
Yahweh's acceptance of their conciliatory offer (7.8)
until he joined in the battle on their side (7.10-4), so
Yahweh (and the reader) will not be sure of Israel's
allegiance to the new monarchy (Yahweh's conciliatory
offer) until Israel responds to the victory wrought by
Yahweh (11.11; cf. v. 13). It is a significant comment
on the relationship that it should depend so completely
on the performance of Yahweh (or his designate Saul)
on the battlefield. Without assured military victory,
it seems, there would be no ties between Israel and
Yahweh.

Verse 1

The reader is made aware of the new scene by the
introduction of a new character, Nahash, and a new
setting, the location at Jabesh-gilead. The scene, as
scholars have noted, opens without explicit connection
to prior events. Even following LXX one only gets a
limited temporal connection that can be read as a connector to 9.1-10.16 (eg. Gressmann 1921:43; Hylander
1932:159). The narrator jumps from Saul's silence at
Mizpah into the middle of ongoing actions at Jabesh-
gilead. The sudden switch reinforces the reader's sense
of unfinished business in ch. 10.

Buber has correctly described the literary dynamic
of this abrupt opening. With the change of scene the
narrator goes back to an earlier point in time and
traces the course of action up to a crucial moment.
At this point the hero is introduced and allowed to
demonstrate his prowess in the opportunity afforded
to him by the time-structuring narrator (1956:150).

With respect to Saul's kingship, the reader is
struck by the complete disregard paid to Saul in the
description of the initial exchange between Israelites
and Ammonites at Jabesh-gilead. Since all the people
had acclaimed Saul (*wayyari'û kol-ha'am*, 10.24), the

reader must take the Jabesh-gileadites' suggestion
that they would like to become Ammonite vassals under
an Ammonite covenant (cf. McCarter 1980:203) to imply
that they have no trust in the new king, and no longer
feel any allegiance towards Yahweh and their covenant
with him (cf. Gutbrod 1956:79f). A king had been requested that would make Israel 'like all the nations'
(8.5, 20). When a king was set over Yahweh's 'inheritance' (10.1) to maintain Israel's identity as Yahweh's 'people' (9.16) and the Jabesh-gileadites were
faced with the Ammonite threat, they decided that it
was better to subjugate themselves to 'the nations'
in a covenant, than to risk a reliance on the bruised
reed of a theocratically subordinate kingship.

It seems that the Jabesh-gileadites have forgotten
neither the request for a profane king, nor the reason
for it, namely the great defeat at the hands of the
Philistines (ch. 4). That previous defeat is alluded
to here by the repetition of the verb *hnh* in v. 1,
last used in 4.1 to describe the Philistine encampment.
Should this *Leitwort* connection seem rather slim, one
might note that this is also the first time that Israel
or a group of Israelites has faced an enemy encampment since ch. 4. The situations are parallel. The first
sight of an enemy encampment and Israel would rather
surrender than fight. The Jabesh-gileadites, at least,
do not seem to regard Saul's monarchy as a suitable
solution to the problem of enemy encampments.

Verse 2

Nahash's reply to the plea for a peaceful surrender
is also used to indicate the weakness of Israel without
an accepted leader. His terms - all the right eyes of
the Jabesh-gileadites - are intended to show his contempt for the weak enemy who give up without a fight.
His suggestion that this disfigurement would be a
reproach to all Israel is based upon the obvious lack
of a national defence program in Israel. Should a city

within a nation be willing to gouge out its eyes in
surrender rather than to fight in expectation of support from its country, the disfigurement would indeed
be a reproach on the whole country /1/. It also indicates a complete lack of political authority and allegiance in the country where such a thing would even be
conceivable.

Verse 3

The portrait of Israel's complete disarray as a
political entity is completed in v. 3. The elders beg
(*herep lanû*) for a seven day period of grace in which
they will send messengers to every corner of Israel
in search of a deliverer (*môšîa'*) /2/. It seems that
the Jabesh-gileadites would disagree with Samuel's
statement that Yahweh is their deliverer (*môšîa'*, 10.19)
and by not turning directly to their new king would
implicitly agree with those 'renegades' (*benê belîya'al*)
who questioned Saul's ability to deliver them (*mah-
yošî'enû*, 10.27; cf. Buber 1956:149). At least for these
Israelites neither the theocracy nor its agents is
worth considering as a source of deliverance. Instead,
they look for help from their fellow Israelites, 'in
every corner of Israel.'

Divine help is neither expected, nor solicited. In
view of Israel's covenant with Yahweh, in which divine
protection (as Samuel has just recalled, 10.17-9) was
the underlying presupposition of the relationship, this
attitude is remarkable to say the least (contrast 4.3).
If anything, Yahweh's concession of a limited monarchy
has worsened the state of affairs. Only once before had
Israel looked for a human leader to deliver them from
an enemy instead of looking to Yahweh (Judg 10.17f)
and that was because Yahweh himself had told them
that he would deliver them no more (Judg 10.11-4) /3/.
Even after the terrible defeat at Aphek (ch. 4), Israel
was still willing to rely on Yahweh's saving action to
deliver them from a renewed Philistine threat (7.8),

though it is only fair to point out that the exigency
of that situation was a great stimulus to their renewed
faith. In 1 Sam 11, on the other hand, Israel disregards Yahweh's help totally on its own initiative. The
people act as if their covenant with Yahweh no longer
existed.

Verse 4

Immediately following the plea to the Ammonites the
narrator describes the travels of the messengers, leading the reader to assume that Nahash did grant the
seven-day reprieve (cf. Gressmann 1921:44). Nahash's
agreement is a further indication of what dire straits
Israelite defence was in. 'He only wants to play with
them as the cat with the mouse' (Schulz 1919:160; cf.
Budde 1902:74).

The description of the messengers' journey is limited
to the one stopping place which is of any importance
in the narrator's eyes, namely Gibeah of Saul /4/.
The town in this visit, Gibeah, is called *gib'at ša'ûl*,
not because the narrator wishes his reader to think
that Saul now owns the town, but in order to remind
the reader that Saul had gone home to Gibeah after
the inauguration (cf. 10.26). The messengers are thus
shown to have pursued their search for a *môšîa'* and to
have arrived in Gibeah of Saul, a man whom Yahweh
had said would deliver (*wehošîa'*, 9.16) Israel, but a
king whose ability to deliver was doubted by some.

As Budde notes, the single destination of the search
suggests that the messengers have come to Gibeah to
get Saul, who is known to Israel and reader alike as
king (1902:74). Perhaps, the reader is led to conjecture, the messengers, unable to find a deliverer, have
finally decided to give Saul a try. Is Saul finally
going to be given a chance to prove himself to the
people? The narrator excites these and other specul-
ations, but he does so only to build up the reader's
expectations and then demolish them with the realities

of the situation.

The messengers relate their mission to the people. Instead of running to tell the news to Saul, who has been left off-stage so that the people can call for him if they want him, the townspeople despair and weep and wail. Even the inhabitants of Saul's own home town do not consider Saul, their elected king, as a possible deliverer. Neither do they make the obvious move and turn to Yahweh for help for their countrymen. Saul's neighbours thus share the Jabesh-gileadites' mistrust of Yahweh, and, like them also, they seem to agree with the doubts of the 'renegades' about the ability of Saul's monarchy to serve as Israel's delivering agency.

Verse 5

While his subjects are lamenting the fate of the Jabesh-gileadites Saul appears, coming up from the field behind the oxen. The reader may recall a previous incident where Saul was following some animals (9.3-14) and ended up being anointed as Yahweh's designate. Could the narrator be foreshadowing Saul's future by putting him in a similar position here?

As J.M. Miller points out (1974:165-7), scholars have often used the description of Saul engaged in agricultural pursuits to separate this scene from 10.17-27, where Saul is the acclaimed king with the army at his side (e.g. Beyerlin 1961:188f; Soggin 1967:41f). Two explanations of Saul's agricultural activity are possible, both of them allowing ch. 11 as an important and logical sequel to 10.17-27. First, it is not entirely implausible that a king should also go out and plough his own fields in a small, disjointed kingdom like Israel. (Smith cites Poole who gives classical parallels, 1899:78). Secondly, and more important, the reader has already been presented with two examples of groups of people who seem to have rejected any notion that either Yahweh or Saul can deliver Israel from the enemy. Perhaps Saul does not act like a king (cf.

10.27) because he is not recognized as one, even when
his help is desperately needed. In a situation where a
new king - the first ever in the nation's history - is
not recognized by his subjects, not event in his home
town, what else can he do but tend to his regular daily
affairs? Without even the recognition of being used as
a king when his help is needed, Saul is a king without
a kingdom.

The description of Saul's agricultural activity
after his inauguration completes the picture of the
stalemate in Israel's struggle for constitutional reform. Yahweh may have foisted his own designate upon
Israel as their king, but they have countered by refusing to recognize Saul - no one even takes the time to
tell Saul about the Ammonite threat so that he, like
the worn out, old priest Eli (cf. 4.14), must ask to
find out why the people are crying (Smith 1899:78).
The people's refusal is apparently regarded by God and
king as at least partially justified, since neither has
yet tried to force recognition. The reader may surmise
that the people's attitude towards the new (theocratically subordinate) monarchy is justified by the devious
methods used to install it.

Verse 6

Into the stalemate rushes the spirit of God, overpowering Saul, who immediately becomes enraged over
what he has just heard (cf. Smith 1899:78: the spirit
is 'the efficient cause of wrath'). 'It is clear that
in 11.6 the possession of the spirit becomes the motivation for all that follows: hence, the impetus is
God's' (Birch 1976:57). Saul's own anger at the situation, which commentators have observed to be separate
from the onrush of the spirit (e.g. Hertzberg 1964:93;
Stoebe 1973:227), is now stirred because the spirit
has overpowered him; hence he is no longer subject to
normal human limitations and is able to disregard and
overcome the lack of recognition from his subjects. He

is angered by the situation because he has just been given the means to surmount it.

Much scholarly effort has been spent on the questions of the historicity and nature of Saul's inspiration by the spirit of God (see Beyerlin 1961; Mettinger 1976:234-8 for discussion and review). In the context of our narrative, however, the implications are fairly straightforward. Saul had experienced the onslaught of the spirit once before (10.10), and had been supplied with the explanation that it, amongst other things, indicated God's presence with him (10.7), empowering him to do whatever circumstance demanded. The reader may, therefore, regard this second rush of the spirit of God onto Saul as a booster shot to stir him into action. By himself, Saul seems incapable of overcoming the people's resistance to his leadership (cf. Fritz 1976:357).

Verse 7

The timing is perfect. The spirit of God comes upon Saul exactly when he hears about the Jabesh-gileadites' need for a deliverer. Thus reminded of Samuel's instruction to do what comes to hand, Saul throws off his role as farmer and takes on the task of deliverer /5/. His first action, with which he signals the end of his farming activities, is to take the pair of oxen and cut them up. What a difference a bit of spirit makes - instead of following the oxen around, Saul now destroys them.

Saul commandeers the messengers who were to have gone to every corner of Israel in search of a deliverer and sends them on the same course (*bekol-gebûl yiś-ra'el*) with pieces of the cut-up oxen. His act is a direct challenge to the people who refuse to recognize him. The search for a deliverer is transformed by that deliverer into a call to all Israel to follow him in the fight against the Ammonites. Saul's bold transformation of the messengers' task carries its own clear message with it. A deliverer, says Saul, has been found.

As a not so subtle reinforcement of his call to arms, Saul issues a threat, promising also to destroy the oxen of anyone that did not come out in support of himself and Samuel /6/. He will no longer tolerate the passive resistance to his leadership. If Israel will not willingly support him, he is now willing to coerce their support for the sake of the threatened Jabesh-gileadites.

As often observed, there are similarities between Saul's use of the pieces of oxen and the Levite's use of pieces of his concubine in Judg 19.29 (e.g. Smith 1899:78; Wallis 1952:57-61; McCarter 1980:203). But the differences between the two incidents are even greater than the similarities (cf. Buber 1956:151; Stoebe 1973:227; J.M. Miller 1974:167f). Saul sends out his pieces as a threat against anyone who would not come to fight under him; the Levite sends out his pieces without any accompanying explanation, request, or command. In response to Saul's action, the fear of Yahweh falls on the people and they come out 'as one man,' but in response to the Levite's action the people independently suggest a conference and independently assemble 'as one man' at Mizpah (Judg 20.1). The essential difference is that Saul seems to have the authority to command an action on the part of the people, whereas the Levite only tries to stir up a public reaction, which is initially a reaction to his own abuse of the corpse (Judg 19.30).

Why do the people, who have so far ignored Saul's kingship, now choose to obey him? Before seeking a specific answer one should note that this is the first explicit command that the new king has issued; so, in fact, this is the first actual trial of Israel's recognition of Saul's authority. Against those who assert that 11.1-11 does not presuppose either Saul's designation (9.1-10.16) or acclamation (10.17-27), J.M. Miller suggests that Saul's threat 'is not the sort of threat that an unknown farm boy is likely to have made, or that the people would likely have taken seriously - unless they were aware that he had some authority or ability to back it up' (1974:167f). Miller pinpoints the source of Saul's authority in the army, which, as the reader knows from 10.26, was God's inauguration present to Saul (1974:168).

The reader of v. 7, though he may share Miller's surmise, is given a more explicit reason for the people's obedience. Saul makes the threat, yet intervening between the threat and the positive response is the narrator's own explanation - 'And the fear of Yahweh fell upon the people' (cf. Zimmerli 1978:87). Saul's prime source of authority, then, is Yahweh himself (cf. Birch 1976:57). As Yahweh's chosen king, Saul must be obeyed. Disobedience of Saul is disobedience of Yahweh and the people are well aware that he is able to enact punishments far more serious than Saul's threat of chopped-up oxen /7/.

With the events of v. 7, then, the stalemate between the theocrats and the people is over, even if the recognition accorded to Saul's leadership is forced. For the moment this is all that is required since it will give Saul, Samuel and Yahweh the chance to prove the advantages of acceptance of and cooperation with the new monarchy.

Verse 8

The narrator apprises his reader of the response in numerical terms /8/. However the reader understands the meaning of *'elep*, 'thousand,' he is predisposed by v. 7 to understand the numbers as a favourable response to Saul's call. If the response to the call was as unified as v. 7 suggests - 'they came out like one man' - then the numbers that are given should be taken to support that description (cf. Schulz 1919:162).

The separate assessment of participants from Israel and from Judah foreshadows the eventual split between

the two regions (Keil & Delitzsch 1880:112). By describing the rally in these terms the narrator includes
a veiled irony in his story of Israel's first king, for
though the king is able to unite all Israelites 'as one
man,' the reader is reminded by the names Israel and
Judah that a subsequent king will also be a cause of
division amongst the people.

Verse 9

The messengers that came (*habba'îm*) from Jabesh-
gilead (cf. v. 4, *wayyabo'û hammal'akîm*) are told
to tell the men of Jabesh-gilead that they will be
rescued the next day. In MT the verb *'mr* is plural,
indicating that it is the assembled people (or a part
thereof) that, with or without Saul, predicts a rescue
for the Jabesh-gileadites. Though the majority of
scholars follow LXX in which the first verb is singular and understood to have Saul as subject, there is no
basis other than interpretational preference for rejecting MT. The reader of the Hebrew text must ask
not whether the verb is singular or plural, but why
the unidentified subjects of v. 9a predict a rescue.

At least three answers are possible. The persons who
make this promise may be army personnel, the hearts of
whom God had touched in 10.26. The reader might understand them to express their faith in their leader.
Alternately, the anonymous authors of the promise
may be people who have changed their minds about the
efficacy of Saul since he now seems to have a new
authority and is obviously taken seriously by all in
attendance. In this case, the reader is given to understand that Saul's authoritative command to come
out, in combination with the fear of God, is enough
to gain the sympathy and support of a previously balky
populace. Finally, the reader might also consider the
possibility that the assembled people feel confident of
their success on account of their perception of their own
strength, Saul, Samuel and Yahweh aside. The anony-

mous subjects thus promise deliverance without any
consideration or desire for divine aid in combat /9/.
The simple inclusion of Saul in each of the aforementioned possibilities alters the understanding of each,
and multiplies the number of readings to a total of
six. The reader is, therefore, forced to wait for subsequent events and perhaps narratorial exposition to
know who made this statement and why.

Though the narrator will not fill in the expositional gap created by the anonymity of the subjects in
v. 9a, the gap causes the reader to reflect upon the
meaning of the assembly and the battle with respect to
the people's perception and acceptance of Saul's designated monarchy. Whether any certainty is reached
about who made this promise is relatively unimportant. As it turns out, however, the narrative will allow Saul a chance to declare unambiguously who really assures deliverance (*tešû'â*) in Israel (11.13) and by
that time the question of the people's allegiances
will no longer be in doubt.

The ambiguity of v. 9 continues in the description
of the Jabesh-gileadites' reaction to the promised deliverance. Do they rejoice because their fellow Israelites feel they have strength enough to save them or
because King Saul now seems capable of acting as a
deliverer in Israel? Only time will tell, and even then
the reader will not be sure whether Saul was accepted
before or only after the victory. By that time, however, the issue will have palled in the light of the
reconciliation and resolutions of the victorious Israelites and their king. The ambiguity is important
only as a technique to prod the reader into a consideration of the manifold possibilities and prospects
of the narrated events with respect to the disputed
kingship.

Verse 10

The Jabesh-gileadites inform the Ammonites that

they will surrender the next day, implying that their messengers have not been successful in their quest for a deliverer. They 'give the Ammonites tidings intended to make them confident. The hidden double meaning of the phrase 'tomorrow we will come out to you' is thus an especially subtle touch, which the ancient audience would have applauded loudly' (Hertzberg 1964:93; cf. Keil & Delitzsch 1880:112).

Verse 11

The attentive reader will note that just as the preceding ceremonies at Mizpah (10.17-27) were parallel to the prior Mizpah meeting (7.5-10), so this battle account also has its counterpart in 7.10-2. In the prior instance Yahweh had thrown the Philistines into confusion so that they were defeated by Israel. That victory was a sign to a conciliatory Israel that Yahweh was once again with them.

Comparing this second battle with the first, however, the reader notes a significant difference. Here Yahweh does not himself exert any overt influence over the course of the battle. Nor does Samuel, whose intervention by sacrifice and supplication played a major role in the previous battle, take any part in the battle itself. Instead, Saul stands alone as commander of the Israelite forces. The campaign, like that of ch. 7 (vv. 10f), turns into a rout with the Ammonites fleeing in total confusion, 'disbanded (*welo' niš'arû-bam šenayim yaḥad*) and dispersed (*wayehî hanniš'arîm wayyapuṣû*).' This similarity in result only serves to emphasize even more, however, that the second post-Mizpah victory is achieved under Saul without any apparent interference from Yahweh. Saul has proved that he is indeed capable of delivering Israel (cf. Knierim 1968:32). Only Saul, the narrator, and the reader know that it was the spirit of God that stirred Saul into action in the first place. From the people's point of view, victory is aided only by their support.

Verse 12

Verses 12-4 are one of those places in the Bible where scholarship has blazed so many different pathways through the material that no 'tree' or, in this case, word is left standing as a solid point to guide the reader through the textual wilderness. A short list of difficulties that have been encountered by historical-critical readers is as follows:

1. The people in v. 12 want to kill those who have questioned that Saul should be king. Yet nowhere in ch. 11 has Saul acted as king and even in 10.27, presuming momentarily that 10.27 might be read before ch. 11, nobody questions Saul's kingship, but only his ability to 'deliver' (e.g Seebass 1967:165 n.24; Bardtke 1968:298; Stoebe 1973:222, 228; Ishida 1977:46f).

2. Samuel appears out of nowhere in 11.12-4. He does not belong at all in ch. 11, presupposing the 'obvious' excision of the gloss in 11.7 (Wildberger 1957:449; Fritz 1976:357).

3. A question is put to Samuel in v. 12, yet in v. 13 it is Saul who responds. The logic of the discourse requires that we follow LXX and read Samuel in place of Saul as the subject of v. 13 (e.g. Weiser 1962:74 n.60; McCarter 1980:201). The shifting of subjects in vv. 12-4 may be the result of redactional disturbances in the narrative (Stoebe 1973:222, 228).

4. The request to kill some people who reject Saul's kingship in v. 12 makes sense only when 10.27 is presupposed (Weiser 1962:73-7; Kegler 1977:82; Crüsemann 1978:56f). Yet 11.12 seems to reflect a personal rejection of Saul, while 10.27 questions the type of monarchy established (Bardtke 1968:298; Crüsemann 1978:59)

Though the list could be extended considerably, the relevance of these considerations for a synchronic reading is limited, since in all cases the literary-critical discussion of vv. 12-4 presupposes various dissections and rearrangements of the material in chs. 8-10. Because it has proven possible to find coherence in the preceding scenes, it seems plausible that vv.

12-4 may also be understood as integral elements of a
unitary literary context (cf. Buber 1957:153; J.M. Miller
1974:166).

The first thing that the reader notices in v. 12 is
a definite shift in the attitude of the people towards
King Saul. In 10.27, some had expressed serious misgivings about the chances of such a monarch ever proving
a capable deliverer. Then in 11.1-5 there is widespread
lack of recognition for Saul's kingship. Following the
victory, however, it seems that the majority of people
(*ha'am*) have changed their views and wish publicly to
proclaim their allegiance to the crown. These people
therefore jump in at the first opportunity - just after
the last single Ammonite disappears over the horizon in
v. 11 - to profess this new-found allegiance; and they
do so by a clever rhetorical contrast drawn between
themselves, loyal defenders of the crown, and those
base individuals who had dared to question Saul's
kingship over them /10/. The new converts attempt to
hide their past disregard for King Saul behind their
accusing fingers, which are pointed at those who dared
to *voice* (*ha'omer*) their misgivings about the new
constitution.

The rhetorical intent of the people's question and
request also explains the much queried change in the
nature of the questions in 10.27 and 11.12. In 10.27,
the 'renegades' had questioned the efficacy of Saul's
kingship when they heard Samuel's constitutional declaration (10.25). Now, however, the people rephrase
the expression of doubt so that it becomes more serious in its implied rejection of King Saul. Rather than
a question about efficacy, it becomes a rejection of
Saul's kingship, kingship already acclaimed and constitutionally supported (10.24-5).

In their desire to appear as loyal supporters the
people have turned an expression of misgiving into an
offence of treason, the outright rejection of the monarchy. The 'renegades' had not, in fact, questioned the
legitimacy of Saul's kingship, even though they had

been duped. They questioned only the ability of a theocratically designated monarch to 'deliver' what they
had in mind. The psychology behind the people's reformulation of the question is at least as old as this
example. The paradigmatic biblical example of this
blame-shifting technique is, of course, found in Gen
3.11-3.

To make matters worse, at least from the reader's
perspective, the people express their intention to
slay these villains for their calumny against King
Saul. The hypocrites will have scapegoats to absorb
the punishment due to all for failing to treat Saul
as the king acclaimed by all. The reprehensibility of
the people's call for scapegoats is not alleviated by
Knierim's observation that they base their call for
the death of the vocal opposition on the dictates of
sacral justice:

> The people, in asking Samuel for the execution of
> the judgement, do not turn to the *avenger* but to
> the representative of Yahweh and to the judge of
> Israel. The desire of the people has, therefore,
> nothing to do with vengeance and it is not 'petty'.
> It is a legitimate and necessary demand to execu-
> tive judgement against the convicted slanderers of
> Yahweh. (1968:33; cf. Birch 1976:61f).

While Knierim's suggestion is probably correct, especially since it is supported by the narrator's own
sacro-legal characterization of the dissenters as *benê
belîya'al* (10.27) /11/, the people's call for justice is
thereby no less hypocritical. The *benê belîya'al* may
even legally deserve the death penalty for what they
did say against Saul's kingship, but the fact remains
that the quotation of v. 12 is a fabrication that reveals more about the people who utter it than it does
about the reaction of the dissenters to Samuel's constitutional proclamation.

Knierim's observation that the people bring their

sacral legal grievance to Samuel because he is Yahweh's
representative and Israel's judge is argument enough
against the frequent attempts to oust him from v. 12.
The reader will recall that Samuel had officiated over
Saul's public installation. It is natural that the
newly confirmed adherents should address their self-
justifying incriminations to the human representative
of the divine architect who designed Saul's monarchy
(cf. Weiser 1962:75).

Verse 13

It seems odd that in v. 13 Saul should answer the
question posed to Samuel in v. 12. Some commentators
have followed LXX in v. 13, which reads 'Samuel' instead of Saul as subject of the first sentence, thus
resolving the incongruity (e.g. Weiser 1962:74 n.60;
McCarter 1980:201). Others have regarded LXX as a
harmonistic alteration to circumvent the incongruity
(e.g. Dhorme 1910:94; Stoebe 1973:222), all to the
greater glory of Samuel (Budde 1902:76).

If the people's utterance in v. 12 served to characterize them is it possible that Saul's interruption
is also used to characterize him? Birch has observed
one aspect of characterization in Saul's interruptive
response to the question posed to Samuel: the response
is apodictic in form, a legal pronouncement based upon
Yahweh's deliverance and not on Saul's personal magnanimity (1976:61). Saul thus encroaches upon Samuel's
territory in sacral/legal judgements: 'this small fragment of tradition serves to set up the later situation of Saul's rejection precisely because of his lack
of concern for matters of sacral law' (1976:62; but cf.
Gunn 1980:34f, 46-55)).

It would, however, be a mistake to regard this brief
passage as a criticism of Saul. On the contrary, Saul's
impetuosity in v. 13 offers, if anything, a mitigation
for this and subsequent trespasses on Samuel's theocratic province. The mitigation is supplied within the

answer that Saul gives to the request for summary justice to be meted out to his own erstwhile detractors.

Saul orders the stay of execution and immediately
supports his command with a profession of his own /12/.
Though Yahweh played no obvious part in the battle,
Saul gives him all the credit for the victory. Saul
implies that his own command over the Israelite forces
is, in fact, the command of Yahweh. Saul witnesses to
the fact that he is Yahweh's designate, that he had
acted on the impulse of his inspiration, and so he
testifies to his own belief that Yahweh was with him
as he directed the Israelite army to a sound victory
over the Ammonites. Saul's impetuous interruption is,
therefore, the result of his honesty and self-effacement. He wants everyone to know who really brought
victory to Israel /13/. Saul's intrusion into Samuel's
sphere of activity is excused by his enthusiasm and his
open show of allegiance to his theocratic lord exactly
at a time when it would have been easy for him to take
personal credit for the victory. Saul passes his first
test of power with flying colours: he recognizes and
affirms his subordination to Yahweh and at the same
time deals justly and sympathetically with his subjects, especially those who had previously criticized
his kingship (cf. Gunn 1980:64).

Still we would like to know why the fact that Yahweh has given Israel a victory (*'aśâ-yhwh tešû'â*)
should be cause for amnesty for those who had malign-
ed Yahweh's chosen king. The answer lies in the sequence of actions in narrative time. Yahweh chooses
a king who is accepted but then doubted by these vocal dissenters. Nevertheless, Yahweh delivers Israel,
indicating that he has disregarded the slight against
his chosen king. And if Yahweh shows by Israel's deliverance that he has not been offended by the criticisms of the dissidents, then so much the more should
Israel and Saul let them pass. Saul emphasizes the fact
that Yahweh's positive action supercedes the criticism
by stressing the word 'today' first in his justifica-

tion. 'No one will die on this day (*bayyôm hazzeh*) [for former offences] because today (*hayyôm*) Yahweh has given deliverance in Israel.' The fact of 'deliverance' after the offence is enough to overrule any call for punishment.

Saul directs the attention of both his audience and the reader to an important implication of their victory. That Yahweh should disregard the detractors of his chosen king and still press on to his goal of getting his people to accept his designate is an accurate measure of his priorities. While Yahweh could have anticipated the people's call for the death penalty, perhaps by arranging it so that the 'renegades' would be killed in the battle, a maneuver at which he is accomplished (ch. 4), he does not. Instead he continues his efforts to have Saul accepted, installed and *recognized* as Israel's king. The matter of the detractors is obviously of small importance from Yahweh's perspective, in comparison to the great gain of reconciliation if Saul would be welcomed by the people. For this reason, says Saul, no one shall die, for that would be contrary to Yahweh's wishes as known from the deliverance that he has granted /14/.

Verse 14

Vannoy notes that there is near consensus that v. 14 is the creation of a redactor who tried to harmonize the crowning of Saul at Gilgal (11.15) with the account of his inauguration at Mizpah (10.17-27) (1978:114) /15/. In all cases, the key to understanding the harmonistic redactional intent of v. 14 is seen in the verb 'let us renew (*neḥaddeš*) the monarchy.' (To Vannoy's survey of redactional analyses of v. 14 add McKenzie 1962:8; Langlamet 1970:197 n.195; J.M. Miller 1974:172; Fritz 1976:356; Mettinger 1976:84; Veijola 1977:40; Mayes 1978:16.) Speaking of the relationship between 10.17-27 and 11.14f, Hertzberg suggests that originally the action of 11.15 was no renewal, but a separate description of the first establishment of Saul's monarchy. 'We are also able to see in the sequel that here an editorial hand has tried to represent things as a succession rather than a juxtaposition of accounts' (1964:94).

Before surrending v. 14 to the redactional scrapheap, however, we should examine it carefully to see if it really is so out-of-sorts with its context. Is it possible that the monarchy *was* in need of renewal? The reader will recall that though all the people did acclaim Yahweh's choice in 10.24, there was vocal dissension after the publication of the monarchic constitution (10.27). In fact, only the army, whose hearts were manipulated by God, 'went with Saul' /16/. Subsequently it became apparent that the lack of recognition for Saul's kingship was widespread in Israel (11.1-5; cf. Buber 1956:155). Though Saul had been publicly acclaimed and a monarchic constitution had been proclaimed and installed before Yahweh, the monarchy had been dormant because it was not recognized by the people.

Saul matches their zealous defence of his kingship with a proclamation that Yahweh has granted deliverance to Israel and so all former detractors are pardoned. Both sides of the monarchic dispute thus show themselves reconciled, forgiving, and ready to act together under the auspices of the new monarchic constitution.

Could anything be more appropriate than for Samuel, theocratic mediary and official installer of the conditional monarchy, to suggest that everyone now go *together* (*lekû wenelekâ, ûneḥaddeš*) and renew the monarchy (cf. Levine 1974:28f)? As Buber observes, Samuel's name has now appeared three times in connection with the word *melûkâ* (10.16, 25; 11.14) (1956:156). The 'kingdom' (*melûkâ*) that Yahweh establishes for Israel was secretly planned (10.16), perpetrated (10.25) but unaccepted (10.27-11.5), and finally accepted and supported by all (11.14f).

Not only is a renewal of the monarchy possible in the context of chs. 10f, but it is absolutely necessary as an opportunity for the people to affirm their acceptance of and allegiance to the monarchy offered to them by Yahweh (cf. Vannoy 1978:66). The renewal will mark the beginning of a new period in Israelite political history in which the people are willingly governed by a king given to them by Yahweh on the express condition that the theocracy remains, with the king ruling only as Yahweh's designate. The renewal gives the people the chance to say yes to this condition with an unambiguous and unanimous affirmation, not previously given.

The choice of Gilgal as the place to renew the monarchy is apt, since the renewal of the monarchy is also a renewal of allegiance to Yahweh, the divine architect and master of this monarchy. Forever linked with Gilgal was the memory of Yahweh's foundational acts of deliverance on Israel's behalf (Josh 4.19-24). Gilgal was the place of the twelve stones, set up as a permanent reminder of the exodus and the crossing of the Red Sea, 'so that all the people of the earth may know that the hand of the Lord is mighty; that you may fear the Lord your God forever' (Josh 4.24, RSV). A renewed allegiance to the monarchy at Gilgal is a fitting conclusion to the introduction of a monarchy into the theocracy. The combination of a memorial location and renewed allegiance to the conditional monarchy signals the end to any aspirations of becoming 'like all the nations' with a leader other than Yahweh /17/.

Verse 15

In response to Samuel's suggestion all the people, together again (cf. 10.24, the last explicit description of their unity), go to Gilgal (cf. Buber 1956: 154). The victory, their perception of the possibilities in Saul's kingship, and Samuel's suggestion to renew the monarchy have together brought about the reunification.

As many readers have observed, there is a pronounced emphasis on the fact that the people alone make Saul king (*wayyamlikû šam 'et-ša'ûl*) (Wildberger 1957: 449; Alt 1967:254; Speiser 1971:284; Birch 1976:60; Fritz 1976:357). This emphasis is cited to support the argument that v. 15 and indeed all of ch. 11 represents a separate account in which Saul is made king solely on the initiative of the people (e.g. Birch 1976: 60). As Birch is well aware, however, the influence of 11.14, which suggests renewal, makes the people's action an expression of their support for a king already designated and chosen by Yahweh. In v. 15, also, there is an emphasis on the act as confirmation. Five times Gilgal is mentioned (thrice as *sam*) to stress the importance of the site where the new monarchy was finally accepted by the people. The act of making Saul king takes place 'before Yahweh,' indicating that it is under Yahweh's sanction and in agreement with the monarchic constitution previously installed 'before Yahweh' (10.25) /18/.

The emphasis on renewal and reconciliation in response to the previous dissatisfaction with Saul's monarchy (10.27-11.5) is also seen in the description of sacrificial activity. In contrast to the 'renegades' who refused to bring the new king a *minḥâ*, 'tribute' (10.27), the people now sacrifice *šelamîm*, 'offerings of well being,' before Yahweh /19/. In the contrast with the situation in 10.27, in the type of sacrifice, and in the locations 'there' (Gilgal) and 'before Yahweh,' there is strong emphasis on the complete resolution of political conflict between Yahweh and Israel, reconciled as they are by the new monarchy.

In view of the atmosphere of reconciliation created by vv. 12-5, it seems probable that the emphasis in v. 15 on the people alone making Saul king or (with Mettinger 1976:86) 'calling him king' should be understood not as an indication of an alternate conception of the inauguration of Israel's monarchy, but as the proper

and necessary response to Yahweh's conciliatory gesture
of giving Israel victory through Saul. It is important
for the future state of relations between God, king and
people that the people do act alone in this renewal.
They thereby give their uncompromised seal of approval
to Saul's monarchy, and so they eliminate the shadow of
doubt which hung over the prior inauguration due to
Samuel's deceptive procedure.

The final sentence of v. 15 is the narrator's depiction of the peaceful conclusion to this stormy period
in Israel's political history. We see Saul and *all*
the men of Israel together and exceedingly happy about
the conclusion that has been reached. The men of Israel
are happy to have such a king, Saul is happy to be such
a king, and Yahweh has installed the type of king that
maintains the relative positions of himself and Israel:
he as their God and they as his people.

The sequence of events initiated by the misbehaviour
of Samuel's sons has finally come to a conclusion (cf.
McCarthy 1973:404, 'This is the true climax of the
narrative, and it opens the way to a final resolution
in ch. 12 where, with sin acknowledged and repented,
kingship can be accepted into ongoing salvation history'). Not surprisingly, in view of the many instances
of scenic parallelism already observed between chs. 2-7
and 8-11, the concluding resolution of conflicts in ch.
11 parallels the resolution of ch. 7. In both cases
the series of events were initiated by the misdeeds of
Israel's theocratic leaders, and in both cases the
series concludes with a victory given to Israel by Yahweh through a theocratic agent. The only significant
difference in the final analysis is that in the second
resolution a division of labour has been instituted in
the offices of mediator. Saul takes over the role of
military leader and provides some insulation of national defence from the cultic sphere. Perhaps this
division explains why Israel is now satisfied with
the arrangement, even though they obviously knew
(10.27-11.5) that they had not gotten what they asked

for (8.5, 20). At least they will never again be confronted by a disaster like that brought upon them by the sins of the Elides.

PART TWELVE

1 SAMUEL 12

Verse 1

There is general acceptance of Noth's suggestion (1967:5, 10, 47) that 1 Sam 12 is a programmatic outline of prospects for the new monarchy seen against the historical background of Israel's relationship with Yahweh (e.g. Boecker 1969:63f; J.M. Miller 1974:161; Wolff 1975:88f; Fritz 1976:360; Mettinger 1976:82; Veijola 1977:83; Mayes 1978:10 n.40). There is less accord concerning the relationship of the chapter to 1 Sam 1-11 or to chs. 8-11, or even to ch. 11. Veijola, for example, argues, against Muilenburg (1959:364) and Weiser (1962:82), that Gilgal (11.15) is not the locale of ch. 12. The fact that a collector put the disparate traditions and redactions of chs. 11f in their present order with the understanding that the oration of ch. 12 took place at Gilgal 'is no proof at all that Gilgal is the setting of 1 Sam 12' (Veijola 1977:84 n.5). For Veijola it is important that ch. 12 be viewed in isolation from its present context because he regards the chapter as the redactional product of 'DtrN,' a redaction in which geographic locales are characteristically absent (1977:84).

Considered from a literary perspective, 12.1 does not seem to introduce a new scene; in fact, continuity predominates. Three of the four important scenic determinants link 12.1 with 11.15: 1) Topic - the inaugurated monarchy (Keil Delitzsch 1880:115); 2) Characters - Samuel (11.14), all Israel, and Saul (the *melek*

of 12.1); 3) Time - no indication of any lapse between
11.15 and 12.1; 4) Place - no indication of any change
of place (cf Vannoy 1978:9). A separate factor that
argues for the inseparability of chs. 11 and 12 is the
causal connection: Samuel's introductory words in 12.1
are in response to the proceedings described in 11.15
/1/.

The contextual connection of v. 1 extends much further than 11.15: Samuel explicitly recalls the words of
Yahweh in 8.7 (Budde 1902:77): *šema' beqôl ha'am lekol
'ašer-yo'merû 'eleyka* (against Smith 1899: 84). For Samuel, at least, the actions of 11.15 are the fulfillment
of the request made in ch. 8. He has made them a king
(*wa'amlîk 'alêkem melek*) in accordance with Yahweh's
final command (*wehimlakta lahem melek*, 8.22) (Boecker
1969:65; Birch 1976:67; McCarter 1980:212).

Samuel's opening remarks imply that the conditional
monarchy of Saul is 'everything they asked for' (*lekol
'ašer-'amartem*). They also remind the reader of Samuel's initial worries that the people were rejecting him
(8.6), fears that were only allayed when Yahweh told
him to 'listen to the people, to *everything* they say'
(8.7). Samuel's quotation of Yahweh's words at this
point can be understood partly as self-reassurance
in the face of the now firmly established monarchy
which had previously seemed a threat to his own office
(cf. above on 8.6f). He quotes Yahweh as a reminder to
himself that the request for a king was a direct threat
against Yahweh's position, and not his own. Later the
reader will see that Samuel's own position with respect
to the monarchy is of major concern to him: he takes
care to ensure that it is understood and accepted by
the people (vv. 16-25).

Supplementing self-reassurance is his obvious effort
to assert continuing authority over Israel after the
acceptance of King Saul. The first thing Samuel does
after the renewal is to claim credit for the creation
of the monarchy - 'I made a king over you.' As Dhorme
observes, he seems to quote Yahweh (8.22) here, but

makes one small alteration (1910:100). Yahweh said,
'Make a king *for* them (*lahem*),' but Samuel says 'I
made a king *over* you (*'alêkem*).' Emphasis falls on
Israel's subordination to the king and on the authority of Samuel who places the king over them. Through
this statement Samuel is characterized both by what he
says and by what he changes when he quotes Yahweh
(cf. Alter 1981:70, 97). Both quotations reveal him to be
somewhat apprehensive about his own position as theocratic mediator, probably because the people now have
their king.

Verse 2

A switch to a new concern, separate from the details
of installing a king, is marked by the introductory particle *we'attâ* (cf. Veijola 1977:92f; Vannoy 1978: 11
n.5) /2/. Samuel points out that the path to monarchy
has been followed to its conclusion, using the demonstrative particle *hinneh* (cf. Labuschagne 1973:74):
'And now, *take note*. The king walks before you. As for
me, I am old and grey. My sons are with you and I have
walked before you from my youth up to this very day'
/3/. He states the result of the request for a king,
touching noncommittally on the immediate catalyst
for the request in the state of affairs in his own
family.

The presentational order of Samuel's recollections
is a reversal of the actual order in which things
happened: he retraces the steps by which the king
seems to have preempted his place before the people.
Intervening between the king who *now* walks before the
people and Samuel who *has* walked before them is Samuel's painful recollection of the request for a king
('Again we are given a hint of Samuel's sense of personal rejection' - Gunn 1981:64). That Samuel appears
to think that the king has replaced him, or at least
encroached on his monopoly of walking before the people, is indicated by the emphatic juxtaposition of

himself and the king as the past and present 'walkers'
(Langlamet 1978:289 n.12; Vannoy 1978:11; McCarter
1980:212f).

Verse 2 is not a simple recapitulation of the transition, especially as it pertains to Samuel's sons.
Weiser goes so far as to suggest that the author of
12.2 seems neither to presuppose nor even to be aware
of the sins of the sons as they are described in 8.3,
(1962:80; cf. Veijola 1977:95; Crüsemann 1978:61f).
In view of Samuel's concern over his own post-monarchic status (cf. vv. 1, 3-5), it is likely that the
critically unaffiliated reader will see the neutral
presentation of the sons in v. 2 as the biased opinion
of a father trying to maintain family honour in the
community.

Closer examination from this angle uncovers Samuel's defensive tactics ('The first part of his speech
appears defensive, self-protective' - Gunn 1981:64).
The reference to his sons is surrounded by two self-
references, both begun with the words 'as for me'
(*wa'anî*) to contrast himself with the new king. He
tries to hide and protect his sons between the two predominant self-references; he points to his own behaviour as the explanation for the request.

What were Samuel's failings? - he is old and grey
from a lifetime spent walking before the people. The
way Samuel puts it the reasons for the request for a
king are grudging and thankless. He sees everything
in the light of his long career, which he knows is
uncompromised (cf. vv. 3-5).

The sons, moreover, are 'with the people,' a phrase
with which Samuel proposes a camaraderie between sons
and people; they are even paired with the king by the
parallel introductions of both by the particle *hinneh*
and the suggested associations of both with the people;
they are included with the king as joint heirs to his
heritage. Obviously the sons are the chink in his
armor, so he is careful to hide their failing behind
his own merits. 'Old age and his sons he mentions as

though they were incidental to the whole matter. In
the light of chapter 8 they clearly are not' (Gunn
1981:64). More than the neutral mention of the sons in
v. 2 he dares not make.

Verse 3

Samuel redirects his audience's attention to himself, again, with the third repetition of the demonstrative particle, *hinenî*. Having touched lightly
upon the people's reasons, he continues to present a
revised recollection of the conditions surrounding the
inauguration of the monarchy - a recollection having
little in common with the people's perspective as
revealed in ch. 8. In v. 3, he lays the groundwork for
an understanding of his own perspective as Israel's
incumbent theocratic mediator. The people have had
their say about him and his sons, and their request
has been partially granted. Now he sets about the task
of reframing the entire sequence in what he regards as
a proper perspective.

The people are called to testify against Samuel if
he has has committed any of the crimes that he lists.
His specification that testimony be made before Yahweh's anointed as well as Yahweh has sometimes been
considered a secondary expansion, largely on the basis
of grammatical considerations in v. 5 (e.g. Veijola
1977:94; Crüsemann 1978:63) /4/. This inclusion of
'the anointed' accomplishes two things, however, both
important for Samuel's immediate purposes.

First, Samuel implies that the law and legal practises of Israel still remain a theocratic province,
even when it is the theocratic mediator that is being
tried. Though they now have a king (requested, we are
reminded by v. 2, on account of corrupt judges [cf. 8.3-
5]) he is by definition 'Yahweh's anointed' and not an
alternative or separate authority (cf. Gutbrod 1956:
87). The new king has not altered the judicial hierarchy in Israel, even though it had been expected that

a king would do so by judging Israel 'like all the nations' (8.5). The 'anointed' stands with Yahweh.

Secondly, Samuel puts himself on trial with the confident expectation of being cleared. He recruits the new king - requested to replace him - as a witness to the fact that the replacement was uncalled for; the king is thus a witness to his own redundancy in Israel's legal system!

The injustices that Samuel denies having committed have sometimes been regarded as intentional contrasts to both the manner of the king in 8.11-8 (Budde 1902: 78; Schulz 1919:168; Boecker 1969:70; Veijola 1977: 95; Crüsemann 1978: 64f; Vannoy 1978:16) and the provocative misdeeds of Samuel's sons (Boecker 1969: 70; Crüsemann 1978:64f; Vannoy 1978:12 n.12a). Unlike his hypothetical king in 8.11-8, Samuel claims that he has taken (*lqh*) no livestock and has wronged or abused no-one. Unlike his sons, Samuel has taken no bribes /5/.

Samuel sets up the questions, all relating to the abuse of power by a mediator, so that his audience, if they admit his innocence, will be trapped in the implication that nothing was wrong in the pre-monarchic offices of theocratic mediation. Samuel is careful to avoid mentioning any of the specific misdeeds of his sons, neither does he ask their opinion of his sons' performance in office.

Verse 4

The people answer with a complete acquittal for Samuel on all charges.

Verse 5

Samuel capitalizes on his exoneration by reversing the roles of Yahweh and his anointed: instead of witnessing claims of injustice against Samuel, they now stand as witnesses *against* the people (*bakem*) that

Samuel's hands are clean (*lo' meṣa'tem beyadî me'û-mâ*). Though the aim of this public exoneration is not immediately apparent, the fact that Samuel enlists the support of Yahweh and his anointed is reason enough to suspect some further action or claim (cf. Weiser 1962:84). Since it is Samuel's activities as theocratic mediator that are cleared of suspicion, it is a good bet that any further claims will have direct bearing on the question of his partial or complete replacement by the new king (cf. Keil & Delitzsch 1880:116). 'The people without further ado bear witness loyally to Samuel's personal integrity - and thereby appear to put themselves in the wrong. If they have nothing against Samuel why then should they have demanded a king? The prophet now moves easily into a broader attack' (Gunn 1981:64).

The final sentence in v.5 is problematic on account of the unidentified subject of the verb *wayyo'mer*: who says 'witness'? A common solution to the problem is to follow versional readings in which the verb is plural (e.g. Smith 1899:84f; Stoebe 1973:232). The subject is then understood as the people, who express their assent to Samuel's legal claim with the single word 'witness.'

Whether one follows the plural of the versions, or simply understands Israel as a unit to be subject of the singular (so Keil & Delitzsch 1880:116; cf. Vannoy 1978:18 n. 23), the context seems to demand that the subject be understood as the people, who agree to Samuel's claim. In v. 3, Samuel calls for testimony against himself; in v. 4, the people reply (third person plural of *'mr* without specified subject), clearing him; in v. 5a, Samuel replies (third person singular of *'mr* without specified subject) with a citation of witnesses; in v. 5b, the people reply (third person singular of *'mr* without specified subject) in agreement; in v. 6, Samuel replies (third person singular of *'mr* with specified subject, necessary for clarity on account of the singular in v. 5b) with a comment on the people's agreement. Both the alternating dialogue and the explicit subject of v. 6 suggest that the unidentified subject of v. 5b is the people. The fact that Samuel is specified as the new subject of *'mr* in v. 6 also suggests that the verb in v. 5b should be left in the singular: if it were plural, there would be no need to reidentify Samuel as the respondent, since he is the subject of all third person singular utterances in ch. 12 up to v. 5b /6/.

Verse 6

Inextricably linked to the difficulties in v. 5 is Samuel's description of Yahweh in v. 6 (cf. Buber 1956:157f, who eliminates both vv. 5 and 6 as, respectively, insertion and gloss on insertion). Attempts to regularize the syntax of the verb have either followed LXX and inserted *'ed* before *yhwh* (e.g. Thenius 1864:47), or inserted the pronoun *hû'* between the words *yhwh* and *'ašer* (e.g. Ehrlich 1910:207). The syntactic difficulty of v. 6 can also be alleviated (as Keil & Delitzsch suggest [1880:116]) without alteration on the basis of versions by careful attention to context.

Samuel's reidentification as the speaker in v. 6 avoids confusion on account of the last sentence in v. 5. He answers the people's response (*wayyo'mer 'ed*, v. 5) immediately, perhaps even intrusively, so that his first word, *yhwh*, follows immediately after the word *'ed*, voiced by the people in v. 5. The unidentified person or persons who say *'ed* in response to Samuel's call for witnesses are given an impromptu definition of who it is that is called and accepted as witness to Samuel's integrity /7/. As Ehrlich noted against a correction on the basis of LXX, nothing has dropped out of MT before the word *yhwh* (1910:207). 'He (they) said, 'Witness', and Samuel said to the people, '(Is) Yahweh . . .'.'

Verse 6, then, does function, in part, as a concluding answer to vv. 1-5 /8/. Samuel reminds the people that the witness to his integrity as mediator is Yahweh. More specifically, he points out that his divine witness is Yahweh, who 'made' Moses and Aaron and brought the fathers from the land of Egypt - biographical information important to Yahweh's status as witness. (Some, on the other hand, have regarded this information, especially the peculiar note that Yahweh 'established' ['aśâ] Moses and Aaron as justifiable grounds for excising at least v. 6b as a secondary intrusion; e.g. Buber 1956:157f; Noth 1967:59 n.3; Boecker 1969:71; Stoebe 1973:237; Veijola 1977:94; McCarthy 1978:207, 'a gloss as in v. 8?.')

Keil & Delitzsch suggest that the expression 'he made Moses and Aaron,' means 'to make a person what he is to be' (1880:116; cf. Driver 1913:92). What were Moses and Aaron? The answer, provided by the allusion in the second biographical detail, is that they were Israel's theocratic mediators throughout the fundamental event of the exodus. The syntax of v. 6 parallels the making of Moses and Aaron with the bringing of the fathers up from the land of Egypt:

> yhwh 'ašer 'aśâ 'et-mošeh we'et-'aharon
> wa'ašer he'elâ 'et-'abotêkem . . .

The witness to Samuel's integrity is Yahweh, creator of the offices of theocratic representatives in the exodus and 'maker' of Moses and Aaron, the archetypal mediators. Samuel's credentials as an upright mediator must, therefore, be immaculate, testified to by the people, and witnessed by Yahweh.

Vannoy notes that the verb *'śh* in the phrase, 'who made (*'śh*) . . .,' must have been employed to bring out a particular emphasis (1978:23 nn.39f). He observes that the same verb is used in v. 7 with reference to the *ṣidqôt yhwh*, 'Yahweh's acts of justification' /9/. *'śh* also occurs in 11.13 with Yahweh as subject: 'Yahweh has made deliverance' (*'aśâ-yhwh*

tešû'â). Placing all three occurrences together,
it seems that Samuel, following Saul's use of *'sh* in
11.13, places Moses and Aaron in the same category
as 'deliverance' and 'acts of justification.' All are
things 'made' (*'sh*) by Yahweh for Israel's benefit
when in need. The witness to Samuel's integrity as
mediator is the person who created that position for
Israel's benefit.

The political evolution traced by Samuel reveals
a surprising aspect of the succession of a king to a
position previously occupied by the theocratic mediat-
or alone. The people have moved to replace an officer,
whose office is ranked alongside Yahweh's deliverance
and saving deeds, with a king. Moreover, they have
done so while openly admitting the rectitude of Samuel. As regards the specific situation in the mediatory office, this grave development, which in Samuel's
presentation amounts to a rejection of Yahweh's unwarranted graciousness, is made to appear unnecessary and
inexplicable. If the reader or Samuel's audience accepts Samuel's claim, and his audience *seems* bound to
do so by its testimony to his integrity /10/, the request for the monarchy begins to appear less justifiable. The obvious question of why Samuel should
trouble himself to persuade Israel that the request
was not legitimate after the monarchy is already in
place is answered later in his oration.

Just because v. 6 has been shown to function conclusively with respect to vv. 1-5 does not mean that
it does not also serve as an introduction to vv. 7ff.
Verse 6 introduces the topics of the archetypal mediators Moses and Aaron and the exodus event with which
these figures are associated. Boecker argues that the
references to Moses and Aaron in v. 6 (and v. 8) are
conspicuous and without contextual mooring (1969:71;
cf. Veijola 1977:85). Standing against this view are
Samuel's concern with the office of mediator in vv. 1-5
and the important bearing of v. 6 on that subject, as
we have seen. In addition Samuel will continue to trace

both the benefits and the lineage of mediators from the paradigmatic Moses and Aaron down to himself (vv. 6-11). To deny the connection of Moses and Aaron to Samuel's remarks on Yahweh and his beneficial mediators one must ignore the syntactic parallels between the descriptions of Moses and Aaron (v. 8) and the other judges (vv. 10-12). Both form and content speak against the elimination of Moses and Aaron from Samuel's speech.

Samuel's brief recollection of the origins of his office in v. 6 is a turning point at which he shifts from the vindication of his own performance in office to a historical retrospect covering the entire line of theocratic mediators. Having obtained a public acknowledgement of his personal integrity in office, he moves on to defend the office itself.

He begins already in v. 6 with his recollection of the exodus, Israel's birth story as a nation, and the provision of mediators whose important role was known by all Israelites (cf. Vannoy 1978:21). These memories remind Samuel's audience of a time and place when the mediator was of irreplaceable benefit to Israel, as Yahweh worked through Moses and Aaron to bring Israel up out of Egypt.

Verse 7

Samuel marks a complete shift to a new topic in Israel's political affairs by repeating the introductory expression *we'attâ*, so employed at three places in his presentation (vv. 2, 7, 16; cf. Muilenburg 1959: 361-63; 1968:171 n.2; Veijola 1977:92f; Vannoy 1977: 11 n.5, 24f). He proposes to review Yahweh's past performance. Like the previous section introduced by *we'attâ* (vv. 2-5 [6]), vv. 7-12 stand in relationship to v. 1, which gives the basic datum to which all of Samuel's reviews are related. In summary form the relationship is:

v.1   Samuel said, 'I have listened to everything you
        said and set a king over you:

v.2-5 (6)   'And now,' as for Samuel's conduct.

v.(6) 7-12 'And now,' as for Yahweh's conduct.

In contrast to his own case, where he called on the
people to testify against him before Yahweh and his
anointed (v. 3), Samuel expresses his desire to dispute
with Israel, before Yahweh, all the acts of justification that Yahweh has done for them and their fathers /11/. Samuel is open about his bias concerning
Yahweh's irreproachability: he will not even entertain the notion that Yahweh's past behaviour was ever
detrimental to Israel's well-being.

Once again Samuel circumvents the real reasons for
Israel's request for a king. It was not for his performance of any such acts of deliverance that Israel
requested a king to replace Yahweh; rather, it was on
account of Yahweh's failure to perform these covenantally ensured acts (cf. ch. 4). Like Samuel's noncommit-
tal reference to his sons in v. 2, his rehearsal of Yahweh's saving deeds touches on the matter of concern,
but skirts the crucial issues. Samuel's concern is formal vindication for himself and for Yahweh, and not
an impartial review of faults.

Verse 7 begins a section in ch. 12 generally regarded to exhibit the influence of literary covenant forms
(e.g. Muilenburg 1959:360-5; Baltzer 1964:73-76;
Stoebe 1973:237; Birch 1976:68-70; McCarthy 1978:213-
21; Vannoy 1978; McCarter 1980:220f). All are careful
to point out, however, that the covenant form is subordinate to Samuel's particular rhetorical purposes. 'We
do not have a covenant or a treaty document but a
speech by Samuel that shows the influence of the covenant form' (Birch 1976:68). It will pay, therefore, to
devote attention to resemblances to covenant formulas
found in Samuel's presentation without expecting to
find a covenant or covenant renewal as a result. The
reader informed by a knowledge of an identifiable

literary form for describing covenant renewal in the Bible should be prepared to let Samuel's direction of the proceedings override his own understanding of how such a ceremony should go /12/.

The covenantal nature of the business at hand is introduced by Samuel's call to assembly (we'attâ hityaṣṣebû), an expression regarded by Muilenburg as a common feature of covenantal formulations (1959: 361, 363, cf. Baltzer 1964:74 n.1; McCarthy 1978:207; Vannoy 1978:24f). Samuel had last called such a formal assembly in 10.19 (we'attâ hityaṣṣebû) when he installed Saul, initially under the guise of a replacement for Yahweh. The reassembly in 12.7 recalls the assembly of 10.19: at both gatherings Yahweh's history of beneficent acts on Israel's behalf is invoked as a demonstration of the senselessness of the request for a human king (cf. Boecker 1969:74).

Verse 8

Samuel commences his recitation of Yahweh's acts of justification with the exodus. In this presentation it is Israel, represented here by Jacob, that gets itself into trouble in Egypt. Yahweh is excluded from any involvement in the migration to Egypt. Samuel's interest lies in the series of interactions between Yahweh and Israel; he therefore skips over any mention of the Egyptian oppression and moves directly from Israel's entrance into Egypt to Israel's cry to Yahweh for help. The lack of reference to Egyptian oppression is more elegantly explained as a rhetorical feature than as a textual error (against Driver 1913:93) or an alternate tradition about the exodus.

Yahweh's immediate response to the fathers' cries for help is to send Moses and Aaron, his mediators, to their aid. It is Moses and Aaron - not Yahweh - who bring (wayyôṣî'û) the fathers out of Egypt and settle them (wayyošibûm) in the land of Israel (literally 'this place'). In this paradigmatic instance Yah-

weh accomplishes his justifying acts through the agency
of his mediators; the only verb of which Yahweh is subject is *wayyišlaḥ*, 'he sent Moses and Aaron' /13/.
The mediator is indispensable to success.

Samuel brings the implications of the paradigm up
to date with his description of the place where the
fathers of his audience were settled: it is 'this
place' (*bammaqôm hazzeh*), the very place where he
and the people stand and ponder the apparent replacement of the last mediator by a king /14/. By invoking
Yahweh, maker of Moses and Aaron, as witness to his
integrity as mediator, and reminding his audience that
it was Yahweh who sent Moses and Aaron as mediators
of the paradigmatic exodus, Samuel manages to suggest
that by replacing him the people are disrupting Yahweh's mechanism of justification. If the divinely
appointed mediators, Moses and Aaron, brought 'your
fathers' to 'this place,' why replace their successor
to whose untarnished record you have just testified
before Yahweh?

Verse 9

Yahweh arranges for his people to be brought out
of Egypt. Israel expresses its gratitude by forgetting
him! In Samuel's historical concatenation Israel is
allowed only an unequivocal thanklessness in response
to Yahweh's beneficence. According to McCarthy, 'forgetting' Yahweh is destructive of the relationship between Israel and Yahweh (1978:219f). Indeed, this side
of Israel's forgetfulness is highlighted by Samuel
himself, who says, 'They forgot Yahweh, *their* God
. . ..' Samuel draws the contrast between Yahweh and
Israel with bold strokes that pay for unambiguous expression with a lack of accuracy in representation.
Yahweh seeks to build a relationship between himself
and Israel and is, therefore, good; Israel's forgetfulness is destructive of Yahweh's efforts and Israel
is, therefore, bad.

Yahweh's response to Israel's forgetfulness is to
'sell out' (*wayyimkor ... beyad*) Israel to its enemies in warfare - an action which is a direct reflection of their forgetfulness. They forget him so he
abandons them on the battlefield. Like Israel's first
misfortunes in Egypt, these difficulties are presented
as brought on by the people themselves. Though Yahweh is now inextricably linked to all of Israel's experiences, Samuel shows that adversity within the period
of covenantal relationship was the just and necessary
result of Israel's own failings. The point is important
to Samuel's presentation because it establishes a historical precedent for an alternate interpretation of
Israel's disastrous defeat at the hands of the Philistines. If Israel's military failings were previously caused by Israel's own misbehaviour, why should
the recent case be different?

The brief list of enemies to whom Israel is sold out
does not correspond to the fuller enumeration given
in the book of Judges. Though McCarthy sees the sequence of names as an example of the conservation of
a tradition by the deuteronomist(s) that did not agree
with his (their) own portrayal in Judges (1978:208f;
cf. Stoebe 1973:237f), it is possible to forego the
conjecture; following Smith, 'The list of oppressors
here, 'Sisera, the Philistines, the king of Moab', does
not pretend to follow the order of the Book of Judges'
(1899:86; cf. Vannoy 1978:36f; McCarter 1980:215). As
in v. 8, Samuel takes liberties with the traditional
stories both to make new points and to direct his audience's attention to those new points. Here he only
alludes to the tales from the period of judges because
his concern is not to recite history or tradition.
Rather than diverting his audience's attention onto
irrelevant reveries or sad memories, Samuel mentions
only three representative examples. These serve as
paradigmatic characterizations of the whole period of
the judges as a continual cycle of Israelite forgetfulness met by Yahweh's remedial response. Samuel's

inclusion of the Philistines might imply that even the defeat of ch. 4 should be interpreted as an example of this paradigmatic cycle.

Verse 10

Not surprisingly, given that we know that Yahweh has delivered Israel to its enemies, Israel is pictured as completely helpless after the battle (*wayyillahamû bam wayyiz'aqû 'el-yhwh*, vv. 9f). The people are in the same straits that their fathers found themselves in in Egypt, and like their fathers, their only recourse is to 'cry to Yahweh' (vv. 8, 10). Suffering alone turns Israel towards Yahweh. With admissions of sin and apostasy the people promise renewed service to Yahweh if he will deliver them from their enemies.

Samuel borrows both the language and the cycle of forgetfulness and promise of renewed devotion from the books of Deuteronomy and Judges (Birch 1976:70f; McCarthy 1978:208f; Vannoy 1978:33-37; McCarter 1980: 214). The cycle in v. 10 is predicate to the allusion to previous cycles in v. 9 and is, therefore, presented as a summary of the pre-monarchic history of covenantal relations between Israel and Yahweh. That this cycle depicts the customary shape of relations is confirmed by v. 11, which describes a succession of emissaries sent by Yahweh to rescue Israel again and again from the destitution paradigmatically described in v. 10. Samuel emphasizes the respective roles of Yahweh and Israel in the pre-monarchic period: Israel ever the back-slider, and Yahweh ever the forgiving and faithful benefactor (cf. Vannoy 1978:36f).

Verse 11

As in the exodus (v. 8), Yahweh sent various individuals throughout Israel's premonarchic period to rescue Israel. The names of these emissaries, like the names of the adversaries in v. 9, are allusive. The

names Jerubbaal and Samuel establish the chronological
limits for the period in which these emissaries functioned. The middle names, Bedan and Jepthah, represent those mediators sent during this period to deliver
Israel from its enemies: '. . . the fact remains that
Dtr. wishes to remind us of *all* the 'Saviour' figures
of the 'Judges' period' (Noth 1981:51 [=1967:59]) /15/.

Samuel's inclusion of his own name amongst these
agents of Yahweh's acts of justification, though not
in accord with the book of Judges, is in keeping with
his rhetorical intent. He exculpates Yahweh of any failings that could justify the request for a king and ex-
tols the human emissaries who are Yahweh's agents. By
including himself amongst the latter he indicates that
Yahweh had provided for national defense and leadership up to and including his own time 'in order to make
his case relevant to the current situation, and the
request for a king' (Vannoy 1978:37; cf. Hertzberg
1964:99).

The second thing Samuel's self-inclusion achieves is
to number his own actions on Israel's behalf among Yahweh's acts of justification. As Keil and Delitzsch
observe, he is justified in doing so by his role in the
events of ch. 7 (1880:118). And by tracing the continuing acts of justification through emissaries up to the
contemporary moment, he places any defection from this
divinely implemented system in the same class with all
other such defections (Smith 1899:86).

Verse 11 is the capstone of Samuel's historical argument against the validity of the request for a king. He
has established a set of causal principles underlying
Israel's history and has traced their operation into
the contemporary scene. Since the people have already
exonerated his performance as mediator, they are now
set up for the great fall he has prepared for them. By
seeking to replace Yahweh or Samuel, the people have
in fact rejected Yahweh's justifying acts, a sin even
worse than their predecessors' continual forgetfulness.

The last two sentences of v. 11 stand together in a

relationship of cause and effect. Together they offer a picture of Israel's security under Yahweh's protection. Samuel signifies this security with the word *beṭaḥ*, which evokes a sense of the complete peace of mind Israel gained by Yahweh's victories over their enemies. Because *bṭḥ* is only positively toned as a description of human behaviour when Yahweh is its object or inspiration, Samuel must say that Yahweh (the implicit subject), rather than the emissaries, 'delivered' the people (*wayyaṣṣel 'etkem*) /16/. Since he has already established his claim for the importance of the emissaries in the larger framework of the continuing acts of justification, Samuel's shifting of responsibility for the saving acts from the mediators to Yahweh himself should be seen as a shift in focus, from the beneficial acts and actors to the resulting peace of mind given to Israel. Samuel ensures that no one will misunderstand the ambiguous word *bṭḥ* by making it clear that the secure feeling is a response to an act of God.

As Smith notes, the picture of peaceful external relations in v. 11 is similar to the situation with which ch. 7 concludes (1899:86; cf. Schulz 1919:170). Samuel paints this pastoral backdrop in anticipation of his next point, the senseless, unwarranted nature of the request for a king. That much of the final description of Israel's security is dependent on the thought and language of such passages as Deut 12.10, 25.19, and Josh 23.1 supports this reading of its rhetorical purpose as a contrastive backdrop. The attainment of such a state of peaceful security, courtesy of Yahweh, is the goal of Israelite existence; there is nothing more to be achieved /17/. Subsequently, Israel is expected to act in accordance with the wishes of Yahweh, who has fulfilled his covenantal commitment by giving them this secure refuge. Whether there is any truth in Samuel's recollections or not, if he has succeeded in convincing his audience the last thing that could be expected is a response of insurrection or rebellion from Israel (cf. Gutbrod 1956:89).

If Samuel's audience or the reader simply accepts his presentation of the course of Israel's history up to the time of the request - and it is difficult to do otherwise since the unobtrusive narrator allows Samuel to hold the floor - Samuel's evaluation of the request for a king (v. 12) will seem indisputable. Both Samuel's audience and the reader know, however, that his memory is defective because he avoids any mention of the disastrous events of chs. 2-6.

The narrator does not allow anyone in Samuel's audience to object to Samuel's obvious bias. This enforced silence within the narrative goads the reader to express his own objections to Samuel's biased recollections - for the reader has already been supplied with authoritative information contradicting Samuel's presentation (chs. 2-6). The silence of the narrator and Samuel's audience only adds to a sense of the need for protest and of frustration at its absence. Unable, of course, to come to Israel's defence, the reader is at least allowed to evaluate all of Samuel's subsequent rules and regulations for the new political structure from a more sheltered vantage than those in Samuel's audience. Here justice is truly, if only, poetic!

Verse 12

Nowhere is the discrepancy between Samuel's presentation and what actually happened (according to the narrator) more apparent than in v. 12. Though various suggestions about the compositional history of chs. 8-12 have been tendered to explain the differing reasons that are suggested for the request for a king, the most elegant is supplied within the narrative itself /18/.

The reader knows that the request arose out of the particular state of affairs in Samuel's family seen from the perspective of an Israel educated by the Elide affair; and the reader has this information on the authority of the narrator (8.1-3) who has proven to be reliable throughout the narrative /19/. When Samuel contradicts this authoritative version, the discrepancy can only be understood as a product of the character's personal opinions and involvement - as an attempt by Samuel to reinterpret the past, attributing the desire for a monarchy solely to Israel's inexplicable willfulness. Vannoy is a reader who comes close to this very conclusion: 'Samuel's statement in 1 Samuel 12.12 is thus compatible with chapters 8, 10, and 11, [see note 18 above] but more important is that it reveals his own analysis of the motivation behind the initial request of the elders for a king' (1978:39).

As Samuel presents the request, and in this he has adopted Yahweh's perspective (8.7f), it seems to arise as one in the succession of Israelite defections from loyalty to Yahweh. According to Samuel, when the people saw Nahash the Ammonite advancing against them they said, 'No, but a king shall be king over us' - yet Yahweh was their king. Having just rehearsed the usual course of action when faced with an external threat - to cry to Yahweh - Samuel obviously regards Israel's 'No' as a rejection of the theocratic framework for national defense, a framework that he has just shown to be historically proven.

In place of the cry to Yahweh for help, we find 'No - but a king shall be king over us' (Boecker 1969: 76; Veijola 1977:96f). As Samuel stages it, the request is a senseless act. Israel already had a king in Yahweh their God, who, as Samuel has just demonstrated, was not only capable of delivering Israel from any army, but even of giving Israel a secure existence available from no other source (betah). Samuel sees the request for a king, which he quotes from 8.19, as a rejection of Yahweh that is comprehensible only as the fruit of ingrained stubbornness and stupidity, the heritage of their fathers' sins (vv. 9f) /20/.

From the reader's perspective Samuel's recollection of the request reveals a loyal Yahwist refusing to admit the validity of Israel's reasons for that request. Whether or not a reader entertains the historical possibility that the Ammonite threat lay behind the request in ch. 8 (Vannoy 1978:38f), Samuel has omitted its real justification: Yahweh's past behaviour (chs. 4-6) and the immediate danger threatened by the behaviour of Samuel's wayward sons. By avoiding the real reasons and occasion for the request, Samuel exposes his own sensitivity to it (cf. 8.6f). The discrepancy between the request as described in ch. 8 and ch. 12 is a relatively simple matter of a disparity between the way it was, and the way a deeply involved character would like everyone to believe it was.

In spite of the reader's awareness that Samuel is hopelessly biased here (and elsewhere, e.g. 10.17-24), the failing is partially mitigated. Samuel's evasion is the defense of an old man who has spent all his life as a servant of God and people. Both his pride in a lifetime of flawless service and even his continued existence in the office of mediator were jeopardized by the request. Yet he himself had done nothing to deserve dismissal.

Samuel turns to the present result of the request, Israel's new king, introducing him first as 'the king whom you have chosen,' an expression he last used in 8.18 in his attempt to dissuade the people. There is no suggestion here that they have obtained a despot. Rather, his emphasis lies solely on the fulfillment of the people's desire; they have gotten what they wanted. At least, that is what Samuel would like them to think. Next he refers to the king as the one 'whom you requested,' implying, with this play on the name *ša'ûl* and the verb *še'eltem,* that King Saul is in fact a king such as they had asked for (cf. 10.22). Samuel, a master at diplomatic rhetoric, opens his remarks on the behavioural requirements of monarchic Israel with two notes that emphasize that the people have gotten what they wanted /21/.

Finally, however, Samuel must turn to the task of characterizing the new monarchy from the prescriptive theocratic perspective. He signals the important shift by introducing it with the particle *hinneh* (cf. Boecker 1969:77). 'So now, Yahweh has installed a king over you.'

The combination of the verb *ntn* with the preposition '*l* stresses the hierarchy of the new arrangement: Yahweh is over the king, by virtue of being the one to install him, and the king is over 'you,' by virtue of the manner of installation ('*l*) (cf. McCarthy 1978:214; Weiser 1962:86).

With this description, the emphasis shifts from the people's will regarding the king, to Yahweh's. Placing both aspects together, in balance, Samuel presents a summary description of the forces that have gone into the creation of an Israelite monarchy: it is a manifestation of the people's will, which is then actualized, with some reinterpretation, by Yahweh (cf. Vannoy 1978:41 n.95).

Samuel's presentation begins to take on a positive, exhortatory tone with the statement that Yahweh installed the king. Yahweh's action appears to have converted the people's idea of monarchy into something that can be incorporated in the theocratic structure. '[Verse] 13 marks the climax of the formulation and it reverses the history of sin. The king is no longer the sign of a great infidelity; he is Yahweh's gift' (McCarthy 1974:102; cf. Muilenburg 1959:363; Boecker 1969:77; Wolff 1975:88f; Birch 1976:69). As the request for a king was linked to the long history of Israelite defections, so Yahweh's response is to be understood as the most recent in a series of gracious responses. Israel's defection is forgiven and arrangements are made for the continuation of relations between Yahweh and Israel.

Verse 14

Samuel proceeds to lay down the conditions under which the new political organization will function.

McCarthy notes that the conditional protases of both
vv. 14 and 15 are typically deuteronomistic in concern
and formulation, excepting the use of 'rebel' for a
future possibility (1978:209f). All of the conditions
show that Israel remains firmly bound by the same
covenantal stipulations as before. The monarchy has
changed little if anything. In spite of the fact that
they now have a king, Yahweh continues to be the only
one to whom Israel owes its loyalty (cf. Vannoy 1978:
44).

Though v. 14 in MT has often been regarded as need-
ing a conclusion in the form of some reward for accepting the conditions (e.g. Smith 1899:87f; Ehrlich
1910:208; Driver 1913:94; Stoebe 1973:238; McCarter
1980:211f), the necessary apodosis is, indeed, found
in MT. Beginning with the words *wiheyitem,* a grammatically correct introduction to an apodosis (Smith
1899:88), Samuel's audience is promised that they and
their king will follow Yahweh. Boecker has shown
that the expression *hayâ . . . 'aḥar* is a suitable apodosis in v. 14 (1969:77-82). By fulfilling all the conditions mentioned by Samuel, the people and their king
will be true followers of Yahweh. As the phrase reveals
in other contexts (2 Sam 2.10; 15.13; 1 Kgs 12.20;
16.21), to be a true follower of Yahweh means to recognize him as king. *Hayâ 'aḥar,* to be after or behind
a person, is good Hebrew, and is frequently met with,
particularly in the sense of attaching one's self to
the king, or holding to him' (Keil & Delitzsch 1880:
119; cf. Boecker 1969:80; McCarthy 1978:215f; Vannoy
1978:42f).

But how would Israel's and its king's recognition
of Yahweh as their supreme political head be a blessing
to them? By recognizing Yahweh as ultimate authority,
Israel should be able to count on his help as promised
in the covenant (Weiser 1962:86; Boecker 1969:81).
'The implication . . . in terms of the covenant conditional is that Israel and her king can then continue to
expect Yahweh's help in war and enjoy the benefits of

Yahweh's rule as described in the blessings of the covenant (Deut 28.1ff.) which are received as the concomitant of covenant loyalty to Yahweh' (Vannoy 1978: 44f) /22/.

Verse 15

Obviously aiming at strengthening the theocratic position, Samuel characterizes the alternative to accepting his terms as disobedience to Yahweh, and rebellion against his commands. The consequence of such lawlessness is that 'The hand of Yahweh will be against you and against your 'fathers' to destroy you' /23/. If Israel and its king are not willing to be subject to Yahweh, thereby reaping the benefits of being his followers, then they will be treated as an enemy. The same 'hand of Yahweh' that the reader has seen in devastating action against the Philistine enemy will turn against monarchic Israel.

Many scholars have argued that vv. 14f constitute a re-presentation of the covenant blessing and curse, indicating that Israel is being offered a fresh beginning in its relationship with Yahweh (Muilenburg 1959: 363; Weiser 1962:86f; Boecker 1969:81f; Veijola 1977:87f; Vannoy 1978:46f). The choice Samuel offers is clear-cut: Israel and their king can either be for Yahweh or against him. The results of each option are two sides of the same coin: obedience allows unification with Yahweh and disobedience turns him into their enemy (Boecker 1969:82; McCarthy 1978:210).

Considered from the larger perspective of Israel's past relationship with Yahweh, the new conditions, paralleling as they do the blessing and curse portions of the covenant, indicate that the monarchy has changed nothing essential in Israel's political structure. Everything still depends on Yahweh's expressed desires for Israelite behaviour and on Israel's conformity with those stipulations. The king, originally requested as an instrument of political change, is publicly subsumed within the old order /24/.

Verse 16

A new stage in the proceedings is marked by Samuel's opening words in v. 16, *gam-'attâ*, which link up with the previous usage of *'attâ* in v. 7. The emphatic particle *gam* also expresses Samuel's recognition that the formal call to assembly (*hityaṣṣebû*) is made again here, even though it has already been made in v. 7 (cf. Ehrlich 1910:208; against Buber 1956: 158, 'the *gam-'attâ* of v. 16 is completely meaningless'). Both Muilenburg (1959:359, 363) and Harrelson (cited by Vannoy 1978:47 n.106) suggest that the verb *htyṣb* is used in such contexts as a formal expression. The emphasis lies not so much on the physical detail as on the psychological attitudes and religious meaning of the act of assembly.

The people are called to assemble and witness 'this tremendous deed' which Yahweh is about to do before their very eyes. Vannoy has observed that there is a close phraseological resemblance between Samuel's introduction of this phenomenon and Moses' introduction to Yahweh's deliverance at the Reed Sea (1978:47f). Samuel sets himself up as a Moses figure, leading Israel to a new or renewed experience of relationship with Yahweh. The formation of the relationship in Exodus and the reformation in vv. 16-25 are catalyzed by the experience of Yahweh's miraculous deeds. In Exodus the miracle of the Red Sea is enough to make the Israelites fear Yahweh and believe in Yahweh and in Moses (*wayyîr'û ha'am 'et-yhwh wayya'amînû byhwh ûbemošeh 'abdô*, Exod 14.31). Likewise, the thunderstorm convinces Samuel's audience, whose quest for a king has already been compared to Israel's apostasy during and since the exodus (1 Sam 8.8; 12.8-12; cf. 10.18f) /25/, that their request for a king was sinful, and they fear Yahweh and Samuel *wayyîra' kol-ha'am me'od 'et-yhwh we'et-šemû'el* (v. 18) /26/.

The opening phrases show Samuel operating in the role of mediator; once more in a position of dominance, he exhibits an attitude of assurance. Though he began his remarks with intimations that he would step down from his post in deference to the new king and perhaps to the younger generation (v. 2), Samuel's demonstration of power, both Yahweh's and his, if anything puts him back in the position of authority he last occupied by himself in ch. 7.

Excursus on Structure: 1 Sam 7 and 12

Both Buber (1956:158) and Seebass (1965:294f) have perceived a connection between 12.16-25 and ch. 7 (cf. Press 1938:211f; Hertzberg 1964:100). Seebass even argues that this section in ch. 12 is modeled on ch. 7 (1965:294f; cf. Birch 1976:70, criticizing Seebass' proposal). Though the reader (and Samuel's audience) will not realize the full extent of the patterns of contact between the two scenes until Samuel completes his presentation, I shall anticipate that realization in the interests of concise presentation, by summarizing the parallels beforehand /27/.

Ch.7	Ch.12
Israel is exhorted to put away foreign gods and Ashtaroth, to direct its heart to Yahweh, and to serve him only; then he will deliver it from the Philistines (v. 3).	Israel is promised that if they will fear Yahweh and serve him, heed his and not rebel against his command, then Israel and its king will be behind Yahweh, and by implication, Yahweh will be before them (v. 14).
Samuel directs Israel to assemble [qbṣ] at Mizpah, where he will pray to Yahweh for them (v. 5).	Samuel says to assemble [htyṣb] to see the tremendous deed that Yahweh is about to perform for them. Though it is now harvest time, Samuel will call to Yahweh and he will send thunder and rain so that Israel will recognize and

see the great evil that they have done in Yahweh's eyes, by asking for a king vv.16f).

Israel gathers at Mizpah. They draw and pour water before Yahweh, they fast on that day [bayyôm hahû'] and confess their sin against Yahweh (v.6.).

Samuel calls to Yahweh and he sends thunder and rain on that day [bayyôm hahû'] (v.18).

Hearing that the Israelites have assembled at Mizpah, the Philistine leaders go up to Israel. Israel hears about it and fears [wayyir'û] the Philistines (v. 7).

As a result of Samuel's call and Yahweh's response, the people greatly ly fear [wayyîra'] Yahweh and Samuel (v.18).

The Israelites tell Samuel [wayyo'merû 'el-šemû'el]: 'Do not refuse to cry for us to Yahweh, our God ['elohênû], that he may deliver us from the Philistines' (v.8).

The people tell Samuel [wayyo'merû 'el-šemû'el]: 'Pray on your servants behalf to Yahweh, your God ['eloheyka], that we might not be killed because we have added to all our sins the evil of asking for a king' (v.19).

Samuel takes a suckling lamb nad offers it as an an offering to Yahweh. Samuel cries to Yahweh on Israel's behalf, and Yahweh answers him. When the Philistines close for the attack, Yahweh thunders against them with a great voice. The Philistines are duly confused and then routed before Israel (vv.9-10).

Samuel tells the people not to be afraid. Though they have done this evil, they should not turn away from Yahweh; they should serve him with all their heart. They should not turn turn aside after vain things which are profitless and unable to rescue because they are vain. Yahweh will not abandon his people on account of his reputation ('great name') for it was Yahweh's pleasure to make them into a people for himself (vv.20-2).

Yahweh has shown his willingness to be reunited with Israel,

Yahweh will not abandon his people and Samuel promises that he shall not and continues to demonstrate it by giving Israel victory over some neighbours and peace with others. Samuel is established as judge over Israel for the rest of his days (vv. 12-7).

sin against Yahweh by ceasing to offer intercessory prayer on Israel's behalf (cf. 7:8) he will teach Israel to walk the straight and narrow (v.23) and in vv.24f he sets to that task.

In both cases the upshot of the proceedings is that Yahweh sits in firm possession and leadership over a penitent Israel guided by his watchful servant (Israel's intercessor) Samuel. The parallel proceedings support the view that the theocratic superstructure ultimately remains intact and is recognized as legitimate by Israel; the monarchy has not changed the basic political order at all.

The reader must, however, be careful to distinguish between Samuel's meanings and the narrator's. The narrator, who presents us with a third person narration of Samuel's (and Yahweh's) grand finale may shed a different light on Samuel's demonstration through the differences between his third person perspective, and the infra-narrative perspectives expressed by Samuel and the people.

As readers we see Samuel's demonstration of Yahweh's power (at his beck and call) neither from the position of the Israelites, who are frightened into confessions of sin, nor from Samuel's (and probably Yahweh's) point of view, from which the demonstration evokes a proper and needful response from Israel. Instead the reader is the aloof onlooker, viewing things from the distance created by the narrator's external perspective. This distanced viewpoint is undisturbed by the immediate turbulence created by the thunderstorm. The reader easily recalls all aspects of the kingship issue, including the historical causes as presented in the narrative. These powers of recollection are afforded by the narrator's gift of distance.

Verse 17

Samuel sets up a demonstration that will prove two points. It will take the form of a miraculous phenomenon, a thunderstorm in the dry season, an unknown occurrence. According to G. A. Smith (in a chapter appropriately titled 'The climate and fertility of the land, with their effects on its religion'): 'In May showers are very rare, and from then till October, not only is there no rain, but a cloud seldom passes over the sky, and a thunderstorm is a miracle' (1900: 65) /28/. Samuel tells his audience that this weird event, to be enacted at his signal, is intended to convince them that Yahweh viewed their *request* as very evil /29/.

The second purpose of the demonstration, unmentioned by Samuel but obvious to both his audience and the reader, is to prove the strength of Samuel's ties with Yahweh and their agreement concerning the monarchy (cf. McCarter 1980:216). If Samuel's relationship with Yahweh were weak, or if Yahweh did not regard the request as evil, he would not answer the prophet. Samuel shows a great deal of confidence in v. 17. He is so sure of himself and of Yahweh's opinions that he willingly stakes his reputation on the success of the demonstration.

With respect to the parallel between v. 17 and 7.5, several considerations arise. Back in 7.5, Samuel had gathered a scattered Israel which was experiencing a loss of faith in Yahweh on account of his strangeness towards them. Samuel promised to pray for them with the unstated goal of bringing them back together with Yahweh. Now in v. 17, Samuel has called another assembly in which he will effect a communication between Yahweh and Israel, except that this time it is a message from Yahweh to the people who have cast a vote of non-confidence against him and Samuel. Besides the difference in the direction of the communication, there is also a difference in tone: when Israel feels

rejected by Yahweh it seeks reunification through intercessory prayer (at Samuel's suggestion), but when Yahweh feels rejected by Israel he uses the heavy-handed,
direct route of miraculous thunder and rain, which communicates displeasure and smells of coercion, especially against the backdrop of Israel's passive submission
through Samuel's intercession.

This contrast is partly explained by the fact that
reconciliation over the matter of kingship has already
taken place (ch. 11). Yahweh has already given in to
a certain extent by allowing a conditional monarchy.
What is intended by the demonstration of v. 17 is not
so much reconciliation as it is a restoration of a
respectful distance in the existing relationship. Israel has questioned Yahweh and experienced some success in its petition. The demonstration will put Israel back in its proper place through a show of divine
force.

Verse 17 and 7.5 are alike, then, in describing
assemblies for the purpose of a divine-human interchange through the agency of Samuel. Verse 17 differs
in that it describes an effort at restoring *proper*
relationship, while 7.5 describes only a request for
renewed relationship. The difference is caused by the
intervention of the request for a king which, though
granted, is regarded as impudent, improper and in need
of redress.

Verse 18

Having presented Samuel's description of what he was
about, the narrator describes the actual undertaking.
Samuel's actions correspond word for word with what
he said he would do, and so do Yahweh's actions in support of him. The significance of Yahweh's response is
disputed;, some view the thunder (and rain) as an echo
of theophany, especially the Sinai theophany (Weiser
1962:87), others argue that the out-of-season storm is
a visible manifestation of Yahweh's power, a sign in

response to Samuel's call and so an authentification of Samuel as mediator (Boecker 1969:85; Stoebe 1973: 238f; Veijola 1977:98).

As the results of the demonstration show, however, it is likely that aspects of both theophany and sign are present (cf. Vannoy 1978:50f; McCarter 1980:216). The people fear Yahweh and Samuel, a twofold result corresponding to the two sides of the demonstration. On the one side, Birch observes that thunder (*qôl*) is common to theophanies (1976:70); and both the people's fear of Yahweh (v. 18) and their fear that they might die if Samuel did not pray for them seem more in tune with the concept of theophany than that of pure sign (cf. Birch 1976:70). The terrifying thunder and rain do indeed convince Israel that Yahweh was displeased with the request: 'God, who had been shoved aside as a shadowy unreality by Israel with its insistent demand for a king, plainly reveals himself as the living one, who is quite able to annihilate his creature' (Gutbrod 1956:90f). The people certainly see this side of the miraculous thunderstorm; the manifestation of divine power as a displeased reaction to their request seems to them to threaten their very existence (v. 19; cf. McCarthy 1978:217; Vannoy 1978:50f) /30/. While there is, strictly speaking, no theophany, Weiser is justified in saying that there is an echo of it here (1962: 87).

On the other hand, the demonstration does serve to legitimate Samuel by showing the people that they need his services as mediator to pray on their behalf /31/. The storm proves that Yahweh's real power and real domination over Israel continues (cf. Boecker 1969: 85). On account of his intimacy with this powerful God and their shared antipathy towards the request for a king, Samuel is a man to be feared by the people alongside God. Think what he could call down upon them if they angered him by not heeding Yahweh's 'voice' (*qôl*, v. 14 = *qolot* v. 18 'thunder') or rebelling against Yahweh's 'mouth' (v. 14, Samuel?).

Turning now to the parallel with ch. 7, it will be recalled that following the ceremonial downpour of water in v. 6 the Philistines advance against Israel. Given their previous experiences with the Philistines, when Yahweh had proven unreliable, the Israelites are fearful. Despite, however, a victory in that instance, Israel soon finds itself threatened with a repeat of the Elide disaster (8.1-3) and decides to avoid further fiascos by opting out of the theocracy. Now, as a direct result of that request, Israel faces a greater threat than the Philistines, whom it feared because unsure of Yahweh's support; now the people fear Yahweh and Samuel in the knowledge that no human power could ever deliver them from this potential enemy.

Verse 19

There is only one way to soothe Yahweh's ill feelings over the request: Israel hastens to adopt an attitude of humble, repentant submission. In the first words allowed to them since Samuel began his presentation *all* the people tell Samuel: 'Pray on behalf of your servants to Yahweh your God.' The request acknowledges a need for Samuel's legitimate service as intercessor. The people characterize themselves as his servants, subordinate to the theocratic mediator whose prayers are requested. They speak of Yahweh as Samuel's God (*'eloheyka*), in recognition of the fact that their request has alienated God from themselves (cf. Vannoy 1978:52). They express the hope that Samuel's prayers will prevent their death, a punishment that they seem to see lurking in the thunderstorm. Finally they confess that over and above all their sins, they have gone and added to the evil by asking for a king for themselves.

The demonstration is a complete success (Veijola 1977:98f). The people have been frightened into a recognition of their need of Samuel and a confession of their sin in asking for a king (cf. Vannoy 1978:52).

The relative positions of Israel, Samuel, and Yahweh are restored to the order that obtained before the request. In a time of fear and need, Israel confesses to its own sin, suggesting that it has brought this trouble upon itself (cf. 7.6). Fearful for their lives, (cf. 7.7) Israel calls on Samuel to cry or pray to Yahweh for them (cf. 7.8; Hertzberg 1964:100; Mc-Carter 1980:216). The omission of any reference to their king as a possible source of relief indicates their complete return to the theocratic form of dependence.

The parallel with ch. 7 in this instance also reveals a change in Israel's perception of its relationship with Yahweh. In 7.8, the people ask Samuel to cry to Yahweh 'our God' whereas in v. 19 they ask Samuel to pray to Yahweh 'your God.' The change is a result of Israel's perception of the threat contained in the thunderstorm. Having spurned Yahweh by asking for a king, the people no longer think they have the unquestioned right to call Yahweh 'our God' (Vannoy 1978:52). Israel has come full circle back to the position of dependence in which it stood as recently as ch. 7 and from which it had tried to escape by the request. Contrite and repentant, the people plead for a renewal of regular theocratic operations.

The reader's perception of the thunderstorm is influenced by knowledge of the narrative past, and by an understanding of the psychological side of the demonstration - viewed at a fortunate remove. Israel's humble confession is not seen as the utterance of deep reflection and consequent repentance. Rather it is a forced confession, extorted under duress, in fear for life itself (cf. Gunn 1981:65). Only a short time before (10.27-11.5) all Israel had refused to treat Saul as king because he was not a king such as they had wanted. The people were bold then in their demand for a king who would make them a nation like any other nation. When the reader now sees the people humiliated into a condemnation of their seemingly just demand, some explanation for their about-face is demanded. The obvious answer, *supplied by the narrator* in v. 19 (*way-yo'merû*), is that the confession is extracted by the strong-arm tactics used by Samuel and Yahweh. The people beg for Samuel's intercession and confess in order to avoid sudden death (*we'al-namût*).

Yahweh and Samuel may be pleased with their results and Israel may be forced to accept them, but for the reader a question mark hangs over the whole enterprise (cf. Gunn 1981:65). If the subsequent history of the relationship between Israel and Yahweh is based on such a foundation, and it is presented as a foundation for what follows, what will come of it? Can there be a satisfactory sequel to this scene? The reader will have to continue the voyage through the books of Samuel and Kings to get an answer /32/.

Verse 20

Having extorted the confession with a little help from his God, Samuel proceeds to remold the penitents' perception of their request and the meaning of their new political existence as a monarchy under theocracy. As Weiser observes, Samuel again holds a position of recognized authority as mediator between Israel and Yahweh (1962:87). 'Samuel leaps into the breach before the forlorn people together with its king' (Gutbrod 1956:91).

Vannoy notices that Samuel does not immediately pray on the people's behalf, as they request, but suggests that such prayer may be assumed on the basis of v. 23 (1978:52). Plausible as this assumption may be the adoption at this point in the narrative (v. 20) of an assumption based on later material (v. 23) is a defection from the narrated order of description. As Sternberg emphasizes, the reader of narrative must constantly be aware of the effect of sequence on the reading process:

Why has this complex of events been presented first and that delayed? Why has this facet of a character been portrayed before that? Why has this piece of (verbal, actional, structural, or even generic) information been conveyed - or on the contrary, suppressed and ambiguated - at precisely this point? And it is especially imperative to investigate these questions whenever the distribution and ordering of information involve a deviation from a conventional or previously postulated pattern or organization, such as chronological sequence (1978:97).

The people have asked for Samuel's prayers and, if he is favourably disposed towards them, we expect him to pray for them. The people in v. 19 believe that they are in a life or death situation and beg Samuel to intercede that they might live. Instead, Samuel capitalizes on their helplessness to give another repetitious (cf. vv. 14f) lecture on the behaviour required of them.

The fact that Samuel pursues this didactic course reveals that he knows of another side to the demonstration: he views the thunderstorm as an audiovisual teaching aid rather than a threat to life. Samuel does not hasten to pray for Israel because he set up the demonstration for educative rather than punitive purposes (v. 17). His post-thunderstorm lecture is, therefore, the natural consequence of his intention to convict Israel of the great evil it has done in asking for a king.

Samuel's first words to the fearful Israelites are a clear exhibition of his own interests and concerns; 'Fear not! You /33/ have done *all* this evil, but do not turn aside from after Yahweh and serve Yahweh with all your hearts.' They ask him to pray to God because they are scared to death and instead he gives them a lecture on Yahweh's behalf. Passing off their terror with a simple 'Fear not,' he reiterates a portion of their confession - 'you have done all this evil' - and

offers advice for better future performance, again
partially repeating himself (cf. vv. 14f). Samuel's
response reveals that what is of paramount importance
to him, and hence to Yahweh who supports him here, is
that Israel return to a course of strict obedience and
total devotion to Yahweh.

By paralleling the mention of the evil done with the
demand for future obedience, Samuel hints at an evaluation of the request as an act of disobedience. He
plays on his audience's moment of terror to redefine
the legitimate request from the covenantal perspective
as though it were a simple act of unprovoked disobedience and faithlessness.

Verse 21

Though v. 21 is frequently discarded as a late gloss
on account of the supposedly anachronistic word *tohû*
(e.g. Budde 1902:81; Buber 1956:159; Stoebe 1973:239;
cf., however, Deut 32.10) and the ease with which the
verse may be omitted without disturbing the sense of
the context (Budde 1902:81; Boecker 1969:86), it is
not entirely without contextual value. As Boecker observes, v. 21 is connected to v. 20 by the repetition
of the verb *tasûrû*, which is given an expanded interpretation in v. 21 (1969:68; cf. Seebass 1965:295
n.21). It is the expansionistic rhetoric of Samuel's
restatement that also explains the particle *kî*,
which follows after the verb *tasûrû* and has generally been omitted as 'senseless' with the support of
LXX (e.g. Wellhausen 1871:79; McCarter 1980:212; cf.
Vannoy 1978:54 n.128 for a review of other suggestions). The repeated exhortation taken from v. 20 is
'Do not turn aside.' Following the exhortation is a
kî clause explaining why one should not turn (cf.
Muilenburg 1961:157). 'Do not turn aside, for (*kî*)
[it is] after vanities which can neither benefit nor
deliver because they are vain.'

The word *tohû*, though usually understood as a

reference to false gods on the basis of Deutero-Isaiah (e.g. Keil & Delitzsch 1880:121; Hertzberg 1964:100), has a more specific reference in this context. In v. 20, Samuel balances the evil that has been done - the request for a king - against the exhortation not to turn aside anymore from after Yahweh. By a series of associations, then, Samuel equates the anti-covenantal request for a king like the nations with defection (*swr*) from Yahweh: 1. the request for a king is evil (v. 17); 2. the evil (the request) done is not a cause for fear so long as Israel no longer turns aside from after Yahweh (v. 20); 3. one should not turn aside because the things that are so pursued are worthless (v. 21).

In v. 21, Samuel provides more detail. Israel should not engage in such defections: the reason, because all such things are worthless. They are profitless (*lo' yô'îlû*) and unable to deliver (*lo' yaṣṣilû*). In contrast to these worthless things - such as the kingship the people had requested - are Yahweh's actions. He brought Israel up (*he'elêtî*, 10.18) from Egypt, and he delivered (*wa'aṣṣil*, 10.18; cf. 12.11) Israel from all its enemies. No one but Yahweh, according to Samuel, is of any use to Israel as a source of security: in comparison, everything else is *hattohû, 'worthlessness.'*

Verse 22

The introduction of this verse by *kî* indicates that the subsequent information is attached to the preceding as an explanation or motivation for what has been said (Keil & Delitzsch 1880:121; cf. Vannoy 1978:55f). Israel is not to turn aside because Yahweh will not forsake his people. He has a reputation to maintain. It is staked on Israel's fortunes because he made them into his people, and so they need never fear for their political existence. So long as Yahweh's 'great name' means anything to him, Israel's continued

survival as his people is guaranteed. It is this certainty of Yahweh's benefaction that makes the request
for a king a vain thing. Israel sought security from a
king when it was already guaranteed by Yahweh's great
name (v. 11).

From the reader's perspective Samuel's assurances
are less than reassuring. Only a few chapters previously (chs. 5f), Yahweh took action to protect his
reputation, but that action was of no benefit to Israel. Both before and after the Philistines were forced to confess to the greatness of the mighty exodus
God, Israel was subjected to unwarranted abuse at the
hands of Yahweh. So the reader, at least, hears a hol-
low ring to Samuel's assurances in v. 22. The response
of Samuel's audience is left undetermined by the narrative. Perhaps since they were not privy to Yahweh's
name-saving actions in chs. 5f the assurance provided
by the divine reputation might seem more credible to
them.

At any rate, the narrative is focused on Samuel and
on the conditions, promises, and requirements that are
laid down as the basis for Israel's conditional monarchy. But Samuel's tendentious interpretation of the
past and his dubious reassurances about the future do
not seem a firm foundation for the political organization that is being reaffirmed. The inadequate half-
measure of a theocratically designated king only
smooths over the problem raised by the request; Samuel's reassessment of the request only buries the
seeds of legitimate discontent under the facade of
covenant renewal, and Israel is obliged to do all of
the recanting.

It is frequently observed that the language and
ideas of v. 22 draw upon Israel's covenant ideology
(Weiser 1962:87; McCarthy 1974:102; Veijola 1977:
90). In view of the context some scholars have suggested that v. 22 renews the covenant between Israel and
Yahweh (Boecker 1969:87; McCarthy 1973:412; 1978:
217). Certainly it must be admitted that Samuel holds

out the possibility for a fresh beginning to monarchic Israel in ch. 12. But is it accurate to say that v. 22 reestablishes the covenant?

What v. 22 does, in fact, is to point back to the conditions that have always supported Israel's covenantal existence, namely the priority of election and Yahweh, who has a great name to maintain (cf. Muilenburg 1959:364; Payne 1972:324). These *presuppositions* of Israel's covenant do not signal a renewal of covenant, because the covenant has not been broken since ch. 7, when it was last renewed. As ch. 11 concludes Israel has come to terms with Saul's theocratic subordination and signaled its acceptance of Yahweh's terms by renewing the kingdom (11.14f). At that point any rift in the relationship has been mended. Verse 22 explains that Israel should not turn aside from after Yahweh because it is unnecessary; it emphasizes continuity between past, present and future rather than a reestablishment of past conditions. Yahweh *will* not forsake (so Israel should not turn) because he *has* gladly made Israel his people.

Verse 23

Samuel contrasts his own steadfast behaviour as mediator with that of his audience through the use of the emphatic introductory pronouns in vv. 20 and 23: 'You have done all this evil . . . but as for myself . . .' (Ehrlich 1910:209; McCarter 1980:216).

Having criticized Israel's request to the fullest, Samuel finally responds to the people's appeal for his prayers: his response - 'Far be it from me to sin against Yahweh by ceasing to pray on your behalf' - implies that he has never stopped praying on Israel's behalf because it is part of his God-given task as mediator. Though the people have only just recognized their continuing need of Samuel's services, Samuel, like Yahweh, has continued and will continue to fulfill his task within the covenantal framework.

Samuel's reassurance about his continuing prayers
for Israel is paralleled in ch. 7 by Israel's request
that Samuel not cease crying to Yahweh for deliverance
(7.8). His statement here may be taken as a conscious
allusion to that request and as such constitutes a
celebration of personal victory. Threatened with re-
tirement, Samuel has emerged from the crisis with a
public vindication of his integrity (v. 4) as well as
the public recognition of his indispensability as mediator. Samuel remains in authority (cf. E. Robertson
1944:194; Wallis 1972:52f).

Samuel crowns his successful demonstration of the
necessity of his office by electing himself to the task
of directing Israel in the good and upright path. On
the one hand, his audience might well understand this
as an act of kindness on Samuel's part:

> Samuel's pledge in v. 23, therefore, is undeserved
> by its beneficiaries, the Israelites. It amounts to
> a special provision for the succor and preservation
> of the people, which comes on the very brink of
> disaster . . . (McCarter 1980:219).

With Samuel as teacher, the people need not worry that
they will foolishly turn away from Yahweh in pursuit
of some chimerical end. Samuel selflessly undertakes to
keep Israel on the straight and narrow, which, in view
of the ominous threat of divine punishment, must be accepted as a valuable and necessary service to Israel.

The reader cannot help but notice that the installation of the theocratic mediator as the official cen-
sor, dictator of the 'good and upright path,' is the
final blow to Israel's idea of a political system un-
fettered by the minutiae of theocracy. The result of
Israel's quest for independence is a strengthening of
the theocratic hand on this people whom it has pleased
Yahweh to make. Whether the people will always accept
this imposition, and whether the king will be satisfied
with his subordination remain as questions that the

reader must carry into the subsequent scenes of the
monarchic history (cf. Gunn 1980:65).

One thing is certain about v. 23: it marks the end
of the movement for a king like all the nations. Just
as the request for a king was sparked by a recurrence
of a previous circumstance, the dangerous state of affairs in the mediator's family, so the conclusion to
the chain of events resulting from the request is marked by the recurrence of the scene at the end of ch. 7.
In both instances Samuel has brought Israel through
a crisis and stands thereafter ensconced as mediator,
shepherding the people of Yahweh. Both the request for
a king and the conclusion of the issue illustrate the
narrator's technique of using scenic parallels and
allusions to add commentary to scenes that otherwise
appear to lack narrative exposition (cf. Alter 1981:
7). With Samuel's remarks in v. 23 and the parallel
situation in ch. 7, it is almost as though the request
had never been made. Under Samuel's direction, with
special effects by Yahweh, the pursuit of a king like
the nations has now come to seem the pursuit of an
illusion (*hattohû*).

Verses 24-25

Samuel concludes his presentation with a recapitulation of what is required of Israel, balancing his
descriptions of Yahweh's and his own future activity
(vv. 22f) with another prescription for Israel's behaviour. Of the exhortations only the addition of the
adverb *be'emet* 'sincerely' is not a repetition of
things he has already said in vv. 14f, 20. As Buber
has noted, the explanatory clause is linked with the
first part of the exhortation by a wordplay: 'Only
fear (*yer'û*) Yahweh . . . for consider (*re'û*) how gravely
he has dealt with you' (1956:161). The fear of Yahweh and sincere service are motivated by the tremendous deed (*haddabar haggadôl*, v. 16) by which Yahweh showed his evaluation of the request for a king

(Smith 1899:89; Budde 1902:81; Ehrlich 1912:209; cf., however, Keil & Delitzsch 1880:121; Gressmann 1921:46; Stoebe 1973:234). Correct behaviour is motivated by the threat implicit in the thunderstorm.

The alternative to a proper fear of Yahweh and faithful service to him is described by Samuel with the comprehensive words 'If you do evil.' Anything other than obedient subservience to Yahweh is included in this description. The penalty for continued disobedience on the people's part is that both they and their king will be swept away. The people had said about their proposed king 'Even we (*gam-'anaḥnû*) will be like all the nations' (8.20), to which Samuel responds here 'Even you and even your king (*gam-'attem gam-malkekem*) will be swept away.'

Thornton understands v. 25 to be a threat of destruction aimed particularly at Saul himself, if he should behave wickedly (1967:421). Yet, as Boecker observes, Saul is not even mentioned by name in ch. 12 (1969:87 n.3). Moreover, the kingship of Saul is neither questioned nor criticized in ch. 12; only the request for a king like all the nations is reproved. If anything, v. 25 ties the fate of the Israelite monarchy to the behaviour of the Israelite people. If Samuel's audience continues to do evil, the king will be subjected to the same fate as they themselves, without any consideration of his complicity or the lack of it. The installation of a king has changed nothing with regard to Israel's theocratic obligations. They are still governed by the same theocratic duties in their binding covenant with Yahweh. Regarding the Israelite monarchy, Samuel is right: it has become *hattohû*.

CHAPTER FIVE

CONCLUSION

The major hypothesis of this study has been confirmed.
It is possible to read 1 Sam 1-12 as a unitary narrative with a clear, logically progressive plot. Individual points of interpretation may be debated, modified,
or rejected, but the fact that these chapters can be
read as a unity is indisputable.

Within these chapters there are a number of specific
parallels and linkages between the two movements found
in chs. 1-7 and chs. 8-12. These cross connections serve
to unify the narrative while providing implicit commentary on the subsequent incident through allusion to
the prior incident of the linked items. The parallelism
between chs. 1-7 and chs. 8-12 consists of two basic
relationships between the events (actions, occurrences)
and existents (characters, settings). The relationship
may be one of simple repetition of a situation in chs.
8-12 that has already occured in chs. 1-7, or it may be
that the parallel in chs. 8-12 is a response to or development of previous material. Usually such developments in chs. 8-12 resolve tensions and ambiguities
created in chs. 1-7. In summary form the parallels
appear as follows:

	Chs. 1-7	Chs. 8-12
1.	Introduction to Samu-el, the primary human character (chs. 1-3).	
2.	Old Eli the priest (1.9:	Old Samuel (8.1, 5) and

	2.22) and his wicked sons (2.12-17, 22-25).	his corrupt sons (8.2-3, 5).
3.	Yahweh reacts to the Elide abuses (2.25, 30-36; 3.12-14).	The elders of Israel act in anticipation of Yahweh's ahweh's reaction (8.5).
4.	Yahweh punishes the Elides and seems himself to have been defeated (ch.4).	The people request a secular human king who can fight Israel's battles (8.20).
5.	Yahweh displays his powers in a manner similar to the Exodus display (chs. 5-6). Israel's divine warrior has not been defeated.	Yahweh brings Saul to Samuel to be anointed 'nagid' and new Moses. Saul is enlisted in the service of Yahweh, who does not renounce his claims on Israel (9.1-10.16).
6.	Yahweh treats Israel in a manner similar to his treatment of the Philis-Israel responds as the Philistines did (6.19-20; cf. 5-6).	Yahweh seeks to reassure Israel of his commitment to them as his people, his inheritance (9.16, 27; 10.1) He commissions a new Moses to save them (9.1-10.16).
7.	Israel, the rejected covenantal party, makes the first move to renew the relationship (7.3-8).	Yahweh, the rejected party, makes the first move towards reconciliation (9.1-10.16).
8.	The rapprochement takes takes place at Mizpah, where Samuel gathers all the people (7.5).	Cf. 10.17.
9.	Yahweh gives Israel the victory over the Philistines (7.9-14). There is	Yahweh gives Israel under Saul and Samuel the victory over the Ammonites

	even peace with the Amorites (7.14).	(11.7, 11-13).
10.	Samuel acts as covenant mediator for Israel in both political and religious spheres (7.17).	Samuel leads Israel in a covenant renewal that incorporates the monarchy. He pledges continued prayer and instruction to Israel 1on his part (ch. 12).

During the course of reading this episode in Israel's theological-political adventures, it becomes apparent that the greatest failing of historical-critical readings of the narrative is a neglect of the narrative's voice structure. The majority of supposedly irresolvable ideological conflicts in the opinions that find expression in these chapters disappear when careful attention is paid to the simple questions, 'Who says what to whom?' and 'Where and when was it said?'

Along the way, the reading gave rise to several implications for the way in which 1 Sam 1-12 is relied upon as a source of data in various important areas of contemporary biblical scholarship. Obviously a unitary reading of all the twelve chapters calls into question any readings that suggest that a chapter or group of chapters must be read in isolation. Until the suggested unity of the narrative and the supporting evidence thereto is refuted, any further suggestions about the socio-historical settings of the 'pro- and anti-monarchic factions' in chs. 8-12, or about the 'Ark Narrative' in chs. 4-6 must be regarded as unnecessarily complex, both as hypotheses and as explanations of the data. Literary explanations of the narrative are inherently stronger because they are primarily descriptive and so subject to refutation; a holistic literary approach eliminates the undesirable multiplication of historical assumptions, and its conclusions can be accepted or rejected as they agree or disagree with the text (cf. Polzin 1980:5-7). The literary approach

is a way out of the proliferation of studies whose conclusions cannot be compared because they depend on
varying, non-verifiable hypotheses and assumptions. A
descriptive reading of 1 Sam 1-12 can be compared with
other such readings and the comparative strengths and
weaknesses of each reading should appear. Individual
readings may suffer refutation, but scholarly *dialogue*
about the text will increase.

Read as a unit, 1 Sam 1-12 also posed problems for
existing readings of the deuteronomistic history. If
the narrator of these chapters does not condemn kingship, and if the narrator is the deuteronomist, then
it would seem that the generally accepted opinions
about the deuteronomist's negative attitude towards
the institution of monarchy need reconsideration.
Again such reconsideration is made neccessary by a
reading that pays careful attention to the narrative's
hierarchical voice structure, such as was not done by
previous studies of the deuteronomist in 1 Sam 1-12.

The theological implications of these chapters,
especially as regards the characterization of God,
suggest that 1 Sam 1-12 is more comparable to a book
like Job than has previously been accepted. It would,
of course, be question-begging to suggest that these
theological implications reveal the perversity of my
reading when viewed in the wider context of the
known theology of the deuteronomistic history. A
close reading of the remainder of the deuteronomistic history is necessary to evaluate a close reading
of 1 Sam 1-12.

NOTES, ABBREVIATIONS

BILIOGRAPHY & INDEXES

NOTES TO CHAPTER ONE

THE LITERARY ANALYSIS OF 1 SAMUEL 8-12

1   Stoebe (1973:32-44) reviews this period in scholarship.
2   Wellhausen was himself aware of this neglect of the existing narrative but saw no deficiency in his approach. It is the history of Israel and its literature that enables one to understand the Bible and the relationship between its parts. (See Wellhausen's description of his own experiences, 1973:3.) What is important is not the narrative itself, but the more remote social and historical contexts that have given expression to the biblical text (1973:366, 368).
3   Koch explains the reasons for this apparent apriorism:

> Literary [source] criticism begins with the recognition that the period of origin of a biblical writing presents enormous difficulties, and that the situations of the writers have also become greatly obscured through a many levelled process of redaction. Formerly independent sources were linked together, even merged, or torn apart and made up into different and separate units. The literary [source] critic therefore attempts to discover the original writings, to determine exactly their date of origin, and to grasp the personality of the writer as much as is possible. This means that he approaches the text with, so to say, a dissecting knife in his hand, looks out particularly for breaks in continuity, or missing links in the train of thought, and also for disturbing duplications and factual inconsistencies, and for variations in the use of language which will have originated in another set of circumstances or at a period of different religious concepts. The literary [source] critical method leads to a determination of sources . . . Literary criticism is the analysis of biblical books from the standpoint of lack of continuity, duplications, inconsistencies and different linguistic usage, *with the object of discovering what the individual writers and redactors contributed to a text, and also its time and place of origin* (Koch's italics) (1969:69, 70).

4   For criticism of the extrinsic approach to literature see Wellek & Warren 1975:73f, 139-41; Ellis 1974:104-54.
5   Further proliferation of reviews of scholarship on the narrative is unnecessary. For existing treatments see Birch 1976:1-10; Boecker 1969:1-10; Childs 1979:263-77; Eissfeldt 1965:269-71; Fritz 1976:346-9; Ishida 1977:26-9; Jenni 1961:136-41; Kegler 1977:56-70; Langlemet 1970:161-200; 1978:277-300; Mayes 1977:322-31; 1978:1-10; McCarter 1980:12-4; Radjawane 1973:177-216, esp. 190-200; Ritterspach 1967:16-53; L.Schmidt 1970:58-63; Stoebe 1973:32-52; Veijola 1977:5-14;

Wildberger 1957:442-6.

6   Gunkel discusses the proposed literary history in detail in 'Die Israelitische Literatur,' 1906:51-102. See also Klatt 1969:166-91.

7   Gressmann anticipates here, S. Talmon's observations on synony-mous readings in the Bible (Talmon 1975:226-63, 321-400).

8   See Gunkel 1906:51-102, and Gressmann 1921:xii-xvi for the lat-ter's own summary of the generic history of Israelite literature.

9   Gressmann gives a summary of the histories of Egypt, Meso-potamia, and Palestine, showing how events led to the possibility and actual formation of Israel's monarchy. Since only ch. 11 comes close to agreement with Gressmann's analysis of the historical situation it is probably the only historical tradition (1921:27).

10   The historical period in which a pro-monarchic view is possible is further defined for Noth by the historical fact of the long delay before the institution of a monarchy in Israel. Noth explains the delay, remarkable in view of the external threat from neighbouring kingdoms, as a product of a pre-monarchic theocratic ideology in Israel (1960:164f). Pro-monarchic views, therefore, were not likely to have been common before the crushing defeat of the amphictyonic armies at Aphek (1 Sam 4). The losses in this battle forced the weakened Israelites to resort to a monarchy if they were to continue as a politically independent society.

11   Weiser includes Noth (1967) among those whom he calls literary critics because Noth follows Wellhausen's source divisions of the narrative.

12   For example, Birch divides ch. 9 into 1-14, 18f, 22-4, and ch. 10 into 2-4, 9, 14-16a. These verses represent a separate folk tale of Saul's search for his asses (1976:132).

13   On the role of analogy in historical criticism see J. M. Miller 1976:18.

14   See Buber 1956, 1964. Buber's arguments for the unity of 1 Sam 7-12 are vitiated by his excisions of material that does not conform to what he sees as the unitary narrative.

15   A comprehensive, systematic description of narrative in the Hebrew Bible remains far in the future. Alonso-Schökel's evalu-ation of Hebrew narratology still holds true twenty years after he made it: 'We still do not have a basic systematic, well-rounded description of Old Testament narrative art. Moreover such is hard-ly felt to be desirable' (1961:147). Preliminary work is, however, now underway towards this goal, e.g. Alonso-Schökel 1960:154-64; 1961:143-72; 1975:1-15; Alter 1981; Bar-Efrat 1978:19-31; 1980: 154-73; Buber 1956:113-73; 1964:727-845, 1131-58; Conroy 1980; Culley 1976; Fokkelman 1975, 1981; Gunn 1978, 1980; Kikawada 1977:67-91; Perry and Sternberg 1968/69:263-92 (452-99); Polzin 1980, 1981; Schulz 1923; Seeligmann 1962:305-25; *Semeia* 1975, 1977, 1979; Talmon 1978:9-26; M. Weiss 1963:456-75; 1965:181-206; 1971:88-112.

16   The principle is best known as formulated by William of Ockham who said, appropriately enough, 'Plurality is not to be assumed with-out necessity,' and 'What can be done with fewer [assumptions] is

done in vain with more' (cited from Edwards 1967: Vol. 7/8, 307).
17   Polzin comes to similar conclusions, 'If, on the other hand,
we assume that many gaps, dislocations, and reversals in the biblical
text may profitably be viewed as the result of the use (authorial or
editorial) of several different view-points within the narrative,
then, whether the present text is the product either of a single mind
or of a long and complicated editorial process, we are still responsible for making sense of the present text by assuming that the present text, in more cases than previously realized, does make sense'
(1980:17).
18   Cleanth Brooks suggests that 'it is easy to see why the
relation of each item to the whole context is crucial, and why the
effective and essential structure of the poem has to do with the
complex of attitudes achieved. A scientific preposition [*sic*] can
stand alone. If it is true, it is true. But the expression of an
attitude, apart from the occasion which generates it and the situation which encompasses, is meaningless' (1947:207). Cf. Ellis
1974:118-20.
19   The macro-contextual pattern is the narrative structure that
governs the narrative as a whole (Conroy 1978:89f).
20   The objective of narrative theory '. . . is a grid of possibilities, through the establishment of the minimal narrative constitu-
tive features . . . What can we say about the way structures like
narrative organize themselves? . . . What are the necessary components - and only those - of a narrative?' (Chatman 1978:19).
21   E.g. linguistic: phonology, vocabulary, grammar, syntax, and
rhetorical structures; literary: plot, theme, sequence, suspense and
tensions, time relations, character, and narration and point of view.
22   For examples of the methodologies guiding the literary approach
to 1 Sam 8-12 see Wetherill (1974). His book provides summaries and
examinations of major theories and methods in recent literary studies. Rather than supplying a summary of Wetherill's methodological
summary it seems better, at this point, to avoid further theoretical
discussion. As Wetherill suggests, the individual text must determine
the methodology that will be useful in the comprehension of its meaning and in the description of how it achieves that meaning (1974:
248). Since the object of this study is the interpretation of a specific narrative rather than a general theory of biblical narrative, a
detailed discussion of methodology would be aprioristic with respect
to 1 Sam 8-12, and redundant and superficial in view of Wetherill's
and others' metacritical studies.

NOTES TO CHAPTER TWO

DEFINING THE LITERARY UNIT

1   For example, although most modern scholars agree that the so-
called 'Court History of David' (2 Sam 9-20, 1 Kgs 1-2) is a unit
(e.g. Fohrer 1968:222), it is divided in the Bible between the books

of Samuel and Kings. On the other hand, we find, e.g., the collocation of three literary units - the three Isaiahs - in the single book
of Isaiah.

2   This delimitation was classically formulated by Wellhausen
(1899:240f, 1973:24). Although there have been differences amongst
scholars on the boundaries of the narrative - some beginning with ch.
7 (e.g., citing only periodical literature, Ben-Barak 1979, Clements
1974, Langlamet 1970, Mayes 1978, Robertson 1944, Seebass 1965) and
others with ch. 8 (Fritz 1976, McCarthy 1973, Press 1938, Thornton
1967, Tsevat 1980, Wildberger 1957) - there is agreement, however,
that 1 Sam 1-6 (7) are not to be included in the narrative.

3   When chs. 13-5 are included, the theme becomes more specifically the inauguration of Saul's kingship and his subsequent rejection.

4   Rost's study (1926) offers detailed exemplification of stylistic analysis used to support this thematic division. For 1 Sam 4:1b-
7.1, see especially p. 11ff. [= 1982 English transl.: 14-26]

5   Miller and Roberts (1977:20) rejected Willis's literary pattern. Willis replied in a lively polemical rebuttal albeit with
reduced claims of pervasiveness for the convention in biblical narrative (1979:212). In my opinion, Willis's reading remains the more
valid even with the smaller comparative basis for the pattern. The
reading of Miller and Roberts suffers from excessive trimming of
textual data to get a 'text' (1 Sam 2.12-7, 22-5, 27-36; 4.1b-7.1 [Mil-
ler & Roberts 1977:60f]) that fits their explanatory frame. (See
Willis 1979 for extensive criticism of Miller and Roberts on this
issue, esp. 204-7). Even if Willis's literary pattern were evident
only in 1 Sam 1-7, it would still be valid as a logical frame for the
interpretation of the narrative because he meets the first two of
Perry's considerations on frame construction.

6   The question of the historicity of the events is not at issue
here. My concern is only to analyse and describe the text and what it
makes of the events it relates.

7   Samuel himself describes the move towards monarchy as a 'turning aside' out of the path of ordained theocratic politics (1 Sam
12.21).

8   Polzin (1980) proposes to do a literary study of the
deuteronomistic history in two volumes. Obviously he neither intends,
nor is it possible for anyone, to deal with all the individual
exegetical problems posed by the history. Such detailed analysis,
however, is my aim for this study of 1 Sam 1-12.

9   McCarter notes that the use of the word *tešû'â* in 11.13
links the victory over the Ammonites with the pre-monarchic acts of
deliverance via the judges (1980:203f). This link stresses that
regardless of the human agent, deliverance always comes from Yahweh.

NOTES TO CHAPTER THREE

SUMMARY OF THE NARRATIVE

1   The phrase *la'amod lipnê* is also used in covenants of grant
to describe the loyal service of a servant, which is rewarded by a
grant (Weinfeld 1970:185f). In the Bible the phrase occurs several
times in the context of covenantal obedience or priestly service to
Yahweh. In Ezra 9, the Israelite returnees have broken the command-
ment 'by the prophets' (cf. Lev 18.24-30; Deut 7.3) not to intermarry
with non-Israelites. Ezra says, 'Behold we are before thee in our
guilt, for none can stand before thee because of this' (9.15). In
Deut 4.10, the people stand before Yahweh to hear his words and to
learn to fear him. The words that Yahweh speaks are his covenant -
the ten words (v. 13). The priestly service, described as standing before Yahweh, is another aspect of Israel's total covenantal obligation
to Yahweh as 2 Chr 29.10f shows. Hezekiah, wishing to renew the covenant with Yahweh, asks the Levites who have been chosen to stand
before Yahweh as servants (cf. Deut 10.8; 18.5, 7) to be diligent.
2   The question, 'To whom will he/it go from upon us' (6.20), is
pointedly ambiguous, including both Yahweh and his infernal ark.
3   The problematic individuals in both families are the sons and
not the aged fathers, who by implication are too old to keep a tight
rein on their sons' activities. Eli is never accused of active wrong-
doing but is implicated in his sons' sinfulness because he has not
put a stop to their activities (2.29; 3.13).
4   It was essential for both priest and judge, the mediators of
the covenant relationship, to be without sin. The priest represents
Yahweh to man (oracle, ordeal, instruction, blessing and cursing) and
man to Yahweh (sacrifice), (Fohrer 1972:212; cf. Ringgren 1966:204-
10; de Vaux 1965:357). The judge was the official agent to whom the
Israelites brought their cases (Exod 18.13-22, cf. de Vaux 1965:151-
3). Judges were supposed to be God-fearing, trustworthy, and haters
of bribes (Exod 13.21). They not only arbitrated legal disputes, but
also represented the people before God, taught them the statutes and
decisions, and how they were to behave (Exod 18.19f; cf. Samuel's
role as judge described in 1 Sam 7.3, 6, 15-7; 8.10; 10.25; 12.3
(possible abuses of the judgeship), 7, 20-5).
5   The fourfold repetition of 'my people' (*'ammî*) in 9.16f
emphasizes that Yahweh still claims Israel as his covenantal people;
cf. Buber 1956:128.
6   The point of the note, 'and with him went men of valour whose
hearts God had touched' is not, as Buber notes against Budde, to
describe the establishment of a royal court or bodyguard (1956:148).
The expression 'they went with him' (*wayyelekû 'immô*) connotes
more than mere physical accompaniment. In several occurrences, the
idiom is used for Yahweh's covenantal presence with his elect (Exod
33.16; Lev 26.21ff.; Deut 20.4; 31.6; 2 Sam 7.9; Mic 6.8; 1 Chr 17.8;
cf. Helfmeyer 1978:395). Several other occurrences describe a league

between individuals (Num 10.32; Judg 4.8; 11.8; 1 Sam 30.23; Job 31.5; 34.8). Amos, though he does not use the expression, states the principle: 'Do two walk together, unless they have made an appointment?' (3.3).

NOTES TO CHAPTER FOUR: PART ONE

1 SAMUEL 1

1   McCarter notes that the LXX reading is disjunctive, marking the beginning of an entirely new narrative. He cites Job 1.1 as a parallel example. One might just as easily say that the LXX reading is an accommodation to the beginning of other biblical books. Neither genetic explanation would understand either MT or LXX. Interestingly enough, McCarter observes that the LXX reading supports his traditio-historical hypotheses about the prehistory of the text. He makes this observation in a section of his commentary supposedly devoted to textual criticism. Whether it is MT or LXX that is the 'correct reading,' a thing that will never be certain, it is certain that the decisions of text criticism are better made without the influence of traditio-historical hypotheses.

2   Driver's long excursus on the secondary status of the dual ending and the topographical features of Samuel's village (1913:2), though of interest from the theoretical perspective of historical geography, is unnecessarily complex from a literary perspective. An awareness of the poetic parallelism in the genealogy provides a pleasantly parsimonious literary explanation of the dual ending. Needless to say, the literary explanation neither rules out alternatives from other perspectives, nor does it need their agreement. It is a self-sufficient way of looking at biblical narrative. In addition, both E. Robertson (1944:180f) and Aharoni (1979:210) supply geographical arguments that support the dual ending.

3   The names appear elsewhere primarily in Chronicles in various genealogical lists from different periods. Even in these lists they are names of unimportant persons. The occurrences are: (1) *yeroham* - Neh 11.12; 1 Chr 6.12, 19; 8.27; 9.8, 12; 12.27; 27.22; 2 Chr 23.1. (2) *'elîhû'* - 1 Chr. 12.21 [Eng:20]; 26.7; 27.18; and the book of Job. (3) *sûp* - 1 Chr 6.20.

4   The genealogy of Jesus in the gospel of Luke (3.23-38) provides another example of this reversal of the usual function of linear genealogies (Wilson 1979:21).

5   The motif of two wives, one barren and one fertile, usually with the barren wife being favoured over the fertile, is prominent in the patriarchal narratives; see Hauge 1975; J.G. Williams 1980.

6   The textual difficulty produced by the word *'appayim* in v. 5 can be relieved by a philogically and contextually defensible reading suggested by Wellhausen (1871:36) and developed by Driver (1913: 7f). Based on LXXB *plen hoti*, the problematic *'appayim* is read *'epes* and, with the following *kî*, translated 'howbeit.' The

sense of the verse with the emendation is that although Elkanah loved Hannah, he could only give her one portion because Yahweh had
sealed her womb (cf., however, Aberbach 1974:350-3; Deist 1977:
205-9).

7   McCarter's suggestion that MT is expansive by including her
daughters is arbitrary (1980:51). The point of saying 'and all her
sons and daughters' is to emphasize the vexation to Hannah. The sons
and daughters are multiple and they are specifically Peninnah's (3rd
fem. sing. pronominal suffixes).

8   Dhorme labels the repetition in v. 6 as a gloss, simply because it repeats the end of v. 5 (1910:19). Repetition has since been
recognized as an important stylistic device in biblical literature
e.g. Muilenburg 1953:97-111.

9   McCarter's objection to the Wellhausen/Driver solution to 'appayim in v. 5 is that it is contextually unsuitable. It assumes that
Elkanah gives Hannah only one portion thereby leaving Peninnah's
rancor in v. 6 unexplained (1980:52). He suggests that Peninnah's
rancor can be explained by reading 'appayim as kĕpîm, 'prop-
ortionate to them, equal to them,' and understanding that Peninnah
is retaliating on account of Hannah's preferential treatment. The
Wellhausen/Driver reading is, however, perfectly suited to the context and provides a better understanding of Hannah's vociferation in
v. 6. She not only gets a smaller share of the sacrifice because of
her sterility, but is also subject to Peninnah's scorn. Peninnah,
characterized as both the second wife and Hannah's rival, needs no
excuse to vex Hannah; rather Hannah's barrenness and consequent
single portion of the sacrifice provide a prime opportunity for
Peninnah to rub it in.

10   The additional note about Hannah's drinking, 'and after
drinking' (we'aḥarê šatoh) is grammatically anomalous (GKC #113e
n.3) and usually seen as a gloss (Stoebe 1973:91; McCarter 1980:
53). Even if retained it changes nothing. It is difficult to understand why a glossator would add such an anomalous and irrelevant
detail, though. Perhaps it was intended as a small piece of scenic
background by whoever included it.

11   The possibility that the gaps in 4QSama may support LXXB is
insufficient reason to follow the variant, even if the combined versional voice does represent an independent witness and not simply
an amplification of MT (cf. Driver 1913:13; Johnson 1976/77:134).
MT makes sense as it stands and so from a literary point of view,
there is no reason to add or subtract anything. Neither is there any
compulsion to compare variants in order to see what difference the
variant would make to the meaning of the text in such a case. Greenberg suggests that although there is no logical basis for choosing
one version over another when they both make sense, a comparison
of the divergencies, each read in its own context, provides a powerful heuristic resource that can alert us to the particular focus of
each version (1977:140).

  Greenberg does unquestionably demonstrate the heuristic value
of the comparative exercise. But there is a danger here that each

version may be understood and explained according to its distinction from the other. This method of elucidating a text concentrates on a distinctive feature, which is only especially distinctive in view of the other version. Thereby that specific textual feature is given more prominence than it would have had viewed only within its own context (cf. Ellis 1974:116-8). To avoid this danger, and Greenberg is aware of it, it seems better to leave such comparisons aside until a complete interpretation of the narrative has been made. Or if comparison must be made, no special importance should be attributed to LXX or any other version, if our purpose is simply to highlight the text under study. As Wellek and Warren suggest, 'the same end may well be achieved by devising for ourselves alternatives, whether or not they have actually passed through the author's mind' (cit. in Mowatt 1958/59:217f).

12   Although, as Parker states, it is clear from the context that Hannah desires a boy (*ûnetattîw, 'al-ro'šô*) (1979:694; cf. Hertzberg 1964:25), McCarter is correct to reject the translation of *zera' 'anašîm* as male child/offspring (1980:61). The expression occurs only here, where is stands in explicit opposition to the Nazirite whom Hannah gives back to God.

13   Nowack denies that the uncut hair alludes to an association of the future child with the Nazirite life. Instead, he says it was the custom of the priests to leave their hair uncut, citing Ezek 44.20 as an example (1902:5). As Cooke notes, however, the context implies that the reference in Ezek 44 is to the custom of cutting the hair as a sign of mourning. This practise was associated with non-Israelite religious practises and so was prohibited (1936:485; cf. Lev 21.5f; Deut 14.1). The fact that Hannah is making a vow also supports the connection with the Nazirites, who according to Num 6.2 become Nazirites by making a vow, *lindor neder*.

14   Note Hertzberg's response to Hannah. 'Hannah's modest reply so obviously bears the stamp of truth that Eli believes her completely . . .' (1964:25).

15   That the narrative notes Hannah's pregnancy only after the passage of due time may indicate that pregnancy is judged by external appearances rather than the cessation of menstruation.

16   Ellis argues that to go back to prior contexts or usages of a literary document is a contradictory reversal of the process that resulted in the literary work. '. . . to put back all that the poet thought was irrelevant and therefore left out is to destroy the structure of the finished work by virtue of which it has its artistic imact and meaning; that meaning was created precisely by the selective opertion that so many critics seem to be at pains to reverse and remove' (1974:114). Applying these remarks to the case of Samuel's name and its explanation one could agree with the hypothesis that the explanation is well-suited to the name of Saul and yet maintain that the interpretation of the *actual* connection between the explanation of the name Samuel must take precedence as the first concern of readers. Similar observations are made by Childs 1979:75-7.

17   According to Haran, there is no difference between the two

times and sacrifices of vv. 3 and 21; both mean 'the yearly sacrifice' (1978:304-7; cf. Newman 1962:88). Haran cites Exod 13.10; Judg 11.40; 21.19 as support for translating *miyyamîm yamîmû* 'from year to year.' As employed in 1 Sam 1.3 he says it is an event that occurs once a year. But both Exod 13.10 and Judg 11.40 include additional temporal determinants, without which it is not clear that *miyyamîm yamîmû* designates any specific or limited occurrence. Neither is it clear that the *hag* in Judg 21.19 is a once-a-year affair.

The evidence, however, is ambiguous, as Boling's interpretation shows. He reverses Haran's hypothesis, and uses 1 Sam 1.3 to identify the *hag* in Judg 21.19 as the 'important yearly celebration at Shiloh' (1975:293)! Haran deduces the existence of a yearly sacrifice from 1 Sam 1 (esp. v. 21), held once annually. For *yamîm* meaning 'year' he cites Lev 25.29f; Judg 17.10; 19.2.

The occurrence in Lev 25 should not be translated 'year'; the word *yamîm* is set in an appositional explanatory clause that emphasizes the multiplicity of opportunities for redemption of a residence in a walled city. *yamîm* is balanced against *'ad tom šenat*. The use of *yamîm* (pl.) has rhetorical value that is lost when understood simply as synonymic with *šenat*, 'year.'

Judges 17.10 is ambiguous and in 19.2 Haran arbitrarily inserts a 'waw' copulative before *yamîm*, without which there is no reason to translate 'year' (Haran 1978:306 n. 28) (BDB, p. 399, suggests no occurrence of *yamîm* that should be translated a 'year.' Most occurrences actually capitalize on the plurality of the word.)

18   *Ka'ašer* is used similarly to note the fulfillment of promises many times throughout Deuteronomy, e.g. 1.3, 11, 19, 41; 2.1, 14; 4.5; 5.12, 16, 32; 6.3, 19, 25, etc.

19   The reading 'a three year old bull' instead of 'three bulls' is accepted by most commentators, e.g. Driver 1913:20f; Stoebe 1973:99. It is required by the context in v. 25 where a single bull is slaughtered (*'et-happar*; cf. Thenius 1864:8). 'MT *bprym šlš* shows a simple corruption, the *m* grouped with the wrong word' (McCarter 1980:56f).

20   Ehrlich offers the entertaining suggestion that 'the verbs are plural and their subjects undetermined on account of the bull, which Hannah could not lead' (1910:168).

21   The rhetoric of repetition is discussed by Brown 1957; Chatman 1978:78f; Fogle 1974:699-701; Forster 1976:146-50; Genette 1980:113-60; Hartmann 1979 (esp. pp. 4-30); Leech and Short 1981: 257-9.

22   Hylander provides a summary of the discussion of the topic prior to his study, 1932:13 n.1.

23   LXX omits this sentence in 1.28, placing it in 2.11 where MT has Elkanah, rather than Hannah, going home to Ramathah.

24   Keil and Delitzsch hold this view, but for different reasons (1880:28).

NOTES TO CHAPTER FOUR: PART TWO

1 SAMUEL 2

1   Archaic features in the song of Hannah allow only the conclusion that the poem contains certain features of early poetry. Arch-
aizing cannot be ruled out (cf. D.A. Robertson 1972:147f). Even if
an acceptable date could be suggested for the song on the basis of
the proposals of Albright and his followers (cf. Robertson 1972:6;
Willis 1973:140 n.10; Cross and Freedman 1975; McCarter 1980:75f),
it would say nothing about the putative redactional status of the
song. Whether it be early or late, dating cannot answer the questions
of who put the song in ch. 2, and when he did it. If a certain dating
of the narrative context could be determined, then it might be possible to say that the song is redactional - but only if its date were
later than that of the prose context.
2   The syntactic patterning should also indicate to the redaction
critic that the song has not simply been inserted.
3   The connection between B and B' could be further strengthened
assonantally, if the reading of LXX and OL was adopted, as most
scholars do (e.g. Wellhausen, Smith, Driver, Hertzberg, Stoebe,
McCarter): *ramû qarnî be'lohay (!)/ raḥab pî 'al-'ôyebay*
As Willis notes, however, MT is representative of the repetitive
style often seen in early Hebrew and Ugaritic poetry (1973:143f),
and so can be read as is.
4   Ps 18.3 is a particularly interesting parallel since it also
shares both the vocabulary and the conceptual framework of 1 Sam
2.1f.
5   Cf. Zeph 3.11 where *'alilôt* are the rebellious acts of the
proud against Yahweh.
6   Reading *welô* with the Qere.
7   An alternative explanation in terms of class conflicts and
revolution is offered by Gottwald 1979:534-40.
8   Again, the parallel in vocabulary between 1 Sam 2.4 and Ps
18.33 illustrates that Hannah's song expresses a common belief:

> 1 Sam 2.4   *wenikšalîm 'azrû ḥayil*
> Ps 18.33   *ha'el ham'azzerenî ḥayil*

Both passages show the beneficial side of Yahweh's power and incomparability.
9   On the meaning of v. 5b see McCarter 1980:72.
10   Gottwald errs in restricting the poem's critique of human self-
sufficiency to the social elite of Canaan (1979:537f). Nor is it
correct to say, as Gottwald does, that the poem 'hails the elevation
of the poor and destitute to the status of communal leaders and to
the full exercise of sovereign self-rule' (1979:535). The poem is
directed against all expressions of self-sufficiency pointing instead
to Yahweh's graciousness to the helpless and submissive. It is difficult to read a poem that downgrades human ability - 'the warrior's
bows are shattered' (v. 4), and 'a man does not become mighty by

strength' (v. 9) - as revolutionary ideology. The poem exalts only
Yahweh's ability and willingness to rescue the defenseless. The
contrasts are not between people of different nations, or social
classes, but between the humble dependant of Yahweh and the proud,
self-sufficient human.

11   Other occurrences of this metonymic usage of *'apsê-'areṣ*
are Isa 45.22 and Ps 22.28. See Hamp's discussion, 1977:362. On
reading *'alaw* as a divine name in v. 10b see Barr 1968:283.

12   The demand for a human king in 8.5, 20 is not a response resulting from a perception of God's feebleness or incompetence. Rather it
is made in the knowledge of Yahweh's apparently unpredictable and,
therefore, unreliable behaviour when the covenant mediators are sinful (cf. 2.22-5, the resulting disaster in ch. 4, and the note preceding the request (8.1-3), which shows a relapse to the dangerous situation of sinful mediators).

13   This contrast has been discussed often, e.g. Bourke 1954:
82ff.; Hertzberg 1964:34; Willis 1971:289-94; 1972:38; 1979: 208
n.29; Péter-Contesse 1976:313.

14   Samuel acts as though he were a Levite, ministering to Yahweh
before Eli the priest (cf. Num 3.5-13; 8.19, 26; 11.28; Deut 18.7).
The Elides, on the other hand, do not act as the priests they are
supposed to be.

15   The rhetorical effect of narrative exposition is discussed by
Booth 1961; Chatman 1978:228-48; and Sternberg 1978.

16   Two other possible alternatives have been suggested for interpreting vv. 13f. Smith reads the *mišpaṭ hakkohanîm* as object of
the verb in v. 12 (as in LXX), suggesting that vv. 13f describe
cultic abuse (1899:18). Driver, following Wellhausen, also sees vv.
13f as examples of cultic abuse, but reads v. 13 disjunctively from
v. 12, as in MT (1913:29). The interpretation proposed here is not
claimed to be superior to Driver's, but simply accounts for the verse
from a different perspective. Smith's proposal, as well as any other
that follows LXX instead of MT, deals with a different text and so,
a different narrative.

17   The accusative particle here depends on an implicit verbal idea
contained in the preceding context (GKC #117). It also serves to call
attention to the parallel between vv. 12 and 13.

18   In conjunction with the decision to read v. 13 with v. 12 (e.g.
Hertzberg 1964:32, 34) it has been suggested, following LXX, that
the final *m* of *hakkohanîm* should be read with the following
'et as *me'et*. 'They knew not Yahweh, or the right (i.e. the rightful due) of *the priest from* the people' (cit. in Driver 1913:29).
Cf. Stoebe (1973:108) who suggests simply a haplography of *m*. The
chiasmus in MT argues against these emendations.

19   According to Wellhausen the *gam* at the beginning of v. 15
requires that vv. 13f be seen as cultic abuses. 'But since this
(verse) intensifies in the same manner vv. 13f cannot be set against
vv. 15f as right versus wrong; rather, both are counted as abuses of
authority with one being more serious than the other' (1871:44). It
is quite possible, however, to read the *gam* of v. 15 asseveratively

in connection with the priestly lack of patience to wait for Yahweh
to get his share (cf. R. J. Williams 1976:63 #379; GKC #153). When
v. 15 is not seen as a *further* abuse, then, as Wellhausen says,
vv. 13f appear as the customary practice of the priests at that
time.

20   Willis (1972:55) suggests that the priests desecrated the
sacrifice in three ways: taking from the cooking pots what was not
voluntarily given (vv. 13f), claiming choice portions of raw flesh
(v. 15), and intervening before Yahweh got his share (v. 15). The
fact that the priest refuses boiled meat seems to suggest that that
is what was offered to the priest. At best, the receipt of uncooked
as opposed to boiled meat is only a subsidiary issue. In fact, the
priest's desire for raw meat seems more a means of revealing his
character and the reason for his impatience to get his due. Nowhere
is the prohibition against eating on the blood (cf. Gen 9.4; Lev
19.26; Deut 12.16) brought to bear, as one would expect if that were
at issue.

21   In Ps 10.3f, it is also the hybris-filled man who rejects
(*ni'eṣ*) Yahweh. He glories in the desires of his soul (*ta'awat
napšô*). Similarly the priest's servants take whatever they desire
(1 Sam 2.16, *ka'ašer te'awweh napšeka*), and the narrator tells us
that they contemned (*ni'aṣû*) Yahweh's offering. In both cases,
the attitude of self-help is exactly that criticized in Hannah's
song.

22   See above on 1.21 for my reading of *zebaḥ hayyamîm* in this
narrative.

23   The exact meaning of the verb *pll* is as yet undertermined.
For surveys of opinions see de Ward 1976, 1977; Houtman 1977. For
present purposes, however, the context suggests an act of judging
and mediation that lessens the severity of punishment inflicted on
the sinner.

24   Tsevat can list only four instances, including 1 Sam 2.25,
in which failure to repent of sin is traced to divine agency (1964:
357 nn.5-9). He suggests that the explanation of human folly by divine coercion is one extreme in the spectrum of biblical responses
to the problems of unrepentant sinners (pp. 355-8).

25   According to Willis, v. 25 suggests that Eli's sons 'refused
to listen to him because he had not behaved so as to command their
respect' (1971:292). Again, he bases this reading, which contradicts
the plain sense of the text, on 3.13, which states that Eli failed to
rebuke/restrain them (*welo' kihâ bam*), and on 2.29, which states
that Eli honours his sons more than Yahweh. Clearly these last two
verses contradict 2.25, according to which Eli had no chance of
persuading his sons because Yahweh had already predetermined their
response (cf. Smith 1899:20; Press 1938:178f).

The historical-critical solution to such contradictions is com-
mendable in that it admits them, instead of harmonizing them by favouring one at the expense of the other. Press sees 2.22ff., 2.29,
and 3.13 as all contradictory and concludes that, 'that leads to the
supposition that three different hands have worked on 1 Sam 1-3'

(1938:179).

It is, nevertheless, possible and even necessary to relate the two supposedly contradictory views, or better voices, by paying careful attention to two important facets of all narrative, namely the temporal ordering or structure, and the voice structure, as suggested above on v. 23. Attention to these parameters of the narrative puts the conflict into proper perspective as a difference of opinion between the narrator and one of his characters, Yahweh.

26   The three aforementioned keys are: 1. the divine initiative in Samuel's birth; 2. the unquestionable sin of Eli's sons; and 3. the undisputed innocence of the Israelite people.

27   Most commentators follow LXX and now 4 QSama, and insert 'abadîm after bemiṣrayim. Haplography caused by homoioteleuton is the suggested cause of corruption (e.g. Wellhausen 1871:48; McCarter 1980:87). As it stands, though, MT stresses the fact of belonging; the house of Eli's father belonged to Pharoah in Egypt. The revelation came to them in that state and by implication freed them to become priests to Yahweh.

28   The exact meaning of 'iššê is disputed. From LXX on, the term has been translated as 'offering made by fire,' but modern exegetes have suggested that it could mean 'oblation' (Hamp 1977: 424; McCarter 1980:90, citing Hoftijzer 1967:114-34). Whatever the exact meaning of the word, the point is that the priests are granted one specific type of sacrifice or offering as payment for their services.

29   The standard treaty form is discussed by K. Baltzer 1964; McCarthy 1978.

30   As Driver, among others, notes ma'ôn is 'untranslateable' (1913:37). Seebass suggests that we repoint to me'awon reading 'um der Schuld willen' (1966:77). On the causative use of min see GKC #119z. On 'awon as the object of expiation by sacrifice and offering see 3.14.

31   Eli's participation is implied by the 2nd pers. pl. suffix in lehabrî'akem, 'to fatten yourselves.'

32   On the meaning of yithallekû see Keil and Delitzsch 1880: 42; McCarter 1980:90.

33   Cf. McCarter, 'the author is quoting or paraphrasing a traditional maxim' (1980:90).

34   Ruhl has constructed the following algorithm to describe the reading procedures commonly used (by all except historical-critics) to make sense of discourse, including narrative:

If a structure A-and-B can be analyzed as a temporal sequence, it will be. If it can be further analyzed that A is a precondition for B, it will be. And if A can be analyzed as a decisive condition - that is, a cause - for B, it will be. Only if the first stage - the temporal sequence - is not reached, will the co-ordinate structure be analyzed as symmetric (cit. in Pratt 1977:156).

The almost total annihilation of the Elide house in ch. 4 should, according to Ruhl's algorithm, be identified by most readers as the temporal and causal result of the word of God presented in v. 31.

35   Cf. Deut 8.16; 28.63; and 30.5 for further examples of *ytb*
construed with the accusative of person (Keil & Delitzsch 1880:43).
36   Tsevat comes close to suggesting a similar reading of 2.27-36:

> It would not be unreasonable to assume that it is the intention
> of the story of the house of Eli as part of the book of Samuel
> to lead up to the destruction of Shiloh and the capture of the
> ark, to indicate, that, far beyond bringing *kareth* upon their
> family and damaging the institution of the priesthood, the sons
> of Eli brought about national disaster. This assumption, how-
> ever, is not substantiated in the text. Nowhere are the cata-
> strophe of Aphek and Shiloh and the long years of Philistine
> rule over Israel traced in any way, however, devious, to the
> conduct of the Elides (1961:207).

His rejection of the type of reading suggested here for v. 32 cannot
be regarded as well founded in view of the foreshadowing and explicit prophecies of the deaths of Eli's sons (2.25, 34; 4.11). The Israelite defeat is Yahweh's means of killing Eli's sons. We know from 2.25
that Yahweh planned to kill Eli's sons, and from chs. 5f we know that
he was responsible for the Israelite defeat in which they were killed. Tsevat's original intuition is quite reasonable and need not be
called an assumption in view of evidence such as v. 32.
37   The verb *yatab* in the Hiphil is also associated with Israelite military success in Deut 6.18f.
38   Modern commentators in favour of reading vv. 33, 35f in this
way include Budde 1902:21f; Nowack 1902:17; Dhorme 1910:41; Driver
1913:39f; Schulz 1919:52f; Stoebe 1973:117-20; McCarter 1980:87-93.
Others see the supposed references to Abiathar in v. 33 and to Zadok
in v. 35 only as uncertain possibilities (Smith 1899: 23; Hertzberg
1964:38; Mauchline 1971:55; Miller & Roberts 1977: 30).
39   From a typological perspective the identifications of the faithful priest of v. 35 as Samuel (Thenius 1864:15), Zadok (McCarter
1980:92f), 'Theodoret and the Rabbins,' [Keil & Delitzsch 1880:45]),
or Christ (Keil and Delitzsch 1880:47; Gutbrod 1956:30f) are all
valid possibilities.
40   Cf. Michaels who makes the same point using examples from both
legal and literary interpretations. '. . . plain meanings are functions not of texts but of the situations in which we read them' (1979:
33).
41   For *la'adib* we must read *leha'adib* for a grammatically correct text (Driver 1913:39). There is no need to change the suffixes
on the two infinitive constructs to the 3rd masc. sing. The idea of a
man who will continue in the Elides' place at the altar is supposed
to cause Eli severe mental anguish.
42   On the subject of Samuel's multiple roles see McKenzie 1962:3-
18. McKenzie attempts to find the 'real,' historical Samuel lying behind the traditions. He tentatively suggests that the real Samuel is
the leader of the sons of the prophets, as seen in 1 Sam 10 (p. 16).
      As in the case of Moses, however, it is likely that Samuel's
multiple roles should not be regarded as contradictory. Whether the

contradiction is seen in historical terms, or in terms of tradition history is irrelevant. Buber's comments on Moses are equally applicable to Samuel:

> It is true that the way in which he receives the revelation is largely prophetical . . . but his activity in history, as leader of the people, as legislator, is what separates him in character from all the bearers of prophecy known to us. For this reason Moses likewise cannot be comprehended merely as a combination of priest and prophet; moreover, he is not to be comprehended at all within any exclusively 'religious' categories. What constitutes his idea and his task: the realization of the unity of religious and social life in the community of Israel, the substantiation of a ruling by God that shall not be culturally restricted but shall comprehend the entire existence of the nation, the theo-political principle; all this has penetrated to the deeps of his personality, it has raised his person above the compartmental system of typology, it has mingled the elements of his soul into a most rare unity (1958:186).

NOTES TO CHAPTER FOUR: PART THREE

1 SAMUEL 3

1   Cf. above on 1 Sam 2, n.34, and Pratt 1977:156 on Ruhl's algorithm.

2   Stoebe argues that *bimqômô* is a general expression and does not intend to indicate a deviation from correct priestly practise on Eli's part (1973:123). He suggests that if Eli's resting place was supposed to be emphasized, it would have been put more clearly. The contrast is clear, though, between Eli in his place and Samuel in Yahweh's temple, and it is supported by its agreement with the other contrasts noted in vv. 1f. Eli may not be breaking any rules, but neither does he shine when compared with Samuel, as he is in these verses.

3   On the symbolism of the lamp see Funk and Ben-Dor 1962:64; Keel 1978:188f.

4   The first time reader would not be able to appreciate the significance of this mention of the ark. Its appreciation is reserved as a private irony between the narrator and the retrospective reader, who, like Buber and Stoebe, see it as a harbinger of the disaster about to be revealed to and through Samuel. The inability of a first reading to see this meaning is not a point against it, but rather, should be taken to show that scripture is amenable to retrospective reading.

5   Cf. 2 Kgs 21.12; Jer 19.3, where ear-buzzing events are also catastrophes of a national proportion. 'A great misfortune will, therefore, befall the people of Israel' (Schulz 1919:62).

6   The verb *kihû*, translated here as 'rebuke,' poses a problem. McCarter says this translation cannot be right in view of

2.22-5. He suggests, with Freedman, a relationship to *kahâ* 'be weak' (v. 2) - thus *kihâ*, 'weaken, repress, restrain' (1980:98). This reading, however, does little to alleviate the dilemma. Eli's rebuke in 2.22-5 can also be seen as an attempt to restrain his sons. The reader knows from 2.25 that nothing short of death can restrain Eli's sons. Is Yahweh judging Eli because he did not kill his sons himself? The uncertainty about the meaning of *kihâ* prevents a certain answer.

One might posit a textual corruption in *kihâ*, as a result of metathesis (cf. Ehrlich 1910:180). Originally, the verb might have been *hikkâ*, resulting in a known idiom, 'He did not slay them.' (For other occurrences of *nkh* with a direct object modified by *b* see 1 Sam 18.7; 21.12; 29.5; 1 Kgs 20.35; cf. Jer 5.6.) This reading would solve the dilemma. Yahweh would be justified, as Eli did not try to kill his sons. Since MT is conceivable, however, this emendation is only an entertaining speculation.

7   Cf. above on 2.29 and Seebass 1966:77 for discussion of this pointing of *m'wn*.

8   Most recent scholars agree with Wellhausen (1871:53) that *wayyaškem babboqer*, 'he rose in the morning,' should be added, with LXX, after 'he lay down until morning.' This concretization of an indeterminacy (cf. Iser 1978:170-80) is possible but unnecessary, since MT already has *'ad-habboqer*. The preposition implies that the action of the verb ends at morning. The reader does not require the explicitness of LXX to understand that Samuel got up.

9   Cf. Gutbrod (1956:34f) who expresses doubts about the contextual suitability of a pious reply on Eli's lips.

10   The rhetoric of ambiguity is discussed by Rimmon-Kenan 1980/81:185-8 and J. H. Miller 1980/81:189-91. Rimmon-Kenan describes ambiguity as the co-existence of mutually exclusive readings that frustrate the reader's expectation of a univocal, definitive meaning (p. 186).

11   Both Budde (1902:29), and Stoebe (1973:126) suggest that 'his words' (*debarayw*) are God's, not Samuel's. In view of the fact that Samuel does pass them on both to Eli and later to Israel (4.1), it is more likely that the words are Samuel's and Yahweh's, since they originate from Yahweh. Also v. 20, containing Israel's recognition of Samuel's prophetic accuracy, requires a reason for this recognition. What could be more suitable than the immediately preceding reference to the veracity of Samuel's words? Cf. Hertzberg 1964:42.

12   Jepsen discusses the problem of translating *ne'eman* in his article in *TDOT* 1 (1977:296).

13   Seebass regards the portrait of Samuel as a prophet as a superimposition that contradicts the preceding tradition (1967:164 n.40). In that tradition (3.1-18), Samuel's familiarity with Yahweh's word is associated with his cultic duties under Eli (cf. Schunck 1963: 103). The two conceptions of Samuel. as priest and prophet, are products of different socio-historical circumstances according to Seebass.

In fact, Samuel has difficulty receiving the word of God in

his priestly capacity. His master, Eli, only comes to realize that God is trying to speak to Samuel after three attempts. The notice in v. 7 that Samuel did not yet know Yahweh is as much a negative reflection on Eli's tutelage as vv. 1f are on his effect on relations with Yahweh. Hence, Samuel's intimacy with the divine word is not so much connected with his situation amongst the priests in Shiloh as it is in spite of that association. Neither is Samuel's prophetic role necessarily in conflict with his priestly role.

Samuel performs several roles in chs. 1-12. Like Moses, Samuel is one of the great figures of mediation in Israelite literature. It would be surprising if he were not portrayed as a great priest, prophet, judge and seer. Verse 20 says only that Samuel was recognized as a reliable prophet, not that he was no longer a priest (cf. Peter-Contesse 1976:314).

14   Textual emendations and reconstructions abound for v. 21 (see Stoebe 1973:123 for a selection). Noth correctly observes, however, that 'a sufficient reason for an emendation does not exist: therefore it is methodologically requisite to stick with the given wording' (1963:399).

NOTES TO CHAPTER FOUR: PART FOUR

1 SAMUEL 4

1   Mauchline suggests that 4.1b introduces a sudden change of subject. Chs. 1-3 are concerned with the Elides, Shiloh, and Samuel; chs. 4-6 are concerned with politics, the Philistine war, and the national emergency (1971:69). But he has missed the connection between the two episodes, which are only superficially separate. (Cf. Gutbrod, who seems unable to decide how to view the connection between chs. 1-3 and 4-6 (1956:38).) They are linked not only by the theme of priestly sin and its consequent punishment, but also, and to a much greater extent, by the probing of Israel's theological-political order. In chs. 2f, Israel is troubled by the priests, who irresponsibly abuse the sacrificial system, thereby interfering in the regular process of atonement necessary for normal covenantal relations in the theocracy. In chs. 4-6, Israel is made to experience the retributional fruits of its priests' misdeeds in the form of a national military disaster that is interpreted as an end to the theocratic system (4.20f).

2   LXX adds 'Eli grew very old, and his sons continued to act more and more wickedly in the presence of Yahweh. In those days the Philistines gathered to make war against Israel') McCarter 1980: 102). Though the LXX reading has captured the crucial features of the Elide family situation, and though it does make a nice associative implication about the connection between the impending war with the Philistines and Yahweh's wrath at the Elide sin, it cannot be said that it is a necessary correction to any obvious deficiency in MT. LXX offers a slightly different narrative, not a 'better' one.

3   Cf. Booth 1961:154, and Dostoevsky cited by Booth (p. 168),
who explained lapses in his story 'most of all because, as I have
said before, I have literally no time or space to mention everything
that was said and done.'
4   Cf. GKC #125e.
5   The associations of the verb _wattittoš_ are discussed by
Driver (quoted in Jackson 1962:115) and Campbell 1975:59).
6   The placement of the interpretation before the description
makes use of what psychologists call the 'primary effect' (cf. Perry
1979:53). Once a semantic organization of a set of facts is established it will not be altered if subsequent input can be subsumed
within it. Hence the first description of the Israelite defeat has a
greater input into the reader's understanding of the event, and the
second can be subsumed.
7   For detailed examination see von Rad 1951; Stolz 1972; P.D.
Miller 1973; Craigie 1978.
8   Maier's simple assertion that MT [_'arôn berît yhwh_] has been
subsequently deformed and his consequent acceptance of LXX's
'arôn 'elohenû is an example of unsupported textual 'criticism'
at its worst (1965:47f; cf. Buber 1964:823 n.30, whose reason for
deleting the word 'covenant' is that it 'does not suit the elders'!).
Rather than impressionistic selection of one variant or another, the
exegete should endeavour to determine the sense of each variant. In
the case of 'the ark of the covenant of Yahweh,' the description
mentions covenant precisely because it is the covenantal issue of
Yahweh's military duties that is at issue.
9   Taking the ark as subject of the final sentence, the elders' reasoning seems less reasonable. Yahweh has already smitten them. How
can the presence of the ark save them when Yahweh has indicated his
will to defeat them? It is Yahweh who must be with the Israelites;
the ark of the covenant is only a token of his covenanted presence.
10   Schicklberger discusses the various names for the ark and
provides bibliographical information (1973:27f).
11   Although Stolz disagrees with Humbert's analysis of _terû'â_
in other respects, he agrees that it played a part in the so-called
enthronement festival and that is was a sign of Israel's positive
expectations in 1 Sam 4.5 (1972:48f).
12   The statement in v. 6 that the Philistines knew that the ark
of Yahweh had arrived in the Israelite camp is a narratorial description, not of the content of the Philistines' knowledge, but rather of
the Philistines' awareness _that_ (kî) the ark of Yahweh had come
into camp. This knowledge is deduced solely from the sound of the
terû'â. Hence the point of v. 6 is not that the Philistines
know that the ark has come amongst the Israelites, but that they are
aware of the significance of the _terû'â_. As the narrator has
them say in v. 7, the Philistines know only that 'gods have entered
the Israelite camp.'
13   The description of the ark in v. 6 (simply _'arôn yhwh_)
cannot serve as an independent witness to multiple redactions in ch.
4 (as, for example, according to Budde 1902:34). The narrator who

supplies the title as part of his own narrative commentary is concerned only to describe the Philistines' reaction to the entrance of
the ark. He uses a title which appropriately describes the ark with
respect to the Philistines - it is the ark of Yahweh, Israel's
national god.

McCarter's view that the Philistines are somehow aware of the
claim that Yahweh rides upon the ark is unsubstantiated by the text
(1980:106). The Philistines speak of these gods only generally, and,
never as Yahweh. Besides, it is the narrator who calls the ark 'the
ark of Yahweh' in v.6.

14   The Philistine view that God smote Egypt in the wilderness is
neither to be emended as incomprehensible (e.g. Wellhausen 1871:55)
nor viewed solely as a Philistine peculiarity (e.g. Keil and Delitzsch 1880:55). The mention of the wilderness, as more explicitly
that of the exodus, alludes to the saving deeds of Yahweh and the
initial covenantal experiences. The period in the wilderness (*bam-
midbar*, cf. the Hebrew title of the book of Numbers) is recalled by
the Philistines' geographical 'error' and the associations thereby
recalled to the reader are used to indicate the seriousness of Israel's predicament (cf. Jackson 1962:119). 'The people gamble with the
God of the exodus from Egypt and so with him the foundation of
their historical existence' (Timm 1966:521). While it might be
more accurate to say that Yahweh is the one who jeopardizes the
fundamentals of Israelite existence, Timm has correctly apprehended
the impact of the Philistines' reflections.

15   Ahlström observes that *'addîr* usually appears in contexts
of Yahweh's cosmological or other super-human acts (1977:74).

16   On this reading of 2.32 see the discussion above.

17   For a discussion of other passages that utilize such a man-God
contrast see Ringgren 1977:273-5.

18   Rost observes that watching (*meṣappeh*) is to be taken in a
general sense as 'waiting' or 'expecting' (1926:11f; cf. Hertzberg
1964:49). On reading the words *yad derek* as 'atop the gate,' see
McCarter 1980:114.

19   Contrary to those who would excise v. 15 as a suspicious doub-
let of v. 2 that contradicts v. 13 (e.g. McCarter 1980:111), or
those who, like Budde, would regard it as indicating another source
or redaction than that of v. 13 (1902:36), the verse is an integral,
functional, and characteristic example of this narrator's literary
technique. We have already seen several important examples of this
mirroring technique whereby the narrator offers comment upon an
item or event by providing a structural parallel to it elsewhere in
the narrative. The narrator refrains, mostly, from explicit commentary and allows these parallels and literary links to stand as sole
comment. Alter (1981) discusses other examples of this important
literary technique.

20   The messenger's name for the ark is difficult to incorporate
into the framework of previous observations on the significance of
names for the ark in ch. 4. One would expect him to voice concern
for the ark of the covenant of God/Yahweh, given his interest in the

implications of defeat for Israel. It is possible, however, that as in v. 11 'the ark of God' is used to express surprise that the symbol of God is taken by man.

21 Rozenberg, in a study of the title *šopeṭ*, suggests that it often refers generally to 'leadership' without intending further specificity (1975:78). Hence to call Eli a judge after the narrative has made him a priest is not a contradiction between the roles of the priest and 'vindicator' or 'deliverer.' Instead it suggests that both religious and political authority were exercised by Eli as mediator/judge.

22 Cf. Brockington 1962:320 who suggests that 'glory' in vv. 21-2 may anticipate its use in later writers (e.g. Ezekiel) for the concept of God's presence on earth. Cf. Ps 24.7-10.

23 Levine, citing Ginsberg's study of the usage of *kabod* as 'body, person,' suggests that although *kabod* can mean 'glory, honour,' 'in more cases than not, we should eliminate the elements of greater abstraction, so understandably evoked by divine associations, and emphasize rather the element of real presence' (1968:72 n.1). Cf. Rendtorff 1968:36f.

NOTES TO CHAPTER FOUR: PART FIVE

1 SAMUEL 5

1 Cf. Alter, 'The biblical tale might usefully be graded as a narrative experiment in the possibilities of moral, spiritual, and historical knowledge, undertaken through a process of studied contrasts between the variously limited knowledge of the human characters and the divine omniscience quietly but firmly represented by the narrator' (1981:157).

2 Further discussion of the instrumentality of foreign nations in Yahweh's dealings with Israel may be found in Zimmerli 1978:63f, 218f.

3 Detailed treatment of comparative parallels to the capture of the ark may be found in Miller and Roberts 1977, whose special concern is the theological problem raised for a nation by the capture of its gods. Rather than reciting their study, I will presuppose their work and make reference to it when necessary.

4 Discussion of the preposition *lepanayw* may be found in Delcor 1964:148; Stoebe 1973:138f; Miller and Roberts 1977:44.

5 Other biblical examples of prostration as a sign of deference are found in Gen 44.14; 50.18; Josh 5.14; 7.6; 2 Sam 9.6; 14.13, 22; 17.49; 19.19 etc.

6 Several emendations and text-critical explanations for the difficult statement that 'only Dagon was left upon him [Dagon]' have been suggested (e.g. Smith 1899:39; Stoebe 1973:139). It is possible, however, that MT is not 'meaningless' (McCarter 1980:119), and that the significance of the statement will only be understood when we have a better understanding of Dagon's physique. The verse states

that Dagon's head and the palms of his hands were cut off, and then goes on to say that only Dagon was left *on* him (*'alayw*). Perhaps Dagon, a grain god associated with the concept of fertility (Ringgren 1978:142), possessed some distinctive appendage, or anatomical feature that characterized him as the grain god. The point of noting that his hands and head were cut off, but his *dagôn* was left would be to show that he was powerless (i.e. 'palmless') even when still in possession of his distinctive feature, his *dagôn*. Tenuous as this suggestion may be, it does offer a verifiable alternative to the unprovable suggestions of emendation.

7   The literary reading of this etiology is the opposite of what Long calls the 'inferential model' prevalent in historical criticism (1968:88f). The inferential model regards the story as an answer contrived to answer a previous question. In 1 Sam 5.5, for example, the question would be, 'Why do the Philistines skip over the threshold?' The literary reading of etiology, on the other hand, seeks to understand the literary function of etiology in its existing narrative context.

8   Campbell discerns a three part pattern that is repeated three times. In order to get a three part pattern, however, he shifts 5.1 to a position immediately preceding vv. 6-8. Since 5.1 is satisfactory where it is, however, its removal and reinsertion seems dubious.

9   The participation of the so-called gloss, *'et-'ašdôd we'et-gebûleyhâ*, in the chiastic structure supports the rejection of this text-critical label on the grounds of the inherent unverifiability of such pronouncements (against e.g. Smith 1899:40; Driver 1913:52).

10   The great 'confusion' (*mehûmâ*) was the divine weapon used to defeat Israel's enemies (Deut 7.23; 1 Sam 14.15, 20, 22; McCarter 1980:106).

11   Cf. Campbell (1975:101), 'Any triumphalism in the plague stories must needs be tempered by the presence of an unspoken but menacing implication for Israel.'

12   The description of the ark as 'the ark of God' in v. 10a rather than as 'the ark of Israel's God' (vv. 7-9, 10b, 11) has been taken to indicate a separate source or tradition (e.g. Maier 1965: 48). It should be noted that the 'ark of God' in v. 10a occurs in a narrative description immediately subsequent to v. 9 in which there is an emphasis on the divine/human contrast. It may be significant, therefore, that the narrator should say that they sent the 'ark of God' away, rather than the 'ark of Israel's God.' Within ch. 5 one notes that, with the exception of a narrational element in v. 8, the 'ark of Israel's God' is used by the Philistines, for whom it is natural to speak of the ark in political terms.

13   D. Daube (1963:75) discusses this parallel in greater detail on account of the puzzling first person singular expression attributed to the Ekronites in v. 10.

14   Cf. Bourke (1954:99): 'He [the narrator] presupposes the sort of audience that would be steeped in Hebrew tradition, and that would know the story of the exodus off by heart. For such an audience the

significance of this story would emerge spontaneously (and therefore quite compellingly) from the facts themselves.'
15   It should be recalled that Yahweh's non-appearance and passivity in vv. 1-5 meet the specific rhetorical requirements of that particular 'conflict.' He effortlessly dominates Dagon without lifting so much as a finger.

NOTES TO CHAPTER FOUR: PART SIX

1 SAMUEL 6

1   Genette (1980) provides detailed analysis of narrative time relations; cf. Chatman 1978:63-84. For analysis of similar narrative prolepses in the books of Samuel see Willis 1973:294-314.
2   Cf. Milgrom's discussion of the *'ašam* case in Lev 5.17-9:

> He who suffers in body or conscience without knowing the cause suspects that he is being punished by God for trespassing on his sanctums. In this respect, ancient Israel is no different from its environment, where unconscious sanctum trespass was identified as a prime cause for divine retribution (e.g., ANET pp. 34-6, 391f) (1976:768).

Levine, in a discussion of 1 Sam 6.3, notes the appropriateness of the *'ašam* in the Philistine case. The Philistines had inadvertently trespassed on the sanctity of Yahweh's ark in the course of handling it. Although they did intend to capture and keep it, they were ignorant of its sanctity, of the proper procedure for handling it, and of the penalties for trespass. 'The *'ašam* thus emerges as a response to misfortune, when the causes of misfortune are not fully identified, and an element of uncertainty exists' (Levine 1974:94).
    The numerous emendations, literary-critical operations, and unusual readings for the second half of v. 3 are obviated by Levine's observations. (See Stoebe 1973:146; Miller and Roberts 1977:52-4; McCarter 1980:129, 133 for examples.) The priests prescibe an *'ašam* because the people know that something has to be done, but do not know what. The healing of the people after they have sent the *'ašam* will explain the plague to them because the *'ašam* is successful. The final sentence of v. 3 thus predicates the knowledge of why Yahweh's hand is against the Philistines to the successful result of the *'ašam*. The people will know how they have been healed, that is, by an *'ašam*, a sacrifice for inadvertent trespass.
3   See McCarter 1980:135 for a discussion of the correct translation of *'argaz*. Ehrlich (1902:189) offers the plausible suggestion that *'argaz* is simply a textual corruption of *'arôn*.
4   Most scholars have chosen to follow the LXX here, reading 'they rejoiced to meet it' (e.g. McCarter 1980:130, who also adds an unattested verb 'they *ran* rejoicing to meet it'). Given the flexibility of text-criticism, however, one may choose to view the LXX

reading as either 'pregnant . . . [and] so much more forcible and idiomatic' (Driver 1913:57), or as 'a free translation' (de Boer 1938:63). MT is acceptable as is, and makes good sense when *lir'ōt* is translated as a verbal noun, object of the verb *śmḥ* (cf. R.J. Williams 1976:35 #193, GKC #114m).

5 Contrary to Schulz, the double *šam* is not to be reduced to one and explained as dittography (1919:105). The narrator attracted the reader's attention to the divine cart-driver's straight path in v. 12 by multiple descriptions. Now he does the same for the choice of a final stopping place, noting by the double *šam* that the cart stops exactly where a large stone is located. As Wellhausen notes, the stopping place is important (1871:65). It indicates the cart-driver's intentions, which are correctly perceived by those Israelites in attendance in v. 14, who use the cart and cattle to offer a holocaust to Yahweh (Budde 1902:45). It is important to note at this point, however, that the text does not say that the *'olâ* was offered on the stone. Though that action is implied by the text, and inferred by most readers, it is never made an explicit part of the narrative (against Schicklberger 1973:120).

6 Contrary to Mauchline's belief, the notice about the Levites does not 'make it plain that the sacrifice was made by properly authorized persons' (1971:80; cf. Hertzberg 1964:60). The Levites are only subjects of two verbs, both of which describe actions done to the ark and box. As a matter of fact, the only persons who sacrifice at all in v. 15 are the people of Bethshemesh.

7 Discussion of the textual problems in v. 18 may be found in Driver 1913:57f; Stoebe 1973:148f; and McCarter 1980:130f.

8 On the pointing of *'d* see Stoebe 1973:148.

9 Resort to LXX is initially made because Yahweh's devastation of the Bethshemeshites on account of their looking 'on' or 'in the ark' is said to be out of tune with the preceding context (e.g. Mauchline 1971:81). LXX justifies Yahweh's slaughter on account of the sons of Jeconiah, who did not participate in the joyful reception of the ark (*kai ouk esmenisan hoi huioi iexoniou en tois andrasin baithsamys*). As Stoebe has observed, however, if Yahweh has just cause for punishing because of some wrong actions amongst those present, there is no call for the people as a whole to take exception to the punishment (1973:153; cf. Campbell 1979:38). LXX has, therefore, as much or more difficulty with the subsequent context (v. 20), as is suggested for MT and the preceding context. McCarter's ingenious adaptation of LXX is weakened in its dependence on literary-critical hypotheses about the text's pre-history in v. 15, hypotheses that are not supported by versional evidence (1980:131). In any case, the reading with LXX or an adaptation thereof is not warranted when MT is comprehensible as it is here. What is incomprehensible, as the people of Bethshemesh observe in v. 20, is Yahweh, not the text. See Driver 1913:58f, Schicklberger 1973:123-6; Stoebe 1973:149; and McCarter 1980:131 for elaboration on the possibilities of LXX.

10 Both from the preceding context (v. 13) and the usual meaning of the verb *ra'â* with the preposition *b*, it is likely that

nothing more is intended by the expression in v. 19 than that the Bethshemeshites looked at the ark. We know from v. 13 that they did look at the ark from a distance, since it had not yet stopped in the field (v. 14). We also know from v. 15 that the ark was handled only by Levites, in accordance with the prohibition against profaning the ark. Since both of these verses are pieces of narration supplied by the same narrator who gives us v. 19, it is a safe, contextually based assumption that v. 19 means 'because they looked at the ark.' From the numerous other occurences of *ra'â* with *b* it is also safe to say that the preposition functions deictically, indicating the object of perception (BDB 907 #8a-908; cf. 90 IVd; GKC #119k).

The inference made by some commentators that the expression is used in a bad sense in v. 19, signifying 'to gaze at, viz. with an unbecoming interest' (Driver 1913:58; cf. Wellhausen 1871:65f) is unsupported by a consistent occurrence of such usage elsewhere. Neither does the immediate context support such an inference.

> There is, however, no other indication that this author thought it sinful to look upon the Ark. Had he thought so, he would have shown what precautions were taken by the Israelites before the battle to prevent this profanation, and would for this cause have aggravated the plague sent upon the Philistines (Smith 1899:48).

11 In contrast to commentators' attempts to supply the seeing in v. 19 with an adverb that would demonstrate the Bethshemeshites' culpability, the narrator supplies us with an adverb in v. 13 (in verbal form) that demonstrates their good intentions.

12 Cf. Alter, 'Broadly when repetitions with significant variations occur in biblical narrative, the changes introduced can point to an intensification, climactic development, acceleration . . .' (1981:97).

13 Cf. M. H. Pope, 'seven denotes completeness, perfection, consummation' (1962:295).

14 Examples of the phrase used to describe priestly service are Deut 10.8; 18.5, 7; Num 16.9. The connection between the priestly service 'standing before Yahweh,' and the proper maintenance of covenant is explicit in 2 Chr 29.10f. The covenant mediator is also found standing before God in Jer 18.20. In Deuteronomy the covenant is established with Israel standing before Yahweh (4.9-14; 29.14). And in Ezra 9.15, Ezra confesses the inability of Israel to stand before God because it has forsaken the covenantal laws. Cf. Weinfeld 1970:185f; 1972:77.

NOTES TO CHAPTER FOUR: PART SEVEN

1 SAMUEL 7

1 The examples offered by Miller and Roberts (1977:25) to support their claim that Eleazar is designated as a proper priest in 7.1 do not support it. In all cases (Exod 28.3, 41; 29.1, 44; 30.30;

40.13; Lev 8.30; 21.8) *qdš* ... *l* is used of the sanctification of
priests only at the direct command of Yahweh himself. Similarly,
šmr as a description of priestly duties is, in the examples provided by Miller and Roberts, a description of a service commanded
directly by Yahweh (Num. 1.53; 3.10, 31; 18.3; 31.30, 47). Ehrlich's
observation that there is a great difference between the people sanc-
tifying someone and Yahweh doing so, stands against the argument of
Miller and Roberts.

    McCarter also wishes to see Eleazar made a priest in 7.1. He
offers only the weak defense that the names Abinadab and Eleazar are
common in the levitical pedigrees (1980:137). Miller and Roberts and
McCarter see Eleazar's putative priesthood as a satisfactory conclusion to the 'ark narrative.' McCarter understands that the problem in
Bethshemesh was caused by a lack of proper priestly attendance on the
ark. 'But this final difficulty is resolved when Eleazar, a proper
custodian for the ark at last, steps on stage' (1980:139). This may
be true for McCarter, but not for Israel, which continues to mourn
even after Eleazar takes over as custodian (7.2). For a different perspective on the difficulties involved in regarding 7.1 as a satisfactory conclusion to the 'ark narrative' see Willis 1979:209f;
Campbell 1979:38f.

2   There is no vocabulary in the temporal note that has, so far,
been judged the exclusive province of deuteronomistic literary expression.

3   Cf. 1 Sam 13.10 where Samuel's sense of timing also plays an
important part in the story.

4   Only ardent devotees could react like the Bethshemeshites do
when they see the ark: 'They looked up, saw the ark, and were overjoyed at the sight' (6.13). To appreciate this reception, one must
recall that the ark was last seen being taken in a battle that Israel
knew was directed by Yahweh against Israel.

5   I read the participle *šabîm*, 'returning,' as expressive of imminent action as in e.g. Gen 6.17; 20.3; 1 Kgs 20.13; cf. R.J. Williams
1976:39 #214; GKC #116p. Samuel is not describing what Israel is doing. (One does not normally 'return' to someone that one has mourn-
ed as dead.) He is making a suggestion about what Israel might do.

6   On the problem of determining what 'judging' means for Samuel
and throughout the Bible see Rozenberg 1975:77-86. Keil and Delitzsch arrive at a result remarkably similar to that of Weiser and
Budde:

> Judging the people neither consisted in a censure pronounced
> by Samuel afterwards, nor in absolution granted to the penitent
> after they had made a confession of their sin, but in the fact
> that Samuel summoned the nation to Mizpah to humble itself
> before Jehovah, and there secured for it, through his inter-
> cession, the forgivesness of its sin, and a renewal of the
> favour of its God, and thus restored the proper relation bet-
> ween Israel and its God, so that the Lord could proceed to
> vindicate His people's rights against their foes (1880:73; cf.
> Gutbrod 1956:54).

7   Contrary to Veijola the Israelites do not have a mechanical trust in the ark in 4.3, nor is the ark to be taken as subject of the verb *weyoši'enû* in 4.3 (1977:37). They know full well that Yahweh is responsible for their plight and hence are well aware that only he himself can deliver them, if he will.

8   Ehrlich offers an entertaining reason for Samuel's choice of sacrificial animal. He suggests that Samuel chose a tender lamb in view of the imminent threat posed by the Philistines. The small and tender lamb would burn more quickly (than an old goat), thereby allowing Israel and Yahweh to get to the business of fighting more quickly (1910:193)!

9   Buber attempts to use Yahweh's singular action as a solid basis for source analysis in ch. 7. He regards Yahweh's miraculous defeat of the Philistines in response to Samuel's prayer as a late, unhistorical conception (1956:117). Buber suggests that the original narrative ended on the note that Yahweh answered Samuel without supplying a specific content to the answer (p. 118). The answer does not come until 9.16 where Yahweh supplies the true answer to the Philistines' threat in the form of Saul's monarchy (pp. 127f).

Buber's excision of vv. 10-2 from the 'original narrative' falters in the face of the literary connections between this battle report and those in ch. 4 (cf. Willis 1979:211), and on the implications thereby created for the meaning of Yahweh's renewed action on Israel's behalf. When such literary links are evident, the case for compositional layering is weakened and certainly requires more proof than a simple assertion that the theology or ideology of a verse does not agree with one's perception of its context.

10   For discussions of geographical questions entailed by v. 12 see Driver 1913:65; Seebass 1965:293 n.18; McCarter 1980:146f.

11   On the deuteronomisms in v. 14 see Birch 1976:20; McCarter 1980:147. Although the name 'Amorite' is used as a general description of people in Palestine prior to Israel's entry (e.g. Gen 15.16; Deut 1.7; Josh 10.5), it is a name more specifically associated with residents of Trans-jordan (e.g. Deut 3.8; Josh 2.10) (H.B. Huffmon 1976:21).

12   Uncharacteristically, Buber misses this repetition and suggests that the expression in v. 15, 'all the days of his life,' be deleted as a probable replacement for an original numerical description (1964:837). He supplies, however, no grounds for his suggestion.

13   The well-worn paths around the questions of the actual function of the judges and the meaning or meanings of the word 'judge' need not detain us at this time. Within the immediate context of chs. 7f, it is clear enough that Samuel's judgeship consists more importantly in his role as mediator, allowing for renewed covenantal relations between Israel and Yahweh (vv. 6-15). As the temporal paralleling of vv. 13 and 15 shows, Samuel's judging Israel is matched by Yahweh's defensive actions against the Philistines. With regard to covenantal implications, Samuel's judging should be regarded as a maintenance of Israel's commitment by ensuring that stipulations are adhered to. Yahweh's defense of Israel may be seen as the protection promised for

Israel's obedience.

For a recent survey of research on 'judging' and judges, with an attempt at a new historically oriented solution see de Vaux 1978: 751-73. Additional bibliography may be found in Wallis 1968:76 n.37.

14   Cf. Driver, 'Observe the series of *perfects* with *w* conv., descriptive of Samuel's *custom*' (1913:65).

NOTES TO CHAPTER FOUR: PART EIGHT

1 SAMUEL 8

1   Soggin also notes this connection between the sons but draws an unusual and unsupported conclusion:

> Both stories are, in any case, to be separated: in the episode of Samuel's sons we have a parallel to that of Eli's sons (2.11f), both of course had originally nothing to do with the monarchy (1967:31).

Whether or not the sons of Samuel or Eli actually had anything to do with the monarchy is a matter that will probably remain beyond the grasp of anyone. According to the narrative, however, both the sons of Eli and Samuel are intimately and inextricably involved in the initiation of Israel's monarchy, as a first reading of even 8.1-5 alone makes plain.

2   The modern reader must remember that a distance of 80 km. was a greater isolating factor than it is today. Samuel's control over his sons and even his knowledge of their actions would always be at least two days after the fact.

3   Israel's knowledge of the cause of their misfortunes in war comes by way of Samuel's prophecy (4.1) in connection with reflections on the disaster after the fact. That Israel does know of the potential danger of an old mediator with wayward sons is clear enough from 8.5 alone.

4   On the relation of 8.5 to Deut 17.14 see Birch 1976:24, 137f; Veijola 1977:68f; McCarter 1980:161f.

5   Clements observes that the term 'nation' (*gôy*) has strong political colouring. It is never used in construct with the name of a deity. Israel is called the *'am yhwh* but never the *gôy yhwh* (1977:427). The case of Exod 19.6, where God says Israel will be a *gôy* to himself is no exception: Israel is 'a priestly kingdom, a holy nation' (*wegôy qadôs*) indicating that Israel, as a nation, is to be separate from all other nations, sanctified and holy to Yahweh.

Cazelles' reading of Exod 19.6 supports this reading of 1 Sam 8.5. 'Israel is a holy nation that is supposed to draw near to God in the sanctuary, 'because her national life is dependent upon priests . . ., while the other nations have kings' (cit. by Botterweck 1977: 430). The request in 1 Sam 8.5 is for a king so as to become a profane nation.

6   The literary technique of omitting or adding details to dif-

ferentiate between actual narrative circumstances and the characters'
perceptions of the same has already been seen in the case of Eli's
death, where the latter dies before he hears that the ark was taken
(4.17f). Cf. Alter:

> But there is a different kind of biblical repetition, which is
> phrasal rather than verbal or a matter of motif, theme, and
> action. Here entire statements are repeated, either by dif-
> ferent characters, by the narrator, or by the narrator and one
> or more of the characters in concert, with small but important
> changes introduced in what usually looks at first glance like
> verbatim repetition. Many of the psychological, moral, and
> dramatic complications of biblical narrative are produced
> through this technique (1981:97).

7   Buber misses the point when he objects 'that Samuel's distress is not simply a personal reaction, as though the elders had only requested the resignation of a mediator and not an entirely new
constitution' (1964:731). The narrator does not say that the elders
requested only new judges - far from it - but that 'in the eyes of
Samuel' a significant way of putting it - the request initially
boiled down to the simple fact of a king 'to judge' Israel instead of
a judge.

Boecker seeks to buttress Buber's objection against seeing a
technique of characterization in v. 6 by suggesting that one must
take v. 7b, which is seemingly 'directed at Samuel's feelings,' out
of its literary context and read it in the context of its prehistory
(1969:25). While Boecker may or may not be right in his conjectures
about the prehistory of the 'Alternativformel' in v. 7, it must be
maintained that the existing narrative context must serve as the
principal standard of any reading. There can be little surprise that
scholars discover multiple sources and redactions, contradictions and
inconsistencies, and ideological multiplicities in ch. 8 when they
read with strategies such as Boecker's. ('In the interpretation of v.
7b one should not overvalue the immediate context' 1969:25.)

8   Veijola takes the mention of 'the people (*ha'am*) as the
voicers of the request in v. 7 as strong support for separating vv.
6ff. from vv. 1-5 in which it is the elders alone (vv. 4f) who make
the request (1977:55). But the issue is covenantal; what is at stake
is the rejection of Yahweh's rule by his people. Hence it is perfectly appropriate for Yahweh to note that the request for a new sovereign comes from the people, since the covenant is between the god
and his people. In addition, Yahweh does not simply say 'listen to
the people,' but 'listen to *the voice* of the people.' One may understand 'the voice of the people' as a reference to the elders or simply as implying, with divine insight, that the elders speak for the
people.

9   Against Buber, who suggests that the past misdeeds of v. 8
are inappropriate to their context because they describe religious
failures and cannot be compared with the theological-political
treason of the request for a king (1964:733f).

10   This use of connective alliteration to link the rebellion of v.

7, the previous rejection of Yahweh (v. 8), and the making of a king (v. 8) may explain why the verb *'sh* is used to describe the establishment of a monarchy. Cf. Harris 1981:79.

11   This reading of v. 8 goes against the usual reading of similar 'deuteronomistic interpolations' in the deuteronomistic history, all of which are supposed to trace the cause of Israel's downfall to its continual sin and apostasy (see Cross 1973:274-86), and hence might seem contrary to the supposed known intention of its larger literary context. Closer examination of other 'deuteronomisticisms' in their immediate narrative context might reveal a more variegated deuteronomistic idealogy, however. Hence before a close reading of a 'deuteronomistic interpolation' such as v. 8 may be rejected as contradicting the known purposes of the deuteronomist(s), a close rereading of interpolations should be made, in which they are read in relation to their immediate literary context.

It is probable that the single-minded deuteronomist, a hypostasization built from the isolation of all his words from their immediate context (or even worse, from forcing contexts to agree with isolated deuteronomistic interpolations), will appear as a much more complex fellow once he is read in context. The more recent redactional analyses of deuteronomistic literature reveal an increasing awareness of its complexity (e.g. Smend 1971, who saw two differing deuteronomists (DtrG, DtrN), but now (1978:123) sees three (DtrH, DtrP, DtrN). Cf. Dietrich 1972; Veijola 1975; 1977; Bickert 1979; Friedman 1981). As was once the case in Pentateuchal studies, the initial isolation of a unitary literary strand, or in this case, redaction, gives way to a more nuanced reading in which one speaks of J1, J2, J3 . . ., or Dtrs H, P, and N. The literary alternative to this process of redactional *reductio ad absurdum*, which ultimately results in a new deuteronomist with each change in context, is to avoid premature attributions of authorship or redaction, waiting until a detailed contextual reading of all the literature has been made.

12   Veijola has shown that the phrase *ha'ed ta'id bahem* must be understood as covenantal in character. Citing 2 Kgs 17.15, he suggests the expression *'edôtayw 'ašer he'id bam* should be translated 'his covenantal stipulations (respective treaty obligations) which he had imposed on them' (1977:64).

13   Many different translations have been suggested for *mišpaṭ* in v. 9 (cf. Langlamet 1970:186 n.46). No matter which tranlation is preferred, the point I wish to make is that the determination of the king's behaviour is made by Yahweh through Samuel.

14   On the shift from elders in v. 5 to people in v. 10, noted by Wildberger (1957:459), see above on v. 7, and Dhorme (1910:71).

15   Cf. Budde (1902:55); Dhorme, 'The verb *'mr* is not generally used with a direct object' (1910:71).

16   See Langlamet (1970:186 n.146) for a list of scholars who read vv. 11-8 as a description 'habitual behavior of kings.' Cf. Speiser, 'As regards *mishpat* - which has not turned up at Mari - we should now expect it, theoretically, to mean something like "standard,

regulation," and hence conduct, custom, manner, or characteristic behaviour in general' (1971:282).

17   Again a great deal of discussion on the 'manner of the king' in vv. 11-8 has focused on the question of the anti-monarchic tendency that the narrator is thought to be expressing here, while neglecting the simple fact that it is Samuel - not the narrator - who expresses these reservations about monarchic administration. Whether these verses are completely critical of the monarchy (e.g. Boecker 1969: 17; Crüsemann 1978:72f), or contain positive elements (e.g. Press 1938:197; Wildberger 1957:458, 467; Seebass 1965:295 n.22; Stoebe 1973:186f; Ishida 1977:41; Talmon 1979:13); whether the monarchic model for the practises is early Canaanite (e.g. Mendelsohn 1956; cf. Rainey 1975; Weiser 1962:39; Thornton 1967:418; Soggin 1972: 16) or the later kings of Israel (e.g. North 1931:8 [Solomon]; Wildberger 1957:458; Cohen 1965:68 [Solomon]; Clements 1974:409 [Solomon]; Fritz 1976:354f; Mayes 1978:9 [Solomon]), the reader can only misconstrue the narrator's position if he does not distinguish between statements made by the narrator and the characters in the narrator's narrative.

One cannot deny that a narrator may occasionally, or even consistently agree with a specific character, but such agreement must be studied and then demonstrated, rather than assumed.

18   Budde also notes that what Samuel says about the manner of the king is not given to him by Yahweh (1902:55).

19   On the syntax of v. 12 see McCarter 1980:158, who follows Driver's explanation, cf. Driver 1913:67; GKC #114p. Ehrlich regards the entire verse as 'a late tasteless insertion' (1910:194f). His reasoning is that the commissions of officers are honours, the mention of which goes against the negative evaluation of the monarchy's impact.

20   On the nature of the king's 'servants' see Mendelsohn 1956: 20f; Rainey 1975:95-7; and McCarter 1980:158.

21   The emendation, supported by LXX, of *bahûrêkem* to *beqar-kem*, first suggested by Capellus (Stoebe 1973:186), is almost universally accepted (cf. however Stoebe 1973:186, 188). Not only have the 'young men' been implicitly dealt with in v. 11 (Driver 1913:8), but they are incongruous in a list of possessions such as v. 16. Furthermore, their mention here, which Stoebe notes 'represents the strongest encroachment on the family's freedom' (1973:188), is at odds with the ranking of vv. 11-7 from most important to least important items, a rhetorical technique with which Samuel tranquilizes his audience. The same holds true for the order of v. 16 itself, where one would expect the *bahûrêkem* to come before the male and female slaves (cf. McCarter 1980:155 and Deut 5.21).

22   For a parallel rhetorical pattern see Amos 1.3-2.16, and Wolff's comments (1977:149). A similar pattern appears in the prologue to the book of Job (ch. 1), although there the devastations progress from mild to severe with a culmination in Job's personal affliction (2.1-7).

23   Seebass also notes the disjunction between the people's reply

and Samuel's warning, but uses it to draw conclusions about the literary history of ch. 8 (1965:287).
24   Against Talmon's view that Samuel 'took absolutely no exception to the people's wish to be like the other nations in the matter of the monarchy' (1979:10), it must be asserted that Samuel's disobedience of a direct command from Yahweh constitutes the strongest possible expression of Samuel's revulsion at the thought.

NOTES TO CHAPTER FOUR: PART NINE

1 SAMUEL 9

1   For surveys of scholarship on 9.1-10.16, an episode delimited mainly by content, see W. Richter's copious footnotes 1970:13-56 (esp. 13-29), L. Schmidt 1970:58-63, and J. Kegler 1977:56-70.
2   A brief summary of this approach as advanced by Gressmann, Budde, Buber, and Weiser, may be found in L. Schmidt 1970:59f.
3   Weiser comes to much the same conclusion from a historical perspective (1962:47).
4   Wellhausen suggests that the information about Kish's place of residence, *mibbin-yamîn* in MT, is superfluous in view of the subsequent note that Kish's great-great-great grandfather was an *'îš yemînî*. Consequently he inserts, without versional support, *mgb't* before *bin-yamîn,* a suggestion that has been almost universally adopted (1871:70). MT's description is, however, acceptable as is. Benjamin, by itself, is perfectly acceptable as a geographical name (cf. Aharoni 1979:210; G.A. Smith 1900:290). Neither is this geographical information superfluous in view of the subsequent note that Kish had an ancestor who is described as an *'îš yemînî*. The first occurrence of *yamîn* gives Kish's geographical background, the second, his genealogy (cf. Richter 1970:14).
5   The lack of the adjective *'eḥad* after *'îš* in 9.1 marks a deviation from the pattern seen in Judges and in 1 Sam 1.1, the significance of which is uncertain. One might conjecture that it differentiates Saul and Samuel, hinting at the differences in the courses of their divinely initiated careers.
6   Richter's syntactical objection to 9.2b as an original element of ch. 9 is not compelling (1970:25f). 9.2b can be read as a separate sentence, unrelated, syntactically, to the prior comparative.
7   Buber suggests additional reasons for seeing Saul, at this point, as the chosen one (1956:123, 145).
8   Yahweh's remark in 1 Sam 16.7 reflects his own experience with choices made on the basis of appearance and stature. Saul's failings have taught Yahweh the folly of choosing a king that will meet with immediate human approval on account of superficial appearance (cf. Gunn 1980:124).
9   See McCarter 1980:173 for an explanation of the definite article attached to the first occurrence of 'the asses.'

10   Cf. R.J. Williams 1976:67 #409, 100 #593.

11   Symbolic interpretations of the journey have been suggested by Bic 1957:92-7, and Stoebe 1957:362-70; cf. 1973:201f. The most recent attempt to rationalize the itinerary is that of McCarter 1980:174f. Since there is no obvious significance in the itinerary, the problem can be left for topographical and geographical studies; in a specifically literary study such as this, to pursue it would digress too far.

12   The historical-critical division of chs. 8 and 9 is made possible by the narrator's use of uncertainty in the opening of ch. 9. Since historical criticism is predisposed to dissect at the first sign of disjunction, it is unable and unwilling to struggle through the uncertainty and so to achieve the participatory understanding that the narrative affords to a sequential reader. The historical critic is excluded a priori from an appreciation and understanding of any narrative that includes the common literary techniques of suspension and retardation. In anticipation of the objection that the sequential unity is a total creation of the sequential reader, one need point only to the lack of resolution in 8.22. Yahweh had said 'Make a king,' and Samuel said only 'Go home.' The expected resolution of their differences comes, not surprising immediately thereafter, in ch. 9.

13   For the historical-critical position on this situation see the commentaries and Hylander 1932:139-43; Richter 1970:17, 18, 23f, 28, 29, 32-4; L. Schmidt 1970:69-71; Birch 1976:30; and Mettinger 1976:64. Wilson (1980:175-8) provides a sociological perspective on the various terms in 9.1-10.16.

14   Stoebe points to parallel instances in the Elijah narratives where Elijah is called both by name and by the descriptive appellation, 'man of God' (1973:202).

15   Of course the reader will only appreciate the full effect of this irony after he has been told that Saul will be anointed *nagîd*, but this is also true of his appreciation of the entire journey in search of the asses. Once he is told the real meaning of the journey, the reader can make a quick review of the preceding events confirming his suspicions and gaining a full appreciation of the ironies incorporated by the narrator (cf. Sternberg 1978:31).

16   As Dhorme observes (1910:76), the perfect tense of the verbal adjective *'ašer-halaknû* militates against Driver's suggestion that *derek* includes the goal here (1913:71).

17   An example of a reflective reader is Calmet who, following the Vulgate, makes the irony explicit in his translation of v. 6. 'Possibly he will shed some light for us on the subject that has brought us here' (cited by Dhorme 1910:76). Cf., however, GKC #106g.

18   Smith, for example, says that 9.1-10.16 'begins like a separate book, introducing persons hitherto unknown' (1899:xviii).

19   *In medias res* is a simple description of the literary technique of beginning a story 'in the middle.' If we make a distinction between the real, 'historical' order of events (the Russian formal-

ists' *fabula*) and the order in which these events are actually told
(*sjuzet*, plot), an *in medias res* beginning is the opening of a
plot that does not begin where the real, historical events began (cf.
Chatman 1978:19-21, 63-7; Sternberg 1978:8-14, 35-41). In proper
'historical' order, the events of ch. 9 would follow a sequence of:
1. divine revelation to Samuel, predicting Saul's arrival next day;
2. divine intervention, leading the asses astray; 3. human response,
Saul's search; 4. divine guidance and sustenance, Yahweh leads Saul
to Samuel and gives him a quarter shekel, etc. (1 and 2 may also be
reversed).

20   See Richter 1970:19 n.20 for a list of adherents to this view.

21   Richter's response to the wordiness of the reply, in contrast,
is to suggest possible expansions (1970:23f).

22   I follow Stoebe's defence of the 2nd person singular suffix in
MT (1973:195).

23   'A customary sacrificial meal it definitely was not' (Wildberger 1957:453); cf. Stoebe 1973:195.

24   Most translations have not conveyed this idea successfully,
e.g. RSV, 'the people have a sacrifice'; Stoebe (1973:190), 'the
inhabitants celebrated a sacrificial festival'; McCarter (1980:165),
'the people have a sacrifice.'

25   As Richter notes, the supposed discrepancies between vv. 12b,
13a, 13b, and 22 on who participated in the sacrifice - people, invited guests, or 30 guests - are insufficient for purposes of literary-
critical division (1970:20).

26   Wildberger provides an interesting example of a reader who
constructs a provisional frame within which to incorporate and understand all of the exposition hints dropped by the narrator:

> One can easily read between the lines that here a secret
> counsel of representatives of all Israel has assembled under
> Samuel's leadership. This counsel had negotiated about the
> monarchy and now Samuel presents to it the one whom the
> claimants considered of such value (1957:454).

Wildberger is well aware that this explanation is his own construction - it is found 'between the lines' - and even offers a rhetorical explanation for the narrative's pronounced reticence. 'That
little is said here is only natural: the atmosphere of conspiracy
hovers over the congregation' (1957:454).

Unfortunately, as Weiser notes, Wildberger fails to renounce
this provisional frame even when it is contradicted by subsequent
information in the narrative (Weiser 1962:51 n.8). Wildberger does,
nevertheless, offer an example of a reader responding to the literary
dynamics of ch. 9, and so his hypothesis provides tangential confirmation of the analysis presented here.

27   On the arguments for and against emendation of this last
sentence in v. 13 see Wellhausen 1871:72; Driver 1913:72f (both
against); and McCarter 1980:169 (for).

28   Cf. Weiser (1962:50), 'Thereby Saul is legitimated as king in
a way that from the outset excludes any human interference' (1962:
53). 29 Mettinger gives a judicious survey of the various positions

on the significance of anointment in his history of scholarship
(1976:185-8, see p. 185 n.1 for bibliography). He divides biblical
anointing into two categories (1976:192):

1. Instances of anointing performed by the people or their
representatives.

2. Instances performed by a human mediator on behalf of God.
For Saul's anointing, we are concerned only with the latter group.
Although Mettinger denies the historical accuracy of Saul's anointment - 'we can feel entitled to infer that Saul was never anointed'
(1976:197) - the fact remains that in the narrative his anointment
is performed by Samuel.

Mettinger concentrates on the political legitimation accomplished by divine anointment. The king is consecrated to Yahweh and
the anointing becomes a visible sign of divine election (1976:207).
The anointing of a king by Yahweh signals a covenantal relationship
between Yahweh and the king, who becomes a vassal to Yahweh. In
return, Yahweh is obligated to the king as protector (1976:230, cf.
222). In Mettinger's view, the leitmotif of the historical cases of
anointing was to express the idea that God has chosen and was obligated to the anointed (1976:230).

For present purposes and in the context of 1 Sam 1-12, where
the issue is the relationship between theocracy and monarchy, equal
weight must also be given to the other side of the coin, namely that
the act of anointing makes the anointed the vassal of Yahweh. De
Vaux's study exhibits the necessary balance:

> So far then we have shown: that the king of Israel was
> designated by Yahweh; that he was the *nagîd*, the adminis-
> trator appointed by Yahweh over his people Israel; that he was
> the servant of Yahweh; that these facts of choice and
> dependence were expressed in a 'covenant' which guaranteed
> divine protection for the king in return for his fidelity; that
> the terms of this covenant were contained in a pact which the
> king has no choice but to accept and which had similarities,
> both in form and in content, with ancient Oriental treaties of
> vassalage. All of these characteristics make the king of Israel
> Yahweh's vassal (1972:162).

Kutsch (1963), who regards all instances of divine anointing
as unhistorical, theological attempts at monarchic legitimation (p.
58), also recognizes that divine anointing submits the anointed to
divine authority. 'In the Israelite conception of this anointing
Yahweh stands in Pharaoh's place as the suzerain. The anointed is
here as there bound to the order of the suzerain, who invested him.
On the other hand he also enjoys the suzerain's special protection'
(p. 57). Weisman has subsequently attempted to harmonize the two
kinds of anointing as complementary steps in king-making (1976:378-
98).

30   Langlamet (1970:188-92) gives an extensive summary of scholarship on the term *nagîd*, including biographical notes.

31   Cf. L. Schmidt, who reaches a similar conclusion from a
redactional perspective:

> He [the redactor] obviously not only wants to present the
> original narrative (*Grunderzählung*) as dealing with the
> installation of Saul as king. Rather he wants, at the same
> time, to interpret this monarchy. Therefore he dispenses with
> the word *malak* and employs instead *nagîd* (1970:88).

32   On the role of v. 16 as part of a call narrative see Richter
1970:13-56, 136-81; Birch 1976:35-42, and the objections to the
latter's analysis by Walters 1978:69f (cf. Seebass 1967:163 n.36).
Further bibliography is provided by Mettinger 1976:66 n.5.

33   The slight difference in emphasis - Yahweh says that he will
deliver Israel in Exod 3.8, whereas Saul delivers them in 1 Sam 9.16 -
may be accounted for by the purpose of v. 16, which is to define the
role of the new 'king.' The difference is also not as great as it
might seem, since emphasis has already been placed on Saul's role
as Yahweh's anointed designate.

34   From this perspective one may also understand the omission of
the word *'onî* from the quotation. Most scholars insert it in the
phrase 'I have seen (the affliction of) my people' on the basis of
LXX and Exod 3.7 (e.g. Thenius 1864:36f). Without 'affliction,'
Yahweh appears to say that he has 'seen' (had an insight into) his
people on account of their request, which he regards as fear of the
Philistines. For this usage of the verb *ra'â* one may compare Gen
37.,14; Exod 2.25; Num 24:20f. Alternatively, reading with LXX, Yahweh would be saying that he now understands the suffering that his
people underwent in chs. 4-6 on account of their recent cry to him
for a new king. Either reading is possible, but since MT is coherent,
there is no pressing reason to follow the text of LXX, which may or
may not be an accommodation to the Exodus passage.

35   The verb *'anahû* (Yahweh 'answered him') implies that Samuel was watching out for the man and that when he spied Saul Yahweh 'answered' his vigilance (cf. Driver 1913:73f).

36   *'Aṣar* is also used with *b* governing the direct object in Job
4.2; 12.15; and 29.9.

37   L. Schmidt attempts to use Samuel's suggestion that Saul stay
overnight as a means for textual dissection. He suggests that Samuel
originally did not know what he would say to Saul, and required an
evening in which to receive the word from God (1970:68). The revelation of vv. 15f is, therefore, a separate tradition. Schmidt's
suggestion fails, however, to account for the wordplay on *nagîd*
throughout vv. 1-19, and more specifically for Samuel's verbal irony
in v. 19. But is it reasonable to regard such a developed and widespread verbal irony as the happy accident of amalgamated traditions?

38   McCarter's suggestion that Saul's protest of unworthiness is
the customary response of individuals called to divine service fails
to recognize that Saul does not know at this point that he is being
inducted (1980:179). Similarly Birch, who observes that Saul has not
yet been told what he is supposed to do, suggests that Saul's self-
effacement is an integral element in a call narrative (1976:37).
Birch suggests that Saul's objection should be taken to mean that he
feels unworthy of being chosen for divine service (1976:37). But

neither Samuel nor Saul make any mention of induction into divine service (cf. Seebass 1967:163 n.36). Saul, in fact, objects to nothing; he simply remarks on the incongruity of Samuel's rhetorical question and then asks *what the meaning of it is* (*welammû dibbarta 'elay kaddabar hazzeh*) (cf. Walters 1978:69). How can Saul be said to protest or object to a remark, the significance of which he does not even understand (cf. Schulz 1919:137; Gutbrod 1956:71)?

L. Schmidt's reading of v. 21, also influenced by the hypothesis of a 'Berufungsschema' (call schema) in ch. 9, is more congruent with the details of the text:

> The objection in 9.21 makes it clear that Saul came from a tribe and family that in no way seemed to be predestined for this high rank. Thereby the objection also ensures the exclusive initiative of Yahweh (1970:91).

39   Cohen also notes that the choice of Saul was carefully planned but completely ignores the characterization of Saul supplied by the text. In his historical reconstruction, Saul is a military hero before he is chosen. (Cohen places ch. 11 before ch. 9.) 'Saul descended from a family of wealth, to judge from his servants and possessions, and of prestige, to judge from the length and impressiveness of his genealogy' (1965:70; cf. Ishida 1977a:44). According to the text, however, Saul's father possessed an unspecified number of servants and asses. Whether many or few is left to the imagination of readers. His genealogy is not very long and it makes him a man with no impressive familial ties (see above on 9.1). If as Cohen suggests, the 'old guard' chose a king that they could easily manipulate (1965:70), it would make more sense for them to choose the Saul of ch. 9 rather than the military hero and landed gentryman that Cohen reconstructs.

40   Seebass fails to take into account Saul's obvious confusion in v. 21 when he suggests a contradiction between separate narratives seen in vv. 19 and 22 (1967:158). According to v. 19, Saul is to go up to the high place ahead of the seer, while in v. 22 Samuel personally escorts him. The change is most economically explained, however, by Saul's hesitation in the intervening v. 21, rather than by the supposition of two narratives.

41   Buber plausibly suggests that the guests, in view of the events of ch. 8, would see Saul as the requested king (1956:129f). Similarly, L. Schmidt, citing biblical parallels, suggests that the combination of an assembly and an offering with a meal was customary in the election of a new king (1970:84f). The narrator, aware of this custom, incorporated such a scene into ch. 9 by including these aspects in the existing meal of the so-called 'Grunderzählung' (vv. 22a, 24b).

Schmidt seems to suggest that the anachronistic incorporation of this custom, which became familiar only after a succession of monarchies, indicates that the meal was intended to honour the new king. But would the guests, who had never had a king before, know this? My point is not historical but literary, and as such it is not an objection to Schmidt's suggestion but merely a question of mimetic plausibility. In any case, the narrative itself leaves the guests' impressions unstated.

42   The corrupt portion of v. 24 cannot be interpreted as is, nor do I have any alternative to add to the existing list of unsatisfactory emendations.

43   For an example of gap-filling (concretization) see the suggestion of O.V. Gerlach regarding the topic of the roof-top discourse (cited by Keil & Delitzsch 1880:93f).

44   The servant's accompaniment is omitted from description, not because he was not along - he was (v. 27) -, but because the narrator wishes to foreground the bond between Samuel and Saul and the mention of the servant would obscure the otherwise clear description.

NOTES TO CHAPTER FOUR: PART TEN

1 SAMUEL 10

1   The majority of scholars follow LXX in 10.1, which contains a substantial addition (e.g. Wellhausen 1871:72f; McCarter 1980:171; see also Langlamet's review of text criticism on 10.1, 1978:291-4). MT gives, however, no appearance of corruption. Consequently there are some scholars who defend MT and explain LXX as a deviation (e.g. Keil & Delitzsch 1880:96 n.1; Stoebe 1973:197, 205).

Given the lack of accepted principles for reaching agreement on what our text should be in cases such as 1 Sam 10.1, the reader of the biblical text is left with a practical course. Whether one reads the LXX version of the narrative or MT, one should stick with that version unless corruption dictates otherwise. Even faced with an obvious corruption versional support for emendation, however convincing, can never be more than incidental since one can never be sure whether the intelligible reading was formed before (variant) or after (correction) the corrupt reading. When scholars think that they must make a decision between two intelligible variants, the resulting decision will always be beyond proof or refutation and is best described as impressionism.

Examples of text-critical judgements on 10.1 support this judgement:

The text of the Septuagint is nothing more than a gloss formed from ch. ix 16, 17, which the translator thought necessary, partly because he could not clearly see the force of *halô kî*,' but more especially because he could not explain the fact that Samuel speaks to Saul of signs, without having announced them to him as such. But the author of the gloss has overlooked the fact that Samuel does not give Saul a *semeion* but three *semeia* . . . (Keil & Delitzsch 1880:96 n.1).

'As Samuel here for the first time candidly explains (matters) to his guest it is in order that he should be comprehensive. The significance, moreover, of those events of v. 2ff. as signs of the arrival of greater things stands not only belatedly (vv. 7, 9) but as something to be taken for granted. Finally the *ky* after *hl'* in MT betrays a gap between these two words, which has arisen through a scribal error [homoioteleuton] skipping from the first *mšḥk* to the second' (Wellhausen 1871:73).

Both Keil & Delitzsch and Wellhausen use interpretational arguments based on their understanding of context and literary necessities to support their decisions. The impressionistic element in text criticism seems unavoidable.

Before we can see what it is that has occurred when a text has been changed from one version to another, we must look at the effects of the parts of the text concerned on the whole text; that is, we must interpret their function within both complete texts. And only after that can we form any judgement about the nature of the changes, which must be viewed not merely as the change of a few words that can be compared directly to each other, but as a change from a whole text meaning one thing to a whole text meaning another (Ellis 1974:118; cf. Greenberg 1977).

Both the examples of Keil and Delitzsch and Wellhausen exhibit the rudiments of the approach suggested by Ellis.

The point I wish to make, however, is that text criticism is dependent on literary interpretation. As such, a preference for one version over another is partially a product of the preference of one interpretation over another. The science of text criticism is still handmaid to another queen, the art of interpretation. Hence those readers who select a little LXX here, or a mite of MT there, actually compose new texts (variations) on the basis of interpretation and become interpretive composers in their search for the *Urtext* (theme). As Mowatt points out, such textual criticism is self-defeating when it is seen as an interpretational necessity:

The author's version of his own work is a desirable starting point for the literary historian and critic. Where this is not available, however, it is doubtful whether we are justified in trying to reconstruct it. If we do try, we are obscuring our own function, which is the interpretation of the facts as found (1971:26).

2   Mayes also notes that the anointing episode 'was as much to emphasize the role of the prophet in the call and anointing of Saul as it was to indicate that Saul was in fact called and anointed . . .' (1978:14).

3   Knierim also perceives the emphasis on Yahweh's role in the anointing - 'the king is not the anointed of the people, but of Yahweh' (1968:30; cf. Buber 1956:132) - but fails to observe that Saul is the only Israelite given to know this. At this point in the narrative, the characterization of the anointing as a Yahweh anointing is not so much a polemic as it is a definition with which the naive Saul is indoctrinated.

4   Perry discusses the literary uses of the primacy effect in his article on literary dynamics (1979:52-8), as does Sternberg

(1978: index under 'Primacy effect'). It is also an accepted view that Hebrew syntax can lend special emphasis to a word by placing it first in a sentence and so contrasting it with the usual word order, a technique that seems to depend on the primacy effect (cf. R.J. Williams 1976:96-8).

5   Richter explains the difference chronologically; 'over my inheritance' is likely the earlier form and 9.16 contains the extension over Israel' (1970:47). Aside from this assertion, however, he supplies no proof of the relative dating, and his explanation merely serves to show the tendencies of historical criticism. Such commentary, instead of enhancing the reader's understanding of the story, diverts it onto the hypothetical history of the story.

6   It is for this reason that, as Fritz observes (1976:351), the term *melek* is never mentioned in any communications to Saul, who only comes to know that he will be *melek* as well as *nagîd* in 10.21.

7   Tsevat suggests a symbolic meaning for the second sign. 'Whereas the third sign symbolizes Saul's appointment by God, the second points to his recognition by the people . . . Saul is given consecrated food' (1962:117). Although MT does not say that the bread was consecrated, Tsevat's suggestion, based on LXX (and supported by 4QSama, McCarter 1980:172), is in accord with the general sense of the text. Saul has crossed over from a secular to a sacral position; instead of giving bread, he gets it (cf. Wildberger 1957:455).

8   The incidental note that there was a Philistine prefect at Gibeath-elohim prepares for ch. 13, but cannot be labelled secondary on that account alone if one admits that a narrator can include anticipations in his narrative (against e.g. McCarter 1980:182).

9   Cf. Gressmann (1921:33), who unfortunately suggests that Samuel presents the predictions in order to allay Saul's astonishment and doubts. Weiser criticizes Gressmann's reading as over-interpretation without textual basis (1962:58). He suggests that for the narrator and reader, the anointing done by a man with the authority of a Samuel, accompanied by a word of God was sufficient proof and required no additional signs. The signs are, therefore, secondary accretions (1962:57f).

Weiser, however, goes too far in his reaction to Gressmann. The signs are in the text, and though Saul is never explicitly shown to doubt Samuel, the purpose of the signs, like the prearranged sacrificial banquet, is to convince Saul beyond the slightest doubt, that he is predestined to be the designate of Yahweh. The signs, therefore, are part of the plan and not an impromptu response to some doubt that Saul may or may not have had.

10   The series is: *ûmaṣa'ta, we'amerû* (v. 2); *wehalapta, ûba'ta, ûmeṣa'ûka* (v. 3); *weša'alû, wenatenû, welaqahta* (v. 4); *(tabô'), ûpaga'ta* (v. 5); *weṣalehâ, wehitnabbîta, wenehpakta* (v. 6).

11   Veijola, who follows Press's line of reasoning (1938:199), suggests that the connection between 10.8 and ch. 13 was logical only before ch. 11 was inserted between chs. 10 and 13. According to 11.14, Samuel, Saul and the people all go to Gilgal to renew the

kingdom. 'A seven day wait for Samuel in Gilgal would thereafter be senseless' (Veijola 1977:49)! In view of the fact that 10.8 is a prediction that Saul will go down to Gilgal *ahead* of Samuel and wait there seven days, however, there is no contact or conflict between 11.14 and ch. 13. The only thing they share, in fact, is a situation in which Samuel and Saul are both in Gilgal together, but the circumstances are unrelated.

12   Alternative defences of 10.8 are presented by Eissfeldt 1931:8; Irwin 1941:122-4; and J.M. Miller 1974:160f. The reading presented here is partially anticipated by Schulz 1919:150.

13   Had Samuel wanted to give Saul the freedom to do as he saw fit, he could have said, as Jonathan's armorbearer did, 'do all that your mind inclines you to' (*'aseh kol-'aser bilebabeka neṭeh lak*, 1 Sam 14.7), which better conveys a sense of individual freedom. The expression 'do what your hand finds,' on the other hand, carries a sense of action in accord with circumstance.

14   Richter raises a further objection against 10.8, saying that it is in contradiction to 9.13b; in 9.13b Samuel simply blesses a prepared offering but in 10.8 he promises to perform the very specific sacrifices of *'olôt* and *šelamîm* (Richter 1970:19). Were one to admit a connection between Samuel's appearances throughout chs. 1-12, as Richter I think would not, one might note that Samuel has already been trained as a priest (chs. 1-3), has already offered an *'ōlâ* (7.10), and has built a sacrificial altar (7.17). Wildberger's objection to using these passages as proof of Samuel's priesthood depends on rather arbitrary assessments of historicity (Samuel as prophet is historical, but as priest is fictitious) and, in any case, holds only against those who would argue the historicity of Samuel's priestly activity (1957:462f). The lesser claim of the literary approach is simple and incontestable - in the narrative, Samuel sometimes acts as a priest. Furthermore, 9.13 does not say that the seer cannot sacrifice, but only that he blesses the sacrifice before the people eat.

On the topic of Samuel's priestly activity see McKenzie 1962:4-6 (Samuel's priestly character is late and unhistorical), and Willis 1972:44f ('it was natural for traditionist circles to think of Samuel in priestly terminology').

15   Budde believes so strongly that the expectation created by v. 6 should not be anticipated that he rejects the early divine intervention as a 'mistakenly inserted marginal gloss' (1902:69). Hertzberg shows a similar preference for order and transposes the description of the changing of the heart to the end of v. 10 (1964:77f).

16   Cf. Weiser, 'The concluding note (10.9) 'ʌll these signs came to pass on the same day' renders such a narrative superfluous, especially since the narrator understandably held it unnecessary to report, over and above the summary remark of v. 9, the fulfillment of the first two instructions' (1962:59).

17   Abrams defines dramatic irony as 'a situation in a play or a narrative in which the audience shares with the author knowledge of which a character is ignorant: the character . . . says something

that anticipates the actual outcome, but not at all in the way that he means it' (1981:91).

18   Seebass' suggestion that Saul returned to the high place where he attended the banquet (9.19) strains the meaning of the verb *wayyabo'* in v. 13 and conflicts with v. 14 (1967:161 n.28). According to Seebass, Saul's uncle was one of the invited guests at that banquet. In v. 14, however, the uncle asks Saul where he has been and Saul replies that he has been out looking for the lost asses. The implication is that Saul and the uncle have not met since Saul first left home in 9.4.

19   It should also be noted that only a member of Saul's immediate family or a close acquaintance would miss Saul and ask him about his absence. An uncle is neither a better nor worse choice than any other within that circle to perform this task for the narrator.

20   Driver notes the 'awkward and unnatural position of the words,' but suggests only that v. 16b is a misplaced gloss (1913:83).

21   Various socio-historical reasons have been advanced to explain why Mizpah was chosen as the site of the two important meetings in chs. 7 and 10 (e.g. Press 1938:199; Noth 1967:58 n.3; Boecker 1969:36f; Stoebe 1973:215; McCarter 1980:143 n.6, 191). Whatever the historical importance of Mizpah may have been, the reader should first seek to determine the contextual significance of Samuel's choice to reconvene Israel at Mizpah.

Although there is no narrative context that helps us to understand why Samuel held the first convention (ch. 7) at Mizpah, we do gain insight into the second (10.17-27) by comparing it with the first. 'Samuel selected Mizpah for this purpose, because it was there that he had once before obtained for the people, by prayer, a great victory over the Philistines' (Keil & Delitzsch 1880:106). As Keil suggests, Samuel convenes the second meeting at the same place - Mizpah - because the item on the agenda is directly related to the agenda of the prior meeting.

Samuel's prior administration of Israel's victory had led to a restoration of theocratic covenant relations. The installation of a king is held at Mizpah to show that the accomplishment of the prior meeting is now being reversed, or at least apparently so, for one must always bear in mind that the ceremony of 10.17-27 is a show staged to trick Israel into public acceptance of a 'king like all the nations' who is really Yahweh's designate. Israel is led to believe that it is rejecting Yahweh in favour of a king (10.19), and hence annulling the reconciliation previously made at Mizpah (ch. 7).

The choice of Mizpah may, therefore, be viewed as a brilliant ploy on Samuel's part. As director of this sham covenant dissolution, Samuel carefully ensures that the stage setting is suited to the ensuing action.

22   Smith (1899:72) also observes the connection on the basis of Mizpah, but does not draw any significant conclusions therefrom. 23 That Samuel is said to call the people 'to Yahweh' (*'el-yhwh*) may be a subtle intimation about the true purpose of the meeting - to call the people back from their insurrection to Yahweh.

24 No generic, which is to say form-critical, assertions are
intended by the terms covenant renewal or annulment, which are simply aimed at describing what happens in each meeting.
25 Samuel misses no opportunity to criticize the people's desire
for a king. He describes Yahweh's saving acts toward Israel as
rescues from the hands of kings, who oppress Israel. Yahweh saves,
kings oppress.
26 Boecker follows 'most commentaries,' LXX, Vulg., Syr., and
Targ. reading 'No!' (*lo'*) rather than MT's 'to him' (*lô*) (1969:43 n.2).
Since Samuel has just finished saying that Israel spurned (*me'astem*)
its God, however, MT's reading seems most suited to that description.
A pattern in vv. 18f also supports MT:

> v.18   Yahweh (<u>subject</u>)
> brings Israel (<u>direct object</u>) up from Egypt and delivers
> Israel from the hand of all the kings oppressing it.
> v.19   Israel (<u>subject</u>)
> spurns its God (<u>direct object</u>).
>   Yahweh (<u>subject</u>)
> is Israel's deliverer (*môšî'a lakem*) from all its ills and
> hardships.
>   Israel (<u>subject</u>)
> says to him (*lô*), 'Give us a king.'

Reading *lô* rather than *lo'* in v. 19, there is a degree of correspondence (underlined above) between Yahweh's saving acts on Israel's behalf and Israel's spurnful replies. See also below, n.27.
27 Veijola denies that *we'attâ* is an element of a covenant
form, suggesting that it is simply a redactional connector (1977:41
n.19). In support he suggests 'the call to assemble before Yahweh in
a direct speech of Yahweh - the form of which was, at any rate, given
up already in v. 19 - sounds highly inappropriate' (1977:41 n.20).
There is, however, nothing in the narrative to suggest that v. 19b
should be regarded as part of the 'word of Yahweh,' and in fact the
particle (*we'attâ*) itself seems to suggest a new beginning, which
in context is clearly attributable to Samuel alone. As to any 'abandonment' of the 'Yahweh-speech' in v. 19a, by which one must assume
that Veijola refers to the third person references to 'your God' and
'he,' these references are part of a rhetorical pattern in the oracle:
> v.18   *I* brought up *Israel*
>   *I* delivered you
> v.19   But *you* spurned your *God*
>   and you said to him
28 Noth approximates this perspective on the lottery, though he
fails to observe the dramatic, which is to say the staged, aspects of
the lottery: '. . . though Dtr. could have wanted this decision to be
revealed before the public so that 11:1-15 would not look like an aut-
onomous action of the people' (1982:50 = 1967:58).
29 It has been suggested that the question of v. 22 should be regarded as evidence of two traditions in vv. 21f. In v. 21, Yahweh's

will is manifest by lottery, in which answers to questions could only
be yes, no, or silence. In v. 22, on the other hand, the explicit location of Saul could only be given by some type of oracular designation (Birch 1976:44). It is therefore inferred, in conjunction with
other considerations, that the two incompatible types of inquiry belong to separate traditions.

In view of the fact that the lottery process was stalemated by
Saul's absence, however, there is no reason why the people would not
have reverted to the other, more explicit means of divine inquiry. If
we can understand that the words *ša'al byhwh* describe oracular con-
sultation ('by means of the Urim and Thummim,' Keil & Delitzsch
1880:107; cf. Albrektson 1977/78:4), we should also be able to understand that Israel could know which one to use in order to obtain an
answer to a question such as that posed in v. 22.

30   Regarding the significance of Saul's choice of a hiding place,
'el hakkelîm, McCarter also offers the most balanced view. *Hakkelîm* 'can refer to almost any kind of equipment or paraphernalia,
so that exactly where Saul was hiding is something we cannot know
with certainty' (1980:193).

31   See Richter 1970:25 for the redactional argument. He also
lists other proponents of the redactional view on p. 25 n.48. Richter
is willing to admit that 9.2 may function as one of Buber's *Leitwörter,* but only on the level of the final revision.

32   Many have been puzzled by the fact that Samuel, who was vehe-
mently anti-monarchic as recently as vv. 17-19, should now so heart-
ily endorse the monarchy of Saul (e.g. Schulz 1919:156). Once it is
recognized that the endorsement is a trap, however, Samuel's mixed
attitudes are clearly seen as a part of his rhetoric. There is no
need to posit separate Samuels in separate sources or traditions.

33   Birch objects to this reading of v. 24. 'Vs. 24 emphasizes
that it is Yahweh who has chosen Saul, and his stature in vs. 23 acts
as a prior sign attesting to this divine choice. In no way is it
suggested that it is because of Saul's stature that he becomes king'
(1976:46). But nowhere in v. 23 is there any mention of a sign. In
fact, Saul's physical preeminence is made manifest to the people only
because Yahweh has already chosen him (as far back as ch. 9), revealed his choice in the lottery, and thwarted Saul's efforts to evade
public notice as the chosen one.

Birch suggests that 'Yahweh has chosen a king completely apart
from the normal means of cultic designation which have apparently
failed' (1976:46). The failure of the lottery was, however, only
apparent and due to Saul's uncooperative behaviour. Yahweh revealed
his hiding place and hence reinforced the results of the lottery.
Samuel's speech in v. 24 only suggests a plausible reason why Yahweh
chose Samuel, a choice first made manifest in the lottery.

34   I follow Mettinger's recent development of a suggestion by
Clark (1971:275 n.3) that the verb *r'h* is used here (and elsewhere) as a term for election or choice (1976:112f). Numerous parallels are presented and discussed by both Clark and Mettinger. According to Clark, "*bhr* and *r'h* also came to function as technical

terms of royal election' (1971:275).

As Mettinger points out, it is the contextual suitability of this translation of *r'h* in v. 24 that is most compelling. The divine choice has been established in the lottery, and the people are asked if they agree. 'This solemn question was not merely a rhetorical question about whether the people could see (discern) whom the Lord had chosen. What Samuel's question implied was; whether or not the people were prepared to recognize the divine designation of Saul and appoint him king. The formal consent of the people was expressed by means of the acclamation [*yehî hammelek*]' (1976:113).

35   See above n.17.

36   Budde provides an example of a reader who is aware of what Samuel has done - given Israel as king, a man who is only authorized with the anointing of *nagîd* -, but instead of accepting this, he proposes a conjectural emendation to bring the installation into accord with 12.1-3. In 12.1-3, says Budde, Samuel recalls that he installed Saul as Israel's king, and then refers to the latter as Yahweh's anointed (1902:72). Accordingly there might once have been a simple note at the end of v. 24 that said, 'And Samuel anointed him king' (1902:72).

Budde's conjectural emendation is the result of a careful reading of the text, but he errs in attempting to read 10.24 in the light of the subsequent 12.1-3. Read in the natural order, the reader encounters 12.1-3 after Samuel has revealed that King Saul is actually Yahweh's designate. From this perspective for Samuel to identify the king as Yahweh's anointed in 12.1-3 is not surprising at all.

37   Commenting on Josh 24.26, McCarthy suggests that the word *seper* should be translated 'covenant document' on the basis of parallels in a Sefire treaty (1978:223). Given the covenantal context of 1 Sam 10.25, and the parallels between it and the Joshua example, it seems safe to assume that such is also the meaning of *seper* in v. 25.

38   Seebass also perceives the rhetorical differences between the *mišpaṭîm* of chs. 8 and 10, and on that basis suggests they are *parallellüberlieferungen* (1965:286f). Unless one presumes compositional multiplicity, however, a contextual explanation of such rhetorical differences should preclude genetic explanations.

39   The expression 'to go with' (*hlk 'm*) someone is regularly used to show unity and even compact between individuals and groups (Exod 33.16; Lev 26.23f, 28, 40f; Num 10.32; Deut 20.4; 31.6; Judg 4.8; 11.8; 1 Sam 30.22; 2 Sam 7.9; Mic 6.8; Job 31.5; 34.8; 1 Chr 17.8).

40   Stoebe (1973:214) and de Boer (1938:56) defend MT's 'army' (*haḥayil*) against the addition of *benê* before *haḥayil*. On translating *ḥayil* as 'army' see Crüsemann 1978:55 n.9 and Eising 1980:351f.

41   The opinion that any Monarch receiveth his Power by Covenant, that is to say on Condition, proceedeth from want of understanding of this easie truth, that Covenants being but words, and breath, have no force to oblige, contain, constrain, or protect any man, but what it has from the publique Sword; (1968:231).

42   Caspari's attempt to convey the covenantal implications of the
description of transgressors as *benê belîya'al* with the translation 'outlaws' (*Verfehmte*) has not been well received (cit. by
Buber 1956:147 n.3). Even so, Stoebe, though he rejects Caspari's
translation, agrees with his general conception. 'A *belîya'al* is
a violator of divine law' (1973:214).

43   See Levine 1974:16f on this translation of *minhâ*.

44   The majority of scholars have chosen to follow LXX in v. 27b,
correcting the Hebrew from *wyhy kmhryš* to *wyhy kmhdš* (cf. McCarter 1980:191, 199f). Recently the evidence of 4QSam*a* has also been
cited as reason to read *wyhy kmw hdš*, a reading close to that of
LXX (McCarter 1980:199f). From a strictly grammatical, syntactical
perspective, both MT and LXX are possible and neither preeminent
(cf. Keil & Delitzsch 1880:109; Driver 1913:85).

      The reader gains two things from the cross-fertilization of MT
by LXX and 4QSam*a*. First, with the temporal information of the new
reading, 'About a month later' (McCarter's translation), he gets a
transitional note telling him how much time has elapsed between the
last narrated event and the forthcoming one. (The effect is the same
whether the transition bridges 10.27 and 11.1 as in MT and LXX, or
the additional information of 4QSam*a* and 11.1). Secondly, the reader is thereby relieved of the task set by the expositional gap if he
follows MT. And while I would not suggest that scholars have followed
LXX or 4QSam*a* in conscious evasion of the expositional gap in MT's
v. 27, it is quite possible that this *interpretational* complexity
could influence a text-critical decision. As to the first gain to be
had, one notes that temporal transitions in Hebrew narrative may be
explicitly noted (e.g. 1 Sam 3.2; 6.1; 8.1) and they may not (e.g.
1 Sam 2.27; 4.1b; 9.1; 10.17). Without a supporting argument from
narrative technique, it is difficult to see any advantage in the
versional reading, though there is certainly a difference. Greenberg's
comments on LXX and MT divergence in Ezek 2 also apply here:

> The two versions thus convey different messages in this
> paragraph, for which their distinctive formulations are the
> necessary vehicles. Can one message be made a criterion for the
> other? Which one is more original? On what ground will the
> decision be made? (1977:136).

NOTES TO CHAPTER FOUR: PART ELEVEN

1 SAMUEL 11

1   Cf. Gutbrod, 'Behind it [the intended reproach] stands the
well known claim of the Israelite tribes, which the enemy would also
have known, to be something unique and distinct from their neigh-
boring nations as God's chosen people' (1956:80).

2   The seven day period has troubled some scholars as being too
short a time for messengers to cover all of Israel (Wallis 1968:55f;
cf. Gressmann 1921:44; Soggin 1967:42f). Be that as it may, one

might also consider the influence of the symbolic significance of the
number seven on this suggested time period. Cassuto claims that
Akkadian, Hebrew, and Ugaritic examples all prove 'that a series of
seven consecutive days was considered a perfect period [unit of time]
in which to develop an important work . . .' (1961:13). Perhaps the
seven day time period is intended to suggest a 'perfect period.' If
they could not find a deliverer in this period, they would never find
one. The text is, therefore, readable so long as one does not assume
an intention of historicity.

3   The characteristic Israelite response to threatening adversaries, on the other hand, is straightway to 'cry to Yahweh' (e.g.
Judg 3.8f, 13-5; 4.2f; 6.1-6; 10.9f, 14f).

4   Alternatively, Budde suggests that in the redactional process
a description of the wide-ranging travels of the messengers was dropped out to make it look as though the messengers went straight to
Saul (1902:74). Budde, therefore, also arrives at a conclusion about
the 'redactor's' interest, but includes two assumptions in his comment - that there was a separate redaction, and that something has
been omitted from the original narrative. Occam's razor may be put
to good use when the reader faces such alternatives.

5   Beyerlin suggests that Saul's two experiences of the onrush of
the spirit must be separated, one being a temporary prophetic charis-
ma and the other an empowerment similar to that given to the judges
in their battles against Israel's enemies (1961:187-9; cf. Langlamet
1970:193-5). Looking at the differences between the two one also
notes that the prophetic instance was uncontrolled by Saul, and so
functioned for him as a sign that God was with him. The instance in
11.6, on the other hand, leaves Saul in complete control. In fact,
just after the spirit comes on him, Saul gets very angry at what he
has heard. The spirit, in this case, catalyzes Saul into action (cf.
Hylander 1932:158f; Weiser 1962:71).

Turning to the similarities between the two instances, they are
both examples of God's direct intervention in Saul's life for the
ultimate purpose of making him Yahweh's designate and, as such, Israel's king. The first instance aims at convincing Saul that God is
with him, the second, at stirring Saul into effective action and so,
convincing a reluctant people that their new king is an effective
leader in times of military trouble. The different manifestations of
Saul's charismatic experiences are, therefore, the product of the
different contexts within which they appear. They are linked by the
overriding unity of purpose of installing a theocratically designated
king in Israel over a people that accept him and give up their intention to sever their political ties to Yahweh. (Mettinger has also
questioned the absolute separation of 10.10 and 11.6, and presents
other arguments in favour of their compatibility, 1976:236f).

6   The common assumption that the words 'and after Samuel' are
secondary redactional insertions is not favoured by a careful consideration of their context (cf. Willis 1972:53 n.75; Ishida 1977:47f,
against e.g. Smith 1899:78; Fritz 1976:356f; McCarter 1980:203).
Saul's inclusion of Samuel with himself is a statement by Saul to the

people that he intends to uphold his ties with the theocracy. The
people are clearly reminded by Saul that they will be fighting under
Saul, Yahweh's willing designate, and Samuel, the theocratic mediator. Samuel's inclusion in the call to arms is thus an important
preliminary characterization of the significance of the battle.
Though Saul may have been slow to fulfill the role assigned to him
by Samuel, he leaves no doubt in anyone's mind that he is mindful of
it and of the man who stands over him.

7   The fact that Saul's threat should evoke the fear of Yahweh in
the people is a good argument against the suggestion that 11.1-11 does
not presuppose even 10.17-27. If the people were not aware that Saul
was Yahweh's chosen king whom they had acclaimed, why should they
fear Yahweh when Saul, the supposedly unknown farmer, had made
the threat? Only the reader is aware that Saul's behaviour is conditioned by an onslaught of God's spirit (v. 7), since that fact is only
manifest in a narratorial description. That the infusion of the divine spirit was not readily ascertainable by the people is evidenced
already in 10.10f, a manifestation even more obvious than 11.7.

8   Some commentators have regarded the large numbers of v. 8 as
fantastic and hence, spurious (Smith 1899:78f; Budde 1902:75;
Nowack 1902:51; Hertzberg 1964:93). Others have explained that the
turnout was so large because Saul had issued a call for a general
levy of all Israelites (Keil & Delitzsch 1880:112; Stoebe 1973:22).
A third possibility is that the word 'elep, usually translated as
'thousand,' refers to a military unit comprised of a variable number
of men (E. Meyer 1906:498; Mendenhall 1968:52-66; Gottwald 1979:
270-6; McCarter 1980:204). This last possibility would reduce the
response to a more credible level. Finally, it is possible that the
large numbers emphasize the wide extent of the response to Saul's
call, an emphasis already seen in the expression 'as one man' in
v. 7.

9   Ishida also recognizes that the plural wayyo'merû in v. 9a
focuses the reader's attention on the question of the people's response to the call (1977:47). With reference to the question posed in
10.27, 'How will this (Saul's kingship) save us (yoši'enû)?' the
possibilities with respect to 11.9 and the tešû'â promised
therein remain the same. Either the anonymous subjects have decided
that Saul is capable, or they have concluded that their own assembled
strength is sufficient to the task.

10   Defense of the question as it appears in MT is made by Driver
1913:87; cf. GKC #150a. The insertion of a negative particle, following LXX (saoul ou basileusei) is unnecessary.

11   Knierim also notes the legal connotations of the term benê
beliya'al. 'In all Old Testament references 'iš beliya'al is a
slanderer of God or a breaker of the sacral laws, a destroyer of justice, a rebel against the king, or one who destroys life' (1968: 33).

12   The fact that Saul thinks it necessary to bolster his prohibition against executing the vocal dissenters argues against Birch's
assertion that the right to make judgements in the sacral/legal realm
has been transferred to Saul (1976:61). If he did have that right, he

would not have to explain his pronouncements.

Saul's insecurity in this area is manifest when contrasted with David's issue of a similar amnesty. In 2 Sam 19.22, Abishai suggests that Shimei should die for cursing David, Yahweh's anointed. David, whose situation parallels Saul's in that he has just regained his hold on the throne, asks 'Shall any one be put to death in Israel this day? *For do I not know that I am this day king over Israel?*', (2 Sam 19.23). David bases his amnesty proclamation on the fact that he has, once again, a firm hold on the crown. Though the death penalty was suggested because Shimei cursed 'Yahweh's anointed,' David issues the amnesty on his own authority, a far cry from Saul's humble justification.

13   This [Yahweh's deliverance] demonstrated Yahweh's sanction of the choice of Saul to be king, but at the same time it also demonstrated Saul's realization that he was merely an instrument in the accomplishment of Israel's deliverance, which, rightly understood, was to be regarded as a work of Yahweh (Vannoy 1978:68 n.22).

14   Those commentators who have suggested that Saul's amnesty is intended to publicize his magnanimity as king (e.g. Keil & Delitzsch 1880:113; Smith 1899:80; Hertzberg 1964:94) are not as far off the mark as Knierim suggests (1968:33). They have simply shifted the magnanimity that is Yahweh's onto the shoulders of Saul. Goodenough's statement that the object of the amnesty was 'to make Saul's claim to kingship include judicial justice and mercy, as well as prowess in war' (1928:187) needs only minor modification. What the amnesty pays tribute to is Yahweh's merciful granting of deliverance through his designated king, even after the people have voiced their opposition (10.27) and withheld the recognition due to a king (11.1-5).

15   Vannoy also gives a representative survey of the variations that individual scholars have composed on the redactional theme of v. 14 (1978:114-27).

16   Against the argument that only a minority questioned the monarchy after its constitution was described and installed, Buber replies:

> The narrator, by means of his impressive phrase 'the brave men whose hearts God had touched' wanted to prevent such a conception of the facts. A majority is not described in such a manner, but rather a minority, who swim against the stream (1956:155)

In addition, one might note that the impression created by 11.1-5 is one of general disregard for the monarchy, which would seem to confirm Buber's reading of 'those whose hearts were touched' as a minority.

17   Vannoy also notes the significance of choosing Gilgal as the location for the renewal, but suggests that the monarchy (*melûkâ*) that is renewed is Yahweh's over Israel (1978:82-4):

> Precisely because the kingdom of Saul was being formally established, the kingdom of Yahweh must not be forgotten. The introduction of the monarchy in Israel required that it be under-

stood within the framework of the provisions of the Sinaitic covenant so that the continued rule of Yahweh in the new political order would be recognized (1978:81).

Vannoy's suggestion, while plausible within the textual limits he sets to his study (1 Sam 11.14-12.25), illustrates the hazard of interpretation on the basis of a limited context. The reader knows from 9.1-10.16 that Saul's monarchy presupposes the continuing higher authority of the theocracy, a condition that initially caused the people to question and ignore Saul's kingship (10.27-11.5). When the people are finally persuaded to accept the proffered monarchy, their renewal of Saul's kingdom constitutes, and is recognized to constitute, a simultaneous renewal of allegiance to the theocracy to which Saul publicly professes his own allegiance (11.13).

It is, therefore, unnecessary to isolate the usage of *melûkâ* in 11.14 either to have Israel renew its commitment to Yahweh, or, against historical criticism, to show that the Gilgal renewal is not simply a repetition of the Mizpah inauguration (10.19-25) (cf. Vannoy 1978:61-84). *Melûkâ*, in all three of its appearances (10.16, 25; 11.14), refers to Saul's monarchy; when the people finally reaffirm their acceptance of Saul as king, they also accept the fact that Saul stands under the theocratic authority.

18   Mettinger's suggestion that the verb *himlîk* is a 'delocutive' verb, 'to call someone king,' also supports an understanding of the people's act as a confirmation rather than an initiatory act (1976:86).

19   Vannoy, following R. Schmid (1964), suggests that the *šelamîm* are covenant offerings sacrificed to ratify the renewed relationship between Israel and Yahweh (1978:88-91). Objections to the exclusive association of the term with covenantal contexts have, however, been raised by McCarthy (cit. Vannoy 1978:89 n.84) and especially Levine (1974:35-41). Though the context of v. 15 seems to invite an understanding of the sacrifice in covenantal terms, it is equally open to Levine's suggestion that the *šelamîm* are 'gifts' given to the king and by him to God in celebration of his new kingship (1974:28-32).

Milgrom summarizes the suggested etymologies for the term, all of which he notes are conjectural, as peace, covenant, gift, whole or sound, and repay. He offers the tentative suggestion, which more or less encapsulates the general similarity of all the suggestions, 'offering of well-being.'(1976:769). In 1 Sam 11.15, where the emphasis lies on the fact of reconciliation, it seems unwise to be too specific in one's understanding of the term, given the disputed state of the question. Understanding the *šelamîm* as offerings expressing the people's sentiments of acceptance of Saul and so reconciliation with Yahweh also agrees with the generally applicable translation as 'peace offerings' (cf. Keil & Delitzsch 1880:114; Smith 1899:81; Rowley 1967:122f).

NOTES TO CHAPTER FOUR: PART TWELVE

1 SAMUEL 12

1   Both Thenius (1864:46) and Keil & Delitzsch (1880:115) also point to the waw-consecutive imperfect (*wayyo'mer*) in 12.1 as a syntactic support for the connection.

2   The expression *we'atta* is regularly employed (over 220 cases) after digressive explanations, and representations of states of affairs to return tothe contemporary moment. 'And now' links the digression with the consequent contemporary result (Jenni 1972:8).

3   In spite of McCarter's objections (1980:90, 212f), Driver's explanation of the phrase 'to walk before' is adequate. 'To walk before any one is to live and move openly before him' (1913:38; cf. Helfmeyer 1978:393).

4   Birch (1967:67) and McCarter (1980:213) also regard the positive sounding reference to the king as Yahweh's anointed as incongruent with the remainder of the chapter, which does not use the title 'anointed' (Birch; McCarter) and is uniformly critical of the monarchy (McCarter; cf. Veijola 1977:94). The title is appropriate, however, as part of Samuel's rhetorical intent. As for the supposed anti-monarchic stance of ch. 12, *Samuel* is not so much critical of the new monarchy, which is recognized as God-given (v. 13), as he is of the reasons and attitudes displayed by Israel in its bid for political change (cf. McCarthy 1974:102).

5   The contrasts between Samuel and his sons do not consist of the verbal linkages so often used when contrasts and comparisons are made in biblical narrative (cf. Crüsemann 1978:64f). This vagueness is exactly what one would expect. Samuel is trying to prove that the request for a king was not warranted by pointing to his own innocence of the crime of abusing the office of judge while avoiding any mention of the wrongdoing of his sons. Samuel is significantly more specific in his comparison with 8.11-8; he does not take (*lqh*) livestock, but the king does (8.16f; cf. Boecker 1969: 70; Vannoy 1978:16).

6   McCarter offers the interesting suggestion that the last sentence in v. 5 and the first in v. 6 are conflate variants, 'And he said "Witness,"' 'And Samuel said to the people, "Witness . . ."' (restoring a second *'d* after *h'm* with LXX) (1980:210). He opts for a conglomerate reading using elements from both variants - 'Yahweh is witness,' he said, . . . (1980:208, 210), a solution which removes the difficulty by creating a new version. The new version also creates a new problem for the reader, who must now supply a connection between Samuel's discourse on Yahweh's past history and the preceding dialogue. If the reader follows MT, the connection is supplied by the logic of the alternating dialogue between Samuel and the people.

7   In contrast to Keil and Delitzsch, who suggest only that 'the context itself is sufficient to show that the expression 'is witness'

is understood' (1880:116), I would maintain that Samuel's interruption incorporates the last word of v. 5, *'ed*, into his own sentence, and hence that nothing needs to be presumed. In other words, Samuel finishes that last sentence of v. 5 with his own conclusion, thus shaping the admission of 'witness' to suit his own purposes.

8   Against Smith 1899:85; Ehrlich 1910:207; Birch 1976:65; Veijola 1977:94f; Vannoy 1978:21-3; McCarter 1980:214, who all read v. 6 exclusively as an introduction to vv. 7-12.

9   Eichrodt says that the *ṣidqôt yhwh* are Yahweh's military victories on Israel's behalf, which, as proofs of Yahweh's righteousness, suggests why they are labelled *ṣdq* (1961 vol. 1:242). Zimmerli touches on a more appropriate understanding of Yahweh's *ṣdq* with respect to Yahweh's relationship with Israel. 'When the Old Testament speaks of 'Yahweh's righteousness' it means rather the social bond existing between him and his people and Yahweh's actions based on this bond' (1978:142). With respect to Yahweh's *ṣidqôt* in Judg 5.11 and 1 Sam 12.7, both contexts of recitation of Yahweh's military acts on Israel's behalf, it would appear that these acts are called *ṣidqot* because they justify Yahweh's covenantal claim on Israel. Yahweh's *ṣidqôt* are those actions that justify (or make right, and hence 'righteous') Yahweh's status as Israel's political leader, the divine king. 'Yahweh is acclaimed as king in the light of the victories [*ṣidqôt yhwh*] which he and his armies have wrought . . .' (P.D. Miller 1973:84).

10   Again the reader must be careful not to confuse Samuel's presentation and views with those of the narrator. The people are only compelled to admit Samuel's argument if they allow Samuel's suggestion that the request for a king was partly or wholly entailed by his own performance as mediator. That the narrator does not share Samuel's perspective is evident from his authoritative presentation of the problem in 8.1-3. If Samuel's audience accept Samuel's suggestion, the reader can only attribute their acquiescence to the combination of Samuel's persuasive rhetoric and their characteristic docility, for their admission of his innocence can in no way be extended to cover the sins of his sons.

11   Presentations of the two sides to the insoluble grammatical dispute over v. 7 may be found in Driver 1913:92f (favouring LXX) and Vannoy 1978:24-6 (favouring MT). Cf. König 1897:267 #288k.

12   Caution in the matter of perceiving formal literary patterns need not be taken to the extreme of denying such affiliations unless exact replication of all elements is present. Veijola, for example, denies the validity of reading ch. 12 in the light of covenantal forms, 'because here it is neither a matter of a "covenant" nor a monarchic constitution' (1977:95 n.79). McCarthy rightly maintains the covenantal aspects of Samuel's presentation, even though there is no strict adherence to any idealized covenant form (1978:218).

One might add that the story as developed up to this point requires neither a new covenant nor a covenant renewal. The fact that the people have accepted Saul and renewed the kingdom by making Saul king before Yahweh (11.14f) is a sufficient expression of their willingness to remain under and within the theocracy. Covenantal relationship at the end of ch. 11 - Yahweh having given a conditional monarchy and the people having accepted it - is restored and in no need of repair. If Samuel presents his argument in ch. 12 in covenantal terms, it may be that he is seeking to define the relationship that already exists and, more importantly, to *redefine* the whole escapade from the theocratic perspective.

13   Several scholars have objected to the plural verbs in v. 8 and have accordingly followed LXX in which the verbs 'brought out' (LXX*A*, Targum, Vulgate) and 'settled' (LXX*BL*, Syriac, Vulgate) are singular, with Yahweh understood as subject (e.g. Stoebe 1973: 233 and scholars cited by him; McCarter 1980:210). As Driver puts it, the plural verb 'they settled' 'expresses just what Moses and Aaron did not do' (1913:93).

Underlying the text-critical judgement is an exegetical presupposition that Samuel's presentation of the exodus and settlement stories should agree, or be made to agree with the presentations in the Pentateuch and Joshua. It is equally possible, however, that the plurals of LXX are the product of the same harmonistic presuppositions that lead modern scholars to prefer the versional readings. The alternative path is to consider the singular verbs as meaningful, important and integral to the context of Samuel's rehearsal of Yahweh's 'acts of justification.'

Ehrlich recognizes the validity of the plurals in MT, but short-circuits the interpretation of the verb numbers by shifting to tradition history. 'The received text is probably correct here, but it presupposed an older tradition that did not have Joshua as Moses' successor' (1910:207).

14   Veijola's use of the words *bammaqôm hazzeh* to draw redactional conclusions about ch. 12 suffers from inattention to the contextual utility of the words. Before labelling the expression as 'one of the inconspicuous dtr terms that allow dtr rhetoric its timeliness and broad interpretational application because of the minimal concreteness of their content' (Veijola 1977:86), it is desirable, methodologically speaking, to explore the possibility that the expression might be contextually requisite rather than stylistically characteristic.

15   The widely accepted emendation reading Barak (following LXX) rather than the obscure Bedan (e.g. Driver 1913:93) receives support from the widespread use of allusion in the immediate context. If Samuel is trying to convey a general understanding of the whole period, it is difficult to regard the introduction of an almost unknown character amongst the allusions as compatible with this purpose.

The suggestion of Zakovitch would alleviate this difficulty. He suggests Bedan, identified as a Gileadite in 1 Chron 7.17 is actually another name for Jepthah, also a Gileadite (Judg 11.1, 1972: 124f). The existence of two names for the same man is paralleled by the case of Gideon-Jerubbaal. Originally the list in 1 Sam 12.11 contained only the names Jerubbaal, Bedan and Samuel. A copyist or redactor who knew that Jepthah = Bedan inserted the name Jepthah after Bedan to explain the relatively obscure Bedan. Finally a later copyist, not knowing that Jepthah was intended as a gloss on Bedan, added the words *we'et* before Jepthah (1972:125).

Whether the reader follows LXX (Barak) or Zakovitch, the result is much the same: Samuel alludes to the period of the judges. If, on the other hand, one follows MT, one must assume that Bedan was a judge of whom Samuel could assume his audience's knowledge, whose memory has been lost. In any case, Bedan is insignificant enough that no single alternative changes our understanding of Samuel's rhetoric.

16   In passages where derivates of the root *bth* are used to describe relationships between human beings, frequently they describe security that is taken for granted, but which also turns out to be disappointed, i.e. a credulous, frivolous, or even arrogant unconcern and security . . . Frequently *bth* is used to describe a person who thinks he is secure, but is deceived because the object on which his feeling of security is based is unreliable. When we take all the passages in which *bth* is used in this sense, we get a picture of everything to which the heart of man clings and on which he believes he can build his life, but which will end in failure (Jepsen 1977:90).

In contrast to this clear linguistic usage of *bth* there is another that is even clearer. The community of Yahweh can know for sure that it can rely on him (Jepsen 1977:92).

Thus the feeling of being secure in God is the only certain support for human life. When Israel lives securely, it is a result of divine guidance: 1 S. 12.11; 1 K 5.5 (4.25); Ps. 78:53 (Jepsen 1977:93).

17   In Deut 12.9 it is implied that this security is part of the 'rest and inheritance' given by Yahweh to Israel. Only when these are actualized is Israel to establish the place of sacrificial worship that Yahweh shall choose (vv. 8-11). In Josh 23, the achievement of this security signals a moment for recollection and recommitment to maintain the achievement.

18   Among the proposals one sees three variations: 1. Verse 12 is a late insertion (Budde 1902:80), serving to unite chs. 11 and 12 (Schulz 1919:171). Apparently late redactors do not see contradictions or are not bothered by them. 2. Verse 12 is the creation of the deuteronomist, being an interpretive collage of traditions in chs. 8 and 11 (Hertzberg 1964:99; Noth 1967:60; Boecker 1969:75f; Birch 1976:71f; McCarter 1980:215). Boecker explains the discrepancies between v. 12 and chs. 8 and 11 on the reasons for and time of the request with the suggestion that the deuteronomistic redactors were obviously not so concerned with such disparities as the modern reader (1969:76). Veijola, who also suggests that v. 12 is the composition of a deuteronomist (DtrN), recognizes the problem of the contradiction, which Boecker explains away, and suggests that 8.1-5 is the view of DtrG while 12.12 is that of DtrN (1977:97). His solution is the logical conclusion of the diachronic redactional approach and is,

therfore, methodologically preferable to Boecker's apologetic for deuteronomistic literary taste. 3. Verse 12 represents a third unique tradition about the request and occasion for the development of a monarchy (Weiser 1962:72-4, 86; Hertzberg 1964:99; Stoebe 1973: 237f; cf. Mayes 1978:15).

   A fourth position, presented by Vannoy, is that though the request in ch. 8 is not explicitly made with an eye to the Ammonite threat, there is also nothing in the text that would contradict this hypothesis (1978:38f). This suggestion is a good example of the construction of a retrojective frame with which a reader provides a logical explanation for apparent discrepancies in a text. Such hypotheses may stand or fall depending on whether there is any explicit confirmation or disaffirmation in the text itself. If the text leaves the issue unresolved, the reader is forced to hold such possibilities as the presence of the Ammonite threat behind the request for a king (ch. 8) forever in mind but never incorporated in an unequivocal reading.

19   The complex subject of narrator reliability is discussed by (among others) Booth 1961, parts 2 and 3; Chatman 1978:228-37; Sternberg 1978:see index, s.v. 'Reliability'; Stanzel 1979:199-202; Yacobi 1981).

20   Against the counterproposals of Stoebe (1973:238) and McCarthy (1978:214), who suggest that the request is not viewed negatively in v. 12, one must affirm with Veijola (1977:97 n.85) that the context speaks against such a view. The request replaces the cry to Yahweh in a situation of need, and the people are subsequently forced to admit that their *request* was sinful (v. 19). The thunderstorm is staged by Samuel so that Yahweh has a chance to show his displeasure at the request (*ra'atkem rabbâ . . . be'ênê yhwh liše'ôl lakem melek*, v. 17). The monarchy in the form created by Yahweh, where Saul is Yahweh's anointed designate, is not regarded as sinful by Yahweh and Samuel, but the request for a king in place of Yahweh certainly is.

21   Though text critics have argued for the omission of either of the verbs (*š'l*, e.g. Wellhausen 1871:78f; *bḥr*, e.g. Stoebe 1973:233f), the redundancy of Samuel's usage is rhetorically comprehensible and therefore suitable (cf. Vannoy 1978:40 n.94).

22   In support of the semantic arguments for the apodosis in v. 14, Vannoy has marshalled a structural argument based on the parallel structures of vv. 14 and 15 (1978:42; cf. Baltzer 1964:74 n.6). The parallel, in translation, can be briefly illustrated here:

	v. 14	v. 15
protasis	If you fear Yahweh and serve him, and heed his voice and do not rebel against his commands	But if you do not heed Yahweh's voice and you rebel against his commands
apodosis	then (*wiheyitem*) you and your king will be after Yahweh, your God.	then (*wehayetâ*) the hand of Yahweh will be against you and your fathers.

23   The final word of v. 15 is an example of a situation in which
we are forced either to stretch the usual meaning of a word in the
text, to follow another textual tradition, or to resort to judicious
emendation. Examples of all three solutions to MT, which Smith in
his forthright manner calls 'absurd' (1899:87), are:

(1)   The conjunction *û* attached to the last word (*ûba'abotêkem*) is
used in a comparative sense, 'as it was upon your fathers' (Keil &
Delitzsch 1880:119; Stoebe 1973:234; McCarthy 1978:210; Vannoy
1978:46 n.104). Against this option one notes that *w*-comparative is
confined to poetry (R.J. Williams 1976:71 #437), and that when it is
used in poetry the verb from the first item of comparison applies
identically (including tense) to the second item. The tense of the
verb that governs the first object ('against you') is 'will be' but for
the comparison to make any sense one must substitute 'it was' for
the second clause: 'The hand of the Lord will be against you as it
was against your fathers'; 'the substitution of "it was" in the second clause destroys entirely the "parallelism of idea" upon which
the idiom itself essentially depends' (Driver 1913:94 n.1; cf.
Thenius 1864:48).

(2)   Another example of interpretation that depends on expansion of
the usual semantic range of a word is David Kimhi's suggestion that
the word 'fathers' refers to Israel's kings: 'like *wbmlkkm*, for a
ruler is to the people like a father to a son' (the translation is
Alan Cooper's, who brought Kimhi's suggestion and several parallels
to my attention). Kimhi cites Gen 45.8 as a parallel (cf. Isa 22.21,
and the Phoenician parallels in KAI 22, 24). Ringgren discusses
parallels in Egyptian, Akkadian and Ugaritic (1977:2-6). He also
notes the use of *'b* as a royal epithet in Isa 9.5 (p.19). Kimhi's
suggestion is attractive because it requires no adjustments in the
text and because of its contextual suitability. Understanding 'your
fathers' as a reference to Israel's kings, the parallelism of vv. 14f
is clear and forceful.

(3)   The majority of scholars have followed the readings of LXX,
'and against your king' (Wellhausen 1871:79; Nowack 1902:54;
Driver 1913:94f) or LXX*L*, 'and against your king to destroy you'
(Klostermann 1887:39; Smith 1899:88; Budde 1902:80; Dhorme
1910:104; McCarter 1980:212). The reading 'and against your king'
completes the parallelism of the apodoses in vv. 14 and 15, in which
the fate of king and people are linked, but does not explain how MT's
'and against your fathers' might have come about. The reading of
LXX*L*, which in McCarter's retrojection is *wbmlkkm l'bydkm*, is proposed as the possible basis of MT's reading. Whether we accept this
explanation of MT or not, the reading 'and against your king (to
destroy you)' is superior to MT in contextual suitability, if Kimhi's
suggestion about the meaning of *'b* is not accepted.

(4)   At least three different emendations of the problematic conclusion to v. 15 have been suggested. Schulz, who rejects the reading of LXX*L* because he regards the idea of annihilating the people
as an anachronism from the time of the prophets, expressed his wish
to solve the problem by simply ending the sentence with the words

'against you' (1919:172). Goslinga (cited by Vannoy 1978:46 n.104) suggests that the conjunction *w* attached to 'against your fathers' is a scribal error for *k*, so that the conclusion is 'against you even as against your fathers.' The major problem with Goslinga's suggestion is the same as that facing MT (without Kimhi's suggestion), namely that it disturbs the parallelism of vv. 14 and 15. R. Weiss turns the tables on those who follow either LXX reading, suggesting that LXX*B* ('against your king') is a harmonistic exegetical attempt to correct MT, and that LXX*L* ('against your king to destroy you') is obviously an attempt to bridge the gap between LXX*B* and MT (1976:53). He hypothesizes, instead, a minor corruption in which an aleph was mistakenly inserted into the final word *wbbtykm*, 'and against your houses' (1976:54). The copyist was influenced to err by the common expression *'tm w'btykm* and by the three prior occurrences of the word *'btykm* (once in conjunction with *'tkm* [v. 7]) in ch. 12. Incisive as Weiss' arguments against the LXX readings are in revealing the ambiguity of the relationships between the textual traditions, his suggestion does not, in my view, succeed against the strong contextual linkage of vv. 14f, which supports LXX.

Additional support for the LXX in v. 15 is also found in vv. 24f, which reiterate the structural and semantic patterns of vv. 14f. Paraphrased, the pattern is:

A. Fear Yahweh and serve him because he has benefited or will benefit you
B. If you will not acquiesce, you and your king(!) will become Yahweh's enemies and be destroyed.

This parallel, along with the structural argument from the parallelism of vv. 14 and 15, makes the reading of the LXX an attractive alternative.

Only Kimhi's reading of MT allows a retention of the Hebrew text in view of the structural necessities of the parallelism between vv. 14f and the parallel in vv. 24f. And since Kimhi's reading of *'b* allows for the same sense as the reading of LXX, which may be a correct explication of an obscured sense of the word *'b*, I prefer to follow Kimhi, in keeping with the principle of retaining MT when it is comprehensible.

24   It is important to note that at this crucial juncture, when the conditions for Israel's survival under the monarchy are being laid down, no special emphasis is placed on the behaviour of the king as opposed to the people. Rather they stand together under the demand for obedience. When one holds this fact together with the observation that what Samuel criticizes in ch. 12 is not the monarchy, but the request for a king in place of Yahweh, it becomes questionable whether ch. 12 supports the claim that the deuteronomist, supposedly responsible for the construction of ch. 12 (Noth 1967:54f), saw the monarchy as Israel's downfall. According to Noth, the deuteronomist used Josiah as his model for kingship:

His actions had a direct influence on Dtr.: Dtr. elevates the events of Josiah's time to a general norm and makes it the main function of the monarchy as such to uphold the religious pres-

criptions in the Deuteronomic law; indeed, at the beginning of
his account of the monarchy he completely departs from the
intention of the law itself and transfers the responsibility
for the maintenance of the relationship between God and people,
as envisaged by the law, to the monarchy. This is in fact the
central idea in his account of the monarchy. On the one hand,
then, Dtr.'s view of this part of his account is unhistorical,
because he assumes that the Deuteronomic law, which is traced
back to Moses, was familiar from early times and fell into
oblivion only temporarily. On the other hand, his view is inaccurate because he claims that the monarchy was, while it
existed, responsible for the observance of the law and therefore for the preservation of the relationship between God and
people (1982:82 = 1967:94).

The deuteronomist, says Noth, remodels the traditions about
the rise of the monarchy, incorporating within them his own interpretation of Israel's downfall as caused by the failure of monarchy:

In the 'judges' period the continual apostasies of the
Israelites brought them near the abyss (cf. Judg. 10:6-16);
similarly Dtr. now held the monarchy responsible and judged
that it was Israel's kings who, not immediately but finally,
had laid low the Israelite nation (1982:47 = 1967:54).

In view of the obvious contradiction between Noth's understanding of the deuteronomist's views about monarchy and obedience to the
law, and the deuteronomist's own statements on the subject in ch. 12
(assuming that ch. 12 is deuteronomistic), it seems that there is
reason to reexamine the whole question. If the deuteronomist does not
seem to place responsibility for obedience to Yahweh at the king's
doorstep in ch. 12, which is generally regarded as a covenant renewal
that governs the whole of the monarchic period up to Josiah, then we
must either say that vv. 14f (McCarthy 1978:210) and 24f are not
deuteronomistic or we must reevaluate our understanding of the deuteronomistic history.

25   Speiser has also observed that Yahweh and Samuel see the request for a king as comparable to Israel's previous expressions of
a desire to return to a lifestyle such as they had when they were
slaves in Egypt. 'Thus "the manner of the king" as it is stigmatized
in I Sam 8.11-8, could just as aptly have been labeled in that context "the Egyptian manner"' (1971:283).

26   Though Buber finds that 'the combination of Yahweh and Samuel in v. 18b seems almost a travesty in comparison to Exod 14.31'
(1956:159), the fact of the matter is that the parallel is an integral
part of the scene in which Samuel secures the position of mediator,
first held by Moses, for all subsequent Israelite history. The parallel
with Moses in Exodus is, therefore, an important recollection of the
fundamental role that Samuel is playing. The only travesty here lies
in Buber's arbitrary division of ch. 12 into, among other things,
original narrative and inserted miracle story 'which has nothing to
do with the action and so represents a "proof" (*Erweis*) not in the
good sense of fable, but in the arbitrary sense of late legend'

(1956:158). Such occasional exhibitions of homage to historical criticism in Buber's studies are travesties of his otherwise thorough readings of biblical texts.

27 Although this reordering of the reading experience of vv. 16-25 is destructive of the gradual realization created by the temporal sequence of the narrative, it avoids the tedious repetition involved in first describing the gradual realization, then the full structural parallel, and finally, the significance of each point of contact. In addition, the gradual realization of the parallel does not seem to play the important role in 12.16-25 that it did, for example, in Saul's journey in search of his asses (ch. 9).

28 Ehrlich suggests a third possible implication of the out-of-season shower, namely that Yahweh thereby shows 'that he finds his people's wish for a king [equally] untimely' (1910:209).

29 In view of the widespread acceptance of the opinion that ch. 12 is critical of the monarchy, it is worth underlining that Samuel only says that the show of force is supposed to convince the people of the evil of their *request* (*liše'ōl lakem melek*). The thunderstorm expresses no negative views of the monarchy of Saul, which is an institution created and implemented by Yahweh himself.

30 Boecker suggests that this demonstration of divine power at Samuel's disposal was intended simply to show the error of the request. The request was an expression of doubt about the power of Yahweh:

> Israel had no longer wished to rely on the possibility that its cry would be heard by Yahweh as it had always been before. The prompt hearing of the prayer in such awesome circumstances must have stricken Israel with the knowledge that with its request for a king it had wrongfully withdrawn its trust from Yahweh, and so it had become guilty before him' (1969:85).

This suggestion must be rejected on the grounds of two considerations in the narrative and one consideration in Boecker's own argument. First, it is explicitly stated that the thunder and rain are to convince Israel of Yahweh's *displeasure* with the request (v. 17), and that is exactly how Israel takes it (vv. 18f). When creator is displeased with creature's behaviour, there is good reason for creature to experience some insecurity about his position in the world.

Secondly, if Yahweh and Samuel were only trying to demonstrate the continuing viability of the old arrangement for defence, and were not using strong-arm tactics, why would not the show of power be more convincingly vented on one or another of Israel's potential opponents?

As the later examples of Martin Luther and other converts show, the thunderstorm is a particularly effective means of convincing human beings that they are in need of some protection against the fearful power that is revealed in such storms. The psychologically coercive power of the thunderstorm could only be multiplied many times by the weird occurrence in the dry season, at Samuel's call, and after the explanation that it shows the creator's displeasure.

31   McCarter confuses the issue:
      The point of the narrator is clear: a prophet is the proper and
      divinely sanctioned channel between man and God, and in this
      respect the request for a king is a great evil (1980:216).
Nobody has suggested that the king might replace the prophet as channel. The king was intended to replace both prophet and God as Israel's political leader. He obviates this sort of communication with
God in times of need. What the demonstration does show with reference
to McCarter's perspective, is that even though Israel now has a king
it is still in need of Samuel's intercession precisely because it has
made the request and so has displeased Yahweh. King or no king, the
people cannot escape Yahweh. They need a Samuel to pray for them.
32   Noth's reading of the deuteronomistic history is widely accepted. He suggests that the deuteronomistic recognized 'that God
was recognisably at work in this history, continuously meeting the
accelerating moral decline with warnings and punishments and, finally, when these proved fruitless, with total annihilation' (1982:89 =
1967:100). Given the importance of 1 Sam 12 for the history of monarchic Israel, and the suggestion in the narrative that the arrangement is not fair and not *freely* accepted by Israel, it seems fair
to say that a reconsideration of the meaning and purpose of the
history is in order. It would be a simple case of question-begging
to suggest that our understanding of the wider context of the deuteronomistic history allows us to reject this reading of 1 Sam 12.16-25.
The reading may be discarded, but not until a detailed reading of the
entire history, unconditioned by presuppositions borrowed from previous readings, is made.
33   'You' (*'attem*) is positioned emphatically (Driver 1913:95)
as a further means of drawing his audience's attention to its own
culpability.

ABBREVIATIONS

AASF	Annales academiae scientiarum Fennicae
AB	Anchor Bible
AJSL	American Journal of Semitic Languages and Literature
ASTI	Annual of the Swedish Theological Institute
AnBib	Analecta Biblica
BASOR	Bulletin of the American Schools of Oriental Research
BWANT	Beiträge zur Wissenschaft vom A und NT
BZAW	Beihefte zur ZAW
Bib	Biblica
BibOr	Bibliotheca Orientalis
CB: OTS	Coniectanea Biblica: Old Testament Series
CBQ	Catholic Biblical Quarterly
CQR	Church Quarterly Review
FRLANT	Forschungen zur Religion und Literatur des A und NT
HUCA	Hebrew Union College Annual
KAT	Kommentar zum AT
ICC	International Critical Commentary
IDB	Interpreters Dictionary of the Bible
IDBS	IDB, Supplementary Volume
JBL	Journal of Biblical Literature
JSOT	Journal for the Study of the Old Testament
JSOTS	JSOT Supplement Series
OTL	Old Testament Library
RB	Revue Biblique
SBLDS	Society of Biblical Literature Dissertation Series
SVT	Supplements to Vetus Testamentum
TDOT	Theological Dictionary of the Old Testament
TZ	Theologische Zeitschrift
VT	Vetus Testamentum
WHJP	World History of the Jewish People
WMANT	Wissenschaftliche Monographien zum A und NT
ZAW	Zeitschrift für die alttestamentliche Wissenschaft

BIBLIOGRAPHY

Aberbach, D.
  1974   '*Manā 'aḥat 'appayim* (1 Sam. i 5): A New Interpretation.'
          VT 24: 350-3.
Abrams, M. H.
  1981   *A Glossary of Literary Terms.* 4th edn. New York: Holt,
          Rinehart & Winston.
Ackroyd, P. R.
  1971   *The First Book of Samuel.* Cambridge: C.U.P.
Aharoni, Y.
  1979   *The Land of the Bible: A Historical Geography.* Rev. edn.,
          tr. and ed. A. F. Rainey. Philadelphia: Westminster.
Ahlström, G. W.
  1977   "*addîr.*' TDOT vol. 1: 73f.
  1979   'I Samuel 1, 15.' *Bib* 60: 254.
Albrektson, B.
  1977f   'Some Observations on Two Oracular Passages in 1 Sam.'
          ASTI 11: 1-10.
Albright, W. F.
  1969   'Samuel and the Beginnings of the Prophetic Movement.'
          Interpreting the Prophetic Tradition. Intro. H. M.
          Orlinksky. New York: KTAV: 149-76.
Alonso-Schökel, L.
  1960   'Die stylistische Analyse bei den Propheten.' SVT 7: 154-64.
  1961   'Erzählkunst im Buche der Richter.' *Bib* 42: 143-72.
  1975   'Hermeneutical Problems of a Literary Study of the Bible.'
          SVT 28: 1-15.
Alt, A.
  1967   *Essays on Old Testament History and Religion.* Tr. R. A.
          Wilson. New York: Doubleday.
Alter, R.
  1981   *The Art of Biblical Narrative.* New York: Basic Books.
Andersen, F. I.
  1974   *The Sentence in Biblical Hebrew.* The Hague: Mouton.
Ap-Thomas, D. R.
  1961   'Saul's Uncle.' *VT* 11: 241-5.
Baltzer, K.
  1964   *Das Bundesformular.* WMANT 4. 2 Aufl. Neukirchen-Vluyn:
          Neukirchener.
Bardtke, H.
  1968   'Samuel und Saul. Gedanken zur Entstehung des Königtums
          in Israel.' *BibOr* 25: 289-302.
Bar-Efrat, S.
  1978   'Literary Modes and Methods in the Biblical Narrative in
          View of 2 Samuel 10-18 and 1 Kings 1-2.' *Immanuel* 8: 19-31.

1980   'Some Observations on the Analysis of Structure in Biblical
        Narrative.' *VT* 30: 154-73.
Barr, J.
1968   *Comparative Philology and the Text of the Old Testament.*
        Oxford: Clarendon.
Baumann, A.
1977   '*abhal.*' TDOT vol. 1: 44-8.
Ben-Barak, Z.
1979   'The Mizpah Covenant (I Sam 10.25) - The Source of the
        Israelite Monarchic Covenant.' *ZAW* 91: 30-43.
Bentzen, A.
1948   'The Cultic Use of the Story of the Ark in Samuel.'
        JBL 67: 37-53.
Beyerlin, W.
1961   'Das Königscharisma bei Saul.' *ZAW* 73: 186-201.
Bic, M.
1957   'Saul sucht die Eselinnen (I Sam. IX).' *VT* 7: 92-7.
Bickert, R.
1979   'Die Geschichte und das Handeln Jahwes.' *Textgemässe.*
        Aufsätze und Beiträge zur Hermeneutik des AT. [Fs. E.
        Würthwein] Eds. A. H. J. Gunneweg, O. Kaiser.
        Göttingen: Vandenhoeck und Ruprecht: 9-27.
Birch, B. C.
1976   *The Rise of the Israelite Monarchy: The Growth and Devel-*
        opment of I Samuel 7-15. SBLDS 27. Missoula: Scholars Press.
Blank, S. H.
1962   'Kiss.' IDB vol. 3: 39-40.
Blenkinsopp, J.
1969   'Kiriath-jearim and the Ark.' *JBL* 88: 143-56.
Boecker, H. J.
1969   *Die Beurteilung der Anfänge des Königtums in den*
        deuteronomistischen Abschnitten des I. Samuelbuches.
        WMANT 31. Neukirchen-Vluyn: Neukirchener.
Boer, P. A. H. de
1938   *Research into the Text of I Samuel i-xvi.* Amsterdam: H. J.
        Paris.
1955   'Vive le Roi!' *VT* 5: 225-31.
1974   'I Samuel 8, Verse 16b.' *Travels in the World of the Old*
        Testament. [M. A. Beek vol.] Assen: Van Gorcum.
Boling, R. G.
1975   *Judges.* AB 6A. Garden City: Doubleday.
Booth, W. C.
1961   *The Rhetoric of Fiction.* Chicago: U. of Chicago.
Botterweck, G. J.
1977   '*gôy.*' TDOT vol. 2: 430.
Bourke, J.
1954   'Samuel and the Ark: A Study in Contrasts.' *Dominican*
        Studies 7: 72-103.
Brockington, L. H.
1962   'I and II Samuel.' *Peak's Commentary on the Bible.* Rev.

    edn. Eds. M. Black, H. H. Rowley. New York: Nelson: 318-37.

Brooks, C.
1947   *The Well Wrought Urn. Studies in the Structure of Poetry.*
    New York: Harcourt, Brace & World.

Brown, E. K.
1957   *Rhythm in the Novel.* Toronto: U. of Toronto.

Brownlee, W. H.
1977   'The Ineffable Name of God.' *BASOR* 226: 39-46.

Buber, M.
1956   'Die Erzählung von Sauls Königswahl.' *VT* 6: 113-73.
1958   *Moses. The Revelation and the Covenant.* NY: Harper & Row.
1964   'Der Gesalbte.' *Werke* II. München: Kosel; Heidelberg:
    Lambert: 727-845.

Budde, K.
1890   *Die Bücher Richter und Samuel: Ihre Quellen und ihr*
    Aufbau. Giessen: J. Ricker.
1902   *Die Bücher Samuel.* Kurzer Hand-Commentar zum AT VIII.
    Tübingen: Mohr.

Campbell, A. F.
1975   *The Ark Narrative (1 Sam 4-6; 2 Sam 6). A Form-Critical*
    and Traditio-Historical Study. SBLDS 16. Missoula:Scholars.
1979   'Yahweh and the Ark: A Case Study in Narrative.' *JBL* 98:
    31-43.

Carroll, L.
1963   *The Annotated Alice. Alice's Adventures in Wonderland*
    and Through the Looking Glass. NY: World.

Caspari, W.
1926   *Die Samuelbücher.* KAT VII. Leipzig: Deichter.

Cassuto, U.
1961   *A Commentary on the Book of Genesis.* Vol. 1. Tr. I.
    Abrahams. Jerusalem: Magnes.
1967   *A Commentary on the Book of Exodus.* Tr. I. Abrahams.
    Jerusalem: Magnes.

Chatman, S.
1978   *Story and Discourse. Narrative Structure in Fiction and*
    Film. Ithaca, London: Cornell U.

Childs, B. S.
1974   *The Book of Exodus. A Critical, Theological Commentary.*
    OTL. Philadelphia: Westminster.
1979   *Introduction to the Old Testament as Scripture.*
    Philadelphia: Fortress.

Clark, W. M.
1971   'The righteousness of Noah.' *VT* 21: 261-80.

Clements, R. E.
1974   'The Deuteronomistic Interpretation of the Founding
    of the Monarchy in I Sam. VIII.' *VT* 24: 398-410.
1977   '*gôy.*' TDOT vol. 2: 426-33.

Cohen, M. A.
1965   'The Role of the Shilonite Priesthood in the United
    Monarchy of Ancient Israel.' *HUCA* 36: 59-98.

Conroy, C.
1978   *Absalom Absalom!* An.Bib. 81. Rome: Pontifical Biblical
        Institute.
Cooke, G. A.
1936   *The Book of Ezekiel.* ICC. Edinburgh: T. & T. Clark.
Craigie. P. C.
1978   *The Problem of War in the Old Testament.* Grand Rapids:
        Eerdmans.
Cross, F. M.
1953   'A New Qumran Biblical Fragment Related to the Original
        Hebrew Underlying the Septuagint.' *BASOR* 132: 15-26.
1973   *Canaanite Myth and Hebrew Epic. Essays in the History
        of the Religion of Israel.* Cambridge: Harvard U.
Cross, F. M and Freedman, D. N.
1975   *Studies in Ancient Yahwistic Poetry.* SBLDS 21, Missoula:
        Scholars.
Crüsemann, F.
1978   *Der Widerstand gegen das Königtum. Die antiköniglichen
        Texte des Alten Testamentes und der Kampf um den frühen
        Israelitischen Staat.* WMANT 49. Neukirchen-Vluyn:
        Neukirchener.
Culley, R. C.
1976   *Studies in the Structure of Hebrew Narrative.* Missoula:
        Scholars Press; Philadelphia: Fortress.
Daube, D.
1963   *The Exodus Pattern in the Bible.* London: Faber & Faber.
Davies, P. R.
1977   'The History of the Ark in the Books of Samuel.'
        Journal of Northwest Semitic Languages 5: 9-18.
Deist, F.
1977   *''APPAYIM* (1 Sam. 15) < **PM?'* *VT* 27: 205-9.
Delcor, M.
1964   'Jahweh et Dagon ou le Jahwisme face a la religion des
        Philistins d'apres 1 Sam. V.' *VT* 14: 136-54.
Dhorme, E. P.
1910   *Les Livres de Samuel.* Etudes Bibliques. Paris: Gabalda.
Dietrich, W.
1972   *Prophetie und Geschichte. Eine redaktionsgeschichtliche
        Untersuchung zum deuteronomistischen Geschichtswerk.*
        FRLANT 108. Göttingen: Vandenhoeck & Ruprecht.
Dorn, L.
1978   'Chronological Sequence in two Hebrew Narratives.'
        The Bible Translator 29: 316-22.
Driver, S. R.
1913   *Notes on the Hebrew Text and the Topography of the Books
        of Samuel.* 2nd edn. Oxford: Clarendon.
Dus, J.
1963   'Die Erzählung über den Verlust der Lade 1 Sam. IV.'
        VT 13: 333-7.

Edwards, P., ed.
1967   *The Encyclopedia of Philosophy.* New York, London:
        Macmillan & The Free Press.
Ehrlich, A. B.
1910   *Randglossen zur hebräischen Bibel. Textkritisches, Sprach-
        liches und Sachliches.* III: Josua, Richter, I u. II
        Samuelis. Leipzig: n.p.
Eichrodt, W.
1961   *Theology of the Old Testament.* 2 vols. Tr. J. A. Baker.
        Philadelphia: Westminster.
1970   *Ezekiel.* OTL. Philadelphia: Westminster.
Eising, H.
1980   '*chayil.*' TDOT vol. 4: 348-55.
Eissfeldt, O.
1931   *Die Komposition der Samuelisbücher.* Leipzig: Hinrichs.
1965   *The Old Testament. An Introduction.* Tr. P. R. Ackroyd
        New York, London: Harper & Row.
Ellis, J. M.
1974   *The Theory of Literary Criticism. A Logical Analysis.*
        Berkeley, Los Angeles, London: U. of California.
Eppstein, V.
1969   'Was Saul also among the prophets?' *ZAW* 81: 287-304.
Exum, J. C.
1981   'Aspects of Symmetry and Balance in the Samson Sagas.'
        JSOT 19: 3-29.
Fogle, S. F.
1974   'Repetition.' *Princeton Encyclopedia of Poetry and Poetics.*
        Eds. A. Preminger, F. J. Warnke, O. B. Hardison Jr.
        Princeton: Princeton U.: 699-701.
Fohrer, G.
1968   *Introduction to the Old Testament.* Tr. D. E. Green.
        Nashville: Abingdon.
1972   *History of Israelite Religion.* Tr. D. E. Green. Nashville:
        Abingdon.
Fokkelman, J. P.
1975   *Narrative Art in Genesis.* Assen: Van Gorcum.
Forster, E. M.
1976   *Aspects of the Novel.* Markham: Penguin (reprint).
Fretheim, T. E.
1967   *The cultic use of the ark of the covenant in the monarchial
        period.* PhD diss. Princeton U.
Friedman, N.
1955   'Point of View in Fiction: The Development of a Critical
        Concept.' *Proceedings of the Modern Languages Association*
        70: 1160-84.
Friedman, R. E.
1981   *The Exile and Biblical Narrative. The Formation of the
        Deuteronomistic and Priestly Works.* Harvard Semitic
        Monographs 22. Chico: Scholars.

Fritz, V.
  1976   'Die Deutung des Königtums Sauls in den Überlieferungen
          von seiner Entstehung I Sam. 9-11.' *ZAW* 88: 346-62.
Gaster, T. H.
  1969   *Myth, Legend, and Custom in the Old Testament.* 2 vols.
          New York: Harper & Row.
Genette, G.
  1980   *Narrative Discourse. An Essay in Method.* Tr. J. E. Lewin.
          Ithaca: Cornell U.
Good, E. M.
  1965   *Irony in the Old Testament.* Philadelphia: Westminster
          [reprint: Bible & Literature Series 3; Sheffield: Almond,
          1981).
Goodenough, E. R.
  1928   'Kingship in Early Israel.' *JBL* 47: 169-205.
Görg, M.
  1977   '*bazah.*' TDOT vol. 2: 60-5.
Gottwald, N. K.
  1979   *The Tribes of Yahweh. A Sociology of the Religion of
          Liberated Israel 1250-1050 B.C.E.* Maryknoll: Orbis Books.
Gowan, D. E.
  1975   *When Man Becomes God. Humanism and Hybris in the Old
          Testament.* Pittsburgh Theological Monograph Series 6.
          Pittsburgh: Pickwick.
Greenberg, M.
  1977   'The Use of the Ancient Versions for Interpreting the
          Hebrew Text.' SVT 29: 131-48.
Gressmann, H.
  1913   *Mose und seine Zeit. Ein Kommentar zu den Mose-Sagen.*
          FRLANT 18. Göttingen: Vandenhoeck & Ruprecht.
  1921   *Die älteste Geschichtsschreibung und Prophetie Israels.*
          Die Schriften des AT 2/1. Göttingen: Vandenhoeck &
          Ruprecht.
Gunkel, H.
  1906   'Die israelitische Literatur.' *Die Orientalischen
          Literaturen.* Teil I, Abteilung VII: *Die Kultur der Gegen-
          wart.* Ed. P. Hinneberg. Berlin, Leipzig: Teubner: 51-102.
  1928   *What Remains of the Old Testament.* Tr. A. K. Dallas.
          London: Allen & Unwin.
Gunn, D. M.
  1978   *The Story of King David: Genre and Interpretation.* JSOTS 6.
          Sheffield: JSOT.
  1980   *The Fate of King Saul: An Interpretation of a Biblical
          Story.* JSOTS 14. Sheffield: JSOT.
Gutbrod, K.
  1956   *Das Buch vom Könige: Das erste Buch Samuel.* Die Botschaft
          des alten Testaments. XI/1. Stuttgart: Calwer.
Hamp, V.
  1977   '*ps.*' TDOT vol. 1: 361-2.
  1977   '*esh.*' TDOT vol. 1: 423-8.

Haran, M.
1978   *Temples and Temple Service in Ancient Israel. An Inquiry
        into the Character of Cult Phenomena and the Historical
        Setting of the Priestly School.* Oxford: Clarendon.
Harris, S. L.
1981   '1 Samuel VIII 7-8.' *VT* 31: 79-80.
Hartmann, K. -H.
1979   *Wiederholungen im Erzählen. Zur Literarität narrativer
        Texte.* Studien zur Allgemeinen und Vergleichenden
        Literaturwissenschaft 17. Stuttgart: Metzler.
Hauer, C. E. Jr.
1967   'Does I Samuel 9.1-11.15 Reflect the Extension of Saul's
        Dominions?' *JBL* 86: 306-10.
Hauge, M. R.
1975   'The Struggles of the Blessed in Estrangement.' *ST*
        29: I 1-30, II 113-46.
Helfmeyer, F. J.
1977   "*ôth.*' TDOT vol. 1: 167-87.
1978   '*halakh.*' TDOT vol. 3: 388-403.
Hertzberg, H. W.
1964   *I and II Samuel. A Commentary.* Tr. J. S. Bowden. OTL.
        Philadelphia: Westminster.
Hobbes, T.
1968   *Leviathan.* Ed. C. B. Macpherson. Markham: Penguin edn.
Hoftijzer, J.
1967   'Das sogenannte Feueropfer.' *Hebräische Wortforschung*
        [Fs. W. Baumgartner]. SVT 16. Leiden: Brill: 114-34.
Houtman, C.
1977   'Zu I Samuel 2.25.' *ZAW* 89: 412-17.
Huffmon, H. B.
1976   'Amorites.' IDBS: 20f.
Humbert, P.
1946   *La 'Terou'a': Analyse d'un Rite Biblique.* Neuchatel:
        Secretariat de l'Universite.
Humphreys, W. L.
1978   'The Tragedy of King Saul: A Study of the Structure of I
        Samuel 9-31.' *JSOT* 6: 18-27.
1980   'The Rise and Fall of King Saul: A Study of an Ancient
        Narrative Stratum in 1 Samuel.' *JSOT* 18:74-90.
1982   'From Tragic Hero to Villain: A Study of the Figure of
        Saul and the Development of 1 Samuel.' *JSOT* 22:95-117.
Hylander, I.
1932   *Der literarische Samuel-Saul-Komplex (I Sam. 1-15)
        traditionsgeschichtlich untersucht.* Uppsala: Almquist &
        Wiksell.
Ingarden, R.
1973a   *The Cognition of the Literary Work of Art.* Trs. R. A.
        Cowley, K. R. Olson. Evanston: Northwestern U.
1973b   *The Literary Work of Art.* Tr. G. G. Grabowicz. Evanston:
        Northwestern U.

Irwin, W. A.
  1941   'Samuel and the Rise of the Monarchy.' *AJSL* 58: 113-34.
Iser, W.
  1974   *The Implied Reader. Patterns of Communication in Prose
          Fiction from Bunyan to Beckett.* Baltimore & London:
          Johns Hopkins U.
  1978   *The Act of Reading. A Theory of Aesthetic Response.*
          Baltimore & London: Johns Hopkins U.
Ishida, T.
  1977a   'Ngyd: A Term for the Legitimation of the Kingship.'
          Annual of the Japanese Biblical Institute 3: 35-51.
  1977b   *The Royal Dynasties in Ancient Israel.* BZAW 142. Berlin:
          de Gruyter.
Jackson, J. J.
  1962   *The Ark Narratives: An Historical, Textual, and
          Form-critical Study of 1 Samuel 4-6 and 2 Samuel 6.* ThD
          diss. Union Theological Seminary (New York).
Jenni, E.
  1961   'Zwei Jahrzehnte Forschung an den Büchern Josua bis
          Könige.' *Theologische Rundschau* 27: 1-32, 98-146.
  1972   'Zur Verwendung von *'atta* "jetzt" im Alten Testament.' *TZ*
          28: 5-12.
Jepsen, A.
  1977   '*batach.*' TDOT vol. 2: 88-94.
  1977   '*'aman.*' TDOT vol. 1: 292-323.
Johnson, B.
  1976f   'On the Masoretic Text at the Beginning of the First Book
          of Samuel.' *Svensk Exegetisk Årsbok* 41/42:
          130-7.
Kaufmann, Y.
  1972   *The Religion of Israel From Its Beginnings to the Babylonian
          Exile.* Tr. M. Greenberg. New York: Schocken.
Keel, O.
  1978   *The Symbolism of the Biblical World: Ancient Near Eastern
          Iconography and the Book of Psalms.* New York: Seabury.
Kegler, J.
  1977   *Politisches Geschehen und theologisches Verstehen.*
          Stuttgart: Calwer.
Keil, C. F. and Delitzsch, F.
  1880   *The Books of Samuel.* Tr. J. Martin. Edinburgh: T.&T. Clark.
Kellermann, D.
  1977   '*bs'; besa'.*' TDOT vol. 2: 205-8.
Kikawada, I. M.
  1977   'Some Proposals for the Definition of Rhetorical Criti-
          cism.' *Semitics* 5: 67-91.
Knierim, R.
  1968   'The Messianic Concept in the First Book of Samuel.' *Jesus
          and the Historian.* Ed. F. T. Trotter. Philadelphia:
          Westminster: 20-51.

Knight, D. A.
1975   *Rediscovering the Traditions of Israel.* SBLDS 9. Missoula:
        Scholars.
Koch, K.
1969   *The Growth of the Biblical Tradition. The Form-Critical
        Method.* Tr. S. M. Cupitt. London: A. & C. Black.
1978   '*Derekh.*' TDOT vol. 3: 273-93.
König, F. E.
1897   *Historisch-kritisches Lehrgebäude der hebräischen
        Sprache. Zweite Hälfte. 2. (Schluss -) Theil. Syntax der
        hebräischen Sprache.* Leipzig: Hinrichs.
Krentz, E.
1975   *The Historical-Critical Method.* Philadelphia: Fortress.
Kugel, J. L.
1981   *The Idea of Biblical Poetry. Parallelism and its History.*
        New Haven & London: Yale U.
Kutsch, E.
1963   *Salbung als Rechtsakt.* BZAW 87. Berlin: Töpelmann.
Labuschagne, C. J.
1973   'The Particles *hen* and *hinneh.*' *Oudtestamentische
        Studien* 18: 1-14.
LaDriere, J. C.
1953   'Voice and Address.' *Dictionary of World Literature.* Rev.
        edn. Ed. J. T. Shipley. New York: Philosophical Library.
Langlamet, F.
1970   'Les recits de l'institution de la royaute (I Sam. VIII-
        XII).' *RB* 77: 161-200.
1978   Review of R. Smend, 'Das Gesetz und die Völker'; T.
        Veijola, *Das Königtum in der Beurteilung der deutero-
        nomistischen Historiographie*; B. C. Birch, *The Rise
        of the Israelite Monarchy.* RB 85: 277-300.
Leech, G. N., Short, M. H.
1981   *Style in Fiction. A linguistic introduction to English
        fictional prose.* London & New York: Longman.
Lentricchia, F.
1980   *After the New Criticism.* Chicago: U. of Chicago.
Levine, B. A.
1974   *In the Presence of the Lord.* Studies in Judaism in Late
        Antiquity 5. Leiden: Brill.
Lindblom, J.
1962   *Prophecy in Ancient Israel.* Oxford: Blackwell.
1973   'Saul Inter Prophetas.' *ASTI* 9: 30-41.
Long, B. O.
1968   *The Problem of Etiological Narrative in the Old Testament.*
        BZAW 108. Berlin: Töpelmann.
Lys, D.
1967   'Who is our President? From Text to Sermon on I Samuel
        12.12.' *Interpretation* 21: 401-20.
Maag, V.
1960   'Malkût Jhwh.' SVT 7: 129-53.

Maier, J.
  1965   *Das altisraelitische Ladeheiligtum.* BZAW 93. Berlin:
          Töpelmann.
Martin, W. J.
  1968   '"Dischronologized" Narrative in the Old Testament.' SVT
          17: 179-86.
Mauchline, J.
  1971   *1 and 2 Samuel.* New Century Bible. London: Oliphants.
Mayes, A. D. H.
  1977   'The Period of the Judges and the Rise of the Monarchy.'
          Israelite and Judaean History. Eds. J. H. Hayes, J. M.
          Miller. Philadelphia: Westminster:
          285-331.
  1978   'The Rise of the Israelite Monarchy.' *ZAW* 90: 1-19.
McCarter. P. K. Jr.
  1980   *I Samuel.* AB 8. Garden City: Doubleday.
McCarthy, D. J.
  1973   'The Inauguration of Monarchy in Israel: A Form-Critical
          Study of I Samuel 8-12.' *Interpretation* 27: 401-12.
  1974   'The Wrath of Yahweh and the Structural Unity of the
          Deuteronomistic History.' *Essays in Old Testament Ethics.*
          [J. P. Hyatt memorial vol.] Eds J. L. Crenshaw, J. T. Willis.
          New York: KTAV.
  1978   *Treaty and Covenant. A Study in Form in the Ancient
          Oriental Documents and in the Old Testament.* An.Bib. 21A.
          Rome: Pontifical Biblical Institute.
McKenzie, J. L.
  1962   'The Four Samuels.' *Biblical Research* 7: 3-18.
Mendelsohn, I.
  1956   'Samuel's Denunciation of Kingship in the Light of the
          Akkadian Documents from Ugarit.' *BASOR* 143: 17-22.
Mendenhall, G. E.
  1968   'The Census Lists of Numbers 1 and 26.' *JBL* 77:
          52-66.
Mettinger, T. N. D.
  1976   *King and Messiah. The Civil and Sacral Legitimation of the
          Israelite Kings.* CB: OTS 8. Lund: Gleerup.
Meyer, E.
  1906   *Die Israeliten und ihre Nachbarstämme.* 1 Aufl. Halle an
          der Saale. [Repr. Darmstadt: Wissenschaftliche Buchgesell-
          schaft, 1967].
Michaels, W. B.
  1979   'Against Formalism.' *Poetics Today* 1/1-2: 23-34.
Milgrom, J.
  1976   'Sacrifices and Offerings, OT.' IDBS: 763-71.
Miller, J. H.
  1980f   'A Guest in the House.' *Poetics Today* 2/1b: 189-92.
Miller, J. M.
  1974   'Saul's Rise to Power: Some Observations Concerning 1 Sam.
          9.1-10.16; 10.26-11.15 and 13.2-14.46.' *CBQ* 36: 157-74.

1976   *The Old Testament and the Historian.* Philadelphia: Fortress

Miller, P. D.
    1973   *The Divine Warrior in Early Israel.* Cambridge, Mass.:
        Harvard U.

Miller, P. D. and Roberts, J. J. M.
    1977   *The Hand of the Lord: A Reassessment of the Ark
        Narrative of 1 Samuel.* Johns Hopkins Near Eastern Studies.
        Baltimore: Johns Hopkins U.

Möhlenbrink, K.
    1940f   'Saul's Ammoniterfeldzug und Samuels Beitrag zum
        Königtum des Saul.' *ZAW* 58: 57-70.

Mowatt, D. G.
    1958f   'In the Beginning Was the First Version.' *German Life and
        Letters* 12: 211-21.
    1971   *Friedrich von Husen: Introduction, Text, Commentary and
        Glossary.* Anglica Germanica II. Cambridge: C.U.P.

Muilenburg, J.
    1953   'A Study in Hebrew Rhetoric: Repetition and Style.' SVT 1:
        97-111.
    1959   'The Form and Structure of the Covenantal Formulations.'
        VT 9: 347-65.
    1961   'The Linguistic and Rhetorical Usages of the Particle
        kî in the Old Testament.' *HUCA* 32: 135-60.
    1968   'The Intercession of the Covenant Mediator (Exodus 33.1a,
        12-17).' *Words and Meanings.* [D. W. Thomas vol.] Eds. P. R.
        Ackroyd, B. Lindars. Cambridge: C.U.P.: 159-81.

Newman, M.
    1962   'The Prophetic Call of Samuel.' *Israel's Prophetic Herit-
        age.* [J. Muilenburg vol.] Eds. B. W. Anderson, W. Harrelson.
        New York: Harper & Row: 86-97.

North, C. R.
    1931   'The Old Testament Estimate of the Monarchy.' *AJSL* 48:
        1-19.
    1932   'The Religious Aspects of Hebrew Kingship.' *ZAW* 9: 8-38.

Noth, M.
    1960   *The History of Israel.* 2nd ed. Tr. P. R. Ackroyd. New York:
        Harper & Row.
    1963   'Samuel und Silo.' *VT* 13: 390-400.
    1967   *Uberlieferungsgeschichtliche Studien.* 3rd edn. Tübingen:
        Niemeyer [Pp. 1-110 = The Deuteronomistic History. JSOTS
        15. Tr. Jane Doull *et al.* Sheffield: JSOT, 1981].

Nowack, W.
    1902   *Richter, Ruth und Bücher Samuelis.* Handkommentar zum
        AT I/4. Göttingen: Vandenhoeck & Ruprecht.

Otzen, B.
    1977   '*beliyya'al.*' TDOT vol. 2: 131-5.

Parker, S. B.
    1979   'The Vow in Ugaritic and Israelite Narrative Litera-
        ture.' *Ugarit-Forschungen* 11: 693-700.

Paul, S. M.
1978   '1 Samuel 9.7: An Interview Fee.' *Bib* 59: 542-4.
Payne, J. B.
1972   'Saul and the Changing Will of God.' *Bibliotheca Sacra*
        129/#516: 321-5.
Perry, M.
1979   'Literary Dynamics: How the order of a text creates its
        meanings.' *Poetics Today* 1.1-2: 35-64, 311-61.
Perry, M. and Sternberg, M.
1968f   'The King Through Ironic Eyes: The narrator's devices in the
        biblical story of David and Batsheba and two excursuses on
        the theory of the narrative text.' *Ha-Sifrut* 1: 263-92
        (Hebr.; Eng. summ. 452-99).
Péter-Contesse, R.
1976   'La Structure de 1 Samuel 1-3.' *The Bible Translator* 27:
        312-4.
Polzin, R.
1980   *Moses and the Deuteronomist. A Literary Study of the
        Deuteronomistic History.* New York: Seabury.
1981   'Reporting Speech in the Book of Deuteronomy: Toward a
        Compositional Analysis of the Deuteronomic History.'
        *Traditions in Transformation: Turning Points in Biblical
        Faith.* [F. M. Cross vol.] Eds. B. Halpern, J. D. Levenson.
        Winona Lake: Eisenbrauns: 193-211.
Pope, M. H.
1962   'Seven, Seventh, Seventy.' IDB vol. 4: 294-5.
1973   *Job.* AB 15. 3rd edn. Garden City: Doubleday.
Pratt, M. L.
1977   *Toward a Speech Act Theory of Literary Discourse.*
        Bloomington: Indiana U.
Preminger, O., Warnke, F. J., and Hardison, O. B. Jr., eds.
1974   *Princeton Encyclopedia of Poetry and Poetics.* Princeton:
        Princeton U.
Press, R.
1938   'Der Prophet Samuel.' *ZAW* 56: 177-225.
Radjawane, A. N.
1973f   'Das deuteronomistische Geschichtswerk. Ein Forschungs-
        bericht.' *Theologische Rundschau* 38: 177-216.
Rainey, A. F.
1975   'Institutions: Family, Civil, and Military.' *Ras Shamra
        Parallels.* Vol. 2. Ed. L. R. Fisher. Rome: Pontifical
        Biblical Institute, 93-8.
Rendtorff, R.
1968   'The Concept of Revelation in Ancient Israel.' *Revelation
        as History.* Ed. W. Pannenberg. Tr. D. Granskou. London:
        Macmillan: 23-53.
Richter, W.
1965   'Die *nagîd*-Formel. Ein Beitrag zur Erhellung des
        nagîd-Problem.' *Biblische Zeitschrift* n.f. 9: 71-84.
1970   *Die sogenannten vorprophetischen Berufungsberichte.*

    Eine literaturwissenschaftliche Studie zu 1 Sam. 9, 1-10, 16,
    Ex. 3f. und Ri. 6, 11b-17. FRLANT 101. Göttingen:
    Vandenhoeck & Ruprecht.

Rimmon-Kenan, S.
1980f 'Deconstructive Reflections on Deconstruction.' *Poetics*
    Today 2/1b: 185-8.

Ringgren, H.
1966 *Israelite Religion.* Tr. D. E. Green. Philadelphia:Fortress.
1977a ''*abh*.' TDOT vol. 1: 1-19.
1977b ''*elohîm*.' TDOT vol. 1: 267-84.
1978 '*daghan*.' TDOT vol. 3: 139-42.
1980 '*chayah*.' TDOT vol. 4: 324-44.

Ritterspach, A. D.
1967 *The Samuel Traditions: An Analysis of the Anti-monarchical*
    Source in I Samuel 1-15. PhD diss. Graduate Theological
    Union & San Francisco Theological Seminary.

Robert, P. H. de
1979 'La Gloire en Exil. Reflexions sur 1 Samuel 4.19-22.' *Revue*
    d'Histoire et de Philosophie Religieuses 59: 351-56.

Robertson, D. A.
1972 *Linguistic Evidence in Dating Early Hebrew Poetry.* SBLDS
    3. Missoula: Scholars Press.
1977 *The Old Testament and the Literary Critic.* Philadelphia:
    Fortress.

Robertson, E.
1944 'Samuel and Saul.' *Bulletin of the John Rylands Library* 28:
    175-206.

Rössler, E.
1966 *Jahwe und die Götter im Pentateuch und im deutero-*
    nomistischen Geschichtswerk. PhD diss. Rheinischen
    Friedrich-Wilhelms-U.

Rost, L.
1926 *Die Überlieferung von der Thronnachfolge Davids.* BWANT
    III, 6. Stuttgart: Kohlhammer [= *The Succession to the*
    Throne of David. HTIBS 1. Intro. E. Ball. Tr. M. D. Rutter,
    D. M. Gunn. Sheffield: Almond, 1982].

Rowley, H. H.
1967 *Worship in Israel: Its Forms and Meaning.* London: SPCK.

Rozenberg, M. S.
1975 'The *šofetîm* in the Bible.' *Eretz Israel* 12: 77-86.

Rylaarsdam, J. C.
1962 'Nazirite.' IDB vol. 3: 526f.

Schicklberger, F.
1973 *Die Ladeerzählung des ersten Samuel-Buches. Eine*
    literaturwissenschaftliche und theologiegeschichtliche
    Untersuchung. FB 7. Würzburg: Echter.

Schmid, R.
1964 *Das Bundesopfer in Israel. Wesen, Ursprung und Bedeutung*
    der alttestamentlichen Schelamim. Studien zum A und NT 9.
    München: Kösel.

Schmidt, L.
1970   *Menschlicher Erfolg und Jahwes Initiative.* WMANT 38.
        Neukirchen-Vluyn: Neukirchener.
Schmidt, W. H.
1966   *Königtum Gottes in Ugarit und Israel.* BZAW 80. Berlin:
        Töpelmann.
Schulz, A.
1919   *Die Bücher Samuel.* Exegetisches Handbuch zum AT VIII/1.
        Münster: Aschendorff.
1923   *Erzählungskunst in den Samuel-Büchern.* Münster:
        Aschendorff [= 'Narrative Art in the Books of Samuel.'
        *Narrative and Novella in Samuel: Studies by Hugo
        Gressmann and other Scholars 1906-1923.* Ed. D. M. Gunn.
        Tr. D. Orton. Sheffield: Almond, 1986].
Schunck, K.-D.
1963   *Benjamin. Untersuchungen zur Entstehung und Geschichte
        eines israelitischen Stammes.* BZAW 86. Berlin: Töpelmann.
Seebass, H.
1965   'Traditionsgeschichte von I Sam. 8, 10:17ff., und 12.' *ZAW*
        77: 286-96.
1966a   'Zum Text von 1 Sam. XIV 23B-25A und II 29, 31-33.' *VT*
        16: 74-82.
1966b   '1 Sam. 15 als Schlüssel für das Verständnis der sogen-
        annten königsfreundlichen Reihe 1 Sam. 9.1-10.16, 11.1-5
        und 13.2-14.52.' *ZAW* 78: 148-79.
1967   'Die Vorgeschichte der Königserhebung Sauls.' *ZAW* 79:
        155-71.
1977   *'bachar.'* TDOT vol. 2: 74-87.
Seeligmann, I. L.
1962   'Hebräische Erzählung und biblische Geschichtsschrei-
        bung.' *TZ* 18: 305-25.
Smend, R.
1971   'Das Gesetz und die Völker: Ein Beitrag zur deutero-
        nomistischen Redaktionsgeschichte.' *Probleme biblischer
        Theologie.* [G. von Rad vol.] Ed. H. W. Wolff. München:
        Kaiser: 494-509.
1978   *Die Entstehung des Alten Testaments.* TW 1. Stuttgart:
        Kohlhammer.
Smith, G. A.
1900   *The Historical Geography of the Holy Land.* 7th edn. London:
        Hodder & Stoughton.
Smith, H. P.
1899   *A Critical and Exegetical Commentary on the Books of
        Samuel.* ICC. Edinburgh: T. & T. Clark.
Smith, W. R.
1969   *Lectures on the Religion of the Semites. The Fundamental
        Institutions.* 3rd edn. New York: KTAV (reprint).
Soggin, J. A.
1967   *Das Königtum in Israel.* BZAW 104. Berlin: Töpelmann.

Speiser, E. A.
1938   'The Nuzi Tablets Solve a Puzzle in the Books of Samuel.'
        BASOR 72: 15-7.
1971   'The Manner of the King.' *WHJP* vol. 3: 280-7.
Stanzel, F.
1971   *Narrative Situations in the Novel. Tom Jones, Moby-Dick,
        The Ambassadors, Ulysses.* Tr. J. P. Pusack. Bloomington &
        London: Indiana U.
1979   *Theorie des Erzählens.* Uni-Taschenbücher 904.
        Göttingen: Vandenhoeck & Ruprecht.
Sternberg, M.
1978   *Expositional Modes and Temporal Ordering in Fiction.*
        Baltimore & London: Johns Hopkins U.
Stoebe, H. J.
1957   'Noch einmal die Eselinnen des Kis.' *VT* 7: 362-70.
1973   *Das erste Buch Samuelis.* Kommentar zum AT VIII/1.
        Gütersloh: Gerd Mohn.
Stolz, F.
1972   *Jahwes und Israels Kriege.* Abhandlungen zur Theologie des
        A und NT 60. Zürich: Theologische-Verlag.
Sturdy, J.
1970   'The Original Meaning of "Is Saul also among the prophets?"
        (1 Sam 10.11, 12; 19.24).' *VT* 20: 206-13.
Szikszai, S.
1962   'Anoint.' IDB vol. 1: 138-9.
Talmon, S.
1975   'Aspects of the Textual Transmission of the Bible in the
        Light of Qumran Manuscripts.' *Qumran and the History of
        the Biblical Text.* Eds. F. N. Cross, S. Talmon. Cambridge,
        Mass.: Harvard U.: 226-63 [from *Textus* 4 (1964) 95-132].
1975   'The Textual Study of the Bible - A New Outlook.' *Qumran
        and the History of the Biblical Text.* Eds. F. M. Cross, S.
        Talmon. Cambridge, Mass.: Harvard U.: 321-400.
1978   'The Presentation of Synchroneity and Simultaneity in
        Biblical Narrative.' *Scripta Hierosolymitana* 27: 9-26.
1979   'Kingship and the Ideology of the State.' *WHJP* vol.5: 3-26.
Thenius, O.
1864   *Die Bücher Samuels.* 2nd edn. Kurzgefasstes exegetisches
        Handbuch zum AT 4. Leipzig: Hirzel.
Thomas, D. W.
1960   'A Note on *wnwd' lkm* in 1 Samuel 6.3.' *Journal of
        Theological Studies* 11: 52.
Thompson, J. A.
1974   *Deuteronomy.* London: Inter Varsity Press.
Thornton, T. C. G.
1967   'Studies in Samuel.' *CQR* 168: 413-23.
1968   'Solomonic Apologetic in Samuel and Kings.' *CQR* 169:
        159-66.
Timm, H.
1966   'Die Ladeerzählung (1 Sam. 4-6; 2 Sam. 6) und das Kerygma

des deuteronomistischen Geschichtswerk.' *Evangelische Theologie* 26: 509-26.

Tompkins, J. P., ed.
1980   *Reader-Response Criticism*. Baltimore: Johns Hopkins U.

Tsevat, M.
1961   'Studies in the Book of Samuel, I.' *HUCA* 32: 191-216.
1964   'The Death of the Sons of Eli.' *Journal of Bible and Religion* 32: 355-8.
1980   'The Biblical Account of the Foundation of the Monarchy in Israel.' *The Meaning of the Book of Job and Other Biblical Studies*. New York: KTAV: 77-99.

Tur-Sinai, N. H.
1951   'The Ark of God at Beit Shemesh (1 Sam. 6) and at Peres 'Uzza (2 Sam. 6; 1 Chron. 13).' *VT* 1: 275-86.

Vannoy, J. R.
1978   *Covenant Renewal at Gilgal. A Study of 1 Samuel 11.14-12.25*. Cherry Hill: Mack Pub. Co.

Van Zyl, A. H.
1969   'The meaning of the name Samuel.' *Biblical Essays*. Proceedings of the 12th meeting of the OTWSA. Ed. A. H. Van Zyl.: 122-9.

Vaux, R. de
1965   *Ancient Israel*. 2 vols. New York & Toronto: McGraw-Hill.
1972   'The King of Israel, Vassal of Yahweh.' *The Bible and the Ancient Near East*. Tr. D. McHugh. London: Darton, Longman & Todd, 152-66.
1978   *The Early History of Israel*. Tr. D. Smith. Philadelphia: Westminster.

Veijola, T.
1975   *Die ewige Dynastie. David und die Entstehung seiner Dynastie nach der deuteronomistischen Darstellung*. AASF. Series B 193. Helsinki: Suomalainen Tiedeakatemia.
1977   *Das Königtum in der Beurteilung der deuteronomistischen Historiographie. Eine redaktionsgeschichtliche Untersuchung*. AASF. Series B 198. Helsinki: Suomalainen Tiedeakatemia.

Rad, G. von
1951   *Der heilige Krieg im alten Israel*. Göttingen: Vandenhoeck & Ruprecht.
1965   *Old Testament Theology*. 2 vols. Tr. D. M. G. Stalker. New York: Harper & Row.

Wallis, G.
1952   'Eine Parallele zu Richter 19.29ff. und 1 Sam. 11.5ff. aus dem Briefarchiv von Mari.' *ZAW* 64: 57-61.
1968   *Geschichte und Überlieferung. Gedanken über alttestamentliche Darstellungen der Frühgeschichte Israels und der Anfänge seiner Königtums*. AT II/13. Stuttgart: Calwer.
1980   '*chamadh*.' TDOT vol. 4: 452-61.

Walters, S.
1978   Review of B. C. Birch, *The Rise of the Israelite Monarchy.*
        JSOT 9: 67-70.
Ward, E. F. de
1976   'Eli's Rhetorical Question: 1 Samuel 2.25.' *Journal*
        of Jewish Studies 27: 117-37.
1977   'Superstition and Judgement: Archaic Methods of Finding
        a Verdict.' *ZAW* 89: 1-19.
Weinfeld, M.
1970   'The Covenant of Grant in the Old Testament and in the
        Ancient Near East.' *Journal of the American Oriental*
        Society 90: 184-203.
Weinfeld, M.
1972   *Deuteronomy and the Deuteronomic School.* Oxford:
        Clarendon.
1977   'Judge and Officer in Ancient Israel and in the Ancient
        Near East.' *Israel Oriental Studies* 7: 65-88.
Weingreen, J.
1976   *From Bible to Mishna.* Manchester: Manchester U.
Weiser, A.
1961   *The Old Testament: Its Formation and Development.* Tr. D.
        M. Barton. New York: Associated.
1962   *Samuel: seine geschichtliche Aufgabe und religiöse*
        Bedeutung. Traditions-geschichtliche Untersuchungen zu 1.
        Samuel 7-12. FRLANT 81. Göttingen: Vandenhoeck &
        Ruprecht.
Weisman, Z.
1976   'Anointing as a Motif in the Making of the Charismatic
        King.' *Bib* 57: 378-98.
Weiss, M.
1963   'Einiges über die Bauformen des Erzählens in der Bibel.'
        VT 13: 456-75.
1965   'Weiteres über die Bauformen des Erzählens in der Bibel.'
        Bib 46: 181-206.
1971   'Die Methode der "Total-Interpretation".' *SVT* 22: 88-112.
Weiss, R.
1976   'La Main du Seigneur sera contre vous et contre vos Peres.'
        RB 83: 51-4.
Wellek, R. and Warren, A.
1975   *Theory of Literature.* 3rd edn. New York, London: Harcourt
        Brace Jovanovich.
Wellhausen, J.
1871   *Der Text der Bücher Samuelis untersucht.* Göttingen:
        Vandenhoeck & Ruprecht.
1899   *Die Composition des Hexateuch und der historischen*
        Bücher des Alten Testaments. Berlin: Reimer.
1973   *Prolegomena to the History of Ancient Israel.* Gloucester
        Mass: Peter Smith (reprint of Meridian Books edn. of 1957).
Wetherill, P. M.
1974   *The Literary Text: An Examination of Critical Methods.*

Oxford: Blackwell.

Whybray, R. N.
1962   'Some Historical Limitations of Hebrew Kingship.' *CQR*
        163: 136-50.

Wildberger, H.
1957   'Samuel und die Entstehung des israelitischen Königtums.'
        TZ 13: 442-69.

Williams, J. G.
1980   'The Beautiful and the Barren: Conventions in Biblical
        Type-Scenes.' *JSOT* 17: 107-19.

Williams, R. J.
1976   *Hebrew Syntax: An Outline.* Toronto: U. of Toronto.

Willis, J. T.
1971   'An Anti-Elide Narrative Tradition from a Prophetic Circle
        at the Ramah Sanctuary.' *JBL* 90: 288-308.
1972   'Cultic elements in the story of Samuel's birth and
        dedication.' *Studia Theologica* 26: 33-61.
1973   'The Function of Comprehensive Anticipatory Redactional
        Joints in I Samuel 16-18.' *ZAW* 85: 294-314.
1973   'The Song of Hannah and Psalm 113.' *CBQ* 34: 139-54.
1979   'Samuel Versus Eli.' *TZ* 35: 201-12.

Wilson, R. R.
1977   *Genealogy and History in the Biblical World.* Yale Near
        Eastern Researches, 7. New Haven & London: Yale U.
1979   'Anthropology and the Study of the Old Testament.' *Union
        Seminary Quarterly Review* 34: 175-81.
1979   'Between "Azel" and "Azel": Interpreting the Biblical
        Genealogies.' *Biblical Archaeologist* 42: 11-22.
1980   *Prophecy and Society in Ancient Israel.* Philadelphia:
        Fortress.

Wimsatt, W. K. and Brooks, C.
1957   *Literary Criticism. A Short History.* 2 vols. Chicago: U. of
        Chicago.

Wittig, S.
1977   'A Theory of Multiple Meanings.' *Semeia* 9: 75-103.

Wolff, H. W.
1977   *Joel and Amos.* Hermeneia. Philadelphia: Fortress.

Yacobi, T.
1981   'Fictional Reliability as a Communicative Problem.' *Poetics
        Today* 2/2: 113-26.

Zakovitch, Y.
1972   '*ypth = bdn.*' *VT* 22: 123-5.
1980   'A Study of Precise and Partial Derivations in Biblical
        Etymology.' *JSOT* 15: 31-50.

Zimmerli, W.
1978   *Old Testament Theology in Outline.* Tr. D. E. Green.
        Atlanta: John Knox.

Zobel, H. -J.
1977   '*galah.*' TDOT vol. 2: 476-88.

INDEX OF AUTHORS

INDEX OF BIBLICAL REFERENCES

INDEX OF NARRATOLOGY